ROBERT BELLARMINE

From the engraving by Valdor of Liège, before

ROBERT BELLARMINE

Saint and Scholar

by

JAMES BRODRICK

S.J.

LONDON

BURNS & OATES

BX
4700
.B25
B73

© James Brodrick, S.J., 1961

MADE AND PRINTED IN GREAT BRITAIN BY
THE DITCHLING PRESS LTD, HASSOCKS, SUSSEX,
AND BOUND BY G. AND J. KITCAT LTD, LONDON, FOR
BURNS AND OATES LIMITED,
28 ASHLEY PLACE, LONDON, S.W.I

To
The Rector, Minister,
Professors and Students
of
Heythrop College, Oxfordshire,
dedicated to
Saint Robert Bellarmine

CONTENTS

PREFACE

THIS book is a condensed and largely rewritten version of a biography of St Robert Bellarmine in two volumes, published in 1928, two years before his canonization. The work, which without its very elaborate index and many appendices ran to over a thousand pages, sold out rapidly and has been unobtainable either at first or second hand for twenty-five years. Requests for republication have been coming in during that long time, but not until recently was the author in a position to do anything to satisfy the legion of kind people who wanted it. As a first step he re-read his two volumes and was somewhat dismayed by the experience, for the hand of time lay heavily upon them. Unless a man is a genius or a fool, what he wrote in his thirties will make him shake his grey head in his seventies. Those two volumes of long ago are much too exuberant for their writer's present taste. He seemed to be addicted then in his relative youth to putting adjectives in front of almost every noun in sight, and he flaunted his love for his hero, which was quite genuine, in a way that that meek and humble man would have found distressing. He hardly admitted to a single spot on his sun, which was not the best way to honour a saint who, though very lovable, had like all the saints his definite human limitations. The most disconcerting chapter in the old volumes re-read thirty-three years later was that entitled "The first Troubles of Galileo". Myself when young spent many weary months in the Reading Room of the British Museum poring daily over the twenty volumes of Favaro's *Opere di Galileo Galilei*, but the labour did not cure my romantic determination to justify Roberto even in the esoteric realms of physical science where I see now rather ruefully that he possessed no competence whatever. That chapter has been entirely rewritten and so, to a very large extent, has the one dealing with the much more mysterious subject of efficacious grace. The original two volumes were a pioneering effort, as nothing of any consequence had been written about Bellarmine in

English until they appeared. Neither has anything in the same line been written since, except special studies and articles in various periodicals dealing with the volumes themselves. *The Times Literary Supplement* did not like them, but an erudite contributor to *The Tablet* compared them to Lockhart's classical Life of Sir Walter Scott! They contained a very wide range of quotations from Bellarmine's works and letters, as well as from other sources, and it was a considerable relief to find on investigation that the author at that stage of his existence had stuck pretty faithfully to the Latin, Italian, Spanish, French and German of the original documents.

In the present volume footnotes, which swarmed in the two from which it stems, are dispensed with as much as possible or embodied in the text, in order to make it of manageable size. It is the quiet child of rather effusive parents, but not for that reason, one hopes, the less interesting, as it deals with problems that are of perennial concern to Christians. Robert Bellarmine was a great scholar, involved in all the rough-and-tumble of his fiercely argumentative age, but he transcended those unpropitious circumstances to become by his attractive holiness and winning character an inspiration for men of good will in any age. The driving force of his life and the explanation of his almost incredible achievements was just sheer limitless love for God and his fellow men. Once when addressing his Jesuit brethren, he used the following words: "Love is a marvellous and heavenly thing. It never tires and never thinks that it has done enough. It tackles work no matter how arduous, and in its lexicon is nowhere to be found the word impossible".

J.B.

Chapter I

THE BOY AND MAN TO HIS PRIESTHOOD

MONTEPULCIANO is a characteristic hill town of Tuscany, central Italy, and lies twenty-nine miles south-east of Siena. It is a painfully inaccessible place and attainable only by a bad road that spirals like a stripe on a barber's pole. Yet several thousand people live up there today, so it must have some virtues, the chief of which appears to be a remarkable wine. In medieval and earlier times it was simply a place of refuge which, owing to its position and height, had the misfortune to be strategically important in the never-ending squabbles between the republics of Florence and Siena. Patriotism was exceedingly local in those picturesque old times when the axis of the earth ran through every village pump, and Montepulciano fought hard to keep independent of both aggressors. It still wears an austere and martial look, like some seedy pensioned soldier, and is reputed to have been founded by Lars Porsena of Clusium, who swore by the nine gods, if there ever was such a person outside Livy. Anyhow, Clusium or Chiusi is near, a place once famous for its culture, and later notorious for its ferocious mosquitoes. For a town so small and so much preoccupied with the problems of mere existence, Montepulciano, in Latin Mons Politianus, has an impressive record of native worthies, two canonized saints, two popes, twelve cardinals, and thirty-two bishops of various Italian sees. One of the morning stars of the classical renaissance, second only to Ficino in importance, was also born and spent his boyhood on the hill-top, before going to Florence to become in due course a devoted friend of Lorenzo de' Medici and the tutor of his children. He was Angelo Cini but known to fame as Politian, the Man from Montepulciano, a patriotic name which he seems himself to have adopted. He became a disciple of Savonarola and ended his days in the habit of St Dominic. The first of the town's two saints, not to mention its many *beati*, was Agnes of Montepulciano, prioress of a Dominican convent there, so widely revered that the Holy Roman Emperor Charles IV, a peaceable man, properly deferential to the Pope, in strong contrast to the next person of the name and title, climbed the hill to pray at her shrine. When St Catherine of Siena made the same weary pilgrimage at about the same time, fifty-seven years after the holy prioress's death, her body, still untouched by decay, courteously raised its right foot for the visitor to kiss. The early Italian artists loved to depict that charming story. The second saint of Montepulciano was the subject of this book, Robert Bellarmine.

The Bellarmini family had not shone in history until Roberto arrived to immortalize their obscure name. They lived in a big rambling house with a courtyard and well. It is now a sort of tenement accommodating several families, whose picturesque washing dances in the Tuscan breeze, and there is still attached to it a crumbling shield bearing a very simple coat of arms, six falling pine cones arranged in the order of three, two and one. To use with trepidation the jargon of heraldry, the field used to be gules and the pine cones or, but both the red and the gold were washed away ages ago. Almost all the large houses in Montepulciano bore such shields, for it was a foible of the good citizens to imagine themselves patrician. Very few were and they did not include the Bellarmini. In his old age Cardinal Bellarmine remarked in passing to Pope Paul V that he was "born a poor gentleman", and when, at that time, he fell into controversy with King James I of England and was scorned by His Majesty for his mean birth, he did not in any way try to repudiate the charge of this person, certainly of the bluest blood, but not so certainly a gentleman. Easily the most distinguished citizen of Montepulciano at the time of Robert Bellarmine's birth in 1542 was Marcello Cervini, Cardinal Bishop of Nicastro, and one of the leading figures of the Catholic reform movement. Some time after the death of Marcello's mother, his father Riccardo Cervini married again, and had by this second union two boys and five girls whom, in dying, he committed to the care of his eldest son, their half-brother, already eminent in the papal service and one day to be pope himself. The future of his half-sisters gave the learned

Marcello a good deal of concern, as their mother also had died and one of them, Cynthia, was aged only twelve. In Spain and Italy girls mature rapidly in both body and soul, and our Cynthia may well have looked and demeaned herself more like twenty than twelve. Marcello sought advice about her future from his friend Maria Bellarmino who had a son aged twenty-four in search of a wife. So it was that Vincenzo Bellarmino brought his young bride to the altar in 1538 and so, too, that Robert Bellarmino, their third son, came into the world on October 4, 1542, the feast of St Francis of Assisi. At his baptism, the Grand Penitentiary of the Catholic Church, Cardinal Roberto Pucci, stood as his sponsor, either in person or by proxy, and it was in honour of this very influential dignitary that he received his first name. The Pucci were a Florentine family, and three of the clan, Roberto, his brother Lorenzo, and their nephew Antonio, had succeeded by questionable transactions in keeping the Penitenzieria, one of the most important curial offices, and one in most need of reform, in their control for nearly a generation, all the time determinedly opposed to any change. Already at the font, then, Bellarmine came into innocent contact with the abuses in high places which he would spend the best part of his long life endeavouring to remedy.

The child's second Christian name could not have been other than Francis, considering the day and that Assisi was only forty miles to the east, beyond the tranquil blue waters of Lake Trasimene, scene of so much slaughter in 217 B.C. and A.D. 1944. The influence of St Francis in Bellarmine's life went very deep and became very pronounced, especially in his later years when the people of Rome, always handy with nicknames, took to calling him "the new Poverello". In the year 1613, St Robert, then a cardinal and very famous man, jotted down with extreme repugnance, at the entreaty of two close Jesuit friends who could not be denied, a brief account of his life to that date, running to about seven thousand words. Neither he nor his friends dreamed that it would ever be published as his "Autobiography", but such was the fate of the little manuscript after it had lain dusty in the archives of the Gesù, Rome, for 132 years. Its fortunes in print

make a curious story, but it is introduced now because Robert
devotes the first paragraph to his mother's memory. He writes
throughout in the third person, using the initial N. to indicate
himself:

> N. had pious parents, especially his mother named Cynthia
> who was a sister of Pope Marcellus II. She was devoted to alms-
> giving, to prayer and contemplation, to fasting and corporal
> austerities. As a result of these, she contracted dropsy and died
> holily in the year 1575, forty-nine years old. She brought up her
> sons to piety, and bade the three eldest, of whom N. was the
> third, to go about together and not to mix with other boys.
> Each day, she sent them to the church adjoining their home,
> there to pray before the Blessed Sacrament. She accustomed them
> at an early age to make their confessions, to hear Mass, to pray
> and to practise various devotions.

As there were eventually five boys and seven girls in the family,
their mother can be excused the slight sense of the disciplinarian
which Robert's picture of her conveys. Her addiction to alms-
giving is a significant trait because it came out later almost
extravagantly in her third son. It was the more generous, as she
could have done with some alms herself to feed and clothe her
large family, owing to the meagre business capacity of her good
husband Vincenzo. "Times are so bad and expenses so great",
wrote the poor fellow to his brother-in-law Alessandro Cervini in
1556, "that I think I must have despaired had not God in his mercy
come to my aid. . . . May he help us, for other help we have none."

On April 22, 1541, a French secular priest from the diocese of
Amiens named Paschase Broet, who was born with the century,
pronounced his vows as a Jesuit into the hands of St Ignatius
Loyola, recently elected first general of the new religious order.
Broet was among the first nine companions of Ignatius recruited
at the University of Paris and proved to be one of the most
generous, zealous and attractive of them all. That same year of his
vows, he gave an example of his intrepidity by undertaking at the
behest of Pope Paul III a nightmare journey of exploration to
Ireland which entailed a score of hairbreadth escapes from death

on sea and land. On his return to Edinburgh, all kilted and tam-o'-shantered and begrimed with the mire of Irish bogs and caves where he had hidden from the minions of Henry VIII, he wrote a long and moving account of his adventures to his close friend, Cardinal Marcello Cervini. Back in Italy and busily at work in Foligno, Broet was asked by the Cardinal to pay a visit to Montepulciano where he saw Robert Bellarmine in his cradle and made an indelible impression on his mother Cynthia. Four years later, in 1547, he was back again on the hill-top at the request of Cervini, then cardinal legate at the Council of Trent, who had chosen him for his confessor. This time the indefatigable Paschase, suffering from a head-splitting migraine, gave the Spiritual Exercises of St Ignatius, of which he was one of the best masters, to Cynthia and two of her sisters. As a result, wrote her son Robert, "she conceived for the Father a wonderful veneration and a lasting love for the Society of Jesus, into which she earnestly desired that all her five sons should enter". Owing to the fewness of their numbers and the multifariousness of their occupations the Jesuits, though earnestly solicited by Cardinal Cervini, their great friend, were unable to open a school in Montepulciano until 1557. Meanwhile Robert Bellarmine attended a grammar school in the town conducted by lay masters who gave him a good grounding in the Latin language and a certain amount of picturesque ancient history. Latin was still a living language and to be fluent in it was to be educated. Nothing else mattered much in any schools of the period, Catholic or Protestant, except *Eloquentia Latina*. Cicero was the brightest star in the academic firmament, and many would and do contend that there have been more malignant stars. With Cicero Robert Bellarmine bracketed Virgil in his youth. He has left it on record that he lost his heart to that wistful poet and used sometimes to sit up late into the night spellbound over the *Aeneid*. In his own juvenile attempts at Latin verse, which was not such a waste of time as practical people imagine, he never used a word that had not Virgil's authority.

In April, 1555, when Robert was heading towards his thirteenth birthday, Montepulciano went wild with excitement at the news that Cardinal Cervini had been elected pope as Marcellus II.

The hopes of his relatives ran high as nepotism had been an evil feature of the papacy for so very long. But this pope set his face like flint against it. He wrote to Montepulciano that neither Alessandro, his well-loved brother, nor any other of his relatives were to come to Rome on pain of his grave displeasure. Alessandro's two sons, Riccardo and Errenio, who were there already under the guardianship of the great scholar Guglielmo Sirleto, custodian of the Vatican Library, ventured to put on purple hose and silk mantles in honour of their uncle's elevation but were ordered at once to stop the nonsense and behave in the same modest and retired way as before. This was the kind of medicine that the Church needed, but Marcellus, frail from childhood like his other nephew Robert Bellarmine, died only three weeks after his election. His splendid promise and its sudden quenching made a deep impression on Robert and his momentarily purple-hosed cousin, Riccardo.

Montepulciano at this time appears to have had no resident physician. At all events, the townsfolk invited one from outside to come for two years to minister to their ailments. It may have been the appearance of this worthy, who also advertised lectures on logic, that put into Robert Bellarmine's mind at the age of fourteen the idea of following a medical career. He must have spent a good deal of his first years in bed through grave weakness of the lungs, and on at least three occasions came within an inch of death through other maladies. Those who loved him thought sadly that his chances of survival to manhood were extremely slim. Perhaps such experiences also had something to do with his desire to qualify in medicine after he had finished his schooling. His father was delighted at the prospect and eager to put him in touch with the new doctor by attendance at his logic lectures, but was too poor to pay the fees. Alessandro Cervini, the most affluent member of the tribe, was the brother-in-law of Robert's father by a double title, as he had married Vincenzo's sister Girolama and Vincenzo had married his sister Cynthia. He therefore gladly undertook to pay for the lectures and also guaranteed to meet all the bills of the most dearly loved of his many nephews at the medical schools of Padua University later on. Cynthia,

Robert's mother, acquiesced in the plans for her boy, but in her heart of hearts still yearned that he might join the company of the unforgettable Paschase Broet. She even went on foot on the long pilgrimage to Loreto, right across Italy, in order to make her confession to and receive Holy Communion from "those reformed priests, such spiritual men", Broet's brethren, then confessors at the Sanctuary. At long last, the Jesuits opened a modest school in Montepulciano, whereupon Cynthia promptly transferred Robert, aged fifteen, and his brothers to their care, to the understandable indignation of their former schoolmasters, greatly heightened by the fact that the intruders charged no fees. It looked like unfair competition and perhaps it was, but it lightened the burden on Vincenzo's pocket and gave deep satisfaction to his wife, so they were ready to brave the scowls of the other party who had declared open war on the Jesuits. Robert took a lively part in the contest by answering in public the charge that the fathers were incompetent teachers, and Spaniards to boot, a people not much loved in Italy. From close acquaintance he had grown to esteem them and to wonder whether after all God wanted him to make his vows to Hippocrates or to the Society of Jesus. By the time Robert was sixteen in 1558 the Society had won. The boy knew well how much addicted his saintly uncle Pope Marcellus had been to the new order and, even better, his devout mother's hope and prayer that he might be given a vocation. He was an unusual type of boy, spirited, companionable and gay, but also deeply meditative and prayerful, who found in his frequent Communions the aliment of a spirituality beyond his years. He liked his own master, a young Jesuit named Scariglia, very greatly and knew that the affection he bore him was reciprocated. As he related long afterwards, he determined to open his heart to this friendly man. "I knew that he was very fond of me", he wrote, "so I asked him confidentially as between friend and friend to tell me honestly how he found life in the Society. Was he content with his vocation? Or might there not be some hidden evil or peril in the life which did not appear on the surface? For I was afraid lest having embraced the life I might subsequently regret my decision. That good father assured me that all went

excellently well with him and that he was completely contented
—*contentissimus*."

Meantime, news reached Robert that his cousin Riccardo
Cervini, son of his benefactor Alessandro, who was already studying at the University of Padua, had decided to become a Jesuit.
That fact banished Robert's last lingering doubts, for he greatly
admired his cousin, his elder by three years, and exchanged letters
with him as to how they were to accomplish their purpose.
Riccardo anticipated little trouble from his parents, but Robert
had every reason for expecting his father to be recalcitrant. He had
shown great ability at school, and Vincenzo, a good but poor and
ambitious man, pinned high hopes on his future. After all, his
uncle had become pope, so why should not he, of whom everybody even then spoke so well, attain at least the dignity of a
mitre or a red hat? But not among the Jesuits, for Vincenzo had
learned that they were precluded by their constitutions from
accepting ecclesiastical preferment if not strictly ordered to do so
by the Holy See. When at length he was informed of what he
called the *capricio di Roberto*, he angrily forbade him to have anything more to do with the Jesuits. There were Dominicans in the
town and in future he must avail himself of their ministrations.
He even pleaded with him, if he must abandon a promising
medical career, to join the Dominicans, among whom his talents
would have much better scope to attain their legitimate prizes
than in the other upstart order. Robert, who was a very thoughtful young person, held on his way. His uncle had reached the
highest dignity on earth only to die exactly three weeks after
being elected to it. He himself had had a close brush with death
more than once, and the doctors, who believed him to be tuber-
culous, did not expect him to live very long. What on earth, then,
was the point of those fugitive dignities? What was the point of
anything except to love God and do his holy will?

The struggle of wills between father and son persisted for
months, but at length Vincenzo, seeing how badly it was affecting
his wife, gave in. Then, he and his brother-in-law Alessandro
Cervini wrote a joint letter to the vicar-general of the Society of
Jesus in Rome, that Father Diego Laynez who had recently so

much distinguished himself at the Council of Trent, offering him their sons, but begging to be allowed to keep them another year at home as a last test of the genuineness of their vocation. Laynez readily agreed, and added that he would count the year of waiting as the novitiate of the two cousins. There were advantages in being nephews of Pope Marcellus. Alessandro Cervini had inherited from his brother a property set in woods ten miles south-west of Montepulciano where the Camaldolese hermits had once long ago established themselves, loving its seclusion. Hardly a sound is to be heard there except the song of a swift, tumbling stream which the monks had named *Il Vivo*, because it had seemed to them to be alive, so companionable was the muffled thunder of its waterfalls and its drowsier controversy with its pebbles and reeds. In June of the year 1560, Alessandro invited his nephew Robert Bellarmine, then nearly eighteen, to join himself and his son Riccardo for a studious holiday at this delectable spot. Robert spent four of the happiest months of his life in their company. Pope Marcellus had built a church on the estate, with its own priest, for the help of the local peasantry, and in it each morning Cervini and his son and nephew heard Mass and spent much time in prayer. As for study, all three were enamoured of the Latin classics. The pagan Renaissance had perished of its own excesses in the fearful Sack of Rome by the drunken soldiery of Charles V in 1527, but its lively ghost had learned Christian manners and even entered the Society of Jesus. Robert Bellarmine's most notable Latin effort, written at the age of sixteen, was an eclogue on the death of Cardinal Robert de Nobili, who had spoken Latin and Greek fluently at the age of ten, was raised to the purple at thirteen by his uncle Pope Julius III, and astounded not only papal circles but the whole of worldly Rome by the sanctity and austerity of a life that ended in perfect resignation to the will of God at the age of eighteen. The family of "the little Cardinal", as he was popularly called, had originated in Montepulciano which was an added reason for Robert Bellarmine's interest in him, as later in his nephew and namesake, the celebrated missionary to the Brahmins of South India. Our Roberto's eclogue was considered so good that he was required to recite it publicly before all the notables of Montepulciano, and did so "not without the tears of the listeners".

The idyll of Vivo included on Bellarmine's part not only much prayer and delightful discussions on literary topics under the shady trees, but also much strenuous instruction of the peasantry around who, like most country folk of Italy at that time, were deplorably ignorant of their religion. Robert preached to them in Italian, as he had already done several times in Ciceronian Latin to a confraternity of adults in Montepulciano where his oratory was greatly appreciated. Thus early began a pulpit ministry which never stopped until he was too old and feeble any longer to climb the steps. He became in fact one of the most effective and prolific preachers of his age, as his story will disclose. On September 16, 1560, he and his cousin Cervini set out on foot for Eternal Rome. What his mother felt at Robert's departure is indicated in a brief letter which she wrote to Father Laynez: "I thank the divine Majesty who has deigned to call to his holy service one who was dearer to me than the light of my eyes. . . . From the very beginning I rejoiced at his desire, and am happier than ever now that I have dedicated him to God, knowing that we owe him the best we possess. But all the same, I am unable to stop the aching of my heart for my dearest boy, now gone from me. . . ." Laynez gave the shy and somewhat bewildered new-comers, for whom Rome must have been a staggering revelation of bigness and bustle, a very warm welcome at the ramshackle little house attached to the small church of Santa Maria della Strada where is now the magnificent Gesù. It had been the head-quarters of the Society of Jesus for twelve years and in it St Ignatius had lived and died. By an extraordinary concession, Laynez permitted Robert and Riccardo to pronounce their first Jesuit vows before they had slept a single night under his roof, though two full years of novitiate was then and still is the normal law of the Society. The General's indefatigable secretary, Juan Polanco, wrote shortly afterwards to all Jesuit houses announcing among other things the entrance of "two nephews of Pope Marcellus who so greatly loved our Society". He described Robert as "a good humanist and highly talented". After ten days

of prayer apart from the rest of the community, the good humanist was given his Jesuit cassock and sent into the kitchen to prove
his mettle among pots and pans. He had only a fortnight of this
greasy occupation before passing to the Roman College for those
studies which were to have no end but with his life.

The Roman College, ancestor in direct line of the present
world famous Pontifical Gregorian University, had been the
apple of St Ignatius's eye. He had plotted and planned its foundation over many years, had begged for it and fought for it against
a thousand obstacles, and at long last, in February, 1551, had
succeeded with the help of his good friend and future subject
Francis Borgia, Duke of Gandia, in renting a modest house at the
foot of the Campidoglio, over the door of which he had a placard
fixed, bearing the words: *Schola de Grammatica, d'Humanità e
Dottrina christiana, gratis*. The most significant word of the notice
is the last, *gratis*. Not since the time of Romulus and Remus had
Rome ever possessed a school of the humanities and Hebrew too,
where all were welcome and no fees of any kind demanded. The
result was that the small house soon could not contain the crowd
of youths of varying ages who clamoured for admittance and new
premises had to be rented from a Roman nobleman at a cost of
180 *scudi* a year. Very soon lectures in scholastic philosophy and
theology were being given to more mature students, including a
large number of young Jesuits. As subsequently at Montepulciano
and other places, there was hearty and sometimes violent opposition to the Romano from the masters of fee-paying schools, but
this the College lived down by the sheer excellence of its Parisian
methods and teaching. At the petition of St Ignatius in 1555, Pope
Paul IV, who had never loved him much, granted the College the
right to confer its own degrees, thus dignifying it with the status
of a university. It had made its fourth migration to roomy quarters
on the site of the present church of San Ignacio, given to the
Society of Jesus by the Marchesa della Valle, niece of Paul IV,
when Robert Bellarmine joined the large Jesuit community as a
student.

Among his fellow students were Christopher Schlüssel, a
German eminent in mathematics, better known by the Latinized

form of Clavius, who has for his memorial not only the Gregorian Calendar, but the largest "sea" on the visible face of the moon, and a contrasting character, the French Jean Leunis who originated the world-wide sodalities of the Blessed Virgin. Some of the professors at the College in Bellarmine's time were Father Diego Ledesma, a Spanish doctor of theology who was as saintly as he was brilliant and made a distinct contribution to the educational theory of his age; Francisco de Toledo, better known as Toletus, who had held a chair of philosophy at Salamanca at the tender age of twenty-three, before he became a Jesuit, and subsequently carried all before him as a theologian until he was constrained by the Holy See to become the first Jesuit cardinal; Juan Mariana, also very young and on the way already to developing into one of Spain's great all-round scholars as historian, economist, monetary reformer, and much else, including a grave problem to his superiors by his dangerous theories on tyrannicide.

Bellarmine's studies might be summed up under one name—Aristotle, Aristotle revised, of course, to render him orthodox. Alas, that great man was no longer the "master of those that know", but through bad texts and the slavish interpretations of decadent scholasticism had become the dictator and tyrant of those eager minds who wanted to know. As tutor of Alexander the Great, he had been a wonderful pioneer investigator of the fauna and flora which he had come upon in his travels, but when he turned his eyes up instead of down he failed miserably to understand what was going on in the heavens and merely took over the insubstantial dreams of Pythagoras, Plato and other speculators, fascinated by numbers. The stars, incorruptible and immortal by nature, were fixed in crystal spheres which turned in the only perfect motion, which was circular. If Aristotle had only had a telescope, he could have found out for himself that the planets, the stars and even the galaxies do not move in circles, but in eliptical or oval paths, as Kepler was to prove only in Bellarmine's old age, and Galileo to reject like any benighted Aristotelian. To judge by various schemes of study which they excogitated, the professors at the Roman College had to deal with lively, enquiring minds, not given to swearing by any master,

even St Thomas Aquinas. One professor wanted the Arab
Averroes, St Thomas's *bête noire*, adopted as an excellent com-
mentator on Aristotle, but Padre Ledesma would not hear of it
and even discouraged any kind words for that child of the
Prophet. "Let the praise, great praise, go to Albertus Magnus and
St Thomas. It is permitted to those who so wish to revile Averroes."
Robert Bellarmine took Aristotle as he was taught him, physics,
astronomy and all, and consequently retained into the heyday of
Galileo fifty years later the Stagyrite's crystal spheres, fixed
immutable stars, and swiftly moving sun. Sun, moon and stars
really interested him to the end of his long life only in so far as
they showed forth the glory of God. This appears clearly, and,
indeed, comically, to our twentieth-century eyes, in his very
popular little book, *The Mind's Ascent to God by a Ladder of Created
Things*, published in 1615, the very year of Galileo's crusading
irruption into Rome. The sixth step of St Robert's heavenly
ladder is a consideration of the sun, moon and stars. In this section
he speaks of a little experiment which he once made by the sea-
shore to determine the speed of the sun's course around the earth,
seven thousand miles in diameter:

> I was desirous of learning what space of time the sun would
> take in setting. At the beginning of its setting I began to recite
> the Psalm *Miserere mei Deus*, and I had scarce read it twice
> through when the whole sun had set. So in that short space of
> time the sun must traverse in its course a distance much greater
> than seven thousand miles. Who would believe this unless
> reasoning certainly proved it? And if we said that the body
> which moves so quickly is a mass greater than the whole earth,
> and accomplishes this swift movement without break or
> fatigue, . . . certainly every one with any sense at all must
> admire the infinite power of the Creator.

Fair science had certainly not frowned on Bellarmine's cradle.
Robert was ill during his whole time at the Roman College—
toto triennio aeger are his words. For one thing he suffered from
violent and persistent headaches, as who would not, with Aristotle in wretched Latin translations for his intellectual fare all day
long, including five hours of lectures? There was Aristotle's idea

of God, for instance, infinite, loveless, inaccessible, unconcerned with the fate of his poor creature man bowed under the yoke of inauspicious stars. It is significant that in his second year at the Roman College, given over entirely to philosophy, Robert borrowed the voluminous notes of Francisco de Toledo on the *Summa Theologica* of St Thomas and copied them all out for his own use. Theology was his true love, for it spoke of the God of our Lord Jesus Christ who had absorbed his young heart. Nevertheless he was far too intelligent to think lightly of Aristotle's metaphysics, and indeed was chosen in preference to twelve other students completing the course to defend the whole body of peripatetic conclusions, in one of those public disputations to which men of the sixteenth century were as much addicted as their medieval predecessors. They took, to some extent, the place of the theatre in modern life and were staged almost as elaborately as now are plays. Besides that performance in presence of several cardinals and other dignitaries, he was chosen also at the subsequent ceremony of conferring degrees to speak on behalf of all the candidates and elected for the subject of his discourse Aristotle's *De Anima*. After that, he became officially *Il Maestro Roberto*, at the age of twenty-one.

At the end of his course in philosophy, Robert Bellarmine's health was so gravely impaired that his superiors deemed it wiser that he should discontinue his studies and seek solace in his native Tuscan air. Tuscany in 1563 was one of thirteen separate Jesuit provinces set up by St Ignatius and under the genial supervision of his famous biographer, Pedro Ribadeneyra. Pedro had several colleges for the instruction and formation of youth to provide for as best he could, the principal of them at Florence being the ninth of thirty-three such institutions which Ignatius had brought into being in the last decade of his extraordinary life. The Florentine college and little church of San Giovannino had begun in great poverty in the Via di Gori, close to the palace of the Medici. But the Duchess of Florence, wife of Cosimo de' Medici, who had inherited from her father, the Spanish viceroy of the Kingdom of Naples, a liking for the Jesuits, took a motherly interest in the little college next door and helped it to expand considerably in the decade before Robert Bellarmine's arrival, looking so young that he might have been mistaken for a new pupil. For a long time, people were inclined to underestimate his age by anything from twelve to seven years. He was also small of stature, which can be a handicap when dealing with large boys. He made the journey of 188 miles on foot, in the company of two other students bound for different destinations, and they were given four *scudi*, perhaps seventy shillings of current English money, for their common capital. That was all part of the game, as men who had vowed themselves to poverty ought to be ready to feel its pinch. Robert bore with him to his new rector a letter from Juan Polanco, secretary of the Society of Jesus, asking him to be careful how he employed his latest recruit, as his health was very frail. The reasons given by Polanco for sending him are slightly contradictory, as the first is that he may rest and get strong again, and the second that he may make academic speeches in the approved style, write occasional Latin or Italian verses, and teach rhetoric and the Latin poets. "He is an expert at making speeches and verses", the secretary assured his man. In fact, the willing horse began teaching at once, though he was in no condition to face the strapping, liberty-loving youths in his classroom. He soon began to mend, though, under the benign influence of his native air and the care of a competent physician, but his health remained to the end of his life the half-and-half kind which can be a heavy affliction to a man with a great deal to do. In the Roman process of his beatification in 1828, nearly a hundred years before the honour followed, some ingenious advocate of his cause introduced into the evidence two parallel columns, one containing the fluctuating record of his health at various periods and the other crammed with a corresponding list of his labours and achievements. It makes an impressive balance-sheet.

Robert began with only twelve scholars, but they were the seniors of the college and brawny youths who appear to have intimidated him a little at first, "I taught my pupils as well as I knew how", he afterwards wrote, "and in order to acquire some standing with them used to introduce philosophical questions into my lessons on rhetoric." Whatever his initial misgivings, he soon found his feet both in the classroom and outside it. His very real gift for composing and delivering elegant Latin addresses became known within a few weeks of his arrival in Florence and on November 7 he was invited by the authorities of the Duomo to occupy the pulpit from which seventy years earlier Savonarola had thundered his prophecies and denunciations. According to his rector, he looked so boyish in the pulpit at twenty-one, and his discourse in praise of Christian knowledge was so well turned that the Archbishop of Ragusa and other notables who had heard him were "astounded with his performance" and avowed that they had never listened to a finer address. Rectors might be partial in reporting the triumphs of their gifted young men, but one thing seems certain, that Robert Bellarmine, though small in size, must have had a voice almost as big and carrying as Savonarola's, to be heard in the huge spaces under Brunelleschi's dome. There is record of his oratory at Santa Maria del Fiore on two other occasions at this time and of an entire course of sermons preached in the small church attached to the Jesuit college, during the Lent of 1564. Of the first of these sermons he relates: "During the whole time I was preaching, a certain devout woman remained on her knees in prayer. Asked afterwards why she had done so, she answered that when she saw that beardless boy in the pulpit she was afraid that he would presently lose his nerve and so disgrace the Society. As a matter of fact, I used to hold forth with much greater confidence and spirit in those days than in later years, because I felt sure memory would not fail me." He subsequently told the English Jesuit Thomas Fitzherbert that he could memorize a Latin sermon of more than an hour's length by reading it over once. From this time on, he was required to preach wherever he appeared, sometimes at a moment's notice. During holiday time of the year 1564, Robert was invited by a father at the college to go with him on a pilgrimage to Camaldoli where the hermits led their austere, secluded existence, to the great abbey among the pine trees at Vallombrosa, and to the sacred mountain high in the Apennines between Arno and Tiber where his patron St Francis had received the stigmata, then called Alvernia but now La Verna. At each town and village on their winding, flower-strewn route,

Robert preached and the Jesuit priest heard the confessions that were the result of his sermons. At Camaldoli behind its dangerous mountain the superior general of the hermits insisted that they stay for three days. Robert reports what happened: "On the third day, the superior suddenly bade him give an exhortation to the assembled community. He complied unwillingly and under constraint, but those venerable old men listened most attentively, and wanted afterwards to kiss his youthful hand, which he would not suffer them to do." However great Roberto's reputation as a preacher had already become, it could hardly have penetrated the silence and segregation from the world of Camaldoli, so his priest companion must plainly have given the hermits' superior a hint of his remarkable powers.

Robert remained only a year and a month at Florence, and then, to the unconcealed regret and disappointment of the Jesuit community there, departed, on orders from Rome, for the small university town of Mondovì in Piedmont, then a part of the Duchy of Savoy. The Duke, Emmanuel Philibert, had seen his country overrun by the French and, though his wife was the daughter of Francis I, had accordingly sided with Charles V in the everlasting struggle between Habsburg and Valois. A fine soldier, he had won against the French the great victory of St Quentin in 1557, and with it the recovery of his ancestral Savoy, stretching southwards as far as Nice and north, right up to the frontiers of Switzerland. Emmanuel, a strong and aggressive Catholic, determined to rid his dominions of the many Protestants who had infiltrated from Bern and Geneva. To help with the work, he had appealed to the Jesuits for assistance through the Bishop of Geneva, a predecessor of St Francis de Sales, exiled at Annecy. One of the first men sent was Antonio Possevino, subsequently the tutor at Padua, and the life-long friend and counsellor of St Francis, as he was also of St Robert Bellarmine. The Jesuits felt under an obligation to Emmanuel Philibert who had established for them a small college at Mondovì, a place lying about fifty miles almost due south of his capital, Turin, and would send only of their best to that rather obscure destination. So at least said Secretary Polanco in transmitting his marching orders to

Roberto. He assured him, too, that he would be called on to teach only for two hours or so a day, and so would be a man of leisure, with wide pleasant spaces for study, into which neither boys nor other business would be permitted to intrude. Robert, revered by his superiors throughout life for his swift promptness to obey, as for many other qualities, hired a horse on the very day the instructions arrived from Rome and set off on the long, lonely ride to the coast by way of Pistoia and Lucca to the little port of Lerici on the Gulf of Spezzia. It is a place of frequent and sudden storms, of which the poet Shelley was long afterwards the victim, and one was blowing hard when Robert arrived in search of some kind of ship to Genoa. Nothing could he find and was obliged perforce to put up for several days at the only and extremely primitive inn. In his first letter from Mondovì he told Polanco of a predicament that faced him in that inn:

When I was on the way from Rome to Florence and my *denarii* ran out, I met a Spanish gentleman who gave me all I needed without my asking him. The same thing happened to me in Lerici. Very soon my little stock of money was exhausted, as I was given only enough for a six-days journey, which would have been ample had the weather been kind. Alone, then, and penniless in a strange place, I was at my wits' end to know what to do, when suddenly a Spanish doctor arrived at the hostelry where I was sitting racking my brains. Discovering that I belonged to the Society, he was delighted and supplied all my wants. He also escorted me as far as Genoa, and so God found for me not only money, but a companion.

At Genoa Robert transferred his scanty belongings to another coastal ship which took him through the few miles of stormy sea to Savona, where his real troubles began, as he tried to make his way, again on a hired horse, through the passes of the Ligurian Alps in their full winter panoply. In his letter to Polanco he mentioned that his land journey had been one of rain, mud and snow: "To give you an idea of what the going was like, in many places where there used to be a road a torrent swirled which swamped my horse up to its belly, but I did my best to keep cheerful about it all. . . ." At one inn where he put up for the night his hostess caused him acute embarrassment by claiming him as the long-absent husband of her daughter, and at another he was accused of having stolen during the night somebody's purse. The result of such experiences was twofold, a lifelong antipathy to inns which comes out amusingly in his sermons, and a determination, if ever he held a post of authority in the Society of Jesus, not to send the fathers or brothers on journeys alone, no matter what the extra expense. He held every post in the Society, except general, as in the Church, except pope, and he kept his resolution.

The climate of Mondovì agreed with Robert who avowed that he felt better in health than for years. It was just as well, for the college there was wretchedly poor and understaffed, unable to repay even the paltry sum given as journey money to the new master by the brethren in Florence. Robert admitted that he had to fill almost every post, taught daily in the school, read to the fathers during their meals, accompanied them on their business out of doors, preached in the church, gave the regular "domestic exhortations" to the community, took the janitor's place at the door while he had his dinner, and sometimes acted as official knocker-up of the sleeping brethren at daybreak. So much for the studious leisure promised by Polanco. In the programme of the year's lectures he found himself down to teach "Demosthenes the Greek, Cicero and some other matters". That was a startling discovery, as the only Greek he knew was the alphabet of that language. However, there was no way out, as Demosthenes would not wait, so with characteristic aplomb he informed his scholars that he intended to refresh their knowledge of grammar before proceeding to deal with the difficult prose of the world's most celebrated orator. Then, by a tremendous effort in the quiet of his room at night, he learned the nouns or verbs or whatever it was that he had to teach next day. With his formidable memory he soon drew ahead of his boys and was expounding to them not only Demosthenes, but the much more engaging artist in words, a schoolmaster like himself, Isocrates. Cicero's *Somnium Scipionis*, which was the Latin text appointed for study during the summer term, gave Robert an opportunity to expatiate on astronomical and astrological questions, then popular subjects of discussion. Both his grandfather Riccardo Cervini and his uncle Marcellus, the future pope, had been earnest students of science as it was conceived in their time, so Robert was keeping up a family tradition. Riccardo, a devout Christian and admirable administrator of papal estates, believed in the prognostications of the astrologers and employed one of those mountebanks to cast the horoscope of his son Marcellus, but he never succumbed to the superstition in the manner of his friend and patron, Paul III, who kept a private astrologer in his employ and would undertake no important business until the stars had indicated the propitious hour. Robert Bellarmine might discuss the prevalent superstition with his class, but he was much too close to God and much too firm a believer in divine providence to be deluded by the humbug himself.

On Whitsunday and the following two days of that week in 1566, a reluctant Robert, acutely conscious of his unclerical condition, for he had not yet even received the tonsure, was ordered to preach in the cathedral of Mondoví, and did so well that during the subsequent three years of his stay in the town he became its most popular orator for Sundays and special occasions such as Advent and Lent. He used to prepare his sermons with the greatest care and to study closely those which had been published by celebrated preachers of that age. Among them were the discourses of Cornelio Musso, the Franciscan Bishop of Bitonto in Apulia, so widely famed for his oratory that he was selected to preach at the opening ceremony of the Council of Trent. That sermon, published in the Acts of the Council, makes astonishing reading to the sober modern eye, and was much derided for its flamboyance and tastelessness by anti-papal historians in later times. The good Musso, intoxicated by the solemnity of the occasion, certainly let himself go. The Council he compared to the Wooden Horse of Troy from which would spring the soldiers of Christ to slay the Protestant foe. Well might the assembled fathers cry with Caesar, *Venimus, Vidimus, Vicimus*—and that before they had debated a single point of their agenda. It is true "that Musso's hearers were children of a humanistic age for whom the tricks of rhetoric were in their very blood" and that many of them were moved to tears by the spirited delivery of the sermon.[1] Twenty years later, Robert Bellarmine also succumbed for a while to Musso's tinsel charms. He says that he read the Bishop's sermons carefully and tried "not without great labour" to imitate the alliterations, allegories, puns and pedantic allusions with which they were stuffed. The result was so elaborate that, in spite of his fine memory, it took him several days to get it by heart in readiness for Christmas Day at the cathedral. The authorities there pressed him to preach again the following morning, and that circumstance ended his youthful flirtation with Cornelio Musso, for he knew that he could not possibly compose and memorize another sermon in the *stylo alto*, as it was called, at such short notice. So on St Stephen's Day he threw rhetoric to the winds and preached in a very simple, homely style, as his devout heart prompted him, thereby causing a minor sensation. The canons said afterwards that on Christmas Day they had listened to a man in the pulpit, but on St Stephen's Day they had the impression of listening to an angel from Heaven.

In the summer of 1567 Robert's provincial superior, a man of ducal family named Adorno, who was an intimate friend of St Charles Borromeo, heard him preach at Mondovi, and decided there and then that one so gifted and so patently holy ought to be specialized for the pulpit, for he needed only the grace and authority of the priesthood to be an orator after St Charles's heart. Adorno accordingly bade him proceed at once to Padua to complete his theological studies preparatory to ordination. The Jesuits had a flourishing college for boys at Padua where their own young students resided while attending lectures at the famous university. The university belonged to the Republic of Venice and had become notorious for a spirit of free, not to say rash, speculation which made it a hotbed of Averroistic and other heresies. Robert Bellarmine shared the spirit of free inquiry at least to the extent of disagreeing with his Jesuit professor on the mysterious subject of predestination and with his Dominican professor when he found that he was taking everything word for

[1] Jedin, *A History of the Council of Trent*, English tr., London, 1957, pp. 577-8.

word from a commentary on St Thomas which he could read more profitably for himself. Robert became one of the truly great theologians of his age and the outstanding authority on Protestant theology, not by listening to lectures—there were none anywhere in Italy on the theology of the reformers—but by hard, incessant reading on his own account. While thus engaged at Padua and preaching every Sunday in the Jesuit church, he was summoned to Genoa by Adorno, his provincial, to participate in one of those elaborate scholastic disputations which gave a mysterious delight to the doctors and professors of those old times. They were staged in Genoa's black and white cathedral, and for two days Robert defended against all comers various set theses, presented to him at the last moment, taken from the whole corpus of Aristotle, including his curious views on astronomy, as well as from all three parts of the *Summa Theologica* of St Thomas Aquinas. By all accounts, he made a deep impression on the throng of Franciscans, Dominicans and other professional theologians who came to ply him with difficulties, and it was not only his formidable attainments at twenty-six that won their respect, but the unaffected modesty and courtesy of his bearing.

Just when at the height of his reputation as a preacher in Padua, Robert Bellarmine was instructed by Polanco to proceed to Louvain, from which town and university many appeals had reached the Jesuit authorities for a man to continue the tradition of Latin sermons on Sundays which their best orator, Francis Strada, had started there many years earlier. Louvain University was a key point in the Catholic struggle against further Protestant infiltration and subversion. Robert was to finish his theological studies at this centre of Catholic learning, the only one left in the forlorn North, while helping to stay the Protestant tide by his sermons.

The Paduan fathers were aggrieved when they heard the bad news, and accordingly made use of every legitimate stratagem they could think of to save the situation. A medical veto against the proposed journey to Belgium was obtained and dispatched to Francis Borgia, the Jesuit General, by Padre Adorno. The doctors were of opinion, it ran, that he would never get across Switzerland alive during the winter and, even if he did, his broken health would not long stand the strain of the rough Belgian regime. Besides all this, Padua had its own claims. The Jesuit church there would be left without a preacher if Robert were taken away. Other letters of respectful protest poured into Rome, too, and the result of them was that the evil day of departure was postponed. When the man most concerned heard of those various manoeuvres, he wrote to Borgia on his own account, assuring him that personally he was quite ready and willing to start at a moment's notice. He was told, however, that he might go on with his studies and his sermons until the winter was over. The prolific Jesuit writer Bartoli, famous in his own time, but not now regarded as always trustworthy or impartial, published, among scores of other books, a biography of Robert Bellarmine in which he said: "I certainly know of no other great man among us, in those days when great men were plentiful, who was so much sought after and coveted as Bellarmine, and that, too, by people in far distant places, though he was quite young and not yet a priest. Nor, on the other hand, can I remember anyone who was more jealously guarded by those who had the good fortune to possess him, so much so that they were prepared when arguments and entreaties failed to resort to something like violence rather than give him up." This was true enough as many letters of the time are extant to substantiate it. Hardly had Robert arrived in Louvain, some months later, than the Scot Edmund Hay, rector of the Collège de Clermont, Paris, began to make overtures to the General for his transference there.

Meanwhile, until the spring of 1569, Robert continued his busy round at Padua. Polanco then bade him be on his way to Louvain and mentioned as a consolation that his new rector, a Belgian named Schipmann, held a degree in medicine. The solicitous secretary wrote to this person also in the following terms: "Father General recommends Master Robert to your Reverence's charity as he is not strong and needs a good deal of care. . . . If your beer does not agree with him, will you please see that he has a little wine, and if he finds he cannot manage the coarse salted meat of your country, kindly treat him to a little good

B

fresh meat." He mentions the bread too and says that Robert must have the Italian kind, and not the heavy, dark stuff—*il pane nero*—with which the Belgians contented themselves.

The journey to Louvain, made in the company of another Jesuit and of Dr William Allen, the future cardinal, was without incident. The men travelled on horseback in lay attire to avoid the attention of Protestant soldiery on their route and underwent the usual hardships attendant on a journey across the Alps in the sixteenth century. Towards the end of May the many spires of Louvain came into sight. On arrival at his destination, Robert remarked to his new superior that he had been sent to Louvain for two years but would remain for seven. Why he made the remark he could never explain. "It just came into his head." Seven years was exactly the length of his stay. There are many other instances of similar prevision in his life, but he always strongly maintained that they were not prophecies in the accepted sense, only uncannily accurate guesses. Louvain was the breakwater of the Catholic resistance, and without the embattled theology which Bellarmine absorbed there for seven years, he might never, perhaps, have become the leading champion of the Catholic cause in the sixteenth century.

CHAPTER II

SEVEN YEARS IN LOUVAIN

ON July 25, Robert gave his first sermon in the large parochial church of Saint-Michel, and there was a crowded audience of university men, curious to hear what the young Jesuit from Italy had to say for himself. His appearance aroused much comment, as he wore no stole and looked a mere boy in comparison with other distinguished preachers, to whose post he had succeeded. But the people who packed the church for this and subsequent sermons were not all learned Latinists. Ordinary men and women came, too, for they had at least a smattering of the language. Sermons in Latin were a long-standing institution in Louvain, the magnet of Catholic scholarship at this time, to which so many students were drawn from foreign lands that gradually the town was forced to think in terms of the world. The government officials found Latin a necessity in order to be able to deal with the cosmopolitan population, while the shrewd shopkeepers and innkeepers saw that a little of it might be a good business investment. The Latin that thus became diffused was certainly not the Augustan kind, but it sufficed to enable ordinary men and women to understand the drift of a straightforward sermon.

Of the effect of Robert Bellarmine's sermons at Louvain there are many contemporary witnesses who either heard him or mingled with the crowd converging on Saint-Michel each Sunday in hopes of hearing him. The church had accommodation for about two thousand people and was invariably packed. But the most striking testimony of all came from the professors of the theological faculty of Louvain, who had had many differences in their time with Robert's religious brethren. In 1713, ninety-one years after his death, those men addressed a petition to Pope Clement XI for his beatification, in the course of which they wrote as follows:

Among the wonderful things which by the grace of God Bellarmine achieved here, in the first flower of his youth, were his Latin sermons, sermons all on fire with the divine spirit, and as full of true piety as of learning. So large were his audiences that even the vast spaces of the church could not accommodate them, and such was his success that many men were brought back to the true faith, particularly when, during the octave of Corpus Christi, he demonstrated in the clearest and amplest fashion the real presence of Christ in the Holy Eucharist. . . . His profound erudition, his singular modesty, his uprightness of life, and his sweetness of disposition won for him the love and veneration of the masters of this our University, and these sentiments have endured down to this very day.

Robert in the pulpit and Robert on the ground appeared to be two different people. When preaching he looked a tall, striking figure and, as most men saw him only at such times, the story got about in Louvain that a young giant had come forth from Italy to instruct them in the word of God. In reality he was under-sized, and would have been quite lost in the huge, enveloping pulpits of Flanders had he not by taking thought found a simple means of adding inches to his stature. He stood upon a stool.

After his very first sermon in Louvain, the provincial of the Low Countries wrote to Francis Borgia suggesting the preacher's immediate ordination. In October, the answer came that the event might take place as soon as convenient, but before that Robert was to be solemnly professed of the three vows of religion in compliance with regulations issued by Pope Pius V in 1568. On January 6, 1570, he pronounced the vows in the chapel of the Jesuit college, and eleven weeks later, on Holy Saturday, Corne-lius Jansen, Bishop of Ghent, made him a priest. Shortly after his ordination he devoted a whole sermon to the dignity of the priesthood. Round about him there were many who, forgetful of their high calling, allowed themselves to become entangled in worldly affairs. To these he addressed his first words as a priest:

Let such men think in their hearts a little, and hear God's own voice speaking to them: I have exalted thee and desired thee not to be an angel only but a god among men.

I have made thee the shepherd and ruler of my people. To thee I have committed all my goods, my wealth, my honour, my spouse, myself. . . . I have entrusted thee with the keys of the Kingdom of Heaven, with the Sacraments which I paid for with my Blood, with my Body and Blood themselves, with the souls affianced to me in baptism, for whom I did not hesitate to suffer and die. And I have put my honour and glory in thy hands, desiring to have my praise by thee and through thee and in thee. . .

At the time of Bellarmine's arrival in Louvain, the university, which had played so prominent a part in the Catholic renaissance, was going through a dangerous domestic crisis. For this, its famous alumnus, Dr Michael de Bay, was responsible. De Bay or Baius, as he is usually called, had spent the greater part of his studious and eminently respectable life at the university. But the chancellor, Ruard Tapper, to whose post he succeeded afterwards, detected at the outset a flaw in his otherwise blameless character, his addiction to novelties of speculation. More of a humanist than a theologian, Dr Michael's pet aversion was scholasticism in every shape and form though, as was the case with so many of his predecessors, the contempt he expressed for the medieval doctors was not bred of any notable familiarity with their writings. He took St Paul and St Augustine for his chosen guides, and professed to find in them a series of propositions which were quite at variance with Catholic teaching on grace and free will. In 1567 Pope Pius V condemned seventy-nine of these. The bull did not mention the doctor's name, out of simple charity, and like most documents of its kind spoke "right on", without any punctuation or divisions. Its key-sentence became famous. "These opinions," it ran, "although tenable to a certain extent in the strict and proper meaning of the words intended by those who wrote them we condemn as heretical and erroneous." It makes a great deal of difference to the meaning of this pronouncement whether a comma be placed after the word "extent" or lower down, after the word "them". If put in the first position, the condemnation of Baius and his friends is clearly expressed, but if in the second, there was a good chance left them of arguing their

way out of the tight corner in which they were placed. The
result was that a controversy arose concerning this *comma pianum*
which resembled on a small scale the fierce debates of earlier
times about an iota. Nine years later Bellarmine, then a professor
in Rome, wrote, at request, a brief account of the troubles at
Louvain:

> I found the schools in a state of great excitement. Ravesteyn
> in his lectures, and the Franciscan Godfrey of Liège in his
> sermons, openly attacked the teaching of Dr Michael. But all
> the same, a large section of the University adhered to him, and
> defended his views publicly and privately. On November 16,
> 1570, the bull of Pope Pius V was promulgated in the schools,
> Dr Michael being present as well as the other doctors and
> students. These men were required to take an oath of obedience
> to the bull and did so, but not without a great deal of moaning.
> Michael himself was in tears.

Sound teaching was not likely to thrive in an atmosphere so
stormy, and consequently the same year, 1570, the Jesuits applied
for permission to open a public theological course at their own
house of studies. It was granted without difficulty, and Bellarmine
was appointed at once to be the first Jesuit professor in Louvain,
though he had only given a bare three years to the study of
theology and even during that brief time had had but little
systematic tutoring. His new provincial, François Coster, also
constituted him prefect of studies, consultor, and spiritual director
of the college, his age then being some months short of twenty-
eight.

Robert delivered his first public lecture on October 17, 1570,
to a hundred students, men of all nations and types, and some
doubtless as old as or older than himself. The official textbook in
the theological schools of the university, as in all the other great
centres of Catholic learning, was the *Liber Sententiarum* of Peter
the Lombard, but the Society of Jesus, while allowing that famous
master a certain authority, had adopted St Thomas Aquinas as its
doctor of predilection, and made his teaching law from the
beginning. At the outset of his lectures on the Blessed Trinity
Robert made public profession of his faith in the *Summa Theo-*

logica of St Thomas. "I guarantee," he said, "that any one among you will make more all-round progress in two months devoted to the *Summa*, than in several months' independent study of the Bible and the Fathers." This does not mean that Bellarmine accepted the authority of St Thomas blindly. He dissented from him on many points and gave it as his opinion that, though in general the Angelic Doctor excelled all other theologians, Scotus, St Bonaventure, and Durandus were better guides on a number of debated questions.

Four manuscript volumes of the young professor's Louvain lecture notes are preserved in the archives of the Society of Jesus. They contain more than fifteen hundred double-column pages, every line of which is written in Bellarmine's own neat but rather illegible hand. He follows St Thomas question by question, explaining, developing, supplementing him all the time. The reading involved in the preparation of these notes must have been very great, and they give the first strong hint of what went on behind the placid, outward scenes of their author's unpretentious history. For instance, when he quotes St Augustine in support of an opinion, he is not content with two or three references, but gives no less than thirteen or eighteen, all apparently derived from direct study of that Doctor's voluminous works. His lectures struck a fresh and inspiring note which won him some fame even beyond the frontiers of Belgium. At the English College in Douay the authorities were so much impressed by the reports which reached them that they procured a copy of the lecture notes and had them dictated to their students. The second Diary of the College, under date March, 1577, has the following entry: "Dr Allen, the President, gave instructions for Dr Wright to dictate to us at six o'clock in the morning after Mass, and Dr Bristow at eight o'clock, the learned, concise, and easily intelligible commentaries on the *prima secundae* and *secunda secundae* of St Thomas, which the Reverend Father Robert of Italy delivered not long since in Louvain."

Owing to the official position which he held, Bellarmine felt it his duty to take Baius and his party to task, as papal condemnation had by no means ended their evasive activities. He went to work with great caution, well aware that a single tactical blunder might bring down on himself and his brethren the wrath of the entire university. Baius was the most eminent of its doctors, and good Catholics remembered that he had sat as a delegate at the Council of Trent. A man with such a distinguished personal record might not be attacked lightly, and the youthful David of the Jesuit college was certainly shouldering a heavy responsibility when he began gathering pebbles for his sling, as it were right in the camp of the Philistines. From the reports of some of his students who attended the lectures of Baius, he learned that the man still maintained the erroneous views on grace and free will which had already been condemned in Rome, and, possibly because of that condemnation, was ventilating views on papal authority of an extremely radical kind. A Jesuit colleague of Bellarmine, Jean Willems, once a professor of Scripture at Louvain University and eminent for his knowledge of Hebrew, Syriac and Arabic, told Robert one day that he had personally heard Baius remark, "Who knows but that the Roman Pontiff may not be the Antichrist prophesied to sit in the Temple of God?" Another of his foibles was to designate his opponents as secret heretics because they would not uphold his view that all the works of infidels are sins. Every word which Baius wrote or spoke was carefully scrutinized by his Jesuit critic, who then drew up a long list of the errors he discovered, and refuted them one by one. But he never published his refutation, and in his lectures refrained from ever mentioning Baius or his allies by name. He was fully conscious of the Doctor's good qualities and not slow to praise them. "The aforesaid Michael," he wrote in an official report, "is a man of great ability, and most learned in the study of St Augustine. Furthermore, he seems to be a prudent, pious, and singularly humble scholar." Baius was the real father of Jansenism, and it is interesting to find a Jesuit thus early in the field against that deadly foe of Catholic faith and devotion.

To pass now from Robert on the rostrum to Robert in the pulpit, it has to be said at once that books of sermons are not an attractive form of literature. They belong, as a rule, to the category of "books that are no books", and soon fall into oblivion if they have not been written to be read rather than spoken. Sermons so written can hardly claim to be sermons at all. The real sermon often reads badly because it was meant for the ear rather than the eye. A great orator is not dependent for his effects on the beauty of his style. He has other resources, his hands, his eyes, the tones of his voice, the passion of his heart. And it is the evanescence of these things that makes a tragedy of his art. Painters and sculptors can mould their thought into imperishable forms, the emotions once awakened by great music or poetry can be awakened again by re-reading the poem or re-playing the music, but the sorrow or hope or resolution which were kindled by the living voice are not to be recaptured from a printed record. When the orator dies he dies in a real sense for ever. He himself is his art, and the cold prose of his speech, as set down in books, is only its far-away and lifeless echo.

To judge by the results which Bellarmine obtained from his preaching, he must have been an orator of very great power, but his sermons do not, on the whole, make pleasant reading. They are too rhetorical for modern taste, too much in the tradition of Aristotle and Quintilian, with their proems, enthymemes and perorations. We know only by report the devout earnestness that made these dead cinders of speech once burn and shine like flames, but, dry and dull though they may appear, they still hold many a clue to the character of the man who pronounced them, and for that reason, if for no other, are deserving of consideration. In 1617 the Premonstratensians of Cambrai brought out an edition of the Louvain sermons based on Bellarmine's own manuscript. There are 796 double-column pages of small print in the book, the average length of each sermon being about nine pages. Forty-five sermons are on the Gospels of the Sundays and major Feasts; five are *de Novissimis*; five on the text *Missus est Angelus*, etc.; twelve on faith, the true Church and the evils of heresy; eight on the sufferings and sorrows of life; and twelve on the Psalm *Qui habitat in adjutorio Altissimi*. They were translated into French in 1856, and they form the basis of an excellent handbook for preachers entitled *Sermons from the Latins*, which was published in London by Dr J. Bagster in 1902. Other

BX

large volumes of Bellarmine's sermons, preached in various places, were published in Naples during his lifetime, but not by him, and during the period 1942–1950 a Dutch Jesuit, Sebastian Tromp, professor at the Gregorian University, Rome, brought out nine stout volumes of St Robert's sermons, hitherto in manuscript. They contain his Sunday sermons in Rome 1599–1606, two other volumes of Sunday sermons, a volume of sermons on various occasions, one of sermons in praise of Christ, the Blessed Sacrament, the Blessed Virgin, the Apostles and the Saints. The average length of each volume is 364 pages.

A few years before his elevation to the cardinalate, Bellarmine wrote a short essay on preaching which sums up his ideal of the Christian orator, and incidentally gives the key to his own practice. There are nine points in it, and they make together a little compendium of pulpit wisdom which the passage of time has in no way obscured:

A true preacher should have a twofold aim before him, to instruct men in what they ought to know, and to urge them on in what they ought to do. He must conceive his aims clearly, and then direct his whole sermon and each individual part of it to the attainment of what he has set before his mind. Thus, for example, he should say to himself, today's Gospel is an exhortation to penance, and therefore I want with the help of God to instil the desire of that virtue into my people's hearts. For this purpose, I will collect various motives, proofs, illustrations, etc., which bear on the matter. In the same way, the true preacher must examine each part of his sermon and see whether it conduces to the end specified. It is because they neglect these preliminaries that many men discourse not only uselessly but even with peril to souls, their one idea being to get through an hour of talk.

Secondly, in his instructions the true preacher will not be content merely to say something on each word of the Gospel, or to throw out some thoughts which its phrases have suggested to him. The literal and genuine sense of the text must be made clear, and its bearing on faith and morals emphasized. In a word, the preacher's business is to teach what the Holy Ghost intended to teach when he inspired the sacred writer's pen.

Thirdly, in order to stir in men's hearts the love of holiness, it is not enough to get angry with sinners and shout at them. Empty clamouring of that kind may, indeed, terrify simple folk, but its only effect on the educated is to make them laugh. In neither class will it produce any solid fruit. Therefore we must first of all appeal to the minds of those who listen to us, and endeavour by sound reasons deduced from Holy Writ, by arguments of common sense, by examples and by similes, so to convince them that they will be forced to acknowledge the ideal of living which we propose as the only one becoming a reasonable man. Then by our eloquence and earnestness, and all the aids which rhetoric affords, we must endeavour to waken in their hearts a serious desire for that which their reason has already approved.

Three things are necessary for the attainment of the preacher's ends, three qualities of the soul without which his efforts will be unavailing. They are a great, vehement zeal for the honour of God, wisdom and eloquence. The fiery tongues which appeared above the Apostles when God made them the first preachers of his Evangel are the symbols of these things, the burning fire betokening zeal, the light, wisdom, and the form of a tongue, eloquence. Eloquence without charity and wisdom is only empty chattering. Wisdom and eloquence without charity are dead and profitless. And charity without wisdom and eloquence is like a brave man unarmed.

To obtain the zeal or apostolic spirit which is the very foundation of Christian preaching, nothing avails so much as assiduous prayer, constant and serious meditation, and the careful reading of spiritual books, especially such as contain the lives of saints.

The wisdom required in the preacher after God's own heart is made up of three things, the first of which is knowledge of the Scriptures. Consequently, our "ecclesiastes" ought to read a portion of the sacred text every day so as to make himself thoroughly familiar with it, at the same time diligently consulting the commentaries of the Fathers. The second part of the preacher's wisdom is dogmatic theology. It is not right to propound to the people the mere opinions of learned doctors, because, in sober truth, if they do but know and remember what they are bound to know, we may consider ourselves to have done very well by them. In the third place, pulpit wisdom demands varied erudition in its possessor. He must be provided with a great fund of illustrations, similes, and motives, and be able to support his arguments by the telling testimony of prophets and saints. In this respect, the following works will be found extremely helpful: St John Chrysostom on the Epistles of St Paul, and the same holy orator's sermons to the people of Antioch; the sermons of St Basil; the treatise of St Augustine on the Psalms, and his sermons on the words of our Lord and the Apostles; the Dialogues of St Gregory; and finally the histories of the Church and the lives of the Saints, written with such fidelity by Athanasius, Jerome, the Venerable Bede, and others.

St Robert preached his Louvain sermons at a time of spiritual crisis in Belgium when, owing to heresy and national disasters, the faith and hope of many men were growing dim. His truly apostolic heart bled for these poor people who were so apt to seek comfort for their sorrows in drink and debauchery. It did not take him long to discover that the source of their trouble was lack of confidence in God, and so in the pulpit he insisted tirelessly on the great motives of Christian hope. The problem of human suffering occupied him more than any other subject. He was always reverting to it, arguing and pleading for God, and justifying his ways to the suspicious intellect of man. During the Lent of 1574, his whole course was entitled *De Tribulatione*. "As I made my humble prayer to God today," he began, "I begged him, the Father of orphans, to inspire me with some thought for your consolation," and then in eight long sermons, he proceeded to prove to them, by a thousand arguments, how sweet for the Christian soul might be the uses of adversity. His aim was to give these men he loved right thoughts about God, and to instruct them in the strategy of his Providence which, in his vivid words, sends "sorrows out like soldiers to do battle with our vices". His concern in all these sermons on suffering is to show that love is ultimately its meaning. My Lady Tribulation, his own expression, is love knocking at the door, trying to get in, an inexorable patient love, that sees men always in the perspective of eternity, and has no aim but to purify, enlighten, and perfect them. "In the heyday of youth or prosperity men easily forget God, but sorrow comes, wisest of counsellors, and teaches them that vanity is vanity. Then only do they learn that all is not gold that glitters, nor is everything of great worth which is bought and sold in the market-place of fools."

Even God's sternest visitations are mercifully proportioned to man's strength and need, though it may be doubted whether the following considerations would greatly comfort a person suffering from a violent toothache:

The just man's present sufferings cannot pass with him to the life beyond the grave, and in this life they are permitted to come to him only one at a time and for the briefest space. *Momentaneum et leve*, that is the extent of their commission. We never endure at once the pains of a year, or a month, or a day, or an hour. As in time nothing is present but a brief indivisible now, so the burden we bear can never in a true sense be more than momentary. We sip our chalice slowly and gradually, God putting the tiny drops of its sufferings to our lips one by one. But in the life to come how different will the process be! There we shall drink the torrent of bliss at one great draught, and hold all the riches of eternity in a present without future or past.

In these sermons of his youth St Robert's zeal is at war from the first page to the last with everything that diminishes God's external glory or prejudices the interests dear to his love, and it was the intensity of his zeal which gave such power and point to his imagery when he said: "If a man only understood the reverence due to God's holy Name he would choose gladly to have his two lips stitched together rather than utter it in vain". The sins of his people and, above all, the sins of priests, weighed like a great burden on this priest's heart, as when he asked:

What will become of them, those sad traitors who sell Christ daily for less than Judas did, for a woman's kiss, or a dance, or a cup of wine? When celebrating the tremendous mystery of the Mass, a priest knows right well that he is in the Holy of Holies,

surrounded by choirs of adoring angels who tremble with awe.
Think, then, what a matter for tears it is, to see one so placed,
cold and inattentive, and in such a hurry that it looks as if he
thought there was a band of robbers on his track. We all
proclaim to the world that Christ himself is present in the
Sacrament of the Altar, and still some of us act, when we have
him in our hands, as though there was nothing we believed less,
or as if we held a God of metal or stone, who could neither
hear, nor see, nor feel. . . . We place him—the Lord of Glory,
whose name the angels hardly dare to breathe—on a corporal
which we should blush to see spread on a servant's table, while
his altars are defiled with dust and given over to spiders as a
grand place where they can weave their webs undisturbed and
hunt flies contentedly . . . I could tolerate many other abuses,
which I shall not mention, if only the corporals and purificators
were kept clean, and I beg and implore all good priests, zealous
for the honour of our Lord, to admonish and punish unsparingly
such contemners of his Divine Majesty.

Those were strong words for one so young, but he had even
harsher ones for the exhibitionism of some ministers of the word
of God, as the following passage shows:

Preachers who are anxious to do their duty must not suffer
themselves to be frightened away from wholesome teaching,
merely because by delivering it they may make enemies among
their flock. He is but a sad and sorry evangelist who seeks his
own and not God's glory, and desires to be loved and praised
by the people, instead of bending all his energies to make God
loved and praised by them. Much better would it be for him
to plough in the fields or beg his bread, than preach—*aratorem
potius quam oratorem agere.* Suppose a devoted husband, who is
on a journey, sends his wife some little gift or token by a
messenger, and the fellow uses it to ingratiate himself with the
lady, would we not rightly account him a scoundrel, and an
adulterer at heart? Tell me now, if Christ the Heavenly Spouse
of Holy Church sends her a message through a preacher, and
he, instead of delivering it faithfully, tries to appear a grand
fellow on account of his commission, and uses the very Scriptures themselves to show off his eloquence and win the world's

applause—tell me, I say, what better is he in the eyes of God than an adulterer?[1]

St Robert's sermons are pervaded by the Scriptures of both Testaments, and he uses his multitude of texts, about fifty to each sermon being the average, very sensibly on the whole, never trying to force the meaning, or to get more from the words than they were intended to convey. But perhaps it is in his homelier arguments that he is most effective as the following on the Real Presence of Christ in the Blessed Sacrament:

Accipite et manducate: Hoc est corpus meum. Weigh carefully, dear brethren, the force of those words. Surely laws and decrees ought to be promulgated in clear, precise, simple terms, and not obscurely or ambiguously. Otherwise any man might plead ignorance and say: "Let the legislator speak plainly if he wants his law to be kept". Now what Christian ever doubted that our Lord in instituting this Sacrament gave orders and framed a law that it was to be renewed perpetually in his Church? "Do this", he said, "in memory of me." Since, then, these words of Christ are the expression of a law or command, to read figures and metaphors into them is to make Almighty God the most imprudent and incompetent of legislators. Again, a man's last will and testament should surely be drawn

[1] Concio XXXII, *de Dom 4a post Pascha.* Cf. *De Ascensione Mentis in Deum*, Antwerp, 1615, Gradus sextus, cap. iv: "There are many preachers of the word of God in the Church today, and there have always been many. What is the reason that so few are converted by their sermons and declamations? Why is practically no change observable in the morals of a city where twenty, thirty, or even forty orators preached daily during Lent? . . . The only explanation I can find is that the sermons preached are for the most part learned, elegant, and flowery, but that the soul, the life, the fire is wanting, in brief charity is wanting —that great charity which alone can inspire the words of the speakers, and inflame and change the hearts of the listeners. In saying this, I do not mean that many preachers are without power of voice and vehemence of gesture. . . . What is to be desired is that they should be animated by a great love of God and a great zeal for the salvation of souls, and this, not as a feigned but as a genuine emotion; not forced, but as it were welling up naturally from the depth of the heart. St Peter knew nothing of rhetoric. He was skilled only in steering his boat, in casting and mending his nets, but as soon as the Holy Spirit descended upon him and filled him with burning charity, he began forthwith to speak so powerfully, so eagerly and so effectually in the midst of Jerusalem that by one sermon he converted many thousands to penitence and faith."

up in the straightforward speech of everyday life. No one but a madman, or one who desired to make trouble after his death, would employ metonymy and metaphor in such a document. When a testator says "I leave my house to my son John", does anybody or will anybody ever understand his words to mean "I leave to my son John, not my house itself standing four-square, but a nice, painted picture of it"? In the next place, suppose a prince promised one of you a hundred gold pieces, and in fulfilment of his word sent a beautiful sketch of the coins, I wonder what you would think of his liberality? And suppose that when you complained, the donor said, "Sir, your astonishment is out of place, as the painted crowns you received may very properly be considered true crowns by the figure of speech called metonymy", would not everybody feel that he was making fun of you and your picture? Now our Lord promised to give us his flesh for our food. The bread which I shall give you, he said, is my flesh for the life of the world. If you argue that the bread may be looked upon as a figure of his flesh, you are arguing like the prince, and making a mockery of God's promises. A wonderful gift indeed that would be, in which Eternal Wisdom, Truth, Justice, and Goodness deceived us, its helpless pensioners, and turned our dearest hopes to derision. That I may show you how just and righteous is the position we hold, let us suppose that the last day has come and that our doctrine of the Eucharist turns out to be false and absurd. If our Lord now asks us reproachfully: "Why did ye believe thus of my Sacrament? Why did ye adore the Host?" may we not safely answer him: "Yea, Lord, if we were wrong in this, it was you who deceived us. We heard your word, *This is my Body*, and was it a crime for us to believe you? We were confirmed in our mistake by a multitude of signs and wonders which could have had you only for their author. Your Church with one voice cried out to us that we were right, and in believing as we did we but followed in the footsteps of all your saints and holy ones. . ."

The peroration of the sermon is a plea for frequent Communion, as practical considerations were never very distant from the thoughts of Bellarmine's apostolic heart:

We must not suffer it to be said that this most holy and

saving Sacrament was instituted for us in vain. The wheaten bread which is the food of our bodies was not grown in the fields, reaped, ground, and baked merely to be looked at, but to be eaten and sustain our life and strength. So too, the Bread of Angels was not given to us solely for our veneration, but for our nourishment as well, that by partaking of it often we may refresh and fortify our souls. There are many men in this city of Louvain who speak of the holy Sacrament in the most beautiful and reverent terms. They even compete with one another to see who can do it most honour. But believe me those honour it best who take care to receive it often with pure and upright hearts. Why, I ask you, has charity grown so cold amongst us? Why do our lives and manners so little resemble those of the first Christians that alongside them we seem to be only painted disciples, or Christians on the mantelpiece, who never stir a foot or lift a hand? Is it not that, in the Psalmist's words, we have forgotten to eat our bread? They, on the contrary, learned from the Apostles to take this most profitable and life-giving food every day, and so they became strong, robust, energetic soldiers of Christ, ready and in trim for every labour, and for the last heroic conflict of martyrdom. Let us then try to be like them here on earth, that we may deserve to be their comrades in Heaven.

Robert liked to be as concrete as possible in his sermons, which now and then suggest a real vein of the poet in his imagination. Thus, speaking of love or charity as the soul of eloquence, he says:

Who is there in this illustrious home of learning who does not think daily as he goes to the schools of law, medicine, philosophy, or theology, how best he may progress in his particular subject, and win at last his doctor's degree? The school of Christ is the school of charity. On the last day, when the great general examination takes place, there will be no question at all on the text of Aristotle, the aphorisms of Hippocrates, or the paragraphs of Justinian. Charity will be the whole syllabus.

Or there is this little fable as a substitute for the metaphor of time's winged chariot:

Once upon a time a poor fellow stumbled over the edge of a dizzy cliff. By a lucky chance, he managed in his fall to grasp hold of a little bush which grew from the side of the rock, but hope died in his heart when he peered into the crevice to examine the roots of his frail support. For what was it he saw? Two mice, a black one and a white, gnawing ceaselessly at the roots, and already half way through them. And such is human life, pitched perilously between two eternities. Day and Night eat into it with never a pause. Soon they will be through, and what will happen then?

A final example of his style and equally a reflection of his soul is from a sermon which he preached at Padua when aged twenty-five. It is on the opening verse of Psalm 90, *Qui habitat in adjutorio Altissimi*, or in the new Latin version, *Qui degit in praesidio Altissimi*, which comes to much the same thing:

Let us take each word of the Psalm singly and think it out. In the first place, we notice that the Prophet names no particular class of men, in order to show that God's promises are for everybody. So he does not say, "A rich man that dwelleth in the aid of the Most High", lest the poor should seem to be excluded, nor "A poor man that dwelleth", lest the rich should seem to be left out. But he says in general terms *Qui*, which stands for all the world. No class, nor age, nor sex, nor rank, nor state, but finds a place in that universal relative. God is not an acceptor of persons. He is everybody's friend, providing for and defending each and all who fly to him in their troubles. He that dwelleth in the aid of the Most High, whoever he be, rich or poor, great or small, noble or rustic, prince or commoner, he shall infallibly abide under the protection of the God of Heaven.

The next word, *habitat*, dwelleth, means a great deal. It is a little word, but full of power and energy. Notice that what is said is not "he who trusts" or "he who confides", but "he who dwells". This is to bring home to us that we are not to fly to the divine protection as men do to a tree or a doorway when it rains, but rather as little boys are wont to rush to their fathers' arms when anything frightens them. We see them playing with their companions in the streets, but no sooner does the least thing go wrong, than they are off home as fast as their small legs will carry them. It never occurs to them to doubt the security of home. They know that they have mother and father there who would gladly give their hearts' blood to protect them. But people who seek refuge from rain under a tree, have a good look round first, and it is only when no better shelter offers that they run willy-nilly to the tree. Why is it that some men implore divine assistance without receiving it, and seem to put their trust in God without being protected by him? The reason is that they do not really *dwell* in the aid of the Most High, nor take shelter under the providence of God as in their Father's house. They rather make sporadic dashes to it in time of trouble, as they do to a tree when there is a sudden shower. It is therefore very necessary for us to get into the way of always and instinctively turning to God. We must try by constant exercise of holy confidence to build for ourselves a house where we may abide safely when the dark hours come. And we must carry our trusty house about with us wherever we go, just as we see the snails do. They wander here and there and everywhere, and yet they are always at home. . .

The course of controversies which Bellarmine gave in Rome from 1576 onwards, earned him a European reputation and put him at once in the front rank of the Church's defenders. Like Rome itself, that great work was not built in a day. Its origins go back to the Louvain years and beyond them, for during all the time of his teaching and preaching he was studying, too, and studying with a very definite aim before him. He had no hint that he would be called upon to combat Protestantism directly, nor was the Society to which he belonged founded for such a purpose. Nevertheless, he prepared himself to hit the evil as hard as he could, if ever God should give him an opportunity, but always in charity and fairness. With this end in view, he spent his scanty leisure hours gathering and hewing the stones for his fortress of the faith. To the thoughtful modern mind, the very word controversy, in a religious context, bears an antiquated air. Ever since, in the early nineteenth century, the Tübingen Catholic theologian, Johann Adam Moehler, gave in his classic volume, *Symbolism*, a model of a serene and positive study of an opposing theology, there has been increasing dissatisfaction among Catholics, especially in Germany and America, with the older methods of apologetics which rarely made an effort to enter into the mind of such a man as Luther or to give him credit for retaining so many precious spiritual values, in spite of his revolt. Even the extensive biographies of Luther by such Catholic scholars as Denifle and Grisar are in this respect outmoded. Bellarmine lectured and wrote at a time when the Catholic Church was on the defensive and such an eirenic approach as Moehler's hardly possible, but St Robert did try very hard to understand the Protestant views and to state them fairly. Theology in his day was in a state of decline, due to many causes, and he did as much as any man to spread and stabilize the reform initiated by the great Dominican Francisco de Vitoria at Salamanca. In other words, he stressed the positive elements in theology, the assiduous study and use of Scripture, of the Fathers of the Church, the Councils, and Church history in general. Once, in later life he was invited to a solemn disputation which had for its subject, "Whether it be possible to see the Divine Essence apart from the Divine Persons". He listened patiently to all the finely spun arguments, but as he came away he gave a sigh and said: "Would it not be better to wait for the solution of such conundrums until we get to heaven, and spend the little time God allows us on earth in the study of positive and moral theology, and the holy Fathers?" We know from his own confession that he was a man of action rather than of speculation, a lover of the concrete and practical, who looked upon learning as just one among many ways of serving God. The Society of Jesus, which held his devoted allegiance, encouraged this natural bent. It, too, was built for action, a regiment on a war-footing with definite foes in view, namely, the passions of men, and definite weapons. During his time at the Roman College nearly all his professors were from Spain, and had been deeply influenced by the great scholastic revival in that country. Robert, in his turn, was influenced by them, and theology became for him what God meant it to be, a tool or a sword in the hand, and not a dialectical Catherine-wheel. Already when at Padua, his mind was turning to the great doctrinal controversies of the day, and in his sermons he made frequent references to them. Then providence sent him to Louvain, where he was in immediate touch with heresy of the most live and aggressive kind. He had gone there with no set purpose beyond that of preaching and studying in the ordinary way, but it was inevitable that his environment should react upon one so sensitive intellectually, and turn his interests into new channels. He saw the battle for souls in progress all around him, and being the man he was he could not help wanting to join in the fray. From this time on, the thought of the many fair lands, and of England particularly, which heresy was making desolate, began to trouble his meditations. His sermons are full of it. Sixty-eight different times he broke the thread of his discourse to warn his hearers against the dangers of false teaching. There in Louvain itself, a little group of English exiles, headed by the valiant Dr Nicholas Sanders, were a standing inspiration to his zeal. Year after year, from 1565 to 1572, they produced their telling and vigorously worded answers to the challenges that came to them from the homeland over the seas. He read those books carefully, and became convinced that their militant theology was exactly what the age of conflict required. It was a curious quirk of fate that brought him, one of the gentlest and least aggressive of men, into the battle line, but at any rate he fought chivalrously, too chivalrously, some Catholics maintained.

The great religious debate, if that word is not too mild to describe its thunders, had entered on a new phase with the publication of the first volume of *The Centuries of Magdeburg* in 1559. Luther's most ardent and energetic disciple, Mathias Francowitz, alias Flaccius Illyricus, a Dalmatian like that earlier lively controversialist, St Jerome, conceived the design of undermining the Roman claims by an elaborate appeal to history. He gathered men and money for the purpose, and launched his assault with all the airs of an unbiased scholar. The aim of the "Centuriators", as they were called, was to prove that the Lutheran and not the Roman Church was the Church of the Apostles. Each century in turn was scoured for evidence to support that thesis, and volume after volume appeared until, in 1574, when Robert Bellarmine was in the midst of his labours at Louvain, the work was brought to a triumphant conclusion. Written with a great flourish of documents, dates, and testimonies, the thirteen big folios were welcomed enthusiastically by Protestant Europe as the most deadly blow that had ever been dealt Catholicism. Among Catholics themselves there was a good deal of consternation. There were new features in this method of attack for which they were quite unprepared. Church history and patristic lore were certainly not the strong points of their scholarship, and it seemed doubtful whether a man could be found learned enough to write an effective reply. Meantime, the *Centuries* were doing immense harm. Stanislaus Hosius, the eminent papal legate, considered that no more pernicious work had ever been written. In May, 1567, Francis Borgia wrote to Peter Canisius telling him that the Pope wished the fathers of his German province of the Society of Jesus to undertake the refutation of the Centuriators. But St Peter, though he did eventually write three volumes in reply, considered that he and his brethren in Germany were not the men for such a task. He said that, being sorely distracted by the external affairs of the province, he felt "a distinct repugnance to those graver studies", and remarked also, "Hardly a man among us is even moderately versed in ecclesiastical history". Baronius, the great man who under St Philip Neri's inspiration was destined to pen, if not a perfect, at least a sufficiently good answer, admitted similarly, in the preface of his *Annals*, that "nothing had hitherto been so much neglected in the Church as genuine, sure, and exact study of ecclesiastical history, and its adequate narration in books".

This incident of the *Centuries of Magdeburg* emphasized in an unpleasant way the need for more positive methods in theological study and teaching. For Bellarmine the need was a challenge. Daily the conviction deepened in his mind that theology, if it was to be effective, must come down from the clouds and go out girded like a crusader to do battle with the Church's enemies. Not by syllogisms only was the Lord going to save his people. Catholic scholars must take a leaf from their enemies' book, and make more of history and criticism, for only thus could the Protestant appeal to the past be turned into a victorious argument for the Church of the ages. The Scriptures were his first field, for the proper understanding of which Hebrew was necessary, so

Hebrew he decided to learn. He had not many spare hours in his busy day and learning Hebrew, or, indeed, learning anything in the sixteenth century, was not the straightforward task it is now, when our shelves are loaded with grammars, lexicons, and well-edited texts. Robert had to teach himself everything, digging his information laboriously out of the crabbed, disorderly books of the rabbis, or the hardly more methodical efforts at a grammar which bore the names of Pico della Mirandola and Reuchlin. The best testimony to the success of his endeavours is given by a small manuscript volume which is in the archives of the Society of Jesus. It runs to 114 pages, each containing from eighteen to twenty-five lines, and is partly a kind of Hebrew exercise-book, and partly a commentary on Genesis. Robert wrote it, apparently, for the sake of some students to whom he was teaching the language. One of these men recalled, fifty years later, the "extraordinary enthusiasm" for Hebrew which their young master's encouragement and example had inspired—*permirum discendi ardorem*. The text-book proves in a striking way how wide his reading was at this early date. The authority of the Fathers is constantly invoked, and medieval and more recent commentators are laid under contribution with almost equal frequency, while he adduces also apt testimonies from Virgil, Tacitus, Pliny, Strabo, Josephus, and other pagan worthies. Already he shows the independence of judgment which was afterwards to be a characteristic feature of his scholarship, often incorrect but always his own. Thus, he rejects the two commonest opinions as to the construction of *b'resith*, the first word of the Bible, and puts forward a new explanation. A little later he qualifies St Jerome's construing of a word as "*non valde probabilis*", which is a decidedly bold comment to come from a mere beginner. The extraordinary kind of beginner he was, though, is shown by the long archaeological excursus into which he wanders on the meaning of the word *bega* in Genesis xxiv. 22, which was accorded a different meaning in the various versions of the Hebrew Scriptures. Robert boldly tried to harmonize the conflicting renderings. He even compiled a new Hebrew grammar at this time and, in order to prove to his students that the language was not impossibly difficult, he guaranteed to teach anyone willing to take up the challenge enough of the grammar in one week to enable him to read the Scriptures with the sole aid of a dictionary. Someone accepted the bargain and, before the week was up, found that his professor's promise was not in the least an idle boast. St Robert's *Hebrew Grammar* was subsequently published in 334 pages, and long remained without a rival. All the same, he was only an amateur Hebraist.

Among the treasures of the Louvain University library which perished in the fire of 1914 was a large Latin Bible annotated throughout by this most diligent of students. The notes in his microscopically small script which wriggled between the closely printed lines, and tumbled over one another down the margins and across the blank spaces at the top and bottom of each page, told of many an hour stolen from rest or recreation. Most of them were in tiny Hebrew characters, but even those in Latin were very difficult to decipher because their author, intending them for no eye but his own, used a kind of home-made shorthand to lighten his labours.

Robert's concern with Scriptural questions is very well reflected in a letter which he wrote in April, 1575, to Cardinal Guglielmo Sirleto, prefect of the Vatican Library and the most eminent Catholic scholar then alive. Sirleto had been the tutor of his Cervini cousins and Bellarmine had himself spent his first day in Rome in the great man's house. He wrote with trepidation, and only because learned men in Louvain had begged him to do so. Sirleto was obviously a formidable person to approach. What Robert's friends wanted was that the Cardinal, with all the resources of the Vatican at his disposal, should publish a criticism of various annotations on the New Testament Vulgate that had been made by the very great scholar Lorenzo Valla and put into circulation by Erasmus, as they were tendentious and subversive of Catholic belief. Also, that for the good of souls he would bring his immense learning to bear on the semi-Lutheran notes attached to Le Fèvre d'Etaples' French version of the New Testament published in 1523, and to Theodore Beza's edition of the Vulgate which came out at Geneva in 1556. Robert, with much modesty and deference, tells Sirleto that Beza's *Annotations* are in "every-body's hands" and doing very great harm, for which only the Cardinal can provide the remedy. Then he begs for light on several questions which were troubling his own mind. What precisely did the Council of Trent mean when it styled the Vulgate *authentic*? Opinions were sharply divided, some doctors contending that authenticity implied an almost verbal accuracy in the Latin text, while others more reasonably saw in the term only the Church's solemn approval of St Jerome's work as her official Bible, containing nothing offensive to faith or morals. He would be so grateful for the Cardinal's opinion, as also for his views about the extant Hebrew texts, the unity of authorship so long attributed to the Septuagint, then being widely questioned, the canonicity of the last seven chapters of the Book of Esther, and some other points. As far as can be ascertained Sirleto did not deign to reply to Robert, though he supplied Peter Canisius with transcripts of some Vatican texts about this time. Peter, the general handyman of the papacy in Germany, was twenty-one years older than Robert, and at that time far more widely known, which may be the explanation of Sirleto's rudeness to the eager young person at Louvain.

Lecturing daily to a hundred students, preaching a carefully prepared Latin sermon each Sunday, spending interminable hours in the confessional, giving each fortnight long and truly loving "domestic exhortations" to his Jesuit brethren, poring over his big Bible morning, noon and night, seeing a constant stream of visitors in a cold and draughty parlour, and giving each the impression that he was the only person in Belgium who counted to the frail, infirm little priest of thirty-three, how was he able also to study so intensively the Fathers of the Church and ecclesiastical history in general, that his notes on those far-ranging subjects, when published forty years later to save them from piratical and distorting hands, had to be reprinted no fewer than twenty times, under the title *De scriptoribus ecclesiasticis*? It is the more of a mystery because he was at the same time reading and annotating by special permission the works of the German and Swiss reformers, under difficult conditions, as he was not permitted to

keep any of those books in his own room and had to study them
in the rector's room, where they were kept under lock and key.
He had been appointed a consultor to this rector, Jacques Schipmann, and part of his duty was to report periodically to Rome on
his rule of the house. This is what he said in 1573: "As for Father
Rector, two things occur to me. One of them is, as I mentioned
in an earlier letter, that he does not show externally that benevolence to the brethren which would seem desirable if they are
freely to approach his Reverence as a father and open their hearts
to him on their spiritual needs. He rarely comes to recreation, and
when he does he is much too quick to reprehend with harsh words
every little occurrence. The consequence is that he is more generally feared than loved. . ." Fancy trying to study the works of
Luther or Calvin under that glassy and unsympathetic eye! In
spite of his medical lore, Schipmann was removed from his
office but, strange to say, made rector of the Douay college
instead. Perhaps the General of the time, Everard Mecurian,
himself a Belgian, thought that his temper might improve in the
south-west, but it did not and he had to be reduced to the ranks,
from which, it seems plain, he ought never to have risen.

There is much correspondence at this time as to whether Robert
should not preach courses in Italian to the merchants of his own
country trafficking in Antwerp. He detested the idea, guessing
that they would besiege his confessional and confront him with all
sorts of problems arising out of the swift development of capital-
ism and investment about which the moral theologians were still
at sixes and sevens. The old legislation of the Church on the
subject of interest was breaking down before the onslaught of
bankers and big business, and no new guidance had come from
the popes to replace it. In Germany, the problems nearly drove
St Peter Canisius out of his senses, for the transaction known as
the *Contractus Germanicus*, a form of investment at five per cent,
led to open war between his successor as provincial, the very able
Father Paul Hoffaeus who believed it to be legitimate, and
Peter's friend, the crotchety descendant of St Thomas More,
Father Jasper Heywood, who was ready to go to the stake and to
send Hoffaeus there, in testimony of its iniquity. Father Bellar-

mine was determined not to become involved in such toils unless required by obedience, a fate which superiors spared him. His only other dislike was hearing the confessions of society women, who were too much inclined to talk about anything except their sins.

While Robert was at Louvain, Charles Borromeo, only four years his senior, had begun his great reformation of the huge and scandalously corrupt archdiocese of Milan. In his consuming zeal (he died at forty-six) Charles took little account of the rights of other people and other places. He pestered St Philip Neri to send his comparatively few Oratorians to Milan and, when Philip made excuses for not allowing him his right-hand man, Francesco Maria Tarugi, he charged the Saint with selfishness, disobedience and want of zeal for God's glory. Philip wrote an indignant letter in reply, but it may be doubted whether he dispatched it in its first fiery draft. "You accuse me of not being mortified because I will not let you have Father Baronius, but I am certain, and by your leave I am going to tell you so frankly, that you are far more lacking in detachment. Many people, including the bishops of Rimini and Vercelli, say this about you, and also that you are not above downright robbery. When you set eyes on a capable man, you immediately try to allure him to Milan. You are a most daring and audacious robber of holy and learned men. As the proverb says, you despoil one altar in order to adorn another. . ." All this was perfectly true, and one of the holy and learned men on whom the authoritarian St Charles had set his heart was Robert Bellarmine. He played the same game with the Jesuits as with the Oratorians, exacted a vague promise and then held them rigidly to it. Letter after letter went off to Rome wanting to know when Father Bellarmine was to leave Louvain to take up his post as professor of theology in Charles's new diocesan seminary of Brera. Father Adorno, Robert's former provincial, abetted Borromeo's designs for the good reason that he was rector of the Brera college, and even Polanco gave way before the whirlwind from Milan. But the Louvain fathers succeeded in keeping their prize until 1576, when his ill-health at last obliged Robert's recall to Italy. In any case his services were sorely needed at the ever-expanding Roman College which then numbered two thousand students. Father Mercurian instructed him to return by way of Genoa and carefully to avoid Milan where San Carlo lay in ambush.

CHAPTER III

PROFESSOR OF CONTROVERSIAL THEOLOGY IN ROME

GREGORY XIII sat in the Chair of St Peter when Bellarmine reached Rome. His family name, Buoncompagni, suited him, for he was very good-natured and generous with alms, though far too much attached to his natural son, Giacomo, born before he became a priest. He was fond of glory and liked to be praised, altogether a very different type from his severe, unbending predecessor, St Pius V. Gregory was personally very devout and deeply concerned by the progress of heresy in the North and the incursions of the Turks, who had already recovered from Lepanto, in the South. One of his strongest convictions was that the tide of heresy could best be stemmed by education. The priests especially who had to meet the enemy face to face in the lost lands of England and Germany needed to be thoroughly practised in the strategy of their new warfare. For that purpose he had founded or reorganized no fewer than twenty-three colleges and seminaries in Rome and other suitable places. The first of these institutions to enjoy his liberality was the German College which St Ignatius had established in 1553, but which, twenty years later, was on the point of being closed for lack of funds. Gregory came to the rescue in the nick of time, and endowed the institution out of the papal treasury. In 1579 it was England's turn. The little colony of students who resided with their Welsh rector, Dr Clenock, in the old hospice of St Thomas of Canterbury, was transformed by papal brief into a national college under the direction of the Jesuits. Only one thing more remained to put the crown on the Pope's munificence. The great Roman College, on which the others depended for their instruction, was itself so poor that the fourth general congregation of the Society of Jesus had to appeal for assistance. When Gregory consulted Cardinal Contarelli on the matter, he received for

answer an application of Nabuchodonosor's dream: "Holy
Father, you and your predecessors have built a statue like to that of
the King of Babylon. The German College with its rich endowments is the head of gold; the English College is the breast of
silver; the Greek College is the belly of brass; the Maronite
College the legs of iron, and the Roman College, which supports
them all, the feet of clay." The Pope was greatly impressed by
this parable, and set to work with such energy that by 1584 the
west and south sides of the magnificent Gregorian University
were completed. Buildings and endowments, however, are only
the *corpus vile* of an educational scheme. The teaching is its soul,
and that soul, though vigorous enough on the side of abstract
theology, took, in those days, only a languid interest in the
vicissitudes of Christian truth throughout the centuries.

As far back as 1561, when Robert Bellarmine was himself a
student of the Roman College, a chair of controversial theology
existed among its departments. The men responsible for the
curriculum saw clearly that scholastic theology was not by itself
sufficient equipment for times when every dogma had to pass the
fiery test of history, and when the Centuriators of Magdeburg
were giving a new trend to the religious debate in their efforts to
show the width of the chasm which separated contemporary
Roman usages from the simple rites of primitive Christianity.
Unfortunately, however, the chair of controversies was not a
success. Ten years later another effort was made under the
direction of Ledesma, a brilliant theologian but a rather unprac-
tical professor. His lectures were too disconnected to be of much
service, and after a year of experimenting, the course lapsed once
again until resumed in 1574 by a Father Fernandez. It is quite plain
that the authorities were feeling their way all the time, and while
recognizing the need were puzzled how to meet it. Robert
Bellarmine was appointed to the difficult post shortly after his
arrival in Rome, and began the great work of his life with the
good wishes of both Pope and General to encourage him. The
astonishing thing about this beginning was its assurance. He was
very young, only thirty-four, and he had no long tradition to
guide him. Controversial theology, as found in the books, was a

chaos and not a science, yet he started out on his explorations like one who knew every foot of the ground. A fragment of the inaugural address which he delivered on November 26, 1576, is extant in manuscript, and we have besides the more elaborate version which he prepared later as a preface for the first volume of his *Controversies*. It is an interesting document as showing the spirit in which he faced his task:

Today, gentlemen, we approach those questions which are at issue between the Church of the living God and her rebellious and fugitive sons. . . . My endeavour shall be, with the help of Heaven, to gather all those diverse, multitudinous questions together and weld them into unity. It will not be an easy task. In my poor judgment it would require for its adequate performance knowledge almost limitless, not only of various sciences and languages, but of the length and breadth of human history as well. Since I am sadly aware of the smallness of my own little stock of knowledge, and yet must needs bear the burden imposed upon me, I shall try at least to make up by hard work and diligence for the deficiencies of my learning. Even should you find me lacking in the niceties of learning, you will not be able to reproach me with want of industry and care. . . . The importance of these disputations which I am undertaking may easily be seen from the fact that they comprise the larger and more necessary part of all theology. Our concern will not be with little things that make no difference however they stand, nor with the subtleties of metaphysics which a man may ignore without being any the worse for it, but with God, with Christ, with the Church, with the Sacraments, and with a multitude of other matters which pertain to the very foundations of our faith.

Next he proceeds in a few strokes to unfold his plan of campaign:

The enemy of the human race, though he is the father of confusion, yet goes to work with a certain method in his attack on the Church of Christ. He started in the earliest ages with an assault on the first article of the Creed, having for his allies such heretics as the Manichaeans and Gnostics. The whole aim of these men was to overthrow belief in God, the Father

Almighty, Creator of heaven and earth. When that attack failed, the devil in the third century directed his efforts against the second article, wherein the divinity of Christ is declared. Praxeas, Sabellius, Paul of Samosata, Arius, Eunomius, and others rose to do battle for him, and when their offensive too was frustrated, he succeeded in enlisting a new host to carry on the war against the inter-related, third, fourth, fifth, sixth, and seventh articles. . . . Next, with Photius and his followers, came the great attack on the Holy Ghost. That, too, according to the divine guarantee was a failure, and the devil, seeing all his assaults on Father, Son, and Holy Ghost to be useless, turned with savage fury on the ninth and tenth articles: "I believe in the Holy Catholic Church, the Communion of Saints, the forgiveness of sins". From the year 1000 A.D., those two articles have been the main object of heretical attack. Berengarians, Waldenses, Albigenses, Wyclifites, Hussites, Lutherans, Zwinglians, Calvinists, Anabaptists, etc., each in turn doing their utmost to overthrow them.

Since, therefore, the heresies of this age are practically all concerned with the ninth and tenth articles of the Creed, we shall confine our lectures to those two articles. We shall begin by treating of the Church, and in this disputation we shall have, first of all, to deal with Christ himself who is the Church's head and ruler. Then we shall go on to discuss that part of the Church which is labouring on earth under its visible head, the pope. Next the Church suffering will claim our attention, and finally that part of the Church which triumphs blessedly with Christ in Heaven. At this point we shall have occasion to speak of the veneration and invocation of the saints, of relics, sacred images, and similar matters. Having done so, we shall proceed to treat of the Communion of Saints, under which heading the Sacraments may be grouped. Each Sacrament will have a whole treatise to itself, as there is no part of Catholic dogma so cried down and criticized by the heretics. Last of all, we shall deal with the tenth article of the Creed to which appertain various debatable matters concerning grace, justification, free will, and merit.

There was a time when theories of grace and free will used to stir up the hearts of common men like the blast of a trumpet, but that age of belief, orthodox or heterodox, has long been part of the curious past. The religious debate has passed through many phases since the reformers first began to wield the axe of criticism high up among the branches of the great tree of Catholic tradition. There has been a revolution in men's minds since those brave and relatively innocent old times, brought about by the marvellous progress of scientific discovery and the no less wonderful advances in biblical and archaeological scholarship. The point of view of Bellarmine and his contemporaries is no longer ours. They emphasized arguments with which we find ourselves in no sympathy, and they are very diffuse over matters which, for us, are out of date. Thus the Protestants were given to writing books in proof of the pope's being Antichrist. It was a main contention of Flaccius Illyricus and his band of Centuriators. Bellarmine was of course, obliged to notice that nonsense, and did so to the extent of thirty thousand words which for present-day purposes have no value whatever. Nor are these the only dead pages in his great volumes. Time demands a heavy toll of all such work, dimming its lustre, and blunting the fine edge of its opportuneness. Except where some happy grace of style immortalizes their form, the great prose books of other ages continue to be read and reverenced only because of the constant doctoring to which they are subjected.

Robert's lecture seems to have been the first each day, and was probably delivered at some unearthly hour before the rest of the world took breakfast, as there were several others to follow in the course of the morning. Had we been able to peep through the windows of his classroom in the year 1589 we should have noticed how packed it was, and what a brilliant pattern the cloaks of the audience made. There were red-robed Germans there, side by side with men in white garments from Italian towns, and others in sober black from far-away, tragical England. And those colours were symbolic, for many a confessor, and martyr soon to die, sat then at the feet of Bellarmine. In an English book, we may be pardoned for dwelling a little on his relations with the young men from the English College. It was for them and for the Germans that he chiefly laboured, as he points out himself in a note prefixed to the first volume of the *Controversies*:

C

When Pope Gregory XIII, of blessed memory, in his zeal to assist Germany and England established two great colleges for the young men of those countries, I was appointed to teach them controversial theology in our schools, and thus, as it were, to arm these new soldiers of the Church for the war with the powers of darkness which they should have to wage when they returned home.

It was before Bellarmine and two others that the English students made, on April 25, 1579, their vow of returning to their country to labour and, if needs be, to die, for its salvation. "Mr Sherwin, who was then a priest and student of divinity, was the first to declare his sentiments. With his hands on the Holy Scriptures, he took an oath that he was ready at a sign of his superiors to go, and that, rather today than tomorrow, for the good of souls." Besides Sherwin, Blessed Luke Kirby and Blessed William Hart were also present at that parade before battle, and in addition to them, Bellarmine numbered among his friends and pupils the martyrs John Lowe, Christopher Buxton, Edward James, Edmund Duke, John Ingram, John Cornelius, Henry Walpole, Robert Southwell and Edward Oldcorne. Indeed, he might have been himself an English martyr had he been given his way, for it is on record that "he volunteered to go to England to lecture openly against the heretics". However, the chances of such an offer being accepted were very remote if we may judge by the Salmeron incident, which took place at this time. That distinguished companion of St Ignatius and theologian of Trent was living in retirement at Naples. When invited by the General of the Jesuits to publish his works he agreed to do so on condition of being given some learned father as an assistant in the undertaking. The General, Everard Mercurian, immediately thought of Bellarmine, whereupon a strange thing happened. No sooner did his Paternity set about making the necessary arrangements than peremptory orders arrived from the Pope that Bellarmine was on no account to leave Rome. Being an invaluable man had its drawbacks, for Cardinal Santa Severina, the Grand-Inquisitor, who was a warm admirer of Father Robert and had made use of him in the complex and delicate business of his exalted office, had succeeded in persuading the Pope to issue a veto against the proposed departure from Rome. That meant that Robert was virtually a prisoner and though, as Mercurian wrote to Salmeron, the Holy Father had been implored most earnestly—*con ogni caldezza*—to withdraw his prohibition, prisoner he remained for nearly a year.

When at last set free, he repaired at once to Naples and spent the summer of 1579 there, carefully reading through an allotted portion of Salmeron's endless commentaries on the New Testament. They run to sixteen folio volumes, each page in double columns of relatively small print, and are fascinating to browse in, to see how a fabulously learned man dealt with New Testament problems in the sixteenth century. It was not pleasant work, verifying thousands of references in the blaze of the Neapolitan sun, nor could anyone call it a holiday task to have to point out his mistakes to a distinguished but somewhat easily irritated man. Salmeron was not really old, only sixty-four, but he had worked very hard all his life and was worn out. The first time Bellarmine appeared with his budget of errata he received a very cold welcome indeed, but that did not deter him. He had not come all the way from Rome to waste his breath praising what it would have been an impertinence for him to praise, so next morning he returned boldly with another long list of mistakes. This time the humble-hearted Spaniard did not try to defend them, but accepted all his young censor's suggestions, and that was the beginning of a lasting friendship between them.

On August 28, Mercurian wrote asking Robert to come back soon. The students, he said, who so much appreciated his lectures, would be very distressed if he were not in his place on the day when schools began. He must, then, try to placate Father Salmeron, and obtain his leave to return to Rome by mid-September, where, adds the General, "we await you *con desiderio*". He was back by the twelfth of the month, and at once, without a day's rest, set about scrupulously careful preparation of his lectures for the autumn term. He had plenty of subsidiary occupations to think of also, for he was "professor of eloquence" to the young Jesuits at the College, preached often, as of old, once before Pope Gregory and all his cardinals, gave the customary domestic exhortations to his brethren, as well as regular instructions on Christian doctrine to the lay brothers, which subsequently formed the nucleus of his extremely popular catechism.

It is almost a platitude to say that nothing makes a man more selfish than hard concentrated work, especially of the learned kind. He hates to be interrupted or asked to step out of his groove, even at the call of charity. Robert Bellarmine had acquired in his life of prayer a peculiar detachment and serenity in this respect, which was not the least part of his holiness. Both inside and outside his order he was always helping someone or other, usually some harassed cardinal. Thus, from 1579 onwards, he was busy collaborating on a new edition of the works of St Ambrose which Montalto, the future brusque and mighty Pope Sixtus V, had undertaken. A great deal of his time was spent in doing people similar good turns, or in the case of humbler suppliants, in obtaining for them small favours on which they had set their hearts. One man wants the loan of a much-prized manuscript, another would be grateful if he would kindly obtain expert opinion for him from his friend Clavius on a point of applied mathematics. It was not surprising that he received so many appeals, because his way of answering them made it seem as if he counted it a favour to be asked. He never complained of having too much to do, but once in a very short letter to his brother Nicholas, begging him earnestly to see to the comfort of some fathers who were going to Montepulciano, he ended with a plea to be forgiven the brevity because he was "*occupatissimo*", or as busy as he could be.

Controversy of the kind to which he was devoted is not a fine art like the writing of poems or philosophies. These may be wrought out in fair independence of the hurly-burly beyond one's garden wall, but the first need of a controversialist is to know what the other side is saying. To discover that in Bellarmine's day, when there were no newspapers nor theological journals, meant struggling through a wilderness of arid tomes such as no modern man would have the courage to read. Then, too, these tomes were often very difficult to procure. Booksellers' catalogues had not yet been thought of, and there were hardly any booksellers as distinct from printers. If one wished to see the latest literature on any particular subject, the only way was to go, or get somebody else to go, to the half-yearly bookfair at Frankfurt. Public libraries, as we know them now, did not exist, though, owing to the scholarly zeal of Marcello Cervini, students were permitted to make use of the Vatican's treasures. In Rome it was particularly difficult to obtain possession of heretical books owing to the vigilance of the officers of the Inquisition. Father Claudio Aquaviva, Mercurian's successor as General of the Jesuits, wrote to the vice-provincial of Naples in August, 1586, asking him to send Bellarmine a copy of the latest edition of Beza's New Testament. If the book were too big to be carried by some father of the Society *en route* for Rome, then the vice-provincial must devise an alternative means of getting it through, taking care to have it well packed between boards, sealed, and addressed to Bellarmine himself. These precautions were necessary, the General said, "to prevent trouble should the volume fall into the hands of the customs-officers of the Inquisition". Robert was a member of the commission for the revision of the Vulgate and so naturally interested in Beza's learned work which made use of codices then unexploited, particularly the one called after himself, the *Codex Bezae*, now at Cambridge.

Remembering those initial difficulties we are in a better position to understand what his studies in heresy must have cost this *vir lectionis stupendae*, as a famous Anglican bishop styled St Robert. There was hardly a single contemporary or recent heretic of any note whose writings he did not know thoroughly, as a glance through the pages of his *Controversies* proves. Day by day the fame of the controversial lectures grew and spread, not only throughout Rome but in England, Germany and Poland. The King of this last country, Stephen I Bathori, strove very eagerly in 1584 to acquire their author for service in Warsaw, where there were numerous heretics of various persuasions even in his own court. He wanted him, wrote Cardinal Bolognetti, nuncio to the king, "by hook or by crook".

At length Robert began to be inundated with requests for the publication of his lectures, and some enthusiasts even went so far as to threaten that if he did not soon comply they would take the law into their own hands. The General of the Jesuits, too, showed himself very keen, and so indeed did everybody except the man most concerned, who simply had not the time to prepare a large and complicated volume for the press. Whenever a learned commission was appointed, or learned investigations were set on foot, Father Bellarmine was sure to be found in the thick of them. Thus, prior to 1581, he devoted much attention to questions bearing on the reform of the calendar and, though no mathematician himself, acquired for his intimate friend, Christopher Clavius, such works of the past as might be helpful in the inquiry, particularly the many manuscripts of his grandfather Riccardo Cervini, who had been a notable apostle of calendar reform in the days of Pope Clement VII. At the same time Robert was one of a board charged by the Pope with the wearisome task of revising a large collection of rabbinical writings, and a few years later another board claimed him, this time for the more congenial business of preparing a new edition of the Septuagint. There were grave politico-religious questions, too, such as those of the "Sicilian Monarchy", and the excommunication of Henry of Navarre, which kept his pen busy in defence of papal action. On the Sicilian question, a burning one down to the days of Pius IX, he wrote a little treatise in twenty paragraphs for the benefit of the viceroy of the province, Marcantonio Colonna, nephew of the celebrated Vittoria Colonna. Bellarmine was devoted to the Colonna family, and particularly to Marcantonio, who some years earlier had been accorded a public triumph in Rome for his valour at the battle of Lepanto. Since the days of the Norman Conquest there had been trouble in the two Sicilies because its kings, and afterwards the kings of Aragon, claimed full ecclesiastical authority there, to the exclusion of all papal interference. Bellarmine wrote, he said, "because of the love he bore Marcantonio, and the fear he had lest God should send some terrible calamity on him and his house on account of the Sicilian Monarchy". His charity does not seem to have availed much. Perhaps it even lost him the friendship of that powerful family, for during the conclave in which Paul V was elected there appears to have been a Colonna intrigue to bar the possibility, very remote in any case, of Bellarmine being chosen.

The worst intruders on his scanty leisure in those years of feverish activity were not popes nor prelates, but his own brethren of the Society of Jesus. Whenever they discovered a Protestant book which seemed to be causing more harm than usual, they had a habit of sending the troublesome thing to Rome for refutation, instead of sitting down and doing the work themselves. Thus, in 1584, Bellarmine was burdened with the answering of a long-winded essay by Flaccius Illyricus which endeavoured to prove to the German people that the Holy Roman Empire, of which they were the inheritors, had come to them quite independently of any papal concession. It was a tedious question to have to read up, but Father Robert was nothing if not thorough and his rejoinder occupies nearly a hundred double-column pages in Fèvre's edition of his works (Paris, 1873, vol. VI). It has no value now, except as an illustration of historical methods which have been superseded, and also, perhaps, of St Robert's devotion to the Holy See.

His lively criticism of the Lutheran *Book of Concord* had a similar origin. Someone sent it to him in 1585, and received back a long review in which "six grave blunders and sixty-seven lies" were dealt with trenchantly. He did not intend this document for publication, but the good man for whose private eye he wrote it brought it out of his own accord and thereby fluttered the dovecotes of Wittenberg.

There was another reason too, besides lack of time, which must have made the editing of his lectures seem to him an impossible task. He gives it in a paragraph of his long letter to Salmeron of July 19, 1584:

I had planned to lecture on the sacraments during the coming year, or rather to begin my treatment of them, as I shall not get through the matter in a year, but I am doubtful now whether I shall be able to carry out my programme. Last Whitsuntide, a disease of the nerves attacked me in the head and right arm, and caused me the most dreadful pain I have ever experienced. For some days I was unable to make the

slightest movement in bed, and could not obtain a wink of
sleep, even with the aid of opiates. Several remedies were tried,
such as the removal of much blood from my arms, feet, and
shoulders, and ointments and fomentations of many kinds. As
a result of these the spasms passed away, but I have not yet
recovered the use of my arm. The physicians were thinking of
performing a cautery on my neck to remedy this trouble but,
in order to spare me the nuisance of sticking-plaster and
bandages, they operated on my left arm instead. They have
come to the conclusion that the attack was due to over-study,
so if I do not make a good recovery I may be prevented from
pursuing my course next year. At present, I am in banishment
at Frascati, and not reading very much. Please forgive me,
Father, if I have wearied you with this long letter, and remember me in your holy prayers and sacrifices.

In spite of his illness Robert's lectures on the sacraments began
according to programme and, in addition, he settled down in real
earnest to the perfectly dreadful task of preparing his manuscript
for the press. It was not by his own will, he said, that he undertook
the work, but at the command of his superiors, and because he
hoped that it might prove of temporary service until some better
scholar wrote a better book. Every one of the two million words
which it contained when complete, was written out by the right
arm that had suffered so much and been so roughly used by the
doctors. This we know on the authority of his close friend, the
Cretan Jesuit Andreas Eudaemon-Joannes, who himself saw the
copies. The first volume of the *Controversies* was issued in 1586
from the press of David Sartorius of Ingolstadt, and bore diplomas
from Pope Sixtus V, the Emperor Rudolph II, and the Republic
of Venice. It was dedicated to the Pope who, in return for the
honour, sent its author a gift of four hundred gold pieces to help
defray the costs of publication. Seven treatises were contained in
the huge folio, on Scripture and Tradition; on Christ the Head of
the entire Church; on the Pope the head of the Church on earth;
on the members of the Church militant, clergy, religious, and
laymen; on the Church suffering in Purgatory; and on the
Church triumphant in Heaven. As an indication of the fullness of

treatment accorded to each of these subjects, it may be said that the single controversy on the Pope would make a very substantial modern book, if printed separately. The second volume, containing the lectures on the sacraments, appeared in 1588 or within a little over a year after their first delivery. In it, two hundred and fifty-nine ecclesiastical writers are cited textually, as well as fifty-nine historians, philosophers, and humanists. These quotations are practically all first hand, that is, they were selected from their context by Bellarmine himself. He was not content merely to appropriate the happy findings of other explorers, nor was he satisfied with putting his own findings down in a row and leaving them, as he had been inclined to do at Louvain. He proceeded to explain them, to show how they fitted in with and threw new light on other more recalcitrant texts, and finally, to bring out the real strength of their witness to Catholic belief. Five years were to elapse before the appearance of his last volume containing the three great treatises on grace, free will and justification, a delay due to circumstances entirely beyond the author's control.

Here it may be allowable to pause for a moment on an abstract consideration. It is easy enough to throw oneself into work and not impossible to throw oneself into prayer, but to throw the prayer into the work with vigour and persistence is an adjustment that calls for the rarest kind of courage. The attractiveness of St Robert Bellarmine's story lies precisely here. Without instituting comparisons which *The Imitation of Christ*, his favourite reading from boyhood, deprecated, it might fairly be said that there were many saints more illustrious for virtues and miracles than he, and not a few more learned men, but how rare the artists in living who, like him, combined the two things perfectly. He was a great scholar at least by the standards of his age, and a saint by the unchanging standards of Heaven. The three folios of his *Controversies* were his three vows bound in vellum, because it was the love in his heart for these things that begot the other things in his intellect. We may study now, very briefly, how that love showed itself when challenged by his life's circumstances. In 1588 the Society to which he belonged was passing through

CX

one of the worst crises of its chequered history, for Pope Sixtus V
seemed bent on changing its constitutions and its name. In the
thick of the trouble one of its own sons turned traitor. Julian
Vincent, an eccentric priest of the College of Bordeaux, had for
various reasons conceived a grudge against his superiors. He wrote
a preposterous paper in which the General of the Jesuits was
declared to be infallible, and then, coming to Rome without any
leave, he persuaded a simple-minded old father to sign the document. No sooner was this done than he denounced his dupe to the
Inquisition, and backed up the charge with an elaborate attack
on the Jesuit doctrine of obedience. The accused man, notwithstanding his age, was thrown into prison and the Pope himself
did not disdain to take part in the judicial proceedings. Aquaviva
turned for help to Robert Bellarmine, who promptly composed a
little treatise *On the Obedience designated Blind*, wherein Vincent
and his friends were duly and decently annihilated.

No better defence of the third vow of religion was ever
written, and few of Bellarmine's innumerable pages are so finely
reasoned, incisive, and victorious. It could not have been otherwise, because the enthusiasm of a life's convictions went to their
making. After extolling the virtue itself, and tearing Vincent's
travesty of it to pieces, he went on to show that it implied no
irresponsible right to command, that it was the necessary attitude
of all good Christians in the face of any precept of the Church,
that it was plainly commended in the Scriptures and the writings
of the Fathers, of whom he quoted fourteen passages, that it was
taught by all masters of the religious life, and that the similes
of a corpse and a staff, which offended many people's sensibilities,
were not the original invention of St Ignatius, but borrowed by
him from St Basil and St Francis of Assisi. Just as, when a boy,
Robert had come to the rescue of his school so, when a man, he
played a brave and brilliant part in the saving of his Order. The
imprisoned father was released, and the unfortunate Vincent, who
launched an attack on the Pope, would have lost his head by the
sword if he had not already lost it in another fashion. Bellarmine
had foreseen what was coming and, alluding to the savage taunts
of his antagonist, remarked that the poor fellow obviously

"needed hellebore much more than a refutation", the root of that plant affording a powerful cathartic.

Those who lived with St Robert in Rome relate that he went to almost extravagant lengths in his love for the vow of poverty. Here, indeed, St Francis of Assisi, on whose feast he was born and whose name he bore, marked him for his very own. He would not keep in his possession as trifling a thing as a holy picture or a blessed medal, except the one attached to his rosary beads. At the Roman College they used to have a kind of "clearance day" periodically, when all the fathers and brothers were invited to deliver up whatever superfluous goods they discovered in their rooms. Bellarmine usually had nothing to declare, but on one occasion he came with a little relic given him by some friend, which he had obtained permission to keep. The rector, who obviously knew that the trifle was dear to its possessor on account of its associations, tried to persuade him to retain it, but did not succeed. Similarly, when kind people strove to get him to accept small presents by urging that he would find them useful as gifts for children or his brother Jesuits at Christmas time, his answer was always the same: "A poor man ought not to have anything to give away". In one of his domestic exhortations he makes the same strict point: "People say they are ashamed to have no objects of devotion to give to those who ask for them; they ought rather to be ashamed to have them to give". Even the manuscripts of his own compositions which he kept in his room worried him, and he used to envy the unlettered lay brothers who were privileged to be without such encumbrances.

Professors, in our day, are not expected to be scullions as well, but Bellarmine, it appears, used to fill that role. Thus, a Belgian priest studying under him in Rome reported in 1580: "When I was engaged with him in the service of the kitchen, and in washing and drying dishes, he did all this lowly work as energetically, carefully, and exactly as if it were the big business of theology that occupied him, and never a word did he speak nor once look round". This silence and absorption over the dishes did not come from melancholy or moodiness, for St Robert throughout life was noted and loved for his geniality, which extended occasion-

ally even to the making of atrocious puns. A marked trait
observable was his deference to the opinions of other people. The
Cretan Jesuit Eudaemon-Joannes particularly noticed this.
"When I had to revise any of his books", this priest testified,

> I used to be amazed at the humility with which he handed them
> over to me. I have still by me a note in his hand which runs as
> follows: "To the Reverend Father Eudaemon-Joannes, begging
> him to look over this manuscript and to decide whether it
> deserves to see the light or to remain in obscurity". And this
> was not said out of mere ceremony, for after I had been
> through the work he used to ask me again with the greatest
> earnestness to tell him the unvarnished truth. Speak out boldly,
> he would say, as a brother ought to a brother. Nor did he care
> in the least to know if his work would make a great noise in
> the world, but only whether it would do good. This was all
> he ever asked. He was most exact in noting any suggestions his
> advisers had to offer, however unimportant they might be,
> and if he disagreed with anyone, he always let him know.
> On one occasion he sent me a note saying that he had found
> some matter in St Thomas to be just the reverse of what I had
> found there. A little later he saw that he was wrong and that
> I was right, so what should he do but straightway come along
> in person to tell me that the victory was mine. That was always
> his way, not only with regard to his writings, but in cases of
> conscience and grave questions of theology. He used not only
> to ask advice, but to take it most readily, even though before
> he had held the opposite view. Indeed, many a time he made
> me feel quite ashamed, so like a pupil was he dealing with his
> master.

One way among others of estimating the historical importance
of a book or theory is to notice how the world welcomes it.
Admiration and hate are both good witnesses to the power of the
object that provokes them, and so, without ever looking inside
Bellarmine's majestic tomes, we may gain some notion of their
contemporary estimation if we will but observe the excitement
caused by their appearance. The bugles of Protestantism immediately sounded the alarm. A new style of enemy was in the gate,
one equipped, it was reported, as never a Roman before. In 1588

the greatest of the Elizabethan divines, William Whitaker, was Master of St John's College and Regius Professor of Divinity in the University of Cambridge. His *Disputation on Holy Scripture Against the Papists Especially Bellarmine and Stapleton* appeared that year, with an epistle dedicatory "To the most noble William Cecil, Baron Burghley, High Treasurer of England". This epistle is interesting enough to be quoted at some length:

There have been many heretofore, illustrious Cecil, who have defended the papal interest and sovereignty with the utmost exertion, the keenest zeal, and no mean or vulgar erudition. But they who have played their part with most address, and far outstripped almost all others of their own side, are those men who now, for some years back, have been engaged most earnestly in this Cause; a fresh supply of monks, subtle theologians, vehement and formidable controvertists; whom that strange—and in former times unheard of—Society of Jesus hath brought forth, for the calamity of the Church and the Christian religion. For when, after that black, deadly, baneful, and tedious night of Popish superstition and antichristianism, the clear and cheerful lustre of the Gospel had illuminated with its rays some portions of the Christian world . . , on a sudden these men sprang up to obscure with pestilential vapours, and ravish, if possible, from our view, this light, so hateful to themselves, so hostile and prejudicial to their interests. So indeed had John, that holy disciple of Christ, predicted in the Apocalypse. . . . This pit [of Rome] from the time it was first opened, hath not ceased to exhale perpetual smoke to blind the eyes of men, and hath sent forth innumerable locusts upon the earth, like scorpions, who have wounded with their deadly stings all men upon whose foreheads the Seal of God was not impressed. . . . Amongst these locusts—that is, as very learned men justly deem, amongst the innumerable troops of monks—none, as we before said, have ever appeared more keen or better prepared and equipped for doing mischief than are the Jesuits at this present day; who in a short space have surpassed all other societies of that kind in numbers, in credit, and in audacity. . . . Amongst these Jesuits, Robert Bellarmine, a native of Italy, hath now for several years obtained a great and celebrated name. At first he taught scholastic divinity in Belgium, but afterwards, having removed to Rome, he treated of theological controversies in such a manner as to excite the admiration and gain the applause of all. His lectures were eagerly listened to by his auditors, transcribed, transmitted into every quarter and treasured up as jewels and amulets. After some time, for the sake of rendering them more generally useful, they were epitomized by a certain Englishman. Finally the first volume of these Controversies hath been published at Ingolstadt, printed by Sartorius, and the rest are expected in due time. . . . When you, honoured Sir, demanded my opinion of the writer, I answered, as indeed I thought, that I deemed him to be a man unquestionably learned, possessed of a happy genius, a penetrating judgment, and multifarious reading. . . . Now that Bellarmine hath been published, we shall know better and more certainly what it is [our adversaries] hold upon every subject, the arguments on which they specially rely, and what is, so to speak, the very marrow of popery, which is thought to be as much in the Jesuits as in the Pope himself. Knowing therefore how much our party desire that these Jesuits should be answered, and having fallen in with a manuscript copy of Bellarmine's lectures, I thought it worth my while to handle these same controversies in the schools in the discharge of the duties of my office, to discuss the new sophisms of the Jesuits and vindicate our unadulterated truth from the captious cavils with which the popish professor hath entangled it.

The address which Dr Whitaker delivered before the Cambridge undergraduates at the commencement of his course was couched in similar terms: "The Papists," he said, "have two professors in two of their colleges, Stapleton at Douay and Allen at Rheims, both countrymen of ours (besides other doctors in other academies) who have explained many controversies and published books. . . . But beyond them all, in the largeness wherewith he hath treated these controversies is Robert Bellarmine, the Jesuit, at Rome, whose lectures are passed from hand to hand and diligently transcribed and read by very many. . . . Since Bellarmine hath handled these questions with accuracy and method, we will make him, so to speak, our principal aim, and follow, as it were, his very footsteps." That the learned doctor kept faithfully to his plan is evident from the mere titles of his books. The regularity with which these came from his pen, coupled with the fact that he was the father of a large family, gave rise to a saying, *quod mundo quotannis librum et liberum dedit*—that he presented the world with a book and a baby every year. Bellarmine's work had its purpose inscribed on the front page, "*adversus hujus temporis haereticos*", and Whitaker, copying the caption, advertised his answers as being "*contra hujus temporis papistas*". But he was a precise person, and so added to his titles the significant words: "*imprimis Robertum Bellarminum, Jesuitam*". That little codicil was to become very popular in the anti-Catholic literature of those spacious times, for nearly every Protestant doctor of any consequence, who wrote against the Church, flourished it on his front page.

The Oxford dons do not seem to have been quite so brisk in giving battle as their Cambridge brethren, but they showed no less zeal when at length aroused. Whitaker's counterpart among them was a certain Dr John Reynolds, about whom Fuller in his *Church History of England* tells a good though decidedly improbable story. Dr John's brother, William, was a zealous Catholic, and a professor at Rheims. According to Fuller, in early life it was the other way about, John being a zealous Papist and William an earnest Protestant. They had a great argument on religion one day and "providence so ordered it", says our historian, "that by their mutual disputation, John Reynolds turned an eminent Protestant and William an inveterate Papist". John, who had a clever, ambitious head, and later initiated the project of the Authorized Version, was appointed in 1586 to a temporary lectureship at Oxford, founded by Sir William Walsingham "for the confutation of Roman tenets". "He read this lecture," says Anthony Wood, "in the Divinity School thrice a week in full term, had constantly a great auditory, and was held by those of his party to have done great good." Whether or no it was part of his mandate, Dr John occupied himself almost exclusively with Bellarmine. The first of his books against him appeared in 1596, but not till fifteen years later did his complete course of two hundred and fifty Oxford Lectures *adversus Pontificios, imprimis Bellarminum* see

the light. In addition to Reynolds, Wood relates that Richard
Field, of Magdalene Hall, Oxford, "was for seven years together,
every Sunday, a discusser of controversies against Bellarmine,
before his fellow aularians".

The diffusion of books was as strictly controlled in Elizabethan
England as it was in the Italy of Pope Sixtus V. No Catholic
books in the vernacular could be printed or imported on pain of
imprisonment or even death, but the Archbishop of Canterbury,
who exercised the censorship, occasionally licensed the importa-
tion of Catholic controversial books in Latin that they might be
refuted by English divines. It was thus that Robert Bellarmine's
tomes found entrance and came into the hands of such people as
Whitaker and Reynolds. But the *Controversies* fell into private
hands also, as those of John Donne, the Catholic-born future
dean of St Paul's. If we may believe his biographer, Isaac Walton,
which is not always an easy thing to do, Donne at about the age of
twenty "did show the Dean of Gloucester all [Bellarmine's]
works marked with many weighty observations under his own
hand". If there is any substance in this tale, the *Controversies* in
their three volumes must have come to England immediately
after their publication in 1593, the year of Donne's twentieth
birthday. A more competent English student of St Robert was
Dr Richard Montagu, whose appointment to the bishopric of
Chichester by Charles I in 1628 nearly precipitated the Civil War
at that date. He was a kind of early Tractarian in his views, and
consequently anathema to the Puritan party which was then
beginning to take control of England's destinies. The narrow
evangelical divines flooded the country with abusive tracts about
him, in one of which he was described as "an animal scarce
rational, whose study is to read and applaud Peter Lambard
[*sic*] and John Duns before Peter Martyr and John Calvin, and for
more modern polemics he prefers Bellarmine before Chamierus".
Bishop Montagu gained a very high opinion of Bellarmine's
merits, and expressed it in the following terms:

He was a man, I must say, of wonderful industry and learning, and his reading was stupendous. He was the first and only
one to put his hand with amazing skill to that shapeless mass

and huge chaos of controversies, to reduce its confusion to order, and to give it elegance. And all this was done carefully and accurately after years of study. Outdistancing every rival, he snatched away the palm and won for himself all the praise in the world. Those who treat of controversies in our day borrow practically all their material from his stores, as the poets do from Homer.

During the trial of Archbishop Laud, one of the main charges brought against him by the fanatic Prynne was that he had kept Montagu's books in his study. "Oh yes," answered the Primate scornfully, "I have Bellarmine in my study, therefore I am a Papist! I have the Alcoran in my study, consequently I am a Turk!" Between the years 1608 and 1621, when he became Bishop of St Davids, Laud used his pen with great diligence on the ample margins of Bellarmine's tomes. These annotations were published separately in 1857, and fill a hundred pages of small print in the Oxford edition of his works. In 1622, owing to the influence of the Spanish court and the activity of Jesuit missionaries, the fortunes of Catholicism in England seemed to be mending, and King James became very anxious lest the Marquis of Buckingham and his mother should go over to the Church. The divines whom his Majesty had called in to confirm them in their Protestantism had not been very successful, so he decided, as a final measure, to organize a religious debate or conference at York House on May 24, 1622. If he pitted his best theologian against some well-known Catholic advocate, he thought that he might reasonably hope for victory, and that the occasion being a public and solemn one the defeat of the papist would make all the deeper impression. There was in prison at this time a very capable Jesuit who went by the name of Fisher, and to him an invitation was sent to stand champion for Rome, while Bishop Laud was requested by the King to assume the defence of the Church of England. The two men began their duel in the presence of Buckingham and his mother and wife, as well as a large contingent of the most distinguished lords and ladies in the metropolis. From the beginning to the end of it, Bellarmine was taken, almost as a matter of course, by both parties as the decisive authority, and it would be impossible to

imagine a more significant testimony to his importance in the
theology of that age than Laud's ceaseless endeavours to find
flaws in his arguments. The Countess of Buckingham made known
to the debaters that what she was in search of was an infallible
Church. No one in the wide world could show her that, was
Laud's answer, "No, not Bellarmine himself though of very
great ability to make good any truth which he undertakes for the
Church of Rome". After many pages of stern wrestling with
St Robert's proofs, the Bishop winds up the introductory part of
the debate with a personal declaration: "Indeed could I swallow
Bellarmine's opinion that the Pope's judgment is infallible, I
would then submit without any more ado. But that will never
go down with me, unless I live till I dote, which I hope to God I
shall not." All the way through he makes no secret of his profound
respect for this antagonist and agrees "to be judged by Bellarmine" whose work is so "great and full of art". In spite of all his
efforts Bellarmine won on points, for, though Buckingham
remained where he was, his mother and his wife both became
Catholics after the conference.

The men mentioned so far were large-minded enough to
appreciate Bellarmine and to refrain from abuse, but they were
only a small select corps of the great army of his antagonists.
A very ragged army it was for the most part, composed of clerics
whose language would put a fishwife to the blush. Typical of their
blood-and-thunder methods were the many fierce volumes which
came from the pen of Dr Matthew Sutcliffe, Dean of Exeter, and
chaplain to Queen Elizabeth. Their titles alone are a sufficient
indication of his style: *On the Pope and his iniquitous Domination,
against Robert Bellarmine and the whole tribe of Jebusites; On Monks,
their Mode of Life and Manners, against Robert Bellarmine and the
Kennel of Monks and Mendicants; On the Popish Mass, against
Robert Bellarmine and the universal Cohort of Jebusites and Canaanites,*
etc. The *Controversies,* according to this "petulant railer" as
Theodore Beza contemptuously described him, were but a new
"stables of Augaeus containing an infinite heap of dung", and
their author, "a braggart dunghill of a soldier, a furious and
devilish Jebusite, the Hanniball of all the Jebusites". Scarcely

more restrained in style were the tomes of Robert Abbot, Bishop of Salisbury, and George Downham, Bishop of Derry. Those right reverend gentlemen were as handy with an abusive epithet as the Virgin Queen herself or her redoubtable chaplain. Abbot's *Mirror of Popish Subtleties against Sanders and Bellarmine*, which appeared in 1594, might have been written by a bargee, though its author was a Regius Professor of Divinity. The misrepresentations to which St Robert was subjected may be gathered from the following passage of a book published in 1604, *A Persuasion to the English Recusants to reconcile themselves to the Church of England*, by a certain Dr Dove:

> Cardinal Bellarmine, late divinity reader of Rome, and the learnedest divine of that Church which now liveth, in the course of his controversy lectures, though where he delivereth the state of the question, he bringeth what may be brought on their side, for fashion sake, that he may avoid all suspicion of heresy with them; yet he handleth his matter so cunningly and so doubtfully that in his conclusions he agreeth with us in many things, and in many things he showeth himself to be, as far as he dareth, a Protestant.

Bellarmine became something of an institution in the Church of England from the first appearance of his *Controversies*, a kind of gargoyle on its ecclesiastical architecture. Dr Thomas Brightman, a Cambridge preacher famous in his day, believed devoutly, and persuaded others to believe, that a book which he published against the *Controversies* in 1609 was written under the direct inspiration of the Holy Ghost. Practically all the great Anglican divines made them their target at one time or another, so the non-Catholic writer in the *Encyclopaedia Britannica* (eleventh ed.) spoke but the sober truth when he said that their author was "uniformly taken by Protestant advocates as the champion of the Papacy, and a vindication of Protestantism regularly took the shape of an answer to him". The Catholic Dr William Bishop, himself a doughty defender of the faith, referred to St Robert in 1608 as "that renowned and right famous Father Bellarmine". "So notorious is he," wrote the Puritan William Ames, twenty years later, "that at the bare mention of his name, all men are wont to think straightway of the Philistine champion Goliath, who in helmet, mail and fearful accoutrements, most wickedly terrified the ranks of Israel, the army of the living God." In 1605 the vociferous Thomas Bell proclaimed him to be the man "who hath said all that can be said for Popery, and whose testimony alone is most sufficient in all Popish affairs". In the following century the well-known Protestant Church historian, Mosheim, wrote of him as follows: "The numerous Jesuits who took the field against the enemies of the Romish Church excelled all the others in subtlety, impudence and invective. But the chief and *coryphaeus* of the whole was Robert Bellarmine. . . . He embraced all the controversies of his Church in several large volumes, and united copiousness of argument with much perspicuity of style. As soon, therefore, as he entered the arena, he drew upon himself alone, the onsets and the strength of the greatest men among the Protestants." Jumping another hundred years, we find a Protestant publicist describing the *Controversies*, in the year of Queen Victoria's accession, "as the most authentic and genuine record of the Pope's twin spiritual and temporal power", and continuing in the following strain:

So much importance was there attached to Bellarmine's works, that for nearly a hundred years there was scarcely an eminent or learned Protestant divine in Europe who did not publish answers to his ingenious and alluring sophisms. In England, his tract on "The Notes of the Church" was considered so important from the learning of the man and its sly, cajoling, plausible character, that fifteen of the most distinguished ecclesiastics, including one Archbishop and six Bishops, published formal and elaborate refutations of them, each man taking a separate tract. These tracts were written in a style so masterly that having been circulated rapidly and extensively among the thinking and independent population of England, they awakened the spirit of the nation, and were mainly instrumental in producing that tone of anti-papistical feeling that caused the overthrow of Popery and the ejection of James II.[1]

---

[1] Bellarmine, as is well known, suggested no less than fifteen notes of the Church which, however, he pointed out, could be reduced to the traditional four. The answers of Archbishop Tenison, Bishop Stratford, etc., referred to

Whether or not that is good history, it shows at least that Bellarmine continued to be taken very seriously in England. A fair-minded scholar of our own time who had no sympathy with Catholicism wrote the following sober words about his work: "These volumes exhaust the controversy on all points as it was known in those days, and they are distinguished by their fullness, candour, and lucid arrangement, the absence of disguise and evasion, and the broad and unfaltering statement of theological dogmas. No doubt he presents a truer picture of Catholic opinion than either Bossuet, Moehler or Wiseman, in whose treatises the personal peculiarities and mental characteristics of the authors may be distinctly traced."

On the continent of Europe the *Controversies* were accorded an even more remarkable reception. The second volume appeared in 1588. Writing from Mainz on September 29 of that year, the rector of the Jesuit college gave Aquaviva the following piece of information: "The Frankfurt Fair was not as grand as usual this time, but every copy of Bellarmine's second volume on sale was bought up immediately, and if the booksellers had had two thousand copies for disposal, not one of them would have been left on their hands." Two months later, the well-known Jesuit theologian Leonard Lessius mentioned the first volume in a letter from Louvain: "I hear that it is being studied in every quarter, even by educated laymen such as lawyers and members of parliament. The copies that came to Louvain were all disposed of the day they appeared."

In this scramble for the very expensive tomes Protestants were as eager as Catholics. Close on two hundred full-dress replies appeared in northern Europe during the first century after their publication. Many of those rejoinders ran into three or four volumes, and their writers were as diverse in creed as in nationality, Lutherans, Calvinists, Zwinglians, Anabaptists, Jews, Socinians, all co-operating. The variety of tactics adopted by them resembled

---

above, were first published in 1687, the year before the Glorious Revolution. On January 24, 1839, *The Times* newspaper called for their reissue, apparently as a counterblast to the activities of Daniel O'Connell. It is from the introduction to this reprint that the quotation is taken.

more or less those employed in England, but they had in some cases a special venom of their own, as when they attributed such crimes to St Robert as his German defender Jacob Gretser said had never been laid at the doors of even a Nero or Heliogabalus. One story that went about in print was that he had died in despair at Loreto, "bellowing blasphemously like a lion" and denying God and Christ and Christianity. His attention was called to this cheerful obituary notice. It only amused him, but as the German Fathers wanted a denial he wrote, in 1604, to say that he was not merely alive, but in excellent good health by the grace of God, and even obtained a certificate of his existence for them, drawn up in full legal form by a public notary.

Another favourite allegation of the Saint's Protestant critics was that he had not fathered the *Controversies* singlehanded. As a very earnest French Calvinist, named du Jon, Latinized Junius, put it: "Methinks it is not one Bellarmine who speaks in these pages. It is the whole Jesuit phalanx, the entire legion of them mustered for our destruction." The answer to that contention came from Father Eudaemon-Joannes: "I who lived for years under the same roof as Bellarmine and all my fellow priests in Rome at the same time can swear that he not only wrote his books without assistance but that he never even had a secretary or amanuensis". The truth is that, so far from helping Robert with his gigantic task, a considerable number of his fellow Jesuits manifested a deep dislike and distrust of the *Controversies*. Some, like Cardinal Toledo, may have been motivated by just plain jealousy of their fame; others may have quite sincerely considered their author's honesty and impartiality in argument a danger to the faith. Such a one was the prominent Hungarian Jesuit named Stephen Arator, who wrote as follows to Aquaviva in 1591: "Learned prelates out here in central Europe consider that the *Controversies* have done more harm than good to the Church. Instead of depriving the heretics of their weapons, they do but supply them with new ones. Calvinists and Lutherans would never have had the wit to think out so many and such excellent arguments for their sects as they may now find in Bellarmine. The result is that his volumes are being bought up by

Protestants more than by Catholics." Arator, however, was honest enough to end his protest with a confession that he had "read very little of the *Controversies*", and was merely repeating what he had heard others say. Aquaviva answered the self-constituted censor at once: "I am astounded at what you write about the *Controversies* of Father Bellarmine, as the almost universal estimate of them is so utterly different. It would be a good thing, then, if your Reverence would send me a list of those matters which you consider need correcting." On the receipt of this letter, the rather self-important Stephen mistakenly concluded that he had been constituted an official censor. He read the first volume through hastily, noted down two dozen *corrigenda*, and posted them not only to Aquaviva but also, with unsolicited zeal, to Bellarmine. Much worse, however, than this impertinence was the report which he spread in Vienna that he had been appointed to revise the *Controversies* because they were a suspected and dangerous work. Other Jesuits, too, showed themselves disloyal and unfriendly, some going out of their way to criticize Bellarmine in their lectures, while a few went further and charged him with stealing his matter from no less a person than Dr Michael Baius!

Such domestic differences will always be apt to arise while men are men, nor is it any discredit to Bellarmine that he should have withstood his detractors to their faces. In his remonstrance to the General he disposed of their allegations with considerable warmth, but added that what saddened him most was the disunion those tactics betrayed: "Instead of all pulling together as we ought, we bite one another, and in very truth the enemies of a man are those of his own household". Aquaviva replied in very affectionate and fatherly terms:

I have been not a little grieved to hear of the despondency which Father Arator's letter has caused you. But do not take it too much to heart. . . . I shall not fail to apply the proper remedies. . . . Be it known to your Reverence that your books are welcomed and approved so warmly by those who understand them that such readers would not dream of paying any attention to Fr Arator's effusions. . . . Take good care of your health, and work away at the completion of the volume which

you have in hand. I know for a fact that nowhere is it awaited
with greater eagerness than in those very parts where your
credit is supposed to be at stake.

As so often happens, the most charming part of the letter is in the
postscript:

> *Padre mio*, you must not let this idle gossip make you down-
> hearted, nor must you surrender on account of it one little
> bit of the joy which you take in your work. That is exactly
> what the devil would like to happen. He does not approve of
> your labours.

It cheers us ordinary people a little to see an occasional flash of
the old Adam in the saints, and the following answer from Bellarmine provides us with our consolation:

> I thank your Paternity very much for setting my doubts at
> rest because, to tell you the truth, I could not make out why
> there should have been all this eagerness to pass new strictures
> on my book. Least of all could I understand why this should
> have been undertaken by a man who enjoys no great name as a
> scholar. I knew him in his student days and he was not a star,
> to say nothing else about him. . . . His principal censure is the
> last one, where he says that I provide answers to all the argu-
> ments of the heretics, and even admits that I do the work well.
> Nevertheless, he reprehends me, because, as he puts it, the
> heretics can now dig out of my books the arguments of
> Luther and Calvin, and because there seem to be as many
> arguments given on their side as on the side of the Catholics.
> But if that objection were sound, it would be necessary to
> prohibit the book of the holy Bishop and martyr of Rochester
> in which he gives verbatim the complete text of one of Luther's
> works. And the books of Tapper of Louvain, Sanders, and
> others would also have to be forbidden because they have cited
> the arguments of their opponents in their own words. On the
> other hand, we should have to praise the work of the Spanish
> friar, Orantes, a work which makes all the educated Catholics
> of France and Germany weep, and all the heretics hilarious,
> because the author, after answering a few petty arguments of
> Calvin, pretends that that gentleman has nothing better to say

for himself. I must confess to your Paternity that this censure has wounded me more than the others, as it suggests that I wanted to favour the enemies of our faith, though I am sure my censor did not mean it that way.

At the time of writing this letter, January, 1592, Bellarmine was an invalid at Frascati. Thither, at his request, the first volume of the *Controversies* was dispatched, and having received it he began his long, conclusive answer to the criticisms of his Jesuit brethren. This he sent to Aquaviva, with a covering letter in which the fire of his Tuscan blood is for once allowed to blaze:

I am posting to your Paternity my reply to Father Stephen Arator's censures. It may sound a little harsh, but I thought this necessary in order to repress his insolence. Never have I seen, as far as I can remember, less knowledge combined with more presumption. He is so confident in the expression of his ignorance that he did not consider his censures needed any revision, with the result that the names, places, and events are mixed up and muddled in them again and again. I say nothing about the lack of moderation in his style, nor about the boastful way in which he gives himself out for a master, and proposes to amend mistakes by some occult power of divination. . . . All this would matter little if he had not himself committed more than ten of them in the process, as I have noted in the margin of my manuscript. If I did not feel certain that your Paternity would make him retract these errors, and that he would obey, I would feel bound in conscience to denounce him to the Inquisition as being a dangerous man in these times and in his part of the world. But in any case, I would not take action without your Paternity's knowledge and sanction, because though I am in duty bound to make known to the Church the Church's danger, I have an equal obligation to be prudent in taking such a step, and to be ruled by those whom God has given to me for guides.

Father Bellarmine probably never seriously intended to carry out this rather stern threat, but his grounds for making it and his general strictures were certainly not without some justification, as Arator had misinterpreted and misrepresented the teaching of the *Controversies* on practically all the twenty-four points in question. There was an air of patronage, too, about his censures which would have exasperated the meekest of men. "Good Father Bellarmine" is constantly accused of inadvertence, contradictions, misquotations, opposition to St Thomas and the Fathers of the Church, etc. His worst offence, however, was the attack he made on the *Controversies* for their fair presentation of Protestant opinions. "The Lutherans and Calvinists will have no further need of Luther's and Calvin's books", he wrote. "They can find all they want here, but I trust, nevertheless, that the *Controversies* may do more good than harm to many who read them." Bellarmine's comment on this passage is singularly moderate:

If I had brought forward the arguments of both Protestants and Catholics and left the two sets to stand without further remark, there would be something in what my censor says. But since I have refuted the heretical and strengthened the Catholic position, what room is there for cavil? On the other hand, had I not produced all the arguments I could discover on their side, the heretics would say that the ones I omitted were unanswerable, while the Catholics would accuse me of prevarication. That was the reproach brought by learned men against Erasmus, in his discussion of free will, and against some others, better left unnamed, who brag that they have answered Calvin while leaving his main arguments absolutely untouched. Finally there is the testimony of Pope Innocent IX, lately dead. When he had carefully read through the first volume of the *Controversies* twice, he not only commended me for bringing forward and solving all the difficulties I could find, but said he wished that I would undertake to answer all conceivable difficulties. I think I may be permitted to oppose the judgment of that great Pope to the judgment of my censor.[1]

Arator was not the only Jesuit to take up arms against his dis-

---

[1] Innocent IX was an eminent canonist and theologian, who died on December 30, 1591, after reigning for only two months.

tinguished brother. A Spaniard named Henriquez constituted himself a veritable devil's advocate against the *Controversies*. This man left the Society of Jesus in 1593 to become a Dominican, but returned to his first vocation in later life. It was while he was with the Dominicans, but certainly not inspired by them, that he carried on his long and bitter campaign to get the ban of the Spanish Inquisition imposed on Bellarmine's work. Aquaviva was Robert's stoutest defender in this new crisis. He wrote to the Apostolic Nuncio in Spain, begging him to remind the malcontents of the estimation in which Bellarmine was held by the Pope, and of the splendid welcome which his books had received in every part of the world. Cardinal Santa-Severina, an old friend, was also asked to help by obtaining an injunction from Clement VIII that should restrain the Spanish Inquisitors from taking action before they had first notified the Holy See. Bellarmine won the day but, as a result of the campaign against him, a story went about among the Protestants that their great adversary had been officially silenced. As a contrast to the activities of those Jesuit critics, it may be worth mentioning that a group of far more eminent ones, headed apparently by Antonio Possevino, seriously proposed to Aquaviva in 1599 that no member of the Society of Jesus should in future be promoted to the status of professor until he had carefully read and been examined in Bellarmine's entire course of controversies.

It is possible to be fair in an argument without being exactly courteous or generous. Many of Bellarmine's opponents were honest enough in their controversial dealings, but very few of them had the grace to be polite, and it is worth inquiring whether St Robert himself showed any marked superiority in this respect. Controversy has never been a school for chivalry; in the sixteenth century it was a snake-pit. The depths to which the doctors descended would scarcely be credible were there not abundant evidence in the violently abusive titles of the books and pamphlets which enshrine a little of their elegance. Catholics were almost as adept at abuse as Protestants. It was an inter-denominational and international art, practised by the Tiber as well as by the Thames. Andrew Willet, a rather pompous but very learned Oxford

professor, nicknamed the "walking library", wrote a work in
1593, entitled: *Tetrastylon Papisticum; that is the Foure Principal
Pillers of Papistrie*. In it, the first pillar is made to consist "of
intemperate rayling, with shameful slaunders and untruths", and
that it was not a slender, inconsiderable pillar may be seen from
the scores of examples which Dr Andrew cites. Some of the
choicest of these are from the great Catholic theologian, Thomas
Stapleton, whom Willet, setting up a pillar of his own, calls:
"that black-mouthed Sophister of Louvain". Another Louvain
Doctor, Thomas Harding, is listed there, too, for having described
Bishop Jewel as "a helhound", and "a clawbacke of the devil",
and for having shouted across the sea at him: "As I cannot well
take an haire from your lying beard, so wish I that I could plucke
malice from your blasphemous hart". In the books of Robert
Abbot, Protestant Bishop of Salisbury, the Pope is never simply
the Pope. He is Antichrist, the man of sin, the harpy of Rome,
the filthy harlot, the filthy and unnatural strumpet, the whore of
Babylon. Men with religious vows are idle lossels, filthy belly-
gods, swarms of locusts, Romish vermin, full-gorged friars, and
so on, while his immediate Catholic opponents, such as Bellarmine,
are witless sophisters, false harlots, dumb asses, abominable hypo-
crites, lewd caitiffs, unclean beasts, foul-mouthed hogs, base
fugitives, the seed of the devil, false traitors, and the offscourings
of the theological profession. It is small wonder that Dr William
Bishop, who answered these amenities, should have described
Abbot as "one of the most shallow and beggerliest writers of those
days . . . a fumish and foule-mouthed butter-wench . . . by birth
but a meane tanner's sonne, who at his first coming to Oxford
was gladde to sweep and dresse up chambers and to play the
drudge for a slender pittance". Today, the last part of that indict-
ment would be regarded as entirely to Abbot's credit. During the
long struggle between the Jesuits and the seculars in Elizabethan
and Jacobean times, Anthony Copley described Father Persons as
"being a common ale-house squire and the drunkenest sponge in
all the parish where he lived", while Persons, in his turn, though
a very devout man and author of a spiritual classic, described his
enemy, the conspirator Watson, a secular priest, as "being so

wrong-shapen and of so bad and blinking aspect, as he looketh nine ways at once".[1]

On the Continent matters were even worse. With Luther's awful example as an inspiration, the heretics stopped at nothing in the way of abuse and scurrility, and the majority of Catholic writers paid them back in their own coin. "The foul sayings," wrote the Jesuit Hartmann Grisar in his voluminous life of Luther, "which in his anxiety to achieve popularity, he gathered from the lips of the rabble, swept like a flood over the whole of the German literary field. Foul language became habitual, and during the polemics subsequent on Luther's death was a favourite method of attack." Even great scholars such as Scaliger and Casaubon were not exempt from the general failing. Scaliger indeed was famous for his outbursts, in one of which Bellarmine was the victim, and Casaubon too had his fling, though not so intemperately. Bellarmine, he said, "was a man good for nothing whatever except rhetoric, sophism, and lies, whose norm of truth was not the sacred Scriptures, but the whim of his god, the Pope".

Robert Bellarmine was included in Andrew Willet's book, *Tetrastylon Papisticum*, with Sanders, Stapleton, Harding and others who provided the "first Piller of Papistrie, intemperate rayling", but the author, though writing against him in particular, had to admit that he was "the mildest and most modest child of all that crue". In the two million words of the *Controversies*, the diligent Willet could only discover a dozen which had even the appearance of abuse.

Bellarmine and Stapleton had a common foe in Whitaker. Stapleton, great man though he was, became ill-tempered in debate, and belaboured the doctor furiously. "Should Bellarmine", he says in one place, "once more step into the arena and devote a few hours to cleaning out Whitaker's Augean stables, then will that fellow find himself blacker than the blackest coal ever dug

[1] In his exhilarating though biased book, *The Defeat of the Spanish Armada* (1959), Professor Garrett Mattingly describes Persons' *Christian Directory* as "one of the simplest, sweetest, soundest books of devotion in the English tongue" (p. 72).

out of a mine." All the way through he writes with a pen dipped in gall, Whitaker being addressed constantly as *"doctor indocte"*, *"futilissime disputator"*, *"barbare scriptor"*, *"fatue asine"*, etc., and advised that his "head is thicker than any mallet ever made, a ridiculous head, fitter to wear the cap and bells of a fool than a doctor's boards". As for St Robert's attitude to the same Whitaker, there is the following story told only sixteen years after his death by Lupton, in his *History of the Modern Protestant Divines*:

> I have heard it confessed of English Papists themselves which have been in Italy with Bellarmine, that he procured the true portraiture or effigies of this Whitaker to be brought to him, which he kept in his study. For he privately admired this man for his singular learning and ingenuity; and on being asked of some of his friends, Jesuits, why he would have the picture of that heretic in his presence, he would answer: *"Quod quamvis hereticus erat et adversarius, erat tamen doctus adversarius"*: that although he was a heretic and his adversary, yet he was a learned adversary.

Anthony Wood in his *Athenae Oxonienses* is still more specific. Writing of John Aglionby, Queen Elizabeth's chaplain, he says:

> Afterwards travelling, he was introduced into the acquaintance of Cardinal Bellarmine, who, showing him the picture of the profound William Whitaker of Cambridge which hung up in his library, told him, pointing to the picture, that he was the most learned heretic that he had ever read.

When dealing with the life of Whitaker, that sturdy and entertaining bigot Thomas Fuller describes how he made hay with his Catholic opponents who were excellent only "at the flat hand of rhetoric". These teasers (Campion, Sanders, etc.) did but rouse their game and make him find his spirits. "The fiercest dog is behind," Thomas continues, "even Bellarmine himself, a great scholar and who wanted nothing but a good cause to defend, and generally writing ingenuously, using sometimes slanting, seldom downright railing." Robert never wrote anything against Whitaker who so constantly attacked him, but he procured and read his books. Against other contestants, especially the Centuriators of Magdeburg, he indulged in a certain amount of sarcasm and, by our modern improved debating manners, he is too ready to brand the allegations of Protestant writers as lies. That is about the extent of his failure in good taste throughout his enormous output of books.

At times we find the Saint assuming the defence of some heretical doctor who had been misrepresented in Catholic works. Thus Genebrard, a distinguished Benedictine scholar, had accused Calvin, Beza, and Stancar of teaching that Christ was God of himself and not from the Father. St Peter Canisius also charged Calvin with that fundamental error in the theology of the Blessed Trinity. After pointing out the gravity of the charge, Bellarmine writes:

> I shall say now what I think about the matter. First, I have been unable to find anything of the sort in Stancar, though I must admit that I have not read all his works, but those only which deal with the Blessed Trinity and the Redemption. As for Calvin, his language, I think, is certainly faulty, and so open to the interpretation put upon it by Catholic writers. . . . But even though this be the case, after diligent and very careful examination of his text I am not at all willing to say that he believed or taught the heresy in question, and I shall now briefly explain my reasons for putting a favourable construction on his words.

The criticisms to which, as we have seen, the *Controversies* were subjected by a few of Bellarmine's co-religionists were soon drowned in a universal chorus of praise. It would be an endless task and require a volume by itself to record all the Catholic tributes they received, so the two most illustrious controversialists on whom the mantle of their author fell may be allowed to speak for the rest. They were, beyond the shadow of a doubt, Cardinal du Perron[1] and St Francis de Sales. Bellarmine was told, on one occasion, that du Perron disapproved of his mild tactics in argu-

[1] This famous man was a convert from Calvinism and became the most distinguished of the Church's defenders in France. It was chiefly through his efforts that the conversion of Henry IV was brought about.

ment, and was otherwise dissatisfied with his work. Esteeming the
great French scholar as he did, the news made him very uneasy,
and he communicated his trouble to their common friend,
Cardinal de Joyeuse. Joyeuse was furious when he heard of this
"blasphemy" as he termed it, and straightway reported the
matter to the man whom it most concerned. Du Perron's subsequent letter to Bellarmine blazed in every line of its bad Italian.
He gave him his solemn oath that the story was a diabolical
calumny from beginning to end, a calumny that struck him dumb
with amazement:

> Not only have I never said nor thought such a thing but on
> the contrary have always held your work in the highest esteem.
> No book published in defence of the Church during the past
> thousand years equals, in my judgment, your *Controversies*.
> May God put me to confusion if this is not my sincere convic-
> tion. So far was I from thinking your work harmful to the
> Church that I could imagine no better means for converting
> Protestants than to have a French translation made. All our
> heretics, and especially the Latinless ones, would then be able
> to profit by the *Controversies*. My Secretary, Chatillon, under-
> took the task at my express command, and I hired a printer to
> set up the manuscript in my own house. Your Lordship will
> remember the letter which Chatillon wrote to you in my name,
> asking permission for the publication of the work.

When St Francis de Sales was a young student at Padua in 1588,
the first volume of the *Controversies* was brought to him, hot
from the press, by his Jesuit friend Antonio Possevino. Six years
later he began his famous mission through the wild, mountainous
district of Savoy, known as Le Chablais. The Genevans had forced
their Calvinism on the people, and Francis, at the risk of his life,
determined to see if he could win them back. He knew that he
would have to be often in hiding and always tramping through
the snow, so it was necessary to cut down his equipment of books
and baggage to a minimum. As regards the books he tells us
himself the decision which he made: "*Durant cinq ans en Chablais,
j'ay presché sans autres livres que la Bible et ceux du grand Bellarmin*".

A curious by-product of Bellarmine's notoriety in Protestant circles was the attribution of his name to a type of large pot-bellied jug, with the effigy of a bearded head on its short and narrow neck. These jugs appear to have originated at Frechen, a pottery town which is now a suburb of Cologne, and were nick-named *Bartmänner*, "beard-men". They were exported in large quantities to England among other places, and became particularly popular in London, where they were often called bellarmines from the fancied resemblance of the bearded face to the author of the *Controversies*. Hundreds of specimens dating from the sixteenth century, one of which bears the royal arms and the initials E.R., are on display in London museums and private collections; and there are some references to them as bellarmines in the by-ways of the literature of the period.

Bossuet in the seventeenth century expressed dismay, as a good Gallican, at the extent of St Robert's influence. "Is it possible?" he exclaimed to his friend Diroys in 1682. "Bellarmine reigns supreme and in his own person represents tradition!" The *Controversies* maintained their position at the head of the Catholic Church's apologetic literature *vis-à-vis* Protestantism in all its shapes, regalism as meaning the divine right of kings, and Gallicanism, up to and beyond the date of the Vatican Council (1869-1870). Bishop von Hefele, an opponent of the definition of papal infallibility in the Council, who, however, loyally sub-mitted to the Church's ruling, in contrast with the other great scholar Dr Döllinger, who sarcastically declared the dogma to be "nothing else than a definition of Bellarmine's views", wrote as follows about the *Controversies* in 1883: "It is the most complete defence of the Catholic Faith, especially against Protestant aggression, which has appeared down to the present day, and by its erudition and courtesy has earned for its author imperishable renown".

The *Controversies* were responsible for the return of very large numbers of dissidents to the Catholic Church. To St Robert Bellarmine his fame meant nothing, but that fact gave him intense happiness. It was all the glory he ever sought or wanted, as may be seen in just one story of the many that could be told. A certain

D

Benjamin Antony Carier, canon of Canterbury and chaplain in ordinary to King James I, who considered him to be the most learned theologian in England, studied the *Controversies* anxiously and carefully. He was so deeply impressed that he abandoned his emoluments and his even finer prospects, on pretext of a cure at Spa, to be received into the Catholic Church in Cologne. The King, becoming suspicious of what was in the wind, ordered him to return to England without delay, and directed Isaac Casaubon and other eminent scholars to write to him and endeavour to prevent the calamity of his secession. They were too late. Carier himself addressed a moving little apologia to the King, stating the reasons for the step he had taken:

> As for my returning to England, I can answer no otherwise but this. I have sent Your Majesty my soul in this Missive, and if it may find entertainment and passage, my body shall most gladly follow after. And if not, I pray God I send my soul to heaven and my body to the grave as soon as may be. In the meantime, I shall rejoice in nothing but only in the Cross of Christ which is the glory of your crown. And therefore I will triumph therein, not as being gone from you to your adversary, but as being gone before you to your Mother, where I desire and hope for ever to continue
>
> Your Majesty's true servant and Beadsman,
> B. CARIER.
>
> Liège, December 12, 1613.

A year later, Dr Benjamin addressed the following lines to Cardinal Bellarmine:

> Most Reverend and Illustrious Sir,
>
> Had it been possible for me to remain ignorant of the truth contained in your writings, or to deny it, I think this present letter would never have gone to Italy. But since I could not escape the light of your teaching nor, on the other hand, endure the calumnies of unjust tongues at home, I have left behind me all the books of my library at Canterbury and given up all my other worldly goods, under pretext of taking the waters at Spa, and of travelling in the Palatinate. I have now been received into the Catholic Church by your Fathers at Cologne.

And so, with very good reason, I think I ought to write to your illustrious Lordship, not so much to beg your help in my exile as to thank you for the freedom and salvation of my soul. I was, till recently, for many years preacher to the King . . . But with all my heart I chose the Catholic communion, commended to me by your works more than by any other cause under God, in preference to the position I had already attained and the still brighter hopes that were mine. And so I thank your Lordship with all my heart, not only in my own name but also in the names of very many learned men in England who kindle their lamps and draw warmth daily from your flame. . . . May God renew your old age like unto the eagle's for the peace of His Church and the conversion of England.

Your illustrious Lordship's devoted and humble,
BENJAMIN ANTONY CARIER, D.D.

Liège, January 10, 1614.

Bellarmine answered his new friend immediately.

Very Reverend and Most Learned Sir,
Your letter afforded me immense joy. I thanked God with all my heart for the singular grace which he has given you. It is granted to few to recognize the true Church amid the darkness of so many schisms and heresies, and to still fewer so to love the truth which they have seen as to fly to its embrace, generously despising comfort, honour and, above all, royal favour, the unfailing source of such earthly prizes. If in your voluntary exile you have to endure sorrow and want for our Lord's sake, you will be blessed indeed, being made worthy not only to believe in Christ with your whole heart, but also to suffer for his Name. As in Heaven nothing will be sweeter than to resemble him in his glory, so here on earth nothing is more to our advantage than to be like him in his Passion. Hence arises that solid and perennial joy which nobody can steal from us . . . I do not write this in any spirit of indifference to your present need, which I am more than willing to assist as far as I can, but because I congratulate you from my heart, not only on account of your reception into the Church, outside which there is no salvation, but also for the precious gift of patience with which I think our Lord has adorned your soul.

As for my part in the matter, you owe me no thanks at all, for "neither he who plants is anything, nor he who waters, but God it is who gives the increase". I only pass on to others what our Catholic Mother has herself passed on to me. If there is any lack of learning in my writings, any obscurity of expression or superficial treatment, you may feel sure that it is in such places I am most original. And so farewell, most learned and worthy Sir. Remember me in your holy prayers.

CARDINAL BELLARMINE.

Rome, February 14, 1614.

CHAPTER IV

BELLARMINE AND POPE SIXTUS V

WHILE Robert Bellarmine was peacefully pursuing the study of his Aristotle in 1562, history was being made at a hectic pace on the other side of the Alps. The key to the complicated story was a little independent kingdom called Navarre, which lay along the wild shores of the Bay of Biscay, with its head in France and its heels in Spain. Provocative heels they must have been, which Ferdinand of Aragon liked not to see kicking on his side of the fence. Without more ado, he annexed the Spanish portion of Navarre in 1512, and forced its Queen, Catherine d'Albret, to retire towards the cold, French declivity of her native mountains. Revenge then became the object of the lady's life, and she educated her boy Henry on the lines followed by the stern matrons of Sparta and Carthage. He learned his lessons well and, when he grew up and married the French King's sister, his one great hope was that he might have a boy to carry on the tradition of revenge. However, there was only a girl named Jeanne, and when she in her turn married Antony de Bourbon, her disappointed father had the further sorrow of laying two baby grandsons in the grave.

At last in his old age he was told that Jeanne was going to be a mother for the third time, whereupon his fierce hopes revived, and he summoned the girl home from the French court that the avenger might be born on the soil of Navarre. She came in the depths of winter, and he promised her a casket of gold if she would sing a brave, national song while in labour so that her child might be a sturdy little fellow, indifferent to pain. Jeanne was a bigoted Calvinist, but she chose a hymn to our Lady in the patois of Béarn and, as she struggled gallantly with its music, the best beloved of all the kings of France came into the world. The old grandfather seized the child immediately, and bore him off in triumph to his own apartments, where he rubbed garlic on the

baby lips and forced some strong Jurançon wine through them
to brace up the heart of the unfortunate infant who was then
packed off to the wild storm-battered castle of Coarraze, to have
the scream of winds and wheeling eagles serve him for a lullaby.
As he grew up, he was dressed in the homespun of the peasants
among whom he lived, and fared as they did on bread and garlic.
Their dialect was his only language, and there was not a boy
among them who could beat him in a race or climb a tree or
mountain more daringly.

At length the old King died, and Jeanne d'Albret ascended the
throne. Her Catholic husband was killed fighting against the
Huguenots in the first of the seven religious wars, after which
event she was free to force her Calvinism on the people of Navarre
and on her boy Henry. There was little of the woman about
Jeanne except her name. She adopted the grand airs of Elizabeth I
of England, though, as a Béarnais noble remarked, anybody
could cross her toy kingdom with a hop, skip, and jump. Catholicism was rooted out of it in a fashion more cruel and brutal than
had been followed in any other country, and Henry, its future
overlord, had Calvinism driven into him quite as vigorously.
However, it met with but a sorry welcome in his gay and half-
pagan heart. What he wanted was not a religion but a cause to
champion, and even predestination could provide him with that.
In 1569, after the death of Condé, he became the recognized leader
of the Huguenots, and was the life and soul of their resistance in all
the terrible wars which followed. But though he was ready to
fight for Calvinism, he was by no means prepared to die for it,
and accordingly embraced Catholicism at the time of the Massacre
of St Bartholomew.

By the Peace of Monsieur which ended the fifth religious war
in 1576, the Huguenots were made various concessions that raised
justifiable apprehensions in the minds of the Catholic majority.
To protect themselves the better, they formed leagues and
associations up and down the country with Henry, Duke of Guise,
at their head. Henry III, the King of France, did not like the new
movement, but being powerless to do anything else, gave it, at
last, his reluctant benediction. Finally, there was the third Henry,

"the man of Béarn", who, feeling that his destiny called him to be in the opposite camp to Guise, renounced Catholicism, and once more took his place at the head of the Huguenots. The stage was then set for a very great drama, which developed swiftly when, in 1584, the King's brother, the Duke of Anjou, died, and left him, a wretched childless reprobate, as the last of the Valois line.

Up to this time, the danger of a heretic wearing the crown of St Louis had not seriously troubled the calculations of the Catholic leaders, but with Anjou in his grave and "the man of Béarn" heir-presumptive to the throne, the prospect became decidedly ominous. The League or Holy Union, which hitherto had been but a loose confederation of more or less aristocratic groups, swiftly developed into a powerful and well-organized popular movement. The Guises directed the national enthusiasm very skilfully, and with the additional aid of Spain were soon in a position to dictate terms to their vacillating King. Henry's sympathies naturally leaned towards his kinsman and namesake of Navarre, but he was compelled to repudiate him and to declare Protestantism illegal throughout France. Meantime in Rome Pope Sixtus V had taken the destinies of the Church into his capable hands. In the midst of his splendid administrative work at home, he kept wary eyes on the trend of foreign events, and what was happening in France filled him with gloom. Was the eldest daughter of the Church going the way of England, and what was to be done to prevent such an immeasurable disaster? The emissaries of the League had the answer for him pat, and so had Olivares, King Philip II's haughty ambassador. Excommunicate Navarre, they said, and all will be well. But Sixtus did not want to excommunicate Navarre. Being a strong, resolute man himself, he loved strong, resolute men, and such a one he knew the Béarnais to be. However, he was deceived by the apparent union of the Catholic parties, and in order to cement it effectively issued the desired bull in September 1585. By this document, Henry de Bourbon, King of Navarre, was declared a heretic and incapable of succeeding to the throne of France. In good Gallican fashion the Parlement of Paris, though entirely on the side of the League, refused to register the bull and more or less told the Pope to mind his own business. The bull was repudiated and attacked not only by the leaguers but by the Catholic middle party, called the *Politiques*, who championed the Béarnais claims. Robert Bellarmine wrote a defence of it under a pseudonym, and so dispassionately that only in recent years has his authorship been established. The League and Spain had misled the Pope. They had promised peace and there was no peace. The war of the three Henrys was reducing France to a state of anarchy worse even than in the days of Jeanne d'Arc. In these circumstances the embarrassment of good Catholics became acute, and even the General of the Jesuits found it exceedingly difficult to keep his men in the middle way that became them. One member of the Society, Père Auger, was the confessor and devoted friend of Henry III, while another, Père Mathieu, proved so zealous in the interests of the Guises, that he was nicknamed "the Courier of the League". In 1587 the King conceived a plan which he hoped would rid him once and for all of that hated family, and likewise of the Huguenot complication. He took the field himself at the head of a powerful army, sent the Duke de Joyeuse with a strong force against Navarre and, while directing Guise to head off the German allies of that Prince, provided him with as few reinforcements as possible. But everything fell out contrary to his expectations. Navarre beat Joyeuse badly at the battle of Coutras and, in the north, Guise with his six thousand men annihilated the forty thousand German mercenaries. The feat of the Balafré, or "man with the gashed face", as Guise was called, sent Catholic France wild with delight. At Rome, Pope Sixtus sang the praises of "the new Machabeus" in a special consistory, and granted France a jubilee in his honour. All the pulpits of the land resounded with his glory. "Saul," said the preachers with a sarcastic allusion to the King, "has killed his thousands, and David his tens of thousands." All this incense stank in the royal nostrils, and every day Henry grew more and more jealous.

At length he determined to smash the League, whatever it might cost him, and began with an onslaught on its Paris supporters, the revolutionary "Council of Sixteen". These men appealed to the Balafré, who immediately repaired to the capital in spite of Henry's orders to the contrary. Then followed the *Journée des Barricades*, when the leaguers poured into the streets at the sound of the tocsin, defeated the royal forces, and compelled His Majesty to take refuge in ignominious flight. After this the situation became impossible, so the two parties opened negotiations which resulted in the King's return. By this time, however, he had his mind made up to have the Balafré assassinated, and the Duke with his brother the Cardinal de Guise were duly dispatched by soldiers of the royal bodyguard, on December 28, 1588. At the same time, Cardinal de Bourbon the League's candidate for the succession, was thrown into prison. Henry then thought that his troubles were over, but soon found to his disgust that the blood of the Guises was the seed of a hundred new conspiracies. The entire Catholic world was in an uproar about the murders and the King's highly uncanonical treatment of the two Cardinals would have alienated the Pope completely had not Sixtus felt that the situation was still too obscure for any definite pronouncement on his part.

The next desperate move of the baffled monarch was to throw himself into the arms of the Huguenots. An offensive and defensive alliance was negotiated between him and Navarre, whereupon they joined forces and took the road to the rebellious city on the Seine. Just outside its walls, on August 1, 1589, the dagger of a crazy friar named Jacques Clément closed the long and chequered story of the House of Valois. Henry III had at least one true mourner. When his Jesuit friend and confessor, Père Auger, heard of the assassination he "was so overwhelmed that for two or three whole days he did not touch food or drink but remained in tears all the time, praying without intermission".

Throughout the weary struggle Pope Sixtus had but one object in view, the salvation of the Church in France. With him it was religion first and foremost, and then national interests a long way behind. Being the sovereign of a free state himself, he had the deepest sympathy for all legitimate national feelings, and saw in the sincere conversion of the Huguenot prince the ideal solution of France's difficulties. But that happy event failing, he was ready to tolerate even the dismemberment of the country, rather than witness the triumph of heresy on its soil. Olivares and the Spanish cardinals were forever dinning into his ears that the conversion of Navarre was a dream that could not possibly come true. They had their own master, Philip II, to serve, and that master would have found a slice of French territory decidedly convenient for the furtherance of his ambitious schemes. The aged pontiff did not know what to think. France had two kings now, Henry IV, whose blood was his best ally, and Henry's prisoner, Charles X, sheltering his claim under the purple banner of the League. The position of the Béarnais looked desperate indeed, for he had five-sixths of the country against him. With less than ten thousand men, he fell back on the coast, while Mayenne, brother of the murdered Guise, went in pursuit at the head of thirty thousand, boasting that he would soon "pitch the heretic into the sea".

Pope Sixtus became convinced at last that it was hopeless to look to Navarre for a solution of the Church's troubles, and so, without committing himself irrevocably to either party, decided to send a legate into France who should endeavour to bring about the union of all the Catholic elements in the country. For this exceedingly delicate mission he chose a worthy cardinal named Cajetan, who had the one serious disqualification of being too pro-Spanish in his sympathies. As many thorny questions of canon law and theology were bound to arise in the course of the mission, Robert Bellarmine was assigned to the Cardinal as his adviser-in-chief. Cardinal Cajetan was instructed to visit all the princes whose courts lay along his route, so the journey to Paris was punctuated with audiences at Florence, Bologna, Turin, and other places. Travelling, especially on horse-back, was neither pleasant nor easy, as it rained in torrents most of the time, but Bellarmine, instead of dying of pneumonia as might have been expected, throve wonderfully in the wet.

The many letters that were interchanged between him and Aquaviva while the Legation, which included the Patriarch of Alexandria and three other Italian bishops, was on the road, show how very much they were attached to each other and how solicitous the General was for the safety of his absent son. This he had very good reason to be. Danger lurked at every bend of the road, for Navarre had decided to capture the Legation, Cardinal and all, if he showed the slightest disposition to parley with the League. This he certainly did show but, all the same, Lyons was reached on November 9 without any notable mishap. Robert Bellarmine's fame had gone before him to France, and there were crowds of simple and gentle folk in the towns through which he passed who coveted the distinction of being able to say that they had shaken him by the hand. Judging by the stories they had heard and by the size of his books, they had built up a fancy portrait of him in their imagination. He was to be the *Controversies* made flesh, an awe-inspiring, majestic figure of a man, with an eagle eye and the aloof grandeur of a prophet. They thought at first that there must have been some mistake when a priest very like their own homely *abbés* and *vicaires*, and in stature less than man's average inches, came out to greet them so friendlily.

Meanwhile the Béarnais was making love to France in the west. After the brilliant victory at Arques, and reinforced by a contingent of English and Scots, he moved on with the strides of a conqueror, sweeping the forces of the League before him. Each province, city, and village through which he passed had a party to welcome him and a party to defy him. The country was torn to pieces, and everywhere there were blood and slaughter, ghastly disease, famine, and despair. It was only at the end of November that Cardinal Cajetan dared to take the road once more, and then he was unable to proceed beyond Dijon. The allies of Navarre were skirmishing around Paris, and they knew by this time that the Legate was their sworn foe. He was not a diplomatist and, while adhering conscientiously to the letter of his instructions, he entirely ignored their spirit. The situation had changed greatly since his departure from Rome, but he made no effort to adapt his policy to the new developments, though he was aware that the Pope's sympathies were veering round to King Henry. His Spanish blood was too much for him and, as the days went by, he grew increasingly troubled about the reception he might expect from the fiery Sixtus, if he were to bungle the negotiations. Once when on the road, Bellarmine narrates that he asked him anxiously how long he thought the Pope was likely to live. "He will die this very year" (1590), answered Robert with much assurance, but Cajetan would not believe him. Later, at Paris, the poor, worried Cardinal returned to the question:

"So you really think he will go to Heaven this year?"

"I am sure of it, your Lordship."

"Oh, but you cannot be sure of it; I feel certain he is going to live quite a long time yet."

"No, your Lordship, he will be dead before the end of this year."

So they argued, much, it would seem, to the comfort of the Legate's uneasy mind. The difficulties of the journey are vividly illustrated by another reminiscence of Bellarmine:

When we were at Dijon in Burgundy, and the Cardinal was thinking of pursuing his route to Paris, we were suddenly informed that the Seigneur de Tavines, with a thousand horsemen, was waiting in ambush for us at a fork in the road, his purpose being to capture the Cardinal, kill a certain number of us, and carry off the rest prisoners. But we were also told by other informants that this rumour was a fiction, concocted in order to frighten the Legate into staying where he was. On the morning when we were all due and ready to depart, his Lordship, being unable to discover the truth by any human means, secretly dropped two little pieces of paper into the chalice, when he had finished his Mass. On one was the word "Go", and on the other "Do not go". Then commending the whole affair to God, he drew out one of the folded notes, and opening it, saw that it bore the words: "Do not go". A short time afterwards, we learned that the story of the ambush was true in every detail.

After further alarms and delays, the Legation, under a strong escort provided by the Duke of Mayenne, entered Paris on January 21, 1590, and was vociferously applauded by an immense crowd on its way to Notre Dame. The cheering was deceptive, for even in Paris, which had been all along loyal to the League, considerable numbers had gone over to the rival flag. Many French prelates followed suit, and two cardinals, Vendôme and Lénoncourt, invited these new recruits of Navarre to an assembly at Tours on February 10, 1590. It seemed an ominous move, inasmuch as it was undertaken without the Pope's sanction, and rumour whispered that the intention of the bishops was to set up an independent French patriarchate. Bellarmine, for whom politics as such had only a very academic interest, was all attention when the fortunes of religion were at stake. This little wisp of cloud on the horizon caused him the gravest anxiety, which he expressed in a letter to his friend Father Cresswell, a Londoner, at that time rector of the English College, Rome:

I thank your Reverence for having so kindly sent me an account of the martyrdom of your four holy countrymen.[1] Their constancy has been an inspiration and comfort to us all, and we shall have the story of it translated into French and published soon, in order to encourage the people of this nation. For things have come to such a pass here that unless God quickly intervenes, I fear greatly that France will end up in the same way as England. I was so glad to get news of Father Henry Garnet, a man for whom I have always had the warmest affection. It is my firm conviction that the eventual reward of all his unsparing efforts for the good of souls will be the crown of martyrdom. Should this happen, I hope to have a good advocate in Heaven, but being older than he is, and having been for a considerable time his spiritual director, perhaps the summons will come to myself before it does to him. As for the third volume of the *Controversies*, I am most anxious to get it out, but have to go very slowly for many reasons, and as you know, I have lost four good months in the saddle. Will you please give Cardinal Allen my warm greetings. From Paris, February 19, 1590.

In order to avert any evil consequences that might arise out of the suggested synod at Tours, Cardinal Cajetan determined to proscribe it altogether, and directed Bellarmine to draw up a letter stating and justifying his action. A copy of this document

[1] These seem to have been George Nicols and Richard Yaxley, secular priests from Douay, Thomas Belson, gentleman, and Humphrey Pritchard, servant. All four were apprehended in Oxford, taken to London where they were cruelly treated, returned to Oxford for sentence to be passed on them there, and hanged, drawn and quartered in the City on July 5, 1589.

was then sent to each of the bishops of France, whose ready acceptance of its orders is a clear indication that they were by no means bent on schism but only on putting an end to the anarchy in their country. That, however, was not the last of the unhappy and unwise Legate's apprehensions. Early in March news reached Paris that Mayenne, the new head of the League, had been utterly routed at the battle of Ivry, and that the Béarnais was marching on the capital. On the eve of the great victory, his army, which was numerically much inferior to Mayenne's, had split up into two portions, one going off to confession, and the other to be exhorted by fiery Calvinist ministers. The Legate's eyes were turned too piously towards Spain for him to see the significance of that divided parade. During the battle, Henry's devotees, Catholic and Calvinist, were in a torment of anxiety, for wherever the fighting was fiercest, there he would surely be. When he occasionally emerged from the wild whirl, they could scarcely recognize him, as he was covered with blood and dust from top to toe. Four days afterwards, he was playing tennis and cracking jokes like the merriest monarch that ever sat on a throne. Indeed, except for his nominal Calvinism, and a too great fondness for dice and fair ladies, Henry was a man after Robert Bellarmine's own heart. The most comradely of kings, his gaiety, heroism, wit, and tenderness were precisely the qualities that endeared the homely, reddish-bearded figure of the Legate's theologian to all who knew him.

Few events in the chronicles of the world's disasters were such a pathetic combination of horror and heroism as the siege of Paris by Henry of Navarre. Every historian who has written of it goes back to the siege of Jerusalem by Titus for a parallel, and that they do so with good reason may be seen by glancing through the memoirs of Pierre de l'Estoile, a cynical eyewitness of the tragedy. There were more than 220,000 people locked up in the city, and not enough food to last beyond a month, even with the strictest rationing. At the end of that period, the starving thousands were compelled to adopt expedients such as the dreadful one suggested by the Spanish ambassador, which was to dig up the corpses in the cemeteries, grind their bones into a kind of flour, and bake it, mixed with water, into cakes. Worse even than that, frantic mothers were reported to have devoured their babies. At last even the dogs and cats had to be rationed. The Duchess of Montpensier, being the sister of Mayenne, was exempted from the ruling and, though she was offered golden chains and rings to the value of two thousand crowns for her poodle, she refused to part with him, but not, it is regrettable to record, for any sentimental reasons. "I shall need him for my own table soon", was her answer. De l'Estoile, who tells this story, saw a poor man eating cart-grease one day, and questioning him, learnt that for a whole week he, his wife, and three little children had had no other nourishment but that foul stuff. By further investigations, the diarist discovered that half the poor people were living on it. Before the end of July, 30,000 of them were corpses.

Bellarmine, of course, fared as badly as everybody else, and perhaps worse, on account of his ill-health and his habit of giving things away. When Aquaviva sent him six hundred *scudi* for his private expenses, he immediately made a present of the entire sum to the Paris Jesuits who had 600 pupils in their College to try to keep alive. What he endured may be guessed from the typically laconic paragraph in which he describes the siege:

We remained in Paris from January 20 until the beginning of September, during which time we did practically nothing, but suffered a very great deal. When the King of Navarre beat Mayenne on March 12 we were all terrified, but his Majesty, being unwilling to destroy and ravage so fine a city, preferred a siege to an assault. So he cast his trenches about us and, our food supplies failing, we began to have a very miserable time. A sort of dog-broth, boiled in pots, used to fetch quite a good price. The Spanish Ambassador once made us a splendid present, to wit a haunch of his own charger, that he had slaughtered for food.

In spite of all its sufferings, the spirit of the beleaguered city remained unbroken. The Franciscans, Dominicans, Capuchins and Carmelites worked themselves to death, keeping up the courage of their flocks. They were the League's sturdiest and most devoted allies and, had it not been for them, Paris must soon have hauled down its colours. They preached terrific sermons against the invader, and organized warlike processions that sent the starved populace into ecstasies of enthusiasm. The Jesuits, by Aquaviva's express instructions, did not preach against Navarre, but they and their guest Bellarmine took a leading part in all the non-political activities of the city, the religious processions, the public macerations, the long hours of prayer before the Blessed Sacrament at dead of night, and the unceasing attendance on sick and dying. The superiors of the Carthusians and the four mendicant orders in Paris permitted their subjects to be drilled in arms by the fiery Scottish curé of St Cosmas, a man named Hamilton. Large crowds gathered to see this new type of parade, in which there was much firing of muskets. Cardinal Cajetan also went in his carriage with Bellarmine and others. "Now it fell out", wrote l'Estoile in his *Memoires*, "that one of these new soldiers, who was doubtless unaware that his musket was loaded with ball, wanted very much to salute the Legate as he rode by in his carriage with Panigarol, the Jesuit Bellarmine, and other Italians. This good man accordingly fired his gun point-blank into the carriage and shot the Cardinal's almoner dead, whereupon the Cardinal bade his coachman gallop home in hot haste."

It was not by any will of his own that Bellarmine found himself, the only Jesuit, in that bizarre procession. Wherever the Legate went, he had to go but, as far as was compatible with courtesy, he kept well in the background on such occasions. Once, during a consultation on some political question, Cajetan noticed that his theologian was quietly slipping out of the room. "You are not ill, are you, Father Bellarmine?" he asked. "Oh no, your Lordship," said the fugitive turning back, "but as I was sent to France to give advice only on religious matters, I do not think I would be justified in taking part in such a discussion as that which now occupies you." Casaubon, the famous editor of classical texts, accused Bellarmine in 1611 of being, during his stay in France, "the chief torch, patron, and instigator of the wild public demonstrations connected with the conspiracy called the League". On the contrary, St Robert maintained a singularly prudent reserve throughout all the tedious, turbulent negotiations, and his neutrality must have cost him a good deal, because his sincere love and admiration for Cardinal Cajetan would naturally have inclined him to be a vigorous supporter of that prelate's prejudices in favour of the League. At the beginning of May, 1590, the heads of the League consulted the Sorbonne as to whether it might ever be lawful for Catholics to recognize Henry of Navarre. The answer of the faculty was a decided no, and that even if Henry were to renounce heresy and be absolved by the Pope. Those who aided him or had any dealings with him were guilty *ipso facto* of mortal sin, said the theologians. Three months of the siege took a good deal of its *bravura* out of that rather unwarranted reply. The theologians in a humbler mood requested the Legate to advise them "whether in view of the condition to which Paris was reduced, the penalty of excommunication would be incurred by prelates who approached the King of Navarre with the object of converting him, or at least, of obtaining better conditions for the Catholics". Cajetan immediately submitted the matter to four of his advisers, namely Panigarola, Bishop of Asti, Viceo, an Italian Jesuit, Tyrie, the Scottish rector of the Jesuit college in Paris, and Bellarmine. Panigarola and Viceo were all for the Sorbonne's opinion, but Bellarmine talked them round, and their unanimous final answer was that the prelates would not incur any ecclesiastical censure nor commit sin by undertaking such a negotiation.

Bellarmine's role in the exciting story of the siege was a very quiet and unobtrusive one. He preached a sermon of comfort to the poor people every day, and did all in his power to help his brother Jesuits, who were accused of hoarding food for their boys by the provost of the merchants. Their guest Robert made their cause his own and went personally to explain the situation to the angry official. The older students of the college and the Jesuit lay brothers took an active part in the defence of Paris, and that the fathers also were not averse from holding a gun is evident from the question which a group of them, including Bellarmine, addressed to the General at the worst period of the siege: "Is it permissible and proper for the fathers of the Society to take up arms in the defence of the city against the heretics,

especially as the other religious orders are doing so with everybody's approval?" Aquaviva's prudent answer was that the only
arms which priests ought to lift up were flesh-and-blood ones,
in imitation of Moses, but he did not entirely forbid the use of
the other kind, and it was in fact to ten stalwart members of the
Society that the capital owed its eventual salvation. Early in
September Navarre learned that the Dukes of Mayenne and
Parma were advancing to the relief of the city, and marched away
to meet them. They refused battle, so Henry, on September 10,
suddenly retraced his steps, hoping to find the besieged people off
their guard. To his annoyance, however, the tocsin blared out on
the still night air, and the leaguers swarmed from their beds to the
walls. Henry bade his men keep very quiet, with the result that
the watchers, tiring of their vigil, went home, believing the alarm
to have been a mistake. Only the Jesuits and a handful of soldiers
remained at their posts. About four o'clock in the morning they
heard sounds, as if ladders were being placed against the walls,
and one of them immediately rushed back into the city shouting
at the top of his voice: "To arms! To arms!" Meantime, the
others engaged with the enemy and succeeded by pushing over
the ladders in keeping them at bay till help arrived. That was the
end of the siege of Paris. On the following morning Navarre
marched away for good, and ladders captured by the Jesuits were
taken in triumph to their College of Clermont, where they
remained on exhibit as war trophies for a long time.

Apart from the many hours he spent in prayer, St Robert
occupied himself in visiting the sick, or browsing among the
manuscripts of the Paris libraries, for not even starvation could
kill the scholar in him. In the preface of his book *The Seven
Words* he favours the opinion that our Lord was fastened to the
cross by four nails and not by three. After quoting some authorities
for that view, he continues: "I, for my part, have seen in the Royal
Library at Paris some very ancient manuscripts of the Gospels
which contained many pictures of Christ crucified, and these all
had the four nails". He also tried to learn French and attributed
his lack of success to his advancing years, which were forty-eight.
At the beginning of September a letter arrived from Rome for

Cardinal Cajetan. It was a rare occurrence in those troubled times and there was lively discussion among the Cardinal's suite as to what news it might contain. "The general opinion," wrote St Robert, was "that it contained bad news, because, as we knew already, Pope Sixtus was angry with the Cardinal and his secretary and also with myself on account of a proposition in my books which denied that the Pope was the immediate and sovereign master of the whole world." The letter in fact announced the death of the Pope, as Robert himself had forecast earlier in that year, and also summoned the much-relieved Cajetan to the subsequent conclave. At Meaux, Robert fell dangerously ill of a deadly type of dysentery then ravaging the town. The kindly Cardinal would not leave him to die among strangers whose language he could not speak, and had him carried in a litter until, after a week, he was again able to ride, and so reached Rome on November 11, 1590.

While St Robert was suffering in beleaguered Paris on the business of Pope Sixtus V, that alarming and incalculable Pontiff brooded over a theory propounded in the *Controversies* that denied the Holy See a direct power of interference in the concerns of secular authorities. Temporal rulers, too, Robert maintained, held their authority from God, though in his view it was mediated to them through the consent of the peoples they ruled. Except in his own states, where the Pope enjoyed the same direct temporal power as all other kings and republics, he was not in any sense the overlord of the whole world, as some medieval canonists had maintained and some medieval popes had practised. In fact, Bellarmine contends, the Pope, except in his own states, has no merely temporal jurisdiction, directly and by divine right. In virtue of his office as supreme arbiter of faith and morals, for the protection and supernatural salvation of his flock, the Pope possesses, indeed, by the nature of the case must possess, indirect temporal jurisdiction to be exercised only when the action of secular powers threatened the eternal interests of their subjects. In such cases Bellarmine was even willing to concede to the Holy See the power of deposing such rulers and releasing their subjects from their duty of obedience. That was going very far, but it did not satisfy Pope Sixtus V. St Robert's theory of indirect temporal jurisdiction, which was traditional among theologians and merely systematized and given its full force in the *Controversies*, seemed to Sixtus, who before his election had given an English Protestant visitor to Rome the impression of being "the most crooching humble cardinal that was ever lodged in an oven," a derogation from the plenitude of power claimed by him as by no other Pope since Boniface VIII. He determined to stigmatize the theory as heterodox, and to put St Robert's first volume of the *Controversies*, dedicated to himself, on the Index of Forbidden Books. Robert had good company in condemnation, for the great Dominican Francisco de Vitoria, who had burnished anew the long-dimmed gold of medieval scholasticism, was also included on account of a treatise containing the proposition that it is lawful to resist an unjust command of the Holy See. Count Olivares, the Spanish ambassador in Rome, whose frequent stormy interviews with Sixtus kept the Romans amused, wrote the following very accurate account of the event to his master, Philip II, on August 19, 1590:

> Sir, in spite of all the efforts of which I have informed you, made by the cardinals of the Congregation of the Index, to prevent the Pope from putting Bellarmine's and Vitoria's works on that proscribed list, it has been found impossible to weaken his Holiness's resolution. Finally, as they perceived that he would no longer even listen to them, they sent him a written memorial, a copy of which I am enclosing. All, however, was to no purpose, and the Index is now in the press or has already been printed, but it is not yet possible to obtain it from the booksellers. Special efforts were made to persuade the Pope at least to point out the objectionable passages, and the corrections which were deemed necessary. These, in Vitoria, are the places where he teaches that it is lawful to resist the unjust commandments of popes, and in Bellarmine, the chapters which limit their temporal jurisdiction. It was all in vain, and now everybody is scandalized and afraid. The cardinals of the Congregation of the Index did not dare to tell his Holiness that the teaching of those two authors is drawn from the works of the saints for fear he might give them a bit of

his brusque temper, and perhaps put the saints themselves on the Index.

The edition of the Index referred to was printed in Rome that same August, 1590, a small quarto volume of fifty-nine leaves, numbered on one side only. A few copies of it have survived and in them may be read the entry: "Robert Bellarmine's Disputations on Controversies of the Christian Faith against the Heretics of this Age. Until they shall have been corrected in accordance with the foregoing rules." Six months before the printing of the Index condemning him, St Robert heard on his way to Paris of what was in the wind. He knew that there were men in the entourage of the Pope, mostly canon lawyers of a medieval complexion, who encouraged his high pretensions to universal temporal dominion, and looked on himself and his Society of Jesus with jaundiced eyes. The General of the Society, Claudio Aquaviva, addressed the following letter of comfort to him on February 19, 1590:

Your Reverence will have heard from another source about the noise that has been made in the entourage of the Holy Father over the opinion expressed in your works that the Pope is not lord of the world in temporal matters. I have spoken of it to Cardinal Santi Quattro, who is a man of sound judgment, and he thinks as we do, and I have also approached Cardinal Santa Severina. Since then, a Franciscan friar has presented the Pope with a book on this question in which he attacks your opinion, and the result has been further excitement. The Holy Father has now put the matter in the hands of the cardinals connected with the Index, who are all, thank God, friends of our Society. I have spoken to three of them including Cardinal Allen, and tomorrow I will speak to Cardinal Colonna, senior,[1] my words to each being that you are an obedient son and will carry out whatever is demanded of you. Do not be too anxious, then, Father. I have full confidence that, with the help of God, the affair will turn out well. All these illustrious and prudent gentlemen are on our side, and we have good hopes that once his Holiness has been convinced that your opinion is

---

[1] There were two Cardinals Colonna on the Congregation of the Index.

the common theological opinion on the matter he will permit it to pass. For my own part, I shall not fail to use every means in my power to help, nor shall I forget your interests in my prayers to our Lord.

Aquaviva was unduly optimistic about the results of his strenuous efforts, as when he wrote in April to Robert in invested Paris:

Personally I am convinced that all will be well, but nevertheless I shall continue to do everything in my power. I have the matter deeply at heart owing to its importance, and above all, owing to my regard for your Reverence. . . . When you write to Rome, it will be better not to qualify the opposite opinion as erroneous, because it has its partisans here and it would only damage your cause to offend them. The day before yesterday Cardinal Santa Severina told me that he had studied the question and had come to the same conclusion as your Reverence. To sum the matter up, it is now decided that in future editions the chapter headings should not be put in a negative but problematical form e.g. *Utrum papa habeat*, etc., and that the opinion holding Christ to have exercised temporal jurisdiction should not be styled erroneous, as such a qualification is strongly objected to in these parts.

From the details given in this letter we are enabled to determine not only the book and chapter but the very passage which was responsible for the Pope's annoyance. Some of those who championed the direct temporal jurisdiction of the Holy See used as their main argument the following syllogism: Christ possessed direct temporal jurisdiction, not only as God but as Man, and exercised it during his life on earth; but the Pope is the vicar and the lieutenant of Christ; therefore the Pope possesses and may exercise direct temporal jurisdiction. Bellarmine's answer was to deny the second half of the major, namely that Christ had exercised the jurisdiction which, of course, he possessed. His kingdom was not of this world. From Aquaviva's next letter, dated May 11, it appears that Robert had meantime drawn up a list of patristic passages which taught clearly that the royalty exercised by Christ while on earth was purely spiritual.[1] This he had dispatched to the cardinals concerned, who were stirred by its strong testimonies to new zeal on his behalf. Owing to their efforts the Pope became neutral for a time, but about the beginning of July the opposition canonists were on the warpath again. Aquaviva, however, remained an inveterate optimist, and wrote as late as August 5 to cheer up his despondent friend with the promise of still more strenuous work for the cause. Shortly afterwards he appears to have presented an eloquently-worded memorial to the cardinals of the Congregation of the Index, who in their turn addressed the following supplication to the Holy Father:

> Having diligently examined, by your command, what Father Francis Vitoria and Father Bellarmine have written on the temporal power of the Pope, we have discovered nothing which, in our opinion, could give offence. Consequently, while remitting the whole matter to the wise judgment of your Holiness, we beg of you to take into consideration the reputation of those two good Fathers. Furthermore, even were there to be found in their books some passage less temperate or discreet than is desirable, do we not see that Holy Church has always deemed it better to tolerate the occasional blemishes of good writers than to put them to the great shame of prohibiting their works?

Pope Sixtus, however, had grown increasingly irritated with the legate, Cajetan, and his advisers during the summer of 1590, and was therefore in no mood to listen to pleas on Bellarmine's behalf, especially when they came from Aquaviva, who at this very time was resisting respectfully but firmly the Pontiff's attempts to modify the constitutions of the Society of Jesus. And in addition to all this, there was the persistent clamour of certain

---

[1] The original of this document, entitled *De Regno Christi, quale sit*, is in the Bibliothèque Nationale, Paris. In a recent book, *L'Idée de la Royauté du Christ au Moyen Âge* (Paris, 1959), Jean Leclercq, O.S.B., proves by an enormous wealth of quotations, manuscript as well as printed, including a newly discovered sermon of St Thomas Aquinas, that medieval popes, with few exceptions, medieval theologians, and medieval preachers, all held an idea of the royalty of Christ that was essentially religious, entirely unconnected with temporal jurisdiction.

extremist doctors who knew how to play on the Pope's autocratic temper. Typical of such belligerents was an influential
Spanish canonist named Francisco Peña, an auditor of the Rota
during several pontificates and eventually its dean. Throughout his
long life Peña remained a strenuous champion of the direct power
of the Holy See in temporal affairs and, when Bellarmine attacked
that theory a second time in 1609, addressed the following letter to
the reigning Pope, Paul V, which helps us to divine the sort of
pressure that had been brought to bear on Sixtus V:

> Most Holy Father: In the interests of truth we must needs
> speak out our mind plainly to the Lord and his Vicar on earth.
> If this little Christian [*questo cristianello*, meaning Bellarmine]
> was possessed of solid and truly Catholic zeal, instead of itching
> to write a new book every week in his own defence, he would
> restrain himself and set about correcting those erroneous
> opinions which the public authority of the Church will
> eventually have to correct. This might certainly be expected
> of him, seeing that from the day he published his *Controversies*
> all the heretics of the century have made use of them, and
> employed his arguments word for word against the Church
> and against the authority of the Vicar of Christ. Indeed, as
> long as this seminary [the Roman College] lasts the Church
> will have no peace, unless Christ, the all-powerful King,
> procures it for her by some other means in his power.

Peña even suggested that he might himself be appointed censor of
Bellarmine's offensive book, in which case it would be thoroughly
purged of the error that Christ our Lord had refrained from
exercising temporal jurisdiction during his life on earth. By some
means this determined foe of St Robert had obtained access to his
book before it was published.

With such counsellors to spur him on, Pope Sixtus overcame
his momentary scruples and put the first volume of the *Controversies* on his new Index of Forbidden Books, the worst disgrace
to which any Catholic theologian could be subjected. All that
Aquaviva and the cardinals could obtain from the impetuous
Pontiff was a brief respite before the condemnation was officially
promulgated. That respite was enough. As has been seen from the

letter of the Spanish ambassador, the Index was ready, or almost ready, for publication on August 19, 1590. Eight days later Pope Sixtus was dead, and his successor, Urban VII, who reigned only a dozen days, had the names of Bellarmine and Vitoria immediately removed from the queer company in which they had been listed. Not only did Bellarmine never retract his arguments against the direct power of the Pope, but in the revision of his works which was published in 1607 he brought forward new ones to their support. The saintly but somewhat pugnacious Belgian Jesuit, Leonard Lessius, expressed a strong wish that the dedication of the incriminated volume of the *Controversies* to Pope Sixtus should be utterly expunged in future editions, a view with which his friend St Robert entirely disagreed. The dedication remained intact in all subsequent editions.

The story of the Index was not the only unhappy link which connected Bellarmine's fortunes with those of the great imperious Pope. He was also involved in the very interesting but rather deplorable chapter of Church history which deals with the origins of our present edition of the Latin Vulgate. St Jerome's great revision of the early Latin translations of the Scriptures had won its way into universal favour after a long struggle, and by the twelfth century had routed all rivals from the field. But it had been badly mauled in the fight, and Roger Bacon said that in his day it was already *"horribiliter corruptus"*. When printing was invented, copies of the Vulgate, which did not then boast a capital V, multiplied at a headlong pace, and this rapid succession of new impressions accentuated the evil done by the "drowsy copyists" against whom St Jerome had inveighed. Then came the Reformation with its clamorous appeal to Holy Writ. Latin Bibles, sponsored by both Catholics and Protestants, began to pour from the press in ever increasing numbers, many of them differing in their readings and their interpretation of various dogmagic passages. In this welter of rival versions, each claiming to supersede St Jerome and to be the best ever done, men knew not where to look for the word of God until providence sent the Council of Trent to stay the hand of the free lances who were responsible for the confusion.

After having determined the canon of Scripture in their fourth session (1546), the Fathers went on to declare, in the disciplinary degree *Insuper*, that the Latin Vulgate must be held by all Catholics as the Church's "authentic" version of the Bible and be used by them in public lectures, disputations, sermons, etc. By the word authentic, i.e., officially guaranteed, the Council did not signify that the Vulgate was in every respect an absolutely accurate rendering, but that it was free from error in everything pertaining to moral and dogmatic teaching, and was substantially faithful to the original scriptures. The Fathers of the Council were so well aware of the imperfections of the editions then in circulation that in the same decree *Insuper* they had ordered a new revision to be made with the greatest possible accuracy. But, learned men though they were, they do not seem to have realized fully the enormous difficulties attendant on such a task. Some of them even light-heartedly suggested that the work might be done there and then at Trent in the intervals between the sessions, or that perhaps some encyclopaedic scholar such as Cardinal Sirleto might be given the entire commission. Little did they guess when they sent their request and suggestions to the reigning Pope that neither he nor any of his ten immediate successors would live to see its fulfilment.

Though both Pius IV and Pius V began to prepare the way, nothing of importance was done until the sixteenth century had nearly run its course. Then Sixtus came like a "consecrated whirl-wind", and there was a great stirring of peaceful, academic waters. The flagging energies of the commission for the revision of the Septuagint, which had been appointed by Gregory XIII, immediately revived under his inspiring leadership, and within a year of his election they had brought their labours to a successful end. Bellarmine was one of them, and he had also assisted Sixtus in his edition of the writings of St Ambrose, which was finished at the same time. A document prefixed to the last volume of this work illustrates very well the authoritative and individualistic temper of the Pope. It happens to be the worst edition of St Ambrose in existence, but for all that, he orders the patriarchs, archbishops and bishops of the universal Church to see to it that no part of the holy Doctor's writings be ever again printed in their dioceses unless in conformity with the Roman text which had him for its editor.

After the Septuagint and St Ambrose, the Vulgate. The same commission which had carried through the revision of the Greek text of the Old Testament so successfully was ordered to gird itself for the more difficult and necessary task. It included such eminent men as Cardinal Carafa, the president, Cardinal Allen, and Bellarmine, who devoted the first months to a search for manuscripts which was extremely fruitful and included the Codex Amiatinus, refused by its custodians, the monks of Monte Amiata, until a bolt from the Vatican made them hastily change their minds. The commissioners took the well-known and deservedly popular Louvain Bible of the Dominican scholar Hentenius as their starting point, and wrote in between the lines of its text, or in the ample margins, the corrections they deemed advisable. Their work, to which they had brought immense erudition and the greatest possible devotion, was finished towards the close of 1588, and the revisers began to dream with pardonable pride of the immortality that must surely be the crown of their efforts. But they received a rude awakening when the Pope examined the ten thousand variant readings they had diligently and eruditely chosen. He became so angry at sight of them that he drove Cardinal Carafa from his presence with harsh words and forthwith cashiered the commission. He would revise the Vulgate himself. In the bull which he drafted subsequently to introduce his work to the Christian world, he declared:

> We, weighing the importance of the matter, and considering carefully the great and singular privilege we hold of God, and our true and legitimate succession from Blessed Peter, Prince of the Apostles . . . are the proper and specially constituted Person to decide this whole question.

The Pope set to work with the furious energy characteristic of him and, as he suffered from insomnia, carried on his labours far into the night. Only two assistants were admitted to his counsels, one of whom, an ailing man named Angelo Rocca, was obliged to write out the entire Latin Bible in his own hand, and nearly died under the strain. The other assistant was Bellarmine's old master, Francisco Toledo, to whom Sixtus submitted each sheet of his work as soon as it was completed, but accepted his opinions only when they happened to coincide with his own. These opinions were extremely conservative for, though the Pope followed his discredited commissioners in his choice of the Louvain Bible as a foundation text, unlike them, he clung to its readings as much as he possibly could. The commission had suggested a series of excellent emendations in the last ten chapters of the Book of Genesis, all of which were rejected. Sixtus made, indeed, forty-three changes, but thirty-one of these were merely orthographical. And it was the same way all through the Old Testament. The Louvain Bible more than held its own and, when he turned away from it, as he did only rarely and in matters of little consequence, it was rather to make the sense clear than out of any respect for ancient manuscripts.

But there was one point on which Sixtus showed himself decidedly radical. Robert Stephanus had introduced our present system of verses into his Bible of 1555. The Louvain editors adopted it, and in a short time, owing to its convenience for purpose of reference, it became a settled habit of all Christendom. The Pope now discarded it in favour of a new scheme worked out by himself. It is true that his divisions were more logical than the old ones, and in this they marked progress, but the men of the sixteenth century did not look on the matter in that light. They thought rather of the confusion and worry and waste of time which the change would involve. Preachers and their congregations would be at cross-purposes, and it would be impossible to consult a pre-Sixtine theological book without uncharitable thoughts about the innovator. Learned men, generally, felt that there were more precious things in life than logic, and a uniform system of reference was one of them.

After about eighteen months of Herculean labour, Sixtus had his Bible ready for the printers, the famous firm of Aldus Manutius. At the beginning of 1590 the first copies of the aristocratic folio were brought to the Pope, but his joy at their fine looks was changed to annoyance when he discovered that there were several misprints in the text. With characteristic energy he immediately began to think of some way to remedy the evil and, not liking tables of *errata*, decided to do the corrections with his pen or by means of little square, oblong, or triangular pieces of paper, pasted over the blunders. It was heavy, tedious work, and it took him a full six months to complete, but even then he was not satisfied. The Spanish ambassador relates that no sooner had he been given a copy of the corrected Bible for presentation to his royal master than a monk arrived in hot haste, demanding it back for further retouches. It would seem to be plain enough from these and other indications that the august editor was in two minds about his work. Furthermore, in a few places phrases and whole verses had been accidentally omitted, and no little square, oblong, or triangular devices could restore them. Consequently, publication of the long-expected volume was deferred from day to day and month to month, though the bull which was to introduce it to the Christian world had been drafted, printed, and made ready for posting upon the doors of St Peter's and the Lateran Basilica, much earlier. In it Sixtus said:

> By the fullness of Apostolical power, We decree and declare that this edition . . ., approved by the authority delivered to Us by the Lord, is to be received, and held as true, lawful, authentic, and unquestioned in all public and private[1] discussion, reading, preaching, and explanation.

The learned world remained on the tip-toe of expectation. Everything conspired to whet men's curiosity, the mystery surrounding the Pope's editorial work, his well-known *temperamento focoso*, the inexplicable delays, and the spicy rumours which, as is usual in such circumstances, had soon begun to go their rounds. At last, in the middle of April, 1590, the news-sheets of Rome announced that copies of the Bible had been presented to cardinals and ambassadors. What happened next, nobody knows. Silence resumed its reign until, on August 27, the Romans heard with

---

[1] The adjective "private" is an addition to the ruling of the Council of Trent.

amazement above the familiar notes of the Ave Maria bells, a startling, ominous sound—the solemn tolling from the Capitol which signified that Sixtus the Fifth was dead. Then began an immediate and violent reaction on the part of the fickle mob who, forgetting all that their noble and large-hearted sovereign had done for them, remembered him only as the stern judge of their vices. All night long Rome was given over to wild tumult, and the poor, worn-out corpse of the Pope barely escaped desecration under cover of a terrible storm that had broken upon the ungrateful city. More cruel even than the blind fury of the masses was the cold, calculated hatred with which the Pope's enemies in high places pursued his memory. The insolent Olivares continued to send his hectoring dispatches to Spain in angry denunciation of the new Bible, and there were even some respectable but aggrieved members of Carafa's commission who did not disdain to join in the abuse. Robert Bellarmine was not one of them. He had suffered more than most men from the arbitrary temper of Sixtus, but so little was he inclined to counsels of revenge that he adopted, on the contrary, a line of action which was to bring upon him the heavy charge of having lied brazenly to shield the reputation of the dead Pontiff.

When St Robert reached Rome from Paris in November, 1590, the Sixtine Vulgate was still the topic of the hour. Gregory XIV, who succeeded the short-lived Urban VII at the beginning of December, knew not what course to take in the clamour of conflicting opinions. Robert himself tells how the Pope found a way out of his embarrassment:

During the year 1591, while Gregory XIV was debating what he should do about the Bible of Sixtus the Fifth in which very many regrettable changes had been made, some men, whose opinions had great weight, held that it should be publicly prohibited. I did not think so, and I showed the Holy Father that, instead of forbidding the edition of the Bible in question, it would be better to correct it in such a manner that it could be published without detriment to the honour of Pope Sixtus. The result could be achieved by removing inadvisable changes as quickly as possible, and then issuing the volume with Sixtus's own name upon it, and a preface stating that owing to haste some errors had crept into the first edition through the fault of the printers or some other persons.

Those words of St Robert were to gain almost as much notoriety as the bold statement of Jacob to his father Isaac, and very few advocates would urge on the Jesuit's behalf, as St Augustine had done for the Patriarch, that what he said was not a lie but a mystery.

Pope Gregory immediately acted on Bellarmine's suggestion, and set up a new commission with the elder Cardinal Colonna again at its head, and Robert himself and Cardinal Allen again members. Colonna invited them to his pleasant country-house at Zagarolo among the Sabine hills, eighteen miles from Rome. In this quiet spot they set to work with such a will that the revision was finished by the middle of June. Bellarmine's keen interest and important part in the work may be guessed at from the careful table of "regrettable changes" in the Sixtine Bible which he drew up for the assistance of all concerned. The table has two columns, the left containing the texts that had been omitted, added to, or modified, and the right, his censure based on the Hebrew, Chaldaic, Greek and Latin manuscripts.

The work of revision having been completed, the next practical question was whether it should be made public at once, and if so under what conditions. Bellarmine was again asked for advice, and gave it to the Pope with his usual clarity and frankness. Point number one, the new Vulgate ought to be published immediately as this was the only way to safeguard the honour of the Holy See, and the interests of the Church. The edition of Sixtus was certain to fall into the hands of heretics, and it was greatly to be feared that one or other of them would use it to prove that the Scriptures had been corrupted by a Pope, an argument which he could render plausible by citing many passages that had been omitted, amplified, or changed without rhyme or reason, and against the witness of all codices, Latin, Greek and Hebrew. The best way to forestall such a manoeuvre would be to publish the Zagarolo recension as soon as possible, with a preface saying that Pope Sixtus had published a Bible revised by his orders, the previous year, but on examining it had discovered that many errors had crept into the text owing to excessive haste and other causes, as usually happens in first editions; consequently, that he had decided to have the work done all over again but, death intervening, it fell to his successor to carry out his wishes, which were now realized in the edition before the reader. By proceeding thus, the Holy See would escape the dilemma of seeming either to condemn the acts of Pope Sixtus or to approve the errors which were to be found in his work.

Secondly, it would be better to publish the new Bible under the names of both Sixtus and Gregory, but without any decree giving preference to this over all other editions, or still less, suppressing all others in its favour. "We who laboured at the revision of the Bible," wrote St Robert, "know that we were in a great hurry, and that we had to leave many things alone though they needed emendation, because we did not possess all the necessary Latin codices or because we did not want to trouble the souls of the faithful by too many novelties. We were anxious, too, not to give the impression that we considered ourselves better scholars than our predecessors who preferred to tolerate such blemishes rather than to change them."

Robert's third and last point is an eloquent and effective plea for the retention of variant readings in the margins of the new Bible. St Jerome and St Augustine were both strongly in favour of them, he urges. They are a great help to the understanding of the chosen text, and would afford a second line of defence, if the heretical attack pressed too hardly upon it. Besides this, they would form a sort of library in which everybody could consult the most ancient and rarest of manuscripts.

Much to his disappointment, this advice was not accepted, and the newly revised Vulgate appeared before the end of 1592 without the variant readings and under the name of Pope Sixtus alone, which in many ways was only fair and fitting, seeing how much the great Pope's vigorous initiative and tireless encouragement contributed to the production of the Bible which the Church still uses today, while awaiting the much more thorough and scholarly revision now for many years being carried out by a team of erudite Benedictines in Rome.

The bull which Sixtus V had made ready to launch his own revision of the Vulgate was never promulgated. The revision carried through at Zagarola by Colonna, Allen, Bellarmine and others was published by authority of Pope Clement VIII, and in course of time became known as the Clementine Vulgate, though, as mentioned, it bore only the name of Pope Sixtus. By the wish of Pope Clement St Robert contributed a preface to the new recension which perhaps did not contain the whole truth but enough of it to safeguard the memory and reputation of the very great man whose name it bore. The magnificent folio copies of Sixtus's own revised Vulgate were, as far as possible, retrieved, but some few remained at large in Germany and England to rejoice the hearts of enemies of the Holy See and also of some Catholic detractors of St Robert Bellarmine. The first librarian of the Bodleian, Oxford, a learned but rabidly anti-Catholic person named Dr Thomas James, bought from a soldier a copy of Hentenius's Louvain Vulgate, secured in the plundering of the Jesuit college at Cadiz by Drake. He then had the luck to find in the shop of a London bookseller copies of both the Sixtine and Clementine folios which he diligently compared with their common original, Hentenius. The result was his lively book, *Bellum Papale* or "The Warres of the Popes about the Hierome Bibles". He had written it, he avowed, "to prove by the event that Rome is Babylon and the Pope Antichrist". He made great play with the differing systems of versification in the two Bibles, as Pope Clement had restored that of Stephanus, and he professed to be profoundly shocked that Pope Sixtus had omitted several passages of Scripture from his own revision. Here he cannot have been in completely good faith, for he must have known that those passages were not in the text of Hentenius, but in his margins, or, if in his text, bore a sign indicating that they were not borne out by numerous manuscripts. All were merely trivial questions of scholarship, utterly unconnected with papal infallibility, yet they were taken over lock, stock and barrel from the *Bellum*

Papale, nearly three hundred years afterwards, by the Irish Protestant scholar Dr George Salmon in his well-known and still regularly reissued lectures against the doctrine in question. Dr James of Oxford might be proud of his immortality at Trinity College, Dublin.

CHAPTER V

BELLARMINE IN AUTHORITY

IN 1588 Robert Bellarmine vacated, after twelve years, his post of professor at the Roman College in order to prepare his *Controversies* for publication, and was appointed instead spiritual director of the same institution. In that capacity he had the great ardent soul of Aloysius Gonzaga[1] in his care and became his intimate counsellor and friend. In their record of the life of St Aloysius, the Bollandists say of Bellarmine that "just as no one knew him better, so no one bore such tireless testimony of both word and deed to his holiness, and no one venerated his memory with such tender love as the last of his confessors". About ten o'clock on the night of June 20, 1591, Robert stood by the death-bed of his young friend. "Tell me, Luigi," he said, "tell me when it is time to say the prayers." After a brief space the dying saint whispered, "Now, Father, it is time". After the prayers were done Robert would gladly have remained with his penitent all night, but the Father Minister who was in the room begged him to take some rest, as the infirmarian was convinced that Luigi would not die that night and, in any case, would call him instantly at need. So Robert went sorrowfully away, and Luigi died in great agony shortly afterwards, before he could be

[1] The young saint always signed himself Aluigi or Luigi, never Aloisio or Aloysius. The name Luigi is Italian for Ludovicus or Louis. How the letter A came to be prefixed to it is not known. The strange Latinization, Aloysius, was in use long before his birth in 1568. Thus the French church in Rome, dedicated to St Louis IX, is indicated on Leonardo Bufalini's famous map of the city, published in 1551, as "Sanctus Aloysius Francorum". At least one eminent Italian Jesuit, the excellent early historian of his Society, Francésco Sacchini, objected to the name and tried to introduce the regular Latin form of Ludovicus or Louis in 1612, but he was strongly opposed by Prince Francésco Gonzaga, the saint's brother and head of the family at that time. This same Francésco procured that the form Aloysius should be used in the brief issued by Pope Paul V on October 19, 1605, declaring his brother *Beatus*. It is a pity that Sacchini did not prevail.

recalled. Luigi was himself persuaded that he would die before midnight of that last day within the octave of Corpus Christi, and it was only out of a sense of obedience that St Robert left him, at almost the last moment. Ever afterwards to the end of his life, June 21 was one of his most sacred anniversaries, and he never failed on that day to make a pilgrimage to the grave of his spiritual child at the little church of the Annunziata attached to the Roman College, as well as to the infirmary where he had died. Jesuits of those days, like other religious men, were not buried in coffins, but wrapped in winding sheets and consigned to the bare earth, as is still the custom with Cistercians and Carthusians. It was Robert Bellarmine who procured that Aloysius should be buried in a coffin in a vault of the Annunziata, apart from the graves of the other dead, for he felt certain that Luigi would be glorified by God and honoured by the Church.

On June 21, 1608, when he had been a cardinal for nine years, St Robert was asked to speak on Aloysius at the Annunziata and gave the following address, printed afterwards by the Bollandists:

Three great privileges were his, to which we cannot aspire. The rest of us, like the labourers in the parable, are called at the first or third or eleventh hour, that is when we are boys, or young men, or getting old. But his call came before the first hour, when he was only a child. He used to tell me that he considered his seventh year to have been the year of his conversion. Then again, he never suffered from fleshly allurements, even in his thoughts, and he is the only one I have known who was so singularly blessed. His third privilege was to be free of all distractions in his prayers, and how great a privilege that was, we who try to pray know best.[1] St Augustine says that one of the proofs of God's meekness is the way he puts up with our roving wits. I asked Luigi once how on earth

[1] It is a well established fact that St Aloysius acquired his freedom from distractions in prayer, not only by the grace of God, but by his own persistent heroic efforts to keep his mind and imagination free. Is it not highly likely that his other "privilege" was similarly won in the battle with his naturally passionate nature? "Angelical" might seem to many the least appropriate of adjectives to apply to one who had to fight for his freedom every foot of the way.

he was able so to compose his mind in prayer as to pass a whole hour without the least distraction. Do you know what his answer was? "The real wonder, Father, is, how anybody could possibly turn his mind to other things while standing in the presence of God."

But let us leave those inimitable glories alone, and think rather what we, old and imperfect as we are, can learn from the life of one who was perfect and young. First there was his great strong faith which made him spend the whole week preparing to receive our Lord on Sunday morning. Holy Communion is, indeed, the great test of our faith, for how can anyone believe with all his heart that the Lord of Glory is truly present in the Blessed Sacrament, and yet go to him with a cold distracted heart? About his patience, I scarcely know what to say. During most of his life he was a martyr to headaches, and yet he never uttered a word of complaint. So great was the fever of desire that came over him to spend himself in the service of the stricken poor, that he told me a short time before his last illness, he felt certain that this desire was a sign of his approaching end. In that long last illness itself, he was the very pattern of patience. Scarcely anything remained of his poor, wasted, little body except the skin and bones, and cruel sores, yet when asked how he was he would cheerfully answer, "Grand".

I used to notice how, when out walking with a lay brother companion, he would contrive to give him the place of honour. Indeed his life was all lowliness and he was always longing for the lowliest offices, especially the ones which other men avoided, such as teaching the smallest boys in the schools. Nor was there the slightest trace of affectation in his manner. The desire to be united with God consumed him like a great fire. Once I begged him to pray that his life might be spared as I knew what a holy influence he would exert on the flocks of boys in our colleges. "Father", he answered, "how could I possibly ask to stay?" Death had no terrors for him at all, and he gave me the signal to say the prayers for his departing soul, without a tremor. He answered each of the invocations as calmly and firmly as if it were some other man who lay there dying, for whom he prayed. . . . Yes, indeed, God took delight in his servant Aloysius, and taught us through the miracle of his life

that there is no such thing as coming of age with him, for boys
and girls can beat us greybeards in the race to perfection.
Let us thank God, then, who lit for our guidance such an eager
and splendid flame, and let us keep our eyes on it while our dark
journey lasts. We especially, who were his familiar friends on
earth, should pray to him that by his intercession we may join
him at last in heaven. Amen.

From his knowledge of the special gifts and goodness of
Aloysius, Robert used to say that he was sure that St Thomas
Aquinas, when young, must have looked like his twin brother. In
one part of the *Summa*, that holy Doctor, speaking about vocal
prayer, signalizes three grades of attention which are necessary,
and shows that the most important and highest grade consists in
fixing the mind on God. "Sometimes," he continues, "this
attention becomes so great that the mind forgets everything else,
sicut dicit Hugo de Sancto Victore." That little phrase, "as Hugo of
St Victor says", coming from one whose every prayer, almost,
turned into an ecstasy, is as good as a whole treatise on the divine
self-forgetfulness which we call the virtue of humility. Robert
Bellarmine himself had many of the traits of St Thomas, but this
one of reticence about his own spiritual experiences was the most
marked of all. When he speaks of the converse of God with his
lovers, he must introduce Ignatius, or Aloysius, or Francis of
Assisi to tell about its triumphs and sweetness, and there is
never an *Ego* in the story, except when it deals with struggle
or defeat.

Lancicius, the Polish ascetical writer, and himself a man of no
little holiness, was one of those who attended Robert's weekly
exhortations at this time, and testified in the following enthusiastic
fashion:

I always used to come away from them as inflamed and on
fire with the love of virtue and the horror of all imperfection,
as if I had been through a furnace. These exhortations marked
for me the beginning of a new and far more fervent life than
I had led in the noviceship. Indeed it was a common saying then
that Father Bellarmine had converted me, and the saying was

quite true, because, after the grace of God, his exhortations were the most powerful and efficacious influence which ever came into my spiritual life.

This same saintly witness gives us, in addition, an all-too-rare glimpse of him at his prayers: "I used to watch him while he said Mass, and I noticed his face became so scarlet with the ardour of his devotion that it seemed the blood must burst from his veins. He celebrated with as much fervour, reverence, care, and holy intentness of mind, as if he saw God our Lord standing there before him."

Nine of Father Robert's published exhortations are on the love of God, and from these we may quote a few typical passages to illustrate his quaintly metaphorical style:

Love is the king of all the passions, the first and strongest of them all. Why does a man yearn to possess any object? Because he loves it. Why does he fear and hate anything? Because it is the opposite of some other thing which he loves. Just as a petty prince can never conquer a powerful king, so can the other passions never prevail over love. If the king is to be overcome, it must be by another king greater than he, and if one love is to lower its flag, it will only be to another love more vehement. Ay, and the earthly love in man's heart is a very noble and spirited king, that will not be roughly entreated. Use force and threats, and he will cast them back with scorn; block up one road from his castle, and you will find him riding away by another. What remedy then have we against him? Only one, dear brothers, another love, the love eternal. The little loves of the flesh, of food and drink, and pleasant converse with one's fellows, became like a bitter cross to St Francis because his heart was filled with that love whose horizons are not closed by the Ganges or Caucasus. He used to say that he found it very difficult to attend even to his most ordinary bodily needs, for the more the love of God fills a man's heart, the less room is there in it for any natural desire. . . .

This love of charity is the living water of which our Lord spoke to the woman of Samaria, water which causes all green loveliness and flowers to spring up in the garden of a man's soul. You might plough and dig the desert sands for a thousand years and have never a blade of grass for your pains, but let the rain fall upon them, and immediately the waste places stir into life and clothe themselves with verdure. *Anima mea sicut terra sine aqua tibi*, said David. Without charity our souls remain always unproductive, for even though the habits of virtue may be in us, they are sterile and moribund. . . . Where, then, are we to find a little of this water? We need not wander over the world in search of it, dear brothers, because like the rain, it falls only from Heaven. *Pluviam voluntariam segregavit hereditati suae*. . . . It is a free rain that has no certain seasons of spring-time or autumnal bounty, for it is altogether in God's keeping, and comes only when he chooses to send it. What we must do then is to pray constantly for it with all our hearts. And supposing we find it difficult to pray because our souls are hard and dry and devotionless, then let us do as the parched earth does which yawns open, and so in a manner cries for the rain. A humble recognition of our need is often more eloquent to the ears of God than many prayers.

The brotherly love and forbearance, which is the other side of the love of God, was one of St Robert's favourite themes:

His tender mercies are over all his works, and we show ourselves to be his true sons, if we bear true love to others, especially to those who can make us no return. The kindness of St Francis went out to the poor beasts themselves but, as in the story of our Father Ignatius, it was sick men who experienced the full tenderness of his charity. In this the two men were very like one another. Both of them desired to see their sick quiet and patient, and bearing themselves as poor religious men ought. But meantime both took every conceivable precaution that the sufferers should lack nothing. St Francis was not ashamed to go out and beg meat and other things for the sick, and he used to procure little delicacies for them which he would never have accepted for himself. . . . Indeed he could not look upon anyone in affliction without his heart melting within him, nor could he bide a single minute before running to their assistance. That is the test of real charity, to love the poor, the wretched, and the loveless. It is easy enough to feel drawn to good, healthy people who have pleasant manners, but that is only natural love and not charity. A mother does not love her sick, deformed child because he is lovable, but because she is his mother, and we must pray the Holy Ghost to put into our hearts that selfless devotion which nature has put into hers. And now let us see how even in this life brotherly love will profit us. Peace and union are the most necessary of all things for men who live in common, and nothing serves so well to establish and maintain them as the forbearing charity whereby we put up with one another's defects. There is no one who has not his faults, and who is not in some way a burden to others, whether he be a superior or a subject, an old man or a young man, a scholar or a dunce. If I refuse to put up patiently with your faults, or you refuse to put up with mine, we become strangers to one another, and the results to community life are disastrous. When two pieces of wood are placed together in the shape of an inverted V, if each supports the other, both will stand, but if they do not, both fall to the ground. As this matter is one of such great consequence, try to look upon the defects of your companions as a kind of special medicine and cross prepared for you by God. There are many people who willingly practise penances which they have chosen for themselves, but who refuse to put up with their neighbours' faults, though that is the penance which God wants them to bear. . . . When our bodily health is in question, we are not such fools as to prefer our own medicine to the doctor's. Then again remember that you, too, have your defects, which others mercifully overlook, so it is only fair that you should repay them with an equal tolerance.

On December 18, 1592, St Robert was installed as rector of the Roman College. It was the custom in those days for a rector on assuming office to make known in a public exhortation the policy which he intended to pursue. Bellarmine chose for his text Ecclesiasticus xxxii. 1-5: "Have they made thee ruler [*rectorem*]? Be not lifted up. Be among them as one of them. Have care of them . . . and hinder not music." His commentary amounted to this, that he would try as well as ever he could to act the part of a good *maestro di cappella* who makes little fuss in his conducting, and directs the singers with a scarcely perceptible movement of his baton. "To this end," wrote his sober biographer Giacomo

EX

Fuligatti, who knew him personally, "that perfect harmony might be assured, he begged them all, not only to help him with their prayers, but to tell him plainly if they saw any fault in his conducting, for the common good was his one and only aim. It is impossible to describe the earnestness with which he made this request." No one, it seems, took the rector at his word, so again and again he begged the favour anew. Anyone might come to his room, he said, at whatever hour of the day or night they liked best, or if they did not care to make known their complaint or suggestion by word of mouth, they could write it out and then "push the piece of paper under his door". And they could be quite certain that he would not fail to make its contents the subject of his deepest consideration in the sight of God.

He began the work of reformation with himself. In his room there was a rather fine desk of chestnut wood, and above his prieu-dieu there hung an oil painting of some sacred subject. The desk he sent to the sacristy to hold the altar-linen, and the picture to the corridors. In the process of his beatification, one witness, at a loss for words in which to describe his practice of his first vow, fell back on the delightful privileges of the Italian language, and said that he had always lived *poverissimamente* in religion. Another word much used to express the substance of his life was *hilarità*—he was gay. Those who came to his room were invariably received with smiling courtesy, the rector himself drawing out a chair for them and making them feel at home at once. He did not believe much in ceremony. Sometimes he used to stay away from the public recreations, but this was to give each member of his large community of 220 men a better chance of being able to see him in private should they so desire. There was another reason, too, which caused him to sacrifice the pleasure which he always found in the companionship of his brother Jesuits. His commentary on the text of Ecclesiasticus in his inaugural exhortation was not entirely metaphorical, for, as one who knew him well records, he loved music—*delectabatur musica* —and believed greatly in it as a potent defence against those noonday devils of boredom and irritation from which the best-ordered recreations are not immune. His voice was not very good, but he played the violin, lute, and other instruments with much skill, and was also something of a composer. During those hours stolen from recreation he used to copy out and arrange great numbers of motets for the fathers and brothers to sing together afterwards in the joy of their hearts. It was probably at this time that the Roman College acquired possession of a book published in Venice in 1581, entitled *Madrigals and Neapolitan songs for six voices, composed by Giovanni di Macque.* Just the thing for us, thought the rector, as he hummed the pleasant little melodies, but when he studied the words he thought differently, for they were all about love, and the moonlight, and a certain signorina's blue eyes and golden hair. The signorina plainly had to go, so Robert, remembering, perhaps, the device of Pope Sixtus when correcting his Vulgate, decided to cover up all the references to her with little slips of paper bearing words more suitable for Jesuits to sing. There were a hundred and five pieces to be done, but a large number did not require any changing to "make them talk like Christians". Thus it was sometimes enough to write "*te*" with a capital T, or "*Dio*" instead of "*mio*", and the love-song became straightway a hymn. In the Roman process of 1712, twenty-one specimens of the original and revised versions are printed side by side, from which we may here quote a few lines:

CANTIONES PROPHANAE	CANTIONES SACRAE
Dico spesso al mio Core	*Dico spesso al cor mio*
Solo fuggendo può vincere Amore	*Solo volando puoi trovar Iddio*
Et chi non sà fuggire	*E chi non sà volare*
Resti sicuro di sua man perire	*Resti sicuro di no lo trovare*
La Salamandra se nel foco dura	*La Salamandra se nel foco dura*
Miracolo non è che'l fà Natura	*Miracolo non è che il fa Natura*
Ma che voi nel mio Core	*Ma che Voi gran Signore*
Ch'è tutto fiamme, e foco	*Che sete fiamma, e foco*
Essendo ghiaccio ritroviate loco	*In Cor di ghiaccio ritroviate loco*
Questo si ch'è miracolo d'Amore.	*Questo sì, ch'è miracolo d'Amore.*[1]

[1] I often tell my heart that love can only be conquered by running away from it, and he who has not the wit to

I often tell my heart that God can only be found by those who fly in search of him, and a man who will not

The new rector shared all the common duties of the house with the rest, and insisted on having his turn in the scullery and in sweeping the galleries. During the hot holiday months of September and October he used to send once or twice a week for a few of the hard-worked lay brothers, and give them money for a three-day outing in the country. While they were away he himself took over as much of their work as he possibly could and in this way contrived to give every member of his community a holiday before the summer was over. One day he went out to Frascati himself to see how everybody was getting on and as he trudged back weary and dusty to Rome to his college suddenly remembered that it was his turn to help the cook. He hurried then and went straight into the kitchen on his arrival. Robert's love for his neighbour was strong as well as tender and never took the easy course of letting faults go unchecked. He hated giving admonitions but when he considered it necessary to pull anybody up nothing on earth could stop him. Yet even in this his gentleness found scope and Fuligatti attested that the reproof was invariably given "with much sweetness and compassion". According to the same writer, when, in his public exhortations, he had to call attention to faults against discipline in the house, the tears used to come into his eyes, "and they, rather than the hard words, were his arguments in favour of reform". He would never order a penance before having thoroughly sifted the question and, when anybody lodged an accusation, the other party was always given the fullest opportunity to defend himself. Robert was the most frank and candid of souls, and he did all in his power to make it easy for his subjects to be candid with him. There was nothing he hated more than diplomatic speeches or underhand dealing or, in fact, 'blarney' of any description. He liked a man to say out straight what he had in his mind, and his own habit of doing this

---

run away will surely perish at its hands. . . . If the Salamander lives in the fire it is not a miracle of nature, but that icy you should find a place in my flaming heart, that indeed is a miracle, a miracle of love.

fly may rest assured that he will never find him. . . . If the Salamander lives in the fire it is not a miracle of nature, but that thou, great God, who art all a consuming flame, shouldst take up thy abode in my icy heart, this indeed is a miracle, a miracle of love.

was destined to get him into a good deal of trouble. He had a horror, too, of anything which could breed dissension or party spirit. The Roman College must have been very much exposed to such evils, as nearly every nation under heaven was represented in it, and the rector was correspondingly careful to avoid the smallest show of favouritism, or the least word that could be interpreted as a preference for any particular flag. His only favourites were the sick. For them nothing was too good, and he was quite shameless in the way he mothered them.

Among other of his activities for the promotion of studies, Robert Bellarmine built a new library, and issued an ordinance in 1593, "For the conservation and advancement of mathematical studies in the Society for the greater glory of God our Lord". If he had little ability or liking for mathematics himself, he would encourage those who had. How busy he was during his period as rector is indicated in a brief letter to a correspondent in Louvain:

I will make known your wishes to Father Baronius[1] as soon as I get an opportunity. At present I have scarcely time to breathe—*vix spatium respirandi habeo*—as I have to sit for several hours each day in our general congregation, and when I go home to our college I am overwhelmed with domestic business. In this College there are more than twenty professors, and about two thousand students, of which number two hundred are Jesuits.

The general congregation dealt very largely with a new plan of studies, or *Ratio Studiorum*, for the seminaries and colleges of the Society of Jesus then multiplying at a rapid pace. Bellarmine was intimately associated with this work of capital importance and left his mark on the final text of the *Ratio*, promulgated in 1598, which remained for three centuries the Jesuit code of education for both lower and higher studies.

Owing to his rare friendliness, Robert received visits from cardinals and others almost daily, some of whom invited themselves to dinner at his table. But the person who left the most

[1] The future Oratorian cardinal who become one of St Robert's closest friends.

valuable record of his visit was a rabid English Protestant. In 1617
a huge, posthumous volume of travels appeared in London with
the title: *An Itinerary written by Fynes Moryson, Gent.: containing
his ten yeeres Travell through Germany, Denmarke, Poland, Italy,
etc.* Fynes Moryson was a student of Peter House, Cambridge,
and in 1589, at the age of twenty-three, was appointed one of the
travelling fellows. He then devoted two years to such studies as
would qualify him the better for his tour, and left England in
May, 1591, having first deposited some hundreds of pounds with
an insurance company. The terms which these companies offered
afford telling evidence of the perils of travel in the sixteenth
century, for *if* you came back alive, they were willing to give you
an interest of 300 per cent., on condition that they kept the entire
deposit if you did not. In 1594 the young and very stout-hearted
Englishman reached Rome, giving himself out for a Catholic.
There was no need for him to do that, as Rome did not object to
the presence of Protestants provided they behaved themselves.[1]
Before adopting the disguise he should have asked himself whether
he would be able to live up to it, and then he would not have had
to complain against the authorities for taking him for what he
professed to be. The following is his amusing account of his
adventures:

> I had purposed to see the famous Garden of the Cardinall of
> Ferraria at Tivoli . . . but Easter was now at hand and the
> Priests came to take our names in our lodging and when we
> demanded the cause they told us that it was to no other end but

[1] At a later period, Bishop Gilbert Burnet, chaplain to King William of
Orange, wrote of his Roman experiences in the following strain: "I confess
the Minerva which is the Dominicans where the Inquisition sitteth is that which
maketh the most sensible impression upon one that passeth at Rome for an
Heretick; though except one commit grave follies he is in no danger there. . . .
And I have more than ordinary reason to acknowledge this who have ventured
to go thither after all the liberty I had taken in writing my thoughts freely both
of the Church and See of Rome and was known by all with whom I conversed
there; yet met with the highest civilities possible among all sorts of people and
in particular both among the English and Scottish Jesuits, though they knew
well enough that I was no friend of their Order" (*Travels through France*, etc.
236-237).

to know if any received not the Communion at that holy time, which when we heard, wee needed no spurres to make haste from Rome into the State of Florence. Onely I had an obstinate purpose to see Bellarmine. To which end, having first hired a horse and provided all things necessary for my journey to Sienna, and having sent away my consorts to stay for me with my horse and boots at an Inn in the Suburbs that I might more speedily escape if my purpose succeeded not: I boldly went to the Jesuites Colledge and Bellarmine [*sic*] then walking in the fields I expected his returne at the gate, the students telling me that he would presently come backe; which falling out as they said; I followed him into the Colledge (being attired like an Italian and carefull not to use any strange gestures; yea, forbearing to view the Colledge or to looke upon any man fully lest I should draw his eyes upon me). Thus I came into Bellermine's chambre, that I might see this man so famous for his learning and so great a champion of the Popes: who seemed to me not above forty yeers old[1] being leane of body and something lowe of stature with a long visage, and a little sharpe bearde upon the chin of a browne colour, and a countenance not very grave and for his middle age wanting the authority of grey haires. Being come into his chamber and having made profession of my great respect to him, I told him that I was a Frenchman and came to Rome for performance of some religious vowes, and to see the monuments, especially those which were living and among them himselfe most especially, earnestly entreating to the end I might from his side returne better instructed into my country, that he would admit me at vacant houres to enjoy his grave conversation. He gently answering, and with gravity not so much swallowing the praises I gave him, as showing that my company should be most pleasing to him, commanded his Novice, that he should presently bring me in, when I should come to visit him, and so after some speeches of curtesie, he dismissed me who meant nothing lesse then to come againe to him.[2]

That then was the way in which Father Robert, of the "not very grave" countenance, used to treat his casual visitors. Another

[1] Father Robert was fifty-two at the time.
[2] *Itinerary*, Part I, Book II, pp. 141-142.

Englishman testified on oath, in the process of beatification, that when his countrymen returned home after a visit to the Eternal City, the first inquiry their Protestant friends regularly made was: "Did you see Bellarmine and what is he like in appearance?"

After his hasty departure from Rome in 1594, Fynes Moryson took the road to Naples, and swore heartily all the way along it. It was a terrible road, he says, infested with desperadoes, "vulgarly called banditti", and the only safe and permitted mode of travelling was in company with the postman who had a guard of papal musketeers. The postmen employed mules to carry the mail, and the mules, being mules, did all that in them lay to make everybody thoroughly exasperated and miserable. The travellers, continues Moryson, were obliged "to rise before day and take horse, and so sitting all the day, yet not ride above twenty miles for the slow pace of the mules, and at noon they have no rest, only when they have the inn in sight, they are permitted to gallop before to eat a morsel or rather devour it, for as soon as the mules are past, they must to horse again every man, not only making haste for his own safety, but the soldiers forcing them to be gone, who are more slow than the rest". Towards the close of the same year, 1594, Father Bellarmine, too, found himself unexpectedly in the Rome-to-Naples mule-express, as he had been appointed provincial superior of all Jesuits in the Kingdom of Naples, which stretched from the Papal States to the heel and toe of Italy. That he was missed in Rome is evident from a letter addressed to him shortly after his departure by the Venetian cardinal, Agostino Valiero, an intimate of Philip Neri: "I can never be happy in Rome without your Reverence whom I love so dearly and from whose conversation my old age has learned so much". Father Robert's rule as provincial was so gentle as scarcely to be felt, and we are told that all his orders ran in the subjunctive mood; "Would you please do this for me?" or "Would it be convenient for you to do that?" As of old, he was very much given to asking advice, for he had the meanest opinion of his own judgment. Aquaviva had even to admonish him for his excessive self-depreciation. "I am informed," he wrote, "that your Reverence's great modesty makes you depend too much on your consultors.

This is very well up to a point, but you must keep your liberty of deciding, and show that you, and you alone, are the ruler."

In July, 1596, the General had, for special reasons, transacted some business in connection with the Neapolitan Province without consulting the Provincial. Fearful lest Father Robert might think he had done so from lack of confidence in his discretion, he wrote a most affectionate letter explaining the situation. "If I had been provincial myself," he said, "I would have begun to suspect a general who acted so, but in truth I was driven to it entirely against my will". Bellarmine answered as follows:

Dear Father, I am more sorry than I can say that you should have been worried with a rumour to the effect that I had begun to doubt your trust in me. I feel quite ashamed of myself that in the midst of such important business, and so many anxieties, you should have troubled to write a long letter in your own hand, solely to ease my mind. I will tell you honestly that before I became rector of the Roman College, I did have doubts about your trust in me because of some complaints made to you by one who did not wish me well. All the same, I did not believe that you considered me too far gone in villainy, for you never showed me anything but kindness. Further, I may tell you that I was secretly delighted at the time, thinking that your want of confidence would relieve me for ever from the troubles of government, a position for which I have always thought myself singularly ill-fitted. But when you afterwards gave me care of the Roman College, and I considered what a great treasure you were thus confiding to me, to wit, the souls of so many of your sons, it became as clear as daylight that your distrust of me was entirely gone. Since then I have never doubted again, and with this confidence to support me, I have tried and will always try to serve you faithfully and zealously. . .

At Naples Robert continued his musical experiments and the sick were again the chief objects of his solicitude. One invalid wrote: "Where another provincial would have been content with kind words and exhortations to patience, this one took time and trouble to find out the only remedy which could make me well".

St Robert was ill himself a good deal of the time partly owing to
his rigorous fasting which he tried rather ineffectively to conceal.
"I hear from various sources," wrote Aquaviva in August, 1595,
"that your Reverence's head and general health are suffering
from your heavy work and your fasting. Do try to be more
moderate in both the one and the other." A year later the General
was obliged to return to the charge, and counsel the back-sliding
Provincial to let himself be ruled by the doctors and not write
so many letters with his own hand. This shows us Robert in
trouble for being too hard on himself, but he was also reprimanded
for treating others too lavishly. On September 2, 1595, the
General addressed to him the following admonition:

I have heard something which has astonished me greatly,
knowing well as I do your Reverence's strict spirit of observance. This is that a big feast was held at the house of the
professed on the day of vows, a feast provided by a benefactor
who spent a hundred ducats on it. Now that was far too much,
and on other occasions I have forbidden the acceptance of
delicacies and valuables from outside friends, as such things are
not according to the spirit of religious poverty and frugality.
I would like to hear something more from your Reverence
about this matter, and I hope you will not let it happen again.

But it is important not to overemphasize the Saint's gentleness.
It was while he was superior of the Neapolitan Jesuits that he
wrote one of his most stinging replies to an attack on the Holy
See in the person of Pope Sixtus V, who had purposed to put his
Controversies on the Index. The book that roused his wrath
appeared in Italian and professed to be by a young French nobleman anxious to bring home to Italians that the three proudest
names in their literary history, Dante, Boccaccio and Petrarch,
were all foes of the loathly Antichrist who lifted up his horns in
Rome, and prophets of his imminent destruction. Robert's
answer is lengthy and shows an intimate acquaintance with all
three writers. He had loved and studied Dante from his youth,
and knew enough medieval history to pulverize the "young
nobleman's" contentions. The point of his answer now, however,

is not its Dantean scholarship, but the revelation of its habitually gentle author in a real rage. "Whether the author be a Frenchman or not, is of no consequence," he wrote in his preface. "But he need not have told us that he was young, for the arrogance, pertness, flippancy, and ignorance of his every page are sufficient proof of the fact. As to his being noble, I must say I find it difficult to believe, unless, indeed, the title indicates not a nobleman, but some nobleman's clown. Certainly the foul language and scurrilous abuse with which his book reeks are more suited to the mouth of a stable-boy or tough old salt than to lips with gentle blood in them." The "young nobleman", known to have been a Calvinist named Perrot, had decorated his three morning stars of the Reformation with haloes, which brought from our Robert the following explosion:

> As for the sanctity of Petrarch and Boccaccio, I could scarcely restrain my laughter, when I saw it alleged. Why, their Italian writings, for which this youth has such enthusiastic praise, are almost all on the one theme of lust, so that Petrarch himself grew to be thoroughly ashamed of them. These, save the mark, are the prophets of Luther's and Calvin's new dispensation. I think, Sir, you must have learned this gospel from your bishop, Beza, to whom we are indebted for so many love-songs, some of them to Candida and the boy Audebert being vile enough in all conscience.

So they were, but they belonged to Beza's dissipated youth, and might have been charitably overlooked by Robert, as Beza was at the time an old man and highly respectable. Robert's friend, St Francis de Sales, even cherished hopes of winning him back to the Church which, however, were not realized. To say that butter would not melt in Bellarmine's mouth is plainly an inadequate way of describing him. He was as a rule the most gentle and courteous of men. The people of Naples where he wrote this scathing answer say of the quiescent Vesuvius, "Uncle is smoking his pipe", but "Uncle" has also occasionally blown his top. It was the same way with St Robert, and perhaps we like him the better for it.

During the two years of his provincialate St Robert visited all the widely separated Jesuit houses in the Kingdom of Naples twice over. Among the many places to which he jogged on his horse over very bad roads was the ancient and very attractive city of Lecce in the heel of Italy's boot, two hundred and seven miles from Naples. There he had the intense joy of meeting St Bernardino Realini who, after ten years work among the desperately poor of Naples, had been sent as rector to the Jesuit college in Lecce and remained for the rest of his eighty-six years, the most benign and benevolent counsellor the city ever possessed. Robert fell on his knees before Bernardino, and, when a few days later he mounted his horse to depart, Bernardino exclaimed: "There goes a great saint".

Before the end of the year 1596 Bellarmine had been summoned back to Rome by Aquaviva, at the command of Pope Clement VIII. Clement's principal theological adviser, the Jesuit Francisco Toledo, whom he had raised to the purple, died that year and St Robert was intended to replace him, though he did not win the extraordinary confidence which the Pope had placed in the other man. The Holy Father wished him to live at the Vatican but he never felt at his ease outside a Jesuit house and pleaded with the all-powerful papal nephew, Cardinal Aldobrandini, to be allowed to reside with his brethren who had charge of the polyglot confessionals of St Peter's and had a house called the Penitenzieria quite close to the basilica. For four years, rumours, of which he was well aware, had been circulating that he would soon be made a cardinal. His modern Catholic critics, nearly all pupils of the great Munich scholar, Ignaz von Döllinger, who seceded from the Church on the issue of papal infallibility, endeavoured to establish, on the basis of his correspondence with his elder brother Tommáso, that he felt a grievance at being so long overlooked in promotions of cardinals and, for all his humble demeanour, was a deeply ambitious man. Thomas was certainly ambitious for Robert's promotion and plied him incessantly with questions as to the chances. Robert loved this "Molto illustre Signor Fratello" dearly and dealt very gently with his high hopes. He knew that some of his friends, especially Cardinal Valiero, Bishop of Verona, and Baronius, the right-hand man of St Philip Neri, himself promoted cardinal in 1596, were actively working to have him in the sacred college, and cheered his easily desponding brother with news of their efforts. But he never expressed any approval, and gave Thomas many plain hints that he had no mind whatever for ecclesiastical dignities, which were incompatible with his vows as a Jesuit. Besides, at fifty he conceived himself to be already old. "Behold the pair of us now, both old men", he wrote to Thomas in 1592. "We cannot have much of this temporal life left to us, so it would be a good thing if we both began to think seriously of the life which never ends. If you have made up your mind to take a wife, I have no objection, especially if you can find some widow of reasonable age from whom you might hope to have a son or two." Thomas, who was fifty-two, did not favour the idea of a widow and married a maiden who gave him, not a son or two, but nine of them, as well as five daughters.

Every new child born to Thomas Bellarmine was a fresh inducement to hope that his brother might become a prince of the Church, and—why not?—even Pope, like his uncle Marcellus. In April, 1597, Robert gave questioning, dreaming, doubting Thomas six good reasons why, except under papal compulsion, he would not accept a cardinal's hat:

1°, it would not be good for my soul, which to me is perfectly evident; 2°, it would not be good for my bodily health because, at my age and after so many years of religious life, I have lost zest for temporal business and take pleasure only in study and quietude; 3°, it is not necessary in the family interests because, even though you should have more children, I shall be dead before they reach an age when I could be of any advantage to them; 4°, the change would cause distress to my order in every part of the world, whereas if I escape promotion the relief will be equally widespread; 5°, I could not do the Church any greater service in another state than I can render in my present one; 6°, the change would give those hostile to the Church occasion to blaspheme worse than ever, for they would say that I had written my books solely with a view to ecclesiastical preferment.

In spite of those good reasons against it, Tommáso continued to
nurse his tired hope and make inquiries. A few weeks later Robert
replied: "Ask Mgr Danesi, for he knows more of what is going on
than I do. The cardinals, especially my most intimate friend
among them, Baronius, never broach the question because they
know very well what I think about it." In June of the same year,
he gave Thomas an account of his physical handicaps as a deter-
rence:

> I have had to wear spectacles for the past two years, and the
> hearing of my left ear is almost completely gone. With the right
> one I can hear well enough if people speak up. Cardinal
> Madruzzo [of the Congregation of the Holy Office] always
> speaks in a low voice and this makes it difficult for me to carry
> on business with him. The Pope himself has often to repeat
> what he has said to me, noticing that I have not understood him.
> There was a time when a round of the Seven Churches cost me
> little in fatigue, but now I can scarcely trust myself to do half as
> much. Unlike my old self, I eat very little because of my
> enfeebled stomach. All this seems to me to spell old age.
> Moreover, my hair has turned completely white. If [our
> cousin] Mario had been through what I have been through, and
> if he had to deliver a Latin address every Thursday before the
> Pope, on some thorny problem, perhaps he would not be able
> to boast of so few grey hairs. It seems to me that my deafness is
> a sign that I take after our mother's side of the family, and you
> know how short were the lives of our mother and her brothers
> and sisters. I say this not from any wish for length of days
> because, in truth, I would much prefer to escape as soon as
> possible from the perils which endanger the salvation of my
> soul, but rather that you may consider how little store we
> ought to set by titles and dignities, even should we chance to
> obtain them.

Pope Clement VIII did not have much use for cardinals; he
thought there were too many of them, rarely considered them,
except Toledo the Jesuit, and, as often as not, ignored their advice.
He sought without avail to get St Philip Neri to accept the red hat
but, though he loved and revered Philip, he refused any counsel
from him except such as was strictly spiritual. Philip and his

disciples tried very hard to prevail on the self-willed Pontiff to lift the excommunication launched by Sixtus V against Henry of Navarre, whom they had every reason to believe would become a genuine Catholic. His Calvinism had never been much more than a battle-cry and he had easily shed it once before. On July 25, 1593, he shed it for good and was absolved by the Catholic bishops who supported his claims to the throne of France. But Clement VIII remained adamant. He told the Duke of Nevers who had come to Rome on Henry's behalf that he would not believe in his master's sincerity "unless an angel from heaven came to vouch for him". He was, in fact, terrified of the influence of Spain, then all-powerful in Rome. But the stars in their courses were fighting for Henry, and eventually, in 1595, the Pope summoned up enough resolution to absolve him and recognize his right as King of France, thus ending the religious wars and even allowing, however reluctantly, for the toleration of minority religious opinion in a Catholic country.

Bellarmine, away in Naples, had nothing to do with the negotiations and was not asked for his opinion, but the story shows what he might expect when chosen as theological adviser of the holy, headstrong Pope, said to have had the "gift of tears", whom even St Philip Neri and Clement's confessor, Cardinal Baronius, could not budge, once he had taken up a stand. He did, however, defer to his new theologian in one matter of no special consequence. He had a great liking for Plato and confided to Philip Neri and his disciples that he was thinking of establishing a chair of Platonic philosophy at Rome's university, the Sapienza. The "Filippini' were enthusiastic for the plan, but Bellarmine, when consulted, drowned it in cold water. He had Aristotle in his blood (too much of him by far in the astronomical line), and promptly instanced Origen as an example of what might be expected from involvement with Plato, the enchanter of the *Dialogues* with their subtle mixture of beauty, truth, and gravest error. The Pope was impressed by the onslaught, and Robert came away from the interview with Plato's head on a dish. This did not in the least diminish the love and reverence which old Cardinal Valiero bore him, though he was a passionate Platonist and even wrote a Socratic *Dialogue on Christian Joy*, inspired by his relations with St Philip Neri at the Vallicella. The following year, 1598, Bellarmine, Valiero and Valiero's nephew Peter were in attendance on the Pope at Ferrara. "One day," Peter recorded, "my uncle said that he wanted me to make the acquaintance of the greatest little man in the world—*del maggior piccolò che sia al mondo*. It was Bellarmine he meant, and he continued that if I got nothing else out of my visit to Ferrara, the friendship of such a man would render me estimable in all circles and capable of rising to the loftiest of heights. That was exactly what happened, for I owe all my success in life to the unfailing kindness of God's great servant, Robert Bellarmine".

Meanwhile, in Rome, Bellarmine kept in close touch with his worrying brother Tommáso, who attributed to the malign arts of local witches and wizards the death of his eldest child at the age of five. The abstract possibility of a pact with the devil, on which the whole theory of witchcraft depended, was borne out by the Scriptures and the commentaries of the early Fathers. With this clue for a start, the imagination of pre-scientific Europe, Catholic and Protestant alike, ran riot, with terrible consequences for eccentric old women living alone, and old men addicted to peculiar hobbies as an antidote to their boredom. The book that probably did most harm was published at Cologne in 1487 by two Catholic priests, with the title *Malleus Maleficarum*, or "Hammer of Witches". The authors considered themselves such experts in the field that they were able to warn Europe of the times and seasons when danger from witches and wizards would be imminent, for women the hour of parturition. Few, indeed, were those prepared to withstand the general mania and Robert Bellarmine cannot be numbered of their gallant company. He believed that he had himself in boyhood at Montepulciano witnessed an exhibition of wizardry, which caused a Dominican preacher to be struck dumb in the pulpit until he had made a vow to the local St Agnes. He had his credulous strain, St Robert, but was no worse than the vast majority of his contemporaries. Indeed, his letter to Tommáso on the subject displays a certain amount of charitable caution:

When you have discovered the identity of the wizards and are able to prove that they are such, you will render God a service by denouncing them to the Holy Office, which will not fail to do its duty. However, you must take great care lest your sorrow [for the death of your child] should lead you to make unfounded accusations. I do not know what else I can say to you about the matter. I have not spoken to Father Clavius as he left Germany when quite young and knows nothing about charms and spells. I myself have studied the *Malleus Maleficarum* and the book of Sylvester Mazolino, *De Strigibus*, and I lectured on these questions when I was a professor of theology. The remedies both preventive and restorative are briefly, first and foremost, firm faith in God and the most holy sign of the cross. Many examples might be given in proof of the efficacy of these remedies. 2°, Confession and Communion on the part of the father and mother. 3°, Objects blessed by the Church such as Agnus Dei, holy water, palms, etc. I once possessed a little piece of the wood of the true Cross and several other fine relics, but I gave them all to one of our fathers who was going to the Indies. I will see whether I can find something for you and send it on, but I would like very much to know when the baby is expected so that the relic may arrive in time.

While the wizards were troubling Thomas Bellarmine, another of Robert's relatives, Mgr Herennius Cervini, had brought himself into difficulties of a different kind and also appealed to the family counsellor to help. Mgr Cervini was a distinguished ecclesiastic who, in addition to holding the benefice of an abbey near Sassoferrato, was overlord of the estate of Vivo. In this territory there prowled a brigand named Matthei. Herennius, without any thought of consequences, had the man arrested and handed over to the secular arm, which promptly condemned him to death. Then complications began, for to be the cause of anybody's death is to incur irregularity in canon law, and irregularity may mean the loss of benefices. A scruple arose in Cervini's mind on the point, and to lay it, he had recourse to the wisdom of his always obliging cousin. Father Robert sided with the scruple. Nothing could be done, he said, except to obtain absolution and dispensation from the Holy See, a matter which looks quite simple, but which really requires all manner of tiresome formalities. He undertook the whole process himself, though he was very busy with other work, and only asked Herennius to send him the name of the malefactor, as that had to be entered in the documents. Owing to miscarriage of letters it did not reach him for more than three weeks. As he had filed his petition immediately, the Roman lawyers began to demand what he was about. Did he want the dispensation or did he not? "If this is Monsignor's way of doing business," he told his brother Thomas at the end of March, 1597, "I do not think I shall be in such a hurry over his affairs in future." Not till December of the same year were the troublesome negotiations over. On the fifth of the month he wrote to Herennius: "Your petition has been signed by the Pope, and at the moment a brief is being made out which I shall forward to you next week, if the Holy Father's indisposition does not render it impossible for him to put his signature to the document." On receipt of this letter Cervini wrote back telling of a wonderful cure for the gout which he had discovered and which might benefit the Pope. Robert answered at once:

I went to His Holiness myself and read him the relevant portion of your letter, adding that you were highly qualified in such matters, that your prescription was worthy of all confidence, and that you had no other desire but that his Holiness should enjoy health unto a ripe old age. He heard me very willingly and asked me if I would mind him mentioning the question to his doctor Provenzano, who is a particular friend of my own. I replied that he might certainly do so, but that I did not want your name made known to anybody except himself, in case the doctor might disapprove of the remedy. This official was then summoned, and once again I read over parts of your letter in his presence. He said that it was a good remedy for the gout, but that the use of it was dangerous because in curing the gout it might cause a flux of humours to the vital parts and so occasion death. I replied that according to your Lordship's letter this medicine not only cured the gout, but strengthened the stomach and the head, and arrested the fluxes which are as it were the source of the disease. At length all agreed that the remedy should first be tried on some person here in Rome and, if it succeeded, that the Holy Father might have a dose, should he feel so inclined. In conclusion, his Holiness bade me write to you in his name that you should come to Rome as soon as possible, if you can do so without inconvenience. Otherwise, would you please send on some of those pills with brief directions how they ought to be taken. I told him that your Lordship would willingly suffer any inconvenience in order to be of service to him, but he insisted that I must put the disjunctive in my letter, and leave it to you to decide whether to come yourself or to send the pills. This is the state of affairs. It remains for you now to turn it to good account, and the sooner the better.

The eager way in which Robert seized on the pills as a chance to bring his 'irregular' cousin back into papal favour is typical of him, as is the next letter of March 28, 1597, to a Jesuit who had asked him, the busiest man in Rome, to hunt up some old manuscripts in the Vatican Library:

Dear Father in Christ: My delay in answering you was due to the fact that I could not find anyone to enlighten me on the matter of your request. Cardinal Colonna, senior, the Librarian, is constantly unwell and knows nothing about the Library. That was my chief difficulty, so at last I began investigations on my own account, and by means of the catalogues discovered twelve sermons of St Gregory of Nyssa, partly included in others of his works, and partly in the works of St Basil. In case you might wish to have them examined, the references are numbers 291 and 304 in the Greek section. As for the Breviary Lessons of St Romuald, it is not generally considered that they are so faulty as to need correction, especially since they have been already revised by Father Benico of happy memory, whose linguistic ability was not unknown to your Reverence. Nevertheless, as the Holy Father has given Cardinal Baronius and myself reason to hope that he will go on with the work of correcting the Breviary, if your Reverence has any particular criticism or objection to urge about those lessons of St Romuald you might let me know and it will receive mature consideration. I am here to be of service to your Reverence, and other friends, in whatever way you may wish to use me. I have to confine

myself to my own department, of course, and this is not so
extensive as was Cardinal Toledo's, though people say that I
am his successor. Please give my affectionate good wishes to
Father Superior and all the community. . . . As for news, some
people say that five or six red hats are certain to be disposed of
at Pentecost, but I am of Aristotle's opinion that *de futuris
contingentibus non est determinata veritas*. Pray for me, Father.

People may differ as to what constitutes heroic charity in a
man, but a good case could surely be made out for the dedicated
writer and scholar who never hesitates to drop his pen and forget
his books when his neighbour, often an inconsiderate and tiresome
neighbour, makes a call on his services. At the very time when St
Robert was busily engaged with obstructive curial officials on
behalf of Herennius Cervini and spending hours in the Vatican
Library to satisfy that Jesuit suppliant, he was trying to get
written, by express orders of Clement VIII, a treatise on Indulgences, which, as he explained in his preface, had to be omitted
from its rightful place in the second volume of the *Controversies*:

That which was the first of all the controversies of our age
has had to be dealt with last of all in our pages, not by choice
but by chance. I had originally marked out a place for this
controversy after the books on penance. Those books happened
to be ready for the press about the time of the autumn recess,
and as the printer was in a hurry to get the second volume off
his hands, I had no opportunity of finishing the treatise, though
I was most anxious to have it included. Afterwards I was overwhelmed with business of all kinds, both public and private,
and could scarce steal a few months' leisure in which to bring
the third volume to an end. This present year, however, I found
myself unexpectedly with some free time at my disposal, and
the Holy Year of Jubilee and solemn indulgences being
imminent, I could no longer defer paying a debt which many
men justly demanded of me.

Although I have chiefly in view the exposition of the controversy on indulgences as it is carried on between Catholics
and heretics, still I shall not forget those points which, not being
of faith, are freely discussed among Catholics themselves, in
the search after truth. The following will be the order of the

whole disputation: I shall first say something about the names indulgence and jubilee, and at the same time give a list of those who have written in defence of indulgences or against them. The next step in the argument will be an inquiry whether indulgences exist, and here two matters have to be discussed, namely the spiritual treasury of the Church, and the power of distributing what is contained in that treasury. Thirdly, we shall investigate the precise nature of an indulgence, and here, also, two points have to be explored, to wit, whether an indulgence be simply the payment of a debt or rather a judicial absolution, and if so from what bond the release or acquittal is given. Fourthly, we shall treat of the many forms and varieties of indulgences, and fifthly, of their utility and fruit. In the sixth place, we shall inquire who can grant them, and for what reasons. Then, seventhly, we shall see by whom and under what conditions they may be gained, and finally, whether and how they can be applied for the benefit of the dead. That will end the first book. In the second, I shall expound, discuss, and refute the contrary arguments of Luther, Calvin, Heshusius, and Chemnitz, who are our chief opponents in this matter, and also lay bare their lies, frauds, and impostures.

The treatise runs in its entirety to about 55,000 words. In a confidential letter to his friend John Baptist Carminata, Provincial of the Neapolitan Jesuits, Robert afterwards gave some explanations which illustrate his own attitude and practice where indulgences were concerned. Father Carminata had begged him to obtain from the Pope an indulgence of a hundred years for a new chapel which he had built:

Before speaking to his Holiness I would like to know whether the indulgence you ask for is intended for the living or the dead. I ought to tell you that in spite of numerous requests for indulgences of as great or greater value, the Congregation does not grant such, and readily reduces them from a hundred years to a hundred days. This is because such indulgences are a novelty, and might even be considered as one of the abuses which the Council of Trent ordered to be reformed according to the ancient practice of the Church. It was the custom formerly to grant only very small indulgences. Pope Innocent

III said that the Holy See did not usually grant an indulgence of more than a year and forty days, and blamed the concession of great and disproportionate ones. St Peter Damian relates that, in his times [*c.* 1060], the Roman Church granted to pilgrims from beyond the seas who made a visit to the tomb of the Apostles an indulgence of three years, to pilgrims from beyond the Alps an indulgence of one year, and to pilgrims from Italy an indulgence of forty days.

One reason for conceding only indulgences of small value is that a serious motive is required for their concession at all. Otherwise the discipline of the Church would suffer. Indeed, the grant of a large indulgence for some insignificant act is probably invalid. Consider, I pray you, whether there be any proportion between these two things: attendance at a single Mass and deliverance from a hundred years of the most rigorous chastisement which the justice of God can inflict.

As to the privileged altar, I may tell you that the Pope commissioned two other cardinals and myself to examine the foundation on which the concession of such altars rests. Our answer was that there were no very solid grounds for the custom and that it was not known up to the time of Gregory XIII, who filled the world with these altars. Sixtus V had thought of suppressing them, but refrained for fear of scandalizing the faithful. Moved by such considerations, the present Pope decided to grant the privilege in future only under many restrictions and for a limited time, so that simple Catholics may not get the false notion into their heads that a Mass celebrated at a privileged altar infallibly delivers a soul from Purgatory.

Having explained myself quite frankly, I would ask you to let me know, once again, the precise form in which I should present your petition. Take my advice and be very moderate in your request. The smaller an indulgence is, the surer we are of obtaining its fruit. If the concession of indulgences rested with me, none would be granted except little ones, according to the practice of Pope Pius V.

His first biographer, who knew him personally, recorded that St Robert liked to gain his indulgences *con fatica*, because "it appeared to him that the conditions usually imposed were too easy. He used often to say that since indulgences cost our Lord his precious blood they ought only to be begged for with reluctance and in pressing need."

The rector of the Roman College when Bellarmine went there to write his treatise on Indulgences, was a very saintly man named Pietro Spinelli. It might have been expected that the visitor would receive a privileged welcome, for besides having been rector and provincial in his order, he was considered by everyone to be one of the most distinguished men of his age. It was the very opposite that happened, however, as his friend Eudaemon Joannes relates:

> He was given a tiny little room—*una cameretta molto piccola*— right in front of the house lavatories. These lavatories had afterwards to be abolished because the stink from them rendered the corridor practically uninhabitable. I visited him several times in his little room and never do I remember to have seen two or three books in it at once. He was writing then, if I am not mistaken, a treatise on indulgences by order of the Pope, and used to go to the library whenever he wanted to consult any particular volume. The library was such a very cold and comfortless place that hardly anyone put foot inside it during the winter, yet I remember seeing him come from it many a bitter night of that season. Nor am I aware that a word of complaint, either at the inconvenience of his room or the want of books, ever fell from his lips. He told me afterwards, laughing the while, that the Pope had asked him whether he was satisfied with the *apartments* assigned to him in the College, the idea of apartments in our houses amusing him very much.

Some member of the community went to protest to the rector against the treatment meted out to their eminent guest, supposing that it must have been due to the negligence of an intermediate official. "No," replied Spinelli, "I alone am responsible. Father Bellarmine is a very distinguished man and a saint, and I thought it would be good for the young men of this house to see how distinguished people who are saints behave under unpleasant circumstances."

In the course of the year 1597, Alfonso II, Duke of Ferrara, died childless, having bequeathed his dominions to his illegitimate cousin, Cesare d'Este, Duke of Modena. Ferrara had been for centuries a fief of the Holy See, and St Pius V had decreed some years earlier that if the Este family died out the Duchy should come under the direct jurisdiction of the popes. The pretender Cesare naturally enough refused to acquiesce, and prepared to claim his illegal inheritance by force of arms, with the support of Venice, Tuscany, and Spain. Pope Clement, nothing daunted, excommunicated Cesare, and collected a force of 25,000 men to give point to his bull. Those vigorous proceedings frightened off the claimant's allies, so at the beginning of 1598 he sent in his submission and evacuated Ferrara. The tyranny and grinding exactions of the House of Este had long since alienated the subjects of the Duchy, and the brilliance of the most refined and elegant Court in Europe helped very little to compensate the oppressed lower orders for their own undistinguished sufferings. To win their affections the Pope decided to make a personal tour of his new dominion. Clement had sixteen cardinals and a host of prelates and ambassadors in his retinue, prominent among them being Baronius. Father Bellarmine was there, too, as the Pope's special theologian but relished very little the pomp and pageantry associated with the Pope's triumphal progress, more suited to a pagan emperor than to a pastor of souls. At Ferrara Robert declined the Pope's kindly offer of a suite at the ducal palace, and begged instead to be allowed to stay with his Jesuit brethren at their college in the city. Clement generously paid the fathers whatever expenses they incurred for his keep.

The Jesuits in France had not been enthusiastic for the cause of Henry of Navarre, a fact which gave their opponents a handle when Henry came to the throne. He was not a vindictive monarch but he yielded to the persuasions of persons who desired to be rid of the Jesuits on other grounds. The General, Claudio Aquaviva, wrote in distress to Bellarmine at Ferrara on June 3, 1598:

> *Padre mio*, I would like you to repeat what I am going to say now to the Holy Father and to Cardinal Baronius. I hear from France that the King and his councillors are thinking of

expelling us from that country. Rumours against us are rife, and predictions of our speedy banishment are to be heard everywhere. Public opinion is thus being mischievously affected, and it is necessary that his Holiness should be made aware of the manoeuvres.

Robert sought several interviews with the Pope and persuaded him to write to his legate, the Cardinal of Florence, who wielded much influence with King Henry, on the fathers' behalf, and he sought also the help of the Archbishop of Rennes, later Cardinal d'Ossat, who had always been a stout supporter of the King. Their intercession came too late to prevent the expulsion of the Jesuits, but Henry did not forget and by special edict readmitted them five years later.

At the same time another curious affair was causing the General anxiety. A Spanish father named Pacheco had come to Ferrara with the bizarre notion of founding an order of discalced or barefooted Jesuits. Pacheco had done fine work among the Moors, and Pope Clement in recognition of it might have been ready to see something in his scheme for a reform of the Society of Jesus. Aquaviva was all the more worried because the good man made a great mystery of his negotiations with the Pope. Once again, then, he addressed himself to Father Robert, begging him to keep the conspirator under observation because, though "an honest soul he was simple and of a melancholy nature". The Pope fortunately put the business in the hands of Cardinal Baronius, which was almost equivalent to putting it in Bellarmine's hands, but Pacheco continued to be a nuisance for months until the Pope, tiring of the *episodio semicomico*, as an historian called it, deprived him of his degree of professed father and ordered him back to his Moors. Other discontented Jesuits also arrived in Ferrara, seeking redress from the Pope for imaginary grievances, and the Venetian fathers made a great song when Aquaviva appointed a Neapolitan as their provincial. They complained to the Pope against the indignity of having a subject of the King of Spain placed over them. Bellarmine had little difficulty in counteracting, with the help of Baronius, the manoeuvres of those petty

complainants, and received the following warm letter of thanks
from the General:

> I consider that it was the providence of God that sent you to
> Ferrara to act as our advocate with the charity you bear the
> Society and the holy zeal you have for the common good. . . .
> I thank you with all my heart for your past and present services,
> and I feel very sure that the Divine Majesty will not fail to
> reward your Reverence's love and fidelity to your order.

In August 1598 Robert informed his brother Thomas that
Baronius and he were taking a holiday together: "The Pope goes
to the Villa Bel Riguardo on Monday for ten or twelve days'
vacation, and Cardinal Baronius and myself are going to take a
walk to Venice during his absence, if we can get leave. I shall ask
for it for both of us on Thursday next." Baronius was of a
deeply serious cast of mind and is said to have maintained that
there is nothing more delightful than the thought of death. But
he relaxed in Bellarmine's company, and the story goes that the
pair were in such spirits at Padua that they disguised themselves
as best they could and called upon the most eminent literary man
then in the city, to see what sort of a reception they might obtain.
But Giovanni Vincenzo Pinelli was not deceived and, after some
good-humoured play-acting, cordially invited them to dinner.
"I think," wrote Robert afterwards, "that the thirteen days'
freedom from business and studies did us both a great deal of
good."

When they returned to Ferrara the city was excitedly awaiting
the advent of Princess Margaret of Austria, who was to be married
by proxy, before the Pope, to the new King of Spain, Philip III.
She arrived on November 13 and, among other celebrations in
honour of the wedding, there was a play on the subject of Judith
and Holofernes, acted by the boys of the Jesuit college. Bellarmine, to meet an emergency, wrote the prologue for this affair
in Latin iambics in a couple of hours, a feat of which he was
rather proud. It was at Ferrara that the Holy Father gave solemn
approval to St Robert's two manuals of Christian doctrine, one a
brief catechism for children and the other, also in catechetical

form, a larger handbook for teachers, both of which obtained as much celebrity as and far wider diffusion than his *Controversies*. They were translated into sixty-two different languages and dialects, and maintained their popularity right down to the time of the Vatican Council, at which Pope Pius IX proposed to have a new catechism composed for universal use "on the model of the *Dottrina Christiana breve*, drawn up at the order of this Holy See by the Venerable Cardinal Bellarmine". The Council came to an end before anything could be achieved, so the Church still awaits her universal catechism or manual of doctrine. An extract from St Robert's work for teachers, *An Explanation of Christian Doctrine in Dialogue Form*, which the prim and stupid Austrian Emperor, Joseph II, found such an obstacle to his anti-papal schemes in Lombardy, may give a hint of its power. Robert is dealing with the First Commandment:

Pupil: Would you explain to me how it is that the honour which we give to saints and their relics and images is not contrary to this Commandment, for we appear to adore them and pray to them as we do to God?

Teacher: Holy Church is the Bride of God and has the Spirit of God for her guide. Consequently, there is no danger of her being deceived or doing or permitting anything contrary to God's Commandments. To come to the point, we honour and invoke the saints because they are the friends of God, and can help us by their merits and prayers to him. But we do not account them gods, nor do our genuflexions signify any such thing. A genuflexion is not a mark of reverence peculiar to the service of God, for knees are bent also to persons of great dignity, such as the Pope and kings, and in many places religious men kneel before their superiors. It is not strange, then, that we should show such reverence to the saints reigning with Christ in heaven since we show it to mortal men like ourselves, here on earth.

Pupil: Yes, but tell me why do we genuflect and pray to the *relics* of the saints, which are lifeless things and not persons?

Teacher: The answer is that we do *not* pray to them, knowing very well that they cannot hear us. But we honour them because they were the instruments by means of which the saints did so many good works, and because they will one day be living and glorious bodies again. To us now, they are, as it were, precious tokens of the love which the saints bore and bear towards us. That is why we pour out our prayers to the saints before their relics, begging them, by these dear pledges which we hold, to remember to help us as we remember to do them honour.

Pupil: Is it possible to say the same about images?

Teacher: Yes, because images of our Lord, our Lady, and the saints are not regarded by us as gods, but as mere representations which recall to our minds thoughts of those they represent. Thus they serve people who cannot read in place of books, teaching them many mysteries of our holy faith. The honour which we pay to them is not given because they are figures of paper, or wood, or stone, or metal, or because they are beautifully coloured and moulded, but because they represent Christ, his Mother, or the saints. Knowing as we do that the images are dead, undiscerning things, made by the hands of men, we do not ask anything from them and pray before them only because they picture to our minds, our Lord, our Lady, and the saints, whom we are really addressing.

Pupil: When, then, we hear that someone gained a favour through the use of a relic or by praying before a statue, we are to understand that the prayer was really addressed to the saint whose relic or statue it was, and that God through the intercession of the saint and by means of the relic or statue granted the favour?

Teacher: Exactly; and I am delighted that you have understood so well what I have been trying to explain.

Pupil: One last question. I would like to know why God the Father is represented to us in pictures as an old man, the Holy Ghost as a dove, and the angels as youths with wings. God and the angels, we know, are spirits who have no bodies that can be painted as artists paint men.

Teacher: When God the Father is represented as an old man, the Holy Ghost as a dove, and the angels as winged youths, this is not done because they are really like that. As you said, they are bodiless spirits. But they are given these forms because it was under such that they sometimes revealed themselves to men. Thus God the Father is pictured as an old man because as an old man he appeared in a vision to the prophet Daniel (*Dan. cap. vii*); the Holy Ghost is shown as a dove because it was in that form he appeared at the baptism of our Lord (*John cap. i*); and the angels are represented as youths because they took that shape several times in the Old Testament (*Gen. cap. viii–xix*). Also, you must know that pictures and statues are often intended to show us, not things as they are in themselves, but the qualities of things, or the effects which they produce. Thus faith is represented as a lady with a chalice in her hand and charity as a lady with children about her, though we know well that faith and charity are not women but virtues. So it is not inappropriate to say that God the Father is represented as an old man to teach us that he is "the Ancient of days" or the Eternal, who existed before the foundation of the world; that the Holy Spirit is represented as a dove to signify the gifts of innocence, purity, and holiness with which he endows our souls; and that the angels are represented as young men with wings because their strength and beauty never know decline, and they are always on tip-toe to do God's bidding. Sometimes, too, we see them in white robes and sacred stoles, signifying their sinlessness and service of the Divine Majesty.

Bellarmine was back in Rome before the end of the year and gave his brother Thomas the following items of news:

The Holy Father has returned hale and hearty from Ferrara. I myself had an extremely comfortable journey in Cardinal Cesi's coach, together with Cardinal Baronius and Cardinal Aldobrandini. Such were the Holy Father's instructions, and there was a horse for me, too, whenever I cared to ride, and I had the finest accommodation you could imagine. The Pope is much troubled about the Tiber floods, which are the worst that have ever been known. God grant that nothing more terrible may happen. However, patience is the remedy for every evil.

CHAPTER VI

CARDINAL BELLARMINE

ON March 3, 1599, Robert Bellarmine, then rector of the Jesuit Penitenzieria house, was nominated cardinal by the peremptory Pope Clement VIII, who knew perfectly well that he was utterly averse to the honour. "We elect this man," said the Pope, "because he has not his equal for learning in the Church of God." He was also the nephew of Marcellus II who had befriended Clement's father, Sylvester Aldobrandini, on his banishment from Florence half a century earlier. A Vatican official, the Marquis Sannesio, went to the Penitenzieria to inform the new Cardinal that by the Pope's orders he was on no account to leave the house until summoned to the Vatican. The red hat was conferred the same day at a ceremony during which, according to an eyewitness, Robert wept the whole time. He had begun to hope from various indications, that the Pope, who regarded cardinals as little better than a necessary nuisance, would let him die in his Jesuit gown, and the suddenness of his promotion, after so many earlier false alarms, greatly disconcerted him. Only St Philip Neri, then four years dead, was able to stand up to Clement in his dictatorial hours, and even he failed to save Baronius from the unwanted purple. When the same Clement created his other great stand-by, Francésco Maria Tarugi, Archbishop of Avignon, Philip thought that the Oratory was doomed. For his part Father Aquaviva addressed the following letter to the heads of the thirty-two provinces into which the Society of Jesus was then divided, with 372 colleges and a total membership of 13,112:

> Your Reverence will probably have learned through another channel that God our Lord has brought about the promotion of Father Robert Bellarmine to the cardinalate. Yet I think it

advisable to give you some further details about the matter, for the full story will help to lighten the despondency which such an occurrence is bound to cause us of the Society, who in the spirit of our Institute desire only that God may keep us in the lowliness we have chosen. Be it known to your Reverence, then, that not only did the Society urge seriously on the Pope every motive which our constitutions put forward against the acceptance of dignities, but also that Father Bellarmine himself endeavoured again and again to dissuade him, making evident that his one desire was to live and die as a simple religious. But his Holiness, avowing that he had given the matter mature consideration before God, would not listen to the Father's reasons. When he attempted to urge them once again, just before receiving the biretta, the Pope commanded him in severe tones to accept the dignity and to make no further protest, under pain of excommunication.

I wanted to tell your Reverence all this that both you and your subjects may be gladdened, knowing that neither the Society nor his Illustrious Lordship failed to do all that was proper under the circumstances. In view of this we can hope that God our Lord will be glorified in his promotion, for as the dignity has been thus spontaneously conferred by the Pope on one adorned with the learning, integrity, and saintliness of Father Bellarmine, we have reason to expect that he will be in Holy Church a model cardinal, devoted to the public good, and as friendly to the Society as his long record of faithful service in it promised. To conclude, that God may grant him abundant grace in the performance of his new duties each priest in your province will say one Mass, and those who are not priests one pair of beads for his Lordship. From Rome, March 6, 1599.

The Pope had set aside apartments in the Vatican called the Stanze del Paradiso for the new Cardinal's accommodation, a good suite overlooking a pleasant colonnaded court, where there were shady trees and a splashing fountain to make the summer heats bearable. The same generous hand also presented him with four sets of robes, purple and scarlet, which was three more, the recipient said, than the Gospel allowed. Of these he took such care that they lasted till his death, twenty-two years afterwards, the cuffs only having been renewed when the old ones were past all patching. He had no silks in his possession, and all his garments were made of wool except a cassock of the silvery stuff called *teletta*, which he reserved for very special occasions such as the visits of ambassadors or princes. Pope Clement wished him to buy a pair of horses, and his coachman was instructed by the Vatican officials to bring two very fine ones for his inspection. The good *cocchiere* knew a noble beast when he set eyes on it, and did his very best to persuade the Cardinal to secure the pair. When he asked the price he was told that it was 600 *scudi*, but that need not worry him because the Pope would pay. "Well," said Bellarmine, "if horses at half that price will carry me just as well as these, I do not see why 300 *scudi* of the Pope's money should go on mere show. Buy me a cheaper pair."

He might have been as wealthy as heart could desire by merely nodding his head, for Cardinal Sfondrato pressed several thousand *scudi* upon him, and the Spanish ambassador proffered him a rich pension in the name of King Philip III. Others came forward, too, but he courteously refused all offers and would have nothing beyond the usual allowance given by the Pope to poor cardinals. Clement was extremely generous with money, but Bellarmine would not suffer him to be the judge of what was needful in his case. For his *maestro di casa*, he chose a man named Pietro Guidotti whom he knew well and trusted implicitly. Peter was given complete control and, at the same time, a very serious reminder that the money was not Bellarmine's but the Pope's, so if he wasted it on superfluities he would be responsible before God. Not content with these precautions, he sought the advice of his former superiors and expressed a strong wish to have a Jesuit lay brother to live with him, whom, however, he obtained on loan only for a short period. He was determined to remain a Jesuit as much as he possibly could in the external trappings of his life, as well as in his daily routine, and to make sure of this, he submitted a detailed account of his household for the General's inspection. After St Robert's death his confessor for twenty-three years, Francisco Rocca, showed this report to Fuligatti, from whose pages it is here borrowed:

1°. As to diet, clothing, prayer, Mass, and similar matters, there is scarcely any change.

2°. As to my household, it consists of thirty-five persons: eight or ten would be enough but a cardinal is expected to live up to the conventions. Of this staff, ten are gentlemen in waiting, fifteen are ordinary servants, and the rest servants of the ten gentlemen.

3°. I have three carriages because a horse often gets sick and it is not easy to secure a suitable one at short notice. Yet I must always have two carriages in readiness, for that is the least number that will accommodate my suite when we have to go to public functions.

4°. The furniture of the house is scanty enough. There is no plate, with the exception of a few candlesticks, a ewer and jug, and some forks and spoons. The chairs are covered with leather, three summer apartments are upholstered in the same material, and two of them in winter are hung with old tapestries of little value.

5°. My income goes principally in feeding the household, paying wages and rent, and in clothing the servants. I also give a little to my poor relatives to relieve their greater needs. Anything that is left goes in alms or to the support of churches, and not a farthing is put by.

Letters of congratulation soon began to pour in from all sides, and the subject of their praises hardly knew what to say in reply. To Justus Lipsius, the famous Latinist who had abandoned his Catholic faith while professor at Jena in 1572 and was readmitted, deeply penitent, to the Church at Mainz in 1591, St Robert wrote: "I thank you very heartily for your kindness, and I excuse your mistake. Believe me, the only feeling I have about my elevation is one of anxiety and fright at the extreme danger in which it has placed me."

Father Antonio Talpa, the strong-minded successor of Tarugi as rector of the Oratory of Naples, was answered in similar terms:

Your Reverence speaks and writes according to the dictates of that holy charity which thinks well of all and explains everything in a favourable light. But I who know only too well my many imperfections feel that I have exposed to danger

my peace of soul and my surety of salvation. And so, even
though I did this not freely but constrained by him whom it
was my duty to obey, I cannot remain as I am, save very much
against my will. My Lord Cardinal Baronius, dearest of friends,
professes himself mightily pleased, but I believe the reason of
it is to be found in that Latin tag—*Solatium est miseris socios
habere poenarum*.[1] Have compassion on me, you who enjoy the
peace of holy contemplation, and pray to our Lord for me that
the cloud of human glory may not obscure my vision of him,
the true Sun. I commend myself to all in your holy house and
to each one in particular, for I hold all of your Congregation
to be no less my dear brothers than the members of the Society
of Jesus.

Cardinal Valiero, the most delighted and enthusiastic of all
the well-wishers, had two letters for himself, the second of which
ran:

These things are wonderful and great, if we cleave to earth
and forget our true country. But if we judge aright, like good
scholars of the school of Christ, if we have studied with
attention the Gospels and St Paul, if we seriously consider
ourselves strangers and pilgrims on earth, what are all these
things but a cloud that appeareth for a little time, and what is
our life but grass, and what is its glory but a flower of the
field? I, certainly, dearest Father, can make this confession to
your paternal heart that I have never set any value on the purple,
and now, so far from valuing it, I rather marvel greatly at
those who do. I pity them too, for they seem not to care for
the glory of the Eternal King if only they may gain some
fleeting, counterfeit honours, and the shadow of renown.

Bellarmine could pour out his heart to people who, he knew,
would understand. With others he was laconic and matter-of-fact,
his excitable brother Thomas, for instance, getting only a few
lines of notification:

Rome, March 3, 1599. My dear, distinguished Brother. The
new promotion of cardinals was kept such a close secret that,

[1] It is a comfort to the afflicted to have companions in misery. The saying,
which generally has *solamen* for its first word, comes from ancient times, but its
author is not known.

though there were some plain indications that it was likely, I had no certain knowledge until this very morning when the consistory was held. It has now pleased God to raise me to this dignity, and I hope it will be to his glory. Signor Giuseppe can come to Rome as soon as he cares, but I should like Bartoletto and the rest of our relatives to stay away for the present, as is only fitting. My best wishes. I have now to go to the Vatican for the biretta.

Thomas had his heart's desire at last, and distributed alms with princely generosity. He also begged prayers in many religious houses for the new Cardinal, prayers with the significant twist, "that God the author of his greatness would give it the completion which the world desired", by which he undoubtedly meant the papacy. Montepulciano kept high festival in honour of the event, and so did Taverna, a small town on the promontory of Gargano beyond Foggia, through which Robert had passed on his pilgrim way to the famous shrine of St Michael Archangel there, when he was provincial at Naples. At Rome too there were celebrations, for though Bellarmine's religious brethren had been, like himself, distressed at the original proposal to make him a cardinal, they could not but feel, after the event, that his exaltation reflected glory on their order. Accordingly the superior of the Roman college decided to fête him with the usual round of poems and compositions, and begged him to be present at their little soirée on the feast of the Annunciation. He said that he would come with pleasure provided the poets confined their muse to one theme, namely, "All flesh is grass and all the glory thereof as the flower of the field".

The following details about St Robert in his everyday life are strung together almost entirely in the words of men who belonged to his household. "I who was his servant for seven or eight years," says one, "know that as cardinal he never changed the manner of life which he had followed when a Jesuit." In order that he might wake betimes in the morning without troubling anyone to call him, he accepted a present of a round clock, a little bigger than a piastra, which had an alarm attached to it. He would never buy any such thing for his own convenience. After rising, he put on unattended only his underclothing, and a heavy cloak or a cassock according to the season. Then he immediately said Matins and Lauds, either on his knees or, during Paschal time, standing. When they were finished, he put out his lamp and made an hour of meditation in the dark and at the end rose from his knees to open the shutters and let in the light of dawn. This done, he returned to his prie-dieu to say Prime, and afterwards retired to a back room that he might perform his ablutions and comb his hair. We next helped him to put on his robes but not a word was spoken. Once again he went on his knees to say Terce, and then Mass followed, with thanksgiving and Sext at the foot of the altar. After this he was ready to receive anyone who desired to speak with him.

As soon as his last visitor had departed, he went straight to his carriage and drove off to whatever function required his presence. There was usually some function every morning. On his return home, he at once put aside his robes and began his midday prayer. Then dinner was served, his first meal of the day, after which he knelt down to say None. None was followed by half an hour of recreation which consisted in walking up and down saying the Rosary. It was then time for study, or rather for writing, and it was thus he spent every vacant moment without wasting a single one. As evening approached he recited Vespers and then, after the Ave Maria bell, said the Litanies of the Saints in the chapel with all his household. The Office ended at sunset with Compline, but his prayers did not end, for after supper he walked up and down, saying the Rosary once more. Every day of his life, as soon as he had finished Compline he began the Office of our Lady, and when that was over, the Office of the Dead. So tranquilly did he sleep that he used to tell me neither distracting thoughts, nor heat nor cold could ever disturb his rest.

We are assured that the order of the day, just described, was so regular that important people, such as cooks and chaplains, had never to inquire when their master would be in or out or want to see them. He himself was a living clock, and this "horologiosity" was particularly noticeable in his method of reciting the Breviary. He might have been a choir monk, so careful was he to say each hour at the canonical time, whenever it was in his power to do so. On the rare morning when he was not obliged to go out he was at everybody's disposal and never once refused to see a visitor. Still, no matter who was with him, when the time for Office came he would beg with great courtesy to be excused for a little while, begin the canonical hour, and return to his visitor when it was over. Even Cardinal Pietro Aldobrandini, the most important personage in Rome after his uncle, the Pope, had to wait. "I watched him," this man related, "and he remained as still as a statue until he had finished his prayer."

St Robert's majordomo, Giuseppe Vignanesi, who supplied nearly all the foregoing details on oath to episcopal notaries, gave a further valuable piece of evidence:

I know that apart from his studies and writing he spent nearly every minute of his time in prayer. And this I know because I spied on him and saw it with my own eyes. Many a time during his half-hour of recreation, when he used to say the beads, I have found him all rapt out of himself, as it were in ecstasy, so that though now and then he was repeating the Hail Marys in an audible voice, he neither saw nor heard me, no matter how close to him I came nor how hard I shouted. At the slightest touch, however, a tremor like that of a frightened child passed over him and he was himself again—*dando un tremore come un bambino che pigli paura.*

This habitual intimacy with God bred in the Cardinal's heart a profound compassion for the needs and sorrows of his fellow men. He had not long been a cardinal when he was christened in the Roman slums '*il Padre de' Poveri*', and that affectionate title clung to him with ever-increasing appropriateness to the day of his death. His house became the haunt of all the "down-and-outs" in the city, who crowded daily about its doors and invaded the stairs and his very room. Sometimes on coming back from business he would find as many as three hundred awaiting him, and then he would rub his hands with delight and say to his distracted almoner, Pietro Guidotti: "These are the people, Peter, who will get us to heaven". He refused to have any fixed hours for visitors and insisted that they must be admitted at all hours. If he happened to be writing when someone was announced, his pen would stop poised in the middle of a word that he might welcome the caller instantly. No discrimination whatever was made, and a beggar in shabby clothes was as often seated in his chair as a cardinal in purple. His methods would undoubtedly shock a member of a society for the improvement of the lower classes. Once each month, he and his personal attendant Guidotti went carefully through the household accounts together. If any surplus was discovered, Bellarmine in great delight—*tutto allegro*—got down a book in which the names of various poor families and individuals were registered with details of their position and needs, and on them the surplus was straightway expended. Similarly, on the 31st of each December there was a review of the year's finances and the indigent soon discovered that then was the time to put in their claims, for all that was in hand was at once distributed. The Cardinal even ran into debt for his poor, and he told Father Cepari that he hoped he would die soon after Christmas when his salary was paid, for otherwise he would certainly leave creditors behind him. His standing orders to his almoner, according to this man's own account, were: "Be as close-fisted as possible with me, but as open-handed as you can to the poor". Guidotti must, indeed, have often been driven to despair by the incorrigible generosity of his master. What was a good business man to do with an employer who declared openly that every penny over when necessary expenses had been paid, belonged, not in charity but in strict justice, to the poor; who held that no one really possessed property which they did not give in alms, for such property only was entailed beyond the grave; and who reckoned no alms to be worth the name which did not cost their giver some positive inconvenience? Many and great were the arguments between the master's charity and the prudence of his man, his "Peter of little faith", as he affectionately called him.

Countless stories are told of the devices of his charity. One bitter winter's night he insisted that some hangings of red serge which Guidotti had bought the preceding year should be taken down and given for clothing to the ragged urchins in the street. "The walls won't catch cold", he said. He could not bear to see covers or curtains about the house when there were many poor wretches shivering outside, so on another occasion he packed off a roll of such stuff to the Fathers of the Gesù that they might have them fashioned into garments for the slum-dwellers. His few little valuables were nearly always in pawn. A poor man in sore need of ten or twelve crowns asked his help at the beginning of the month when his pockets were empty. Without hesitation he pulled off his cardinal's ring and gave it to the suppliant with a note stating that it might be pawned in his own name for the man's benefit. Then, as soon as money came in, he sent privately to have it redeemed. The pawnbrokers must have made a good penny out of that ring, for it was often in their hands.

On the morning when Bellarmine received his hat, Cardinal Aldobrandini made him a present of some silver candlesticks, a silver jug, and a silver inkstand and sand-box. The inkstand and sand-box on his desk gave the faithful Guidotti much worry, for they were too temptingly near his master's hand when a cry of distress which he could not otherwise meet reached him, and Pietro had constantly to be redeeming them. The silver candlesticks, too, like those of Victor Hugo's bishop, went off more than once under some shabby coat. An "Oltramontano", who was probably an Englishman, accosted the Cardinal one day as he was getting out of his carriage. When he had told his story, Bellarmine sent for Guidotti and bade him give the man twenty-five *scudi*. "But, your Lordship," answered Pietro, "I haven't as much as twenty-five *giulii*." "Well, then, give him our silver jug", said Bellarmine at once. Guidotti's face fell, but by some means or other he succeeded in raising the twenty-five *scudi* and saving the jug. It was very awkward being almoner to such a master. Twice over, he had to repurchase the very mattress of the Cardinal's bed. A poor old Sienese woman who had been found sleeping on the floor of her attic was the first to have it. She was very infirm, but the second beneficiary was a sturdy sort of beggar and Bellarmine feared that if Guidotti met him carrying away the mattress there would be a row. Consequently, he arranged for a time when Pietro was not about and cautioned his man to steal off with the prize as quickly as possible. He was thinking of his poor people day and night, and if his cook suggested any little delicacy for the table when he was ill or out of sorts, he used to say that it was a fine idea, but that he would enjoy the chicken much better if the extra price went for an alms and he was given mutton instead. Mutton then it would be, and some hungry waif would have a meal. Twice only in the week did he take meat and then it was usually that intolerable veal which is one of the plagues of Italy. He was always stinting himself to help the poor and saving every possible penny for their relief. In September, 1600, his brother Thomas, '*molto magnifico*' as usual, proposed that they should erect between them a grandiose sepulchral monument on their parents' grave. Robert was quite in favour of the monument, but totally opposed to the grandeur. "Let it be a simple memorial," he wrote, "for poor living men have greater need of my money than dead men of rich tombs."

It was not merely what he gave, however, but his manner of giving that made St Robert the idol of the unfortunate. He treated them as gentlemen, always standing and removing his cap when they came in. No matter how late might be the hour or how weary and worn he might be, there was a welcoming smile for them, and a patient ear for the longest of stories. He had no use for the platitudes of officialdom. It was enough for him that a fellow creature was cold or hungry or houseless. It was not his business to judge whether they were deserving, and his charity was of the authentic kind that thinks no evil, believes all things, hopes all things, endures all things. He had quite a good deal to endure for, of course, he was imposed upon and cheated again and again. Beggardom had its professionals and nowhere were they or are they more adept than in Italy. These fellows used to come a second or a third time in disguise, with ever more heart-rending stories. But he didn't mind. Charity is patient, too, and he had a fixed principle that it was better to be deceived a hundred times than miss one genuine case. One cool applicant examined the substantial alms which he had been given with a critical eye, and said: "My Lord, this is not enough. I want a good deal more to put me on my feet." Now Bellarmine had a naturally fierce

temper, but instead of throwing the fellow into the street, he
asked quietly, "How much more, sir?" and paid it as readily as if
he were paying an honest tradesman's bill. The following story in
Guidotti's own words will show how much that harassed
administrator had to endure:

> Whenever my Lord Cardinal went out for a walk or visit,
> he scattered alms right and left as usual. Every morning a
> perfect flood of written petitions were passed on to me, each
> with a note in his Lordship's hand, saying, "Please give such and
> such a number of scudi to this person". One fine day I got a
> note bidding me give thirty scudi to buy out of the army a
> soldier who had deserted from his regiment. I thought this was
> too good, and wrote back to say that I had no money in hand,
> and that if his Lordship went on at this rate we should soon be
> bankrupt, and that the soldier could go back to his regiment
> or find work in some other place. If he were going to pay the
> fines of all such blackguards he would soon have his hands full.
> That was what I said, and I added other arguments too. His
> answer to me was that I ought not to be so terribly cautious
> and strict about the merits of a case, that if we gave freely and
> generously, God would see that we did not become bankrupts,
> and that if I had no money at the moment I could pawn some-
> thing and get it that way. With regard to the matter of alms-
> giving, I could, if I thought well, write a whole book about my
> experiences of his Lordship's instructions and doings.

His Lordship did not wait for misery to come and tell its tale.
He sought it out. Whenever he went driving through the streets,
his head footman carried a purse of money to be distributed to
the casual hard cases for whom his master was always on the
watch. The trouble that appealed to his heart most of all was the
trouble of people, as we say, "in reduced circumstances", whom
a worthy pride made reluctant to ask for help. Fynes Moryson
while on his famous itinerary noticed that there were great
numbers of these respectable poor people in Italy whose "innate
pride is such that they had rather starve for want than beg". The
Cardinal employed secret agents to scent out such cases and then
their names and needs were entered in his book, never to be

forgotten. To a certain poor lady whose frock had seen better days, he sent one of his few fine robes that she might have it adapted for her use, telling her on the same occasion that she must provide herself in good time with all the winter wear she needed and send the bill to him. Once he was informed that a girl of good family had died, rather from starvation than illness. Bursting into tears, he said, "Why, why did nobody speak? If there was no money in the house, you had at least the candlesticks and the jug. Or could you not have pledged my ring or sold a horse or borrowed something in my name?"

In his all-embracing kindness the Cardinal did not forget that charity begins at home. Strict though he was about the morals of his household, he treated his men more as a father than a master. Though his means were small, he tried always to pay their wages in advance and he was ever ready to help them with something beyond their wages when they had need of it. His own physician attended them in illness and he paid all the expenses incurred at such times. In a hundred little ways he proved that their health and happiness were to him as dear a concern as if they were all the sons of his own mother. Any present that might be sent for his table went straight to their hall, and any work of which he could relieve their shoulders was taken upon his own. His orders were all couched as though he were asking a favour—*Mi sarebbe caro*, *Se potete*, etc.,—and it made no difference whether he happened to be addressing a groom or a chaplain. The time of day, the weather, the health of the individual, were all carefully taken into account before he asked anybody to do him a service. These servants themselves testified that he never once suggested the slightest task after dark, or when wet, or at times of meals and siesta. He hated the word servant, never used it himself, and protested when others did. "*Non sono miei servitori ma fratelli e compagni*", he said. He was the most lenient and tolerant of masters to them all, never saying a word if they came late or inconvenienced him by going to sleep when on duty. At such times he would on no account permit the offender to be wakened but quietly did whatever had to be done himself. If any of his suite came to his room to speak to him, he would not let them begin until they had taken a chair. When they had concluded their business, he would remove his cap and accompany them to the stairs with as much ceremony as if they were distinguished strangers.

The spiritual welfare of his men was, of course, his deepest concern. He said Mass for them every day himself, and once each week, for years, personally instructed the under-servants in their catechism. On the greater feasts, he preached to the whole household, and gave them special exhortations for four days preceding the general Communions which were fixed for the Annunciation, Easter, Pentecost, All Saints, Christmas, and Candlemas. Outside those times, he did not administer Holy Communion himself, lest anyone might approach through the wrong motive of pleasing a master they loved rather than pleasing God. He did not meddle with the management of the house or pry into the secrets of life below-stairs, but he was very strict about behaviour. A man might wear what he liked, but he must not swear as he liked. He could whistle or sing to his heart's content and even break things with impunity, but if he was discovered gambling or indulging in scandalous or slanderous talk, he was shown no mercy. Bellarmine, however, was very rarely obliged to be stern, for his men loved him too well to offend him, and behaved so well that to the eyes of Rome they seemed rather a religious community than a prince's suite. Like a true disciple of St Francis the Cardinal had sympathy and compassion not only for men but for all living things. Marcello Cervini,[1] who spent years in his service, recorded that it always made him very angry and sad to see a poor beast ill-used, and that he sometimes preferred to stay at home rather than deprive his horses of their rest and refreshment.

While kind and compassionate towards other men and even towards the birds and beasts, St Robert had no pity on himself. With age creeping upon him, with bad health, with endless work of the most arduous kind, he yet fasted rigorously three times a week all the year round. Throughout Lent and Advent, he tasted

[1] This Marcello was the grandson of Bellarmine's uncle Alessandro Cervini and became Bishop of Montepulciano in 1652.

no food until towards sunset. At the best of times his table was
not very inviting as he liked to dine on the garlic and chicory
which were the usual fare of the poor. He would never permit
more than the equivalent of a shilling or so to be spent on his
dinner, and delicacies of any sort were entirely taboo. But what
he liked best were the mortifications and sufferings that came
uninvited, cold and heat, the ache of rheumatism, headaches. Not
until the very end of his life, and then only at the Jesuit General's
urgent entreaty, would he permit a small fire to be lighted in his
room. "During the whole of winter," wrote Pietro Guidotti,
"he saw to it that there were big fires burning in the hall, the
waiting-room, and the kitchen so that the rest of us might not be
cold. But he would have none for himself." If he expected a
guest, he had a match put to the logs in his grate, but as soon as
ever the guest went out the fire did too, for he used to dismantle
it with his own hands. And yet he was most acutely sensitive to
the cold. His hands became so frost-bitten and covered with
chilblain wounds that towards the end of his life he was obliged
to wear gloves nearly always, though until the damage was done
nothing would persuade him to use them. His steward, Vignanesi,
saw him one day shivering over his books and forced a muff on
him so pleadingly that the Cardinal could not refuse. But he
returned it a few minutes later, saying that he could not write,
if he must also wear a muff. He was always ready with some such
excuse for his austerities. They were good for his health, or they
helped his work, or he just didn't like their opposites. He would
not have a fire, he said, because he could not be bothered looking
after it. In the summer months the flies provided him with
excellent opportunities for penance, as his good friend Cardinal
Crescenzio testified:

He would not brush them from his face, though as everybody knows they are a great torment, and when others wondered at this, he used to answer very sweetly that it was not
fair to trouble the little things, since they had no other paradise
than this liberty of flying about and alighting wherever it
pleased them.

To the end of his life, he kept up with unfailing regularity the various practices of mortification which are customary in the Society of Jesus, and he was so faithful to all his former rules that his friend Fuligatti says he went by the title, *Il Gesuita vestito di rosso*—"The Jesuit robed in red". One curious and out-of-the-way reference to his sanctity and asceticism is interesting enough to be given a few lines in the present section. It occurs in a rare little book entitled, *A New Description of Ireland wherein is described the dispositions of the Irish whereunto they are inclined*, published in London in 1610. Ireland made good copy in those old times. It was the reputed haunt of fearsome savages, and just as modern people like to read about abominable snowmen, so did the Elizabethan and Jacobean ladies like to have their flesh made to creep by tales of the wild Irishry. A Dublin gentleman of Oxford education named Richard Stanihurst wrote a "Description of Ireland" with the assistance of his tutor Edmund Campion, the future martyr, which was published in *The Chronicles* of Holinshed, in 1577. Thirty years later, Barnaby Rich, Gent., late of her Majesty's Irish garrison militia, thought he could improve on Stanihurst, and produced the "New Description" referred to above. Barnaby was a typical swashbuckler of the Elizabethan kind, but he grew tired of slaughtering the Irish and took to literature, incidentally providing Shakespeare with the plot of *Twelfth Night*. He had been brought up, he tells us, "in the fields among unlettered soldiers", and he was wholly self-educated. His book is almost entirely a criticism of Stanihurst who, in his opinion, had not blackened the Irish savages sufficiently. In one place Stanihurst says: "As for Abstinence and Fasting, it is to them [the Irish] a familiar kind of chastisement". Says Rich in his contorted English:

> I think this abstinence and fasting is the holinesse which Maister Stanihurst hath formerly spoken of, for this is a visible holinesse, indeede, which every man may see and wonder at; for let me speak of the most abject Creatures that I think Ireland or the world affoordeth, and those are the *Kearn*[1] of Ireland amongst whom there is not so notable a wretch to bee found

[1] Kern = the lightly-armed foot-soldiers of the ancient Irish clan system.

that will not observe the fasting daies, three daies in a weeke at the least, and those are Wednesdaies, Fridaies and Saturdaies: then they have other Vigiles and such Saints Eeves as I have never heard of but in Ireland nor I think be knowne in any other place, which they observe and keepe with such religious zeal and devotion, *that I am sure Cardinall Bellarmine himselfe cannot be more ceremonious then these bee, nor show himselfe to be more holy nor more honest.*

After becoming a prince of the Church, St Robert began an extensive correspondence with his dear friend John Baptist Carminata, who held, in those days, the post of Jesuit provincial in Sicily. John Baptist was a man of God after Bellarmine's heart, affectionate, simple, and utterly unworldly. When his friend was raised to the purple he was the very first to send congratulations, but this forwardness began to trouble his humble soul when the letter had gone. Who was he to offer his paltry respects, in advance of the great ones of the world? On June 11, 1599, Bellarmine answered:

Dearest Father . . . Since I entered this new order, hundreds of letters have reached me, but none so sweet and welcome as yours. Let me tell you, were there a year's novitiate before entering it, you would never have seen me professed. However, vows have to be taken on the very first day. Like yourself, I too have a great desire to see our holy Father Ignatius canonized but, during the present Pope's time, I see no chance of it at all. It would be easier to get Father Francis Xavier through, but I think the Society does not want him to be canonized before our Father Ignatius. As to Monsignor the Archbishop of Monreale, you have told me nothing I did not know before, as I had already heard much of his zeal and liberality to the poor, and of his other good qualities. To put the finishing touch to his generosity he only needs to give me a serviceable mule as an alms, for I still live on the purses of kind people and am at present enjoying the mule of Monsignor Tarugi, whom the Archbishop knows well. I take this opportunity to tell you that when I consider the many distractions and much worldly pomp of my present position, I envy bishops, because I think their state is safer and more like that of religious, and I find, too, the Calendar full of sainted bishops but can discover only one cardinal, St Bonaventure, and he lived as a cardinal only a few days. *Miseremini mei saltem vos amici mei.* Indeed, I put my trust in nothing so much as in the prayers of my many dear friends, some living and some dead. *Ora pro me, Pater amantissime.*[1]

Five days after the dispatch of this letter, the Cardinal wrote again at great length:

Dearest Father in Christ,

It is very strange that you have received none of the five letters which I wrote to you with my own hand. I will try to make up for their loss by the length of this one. As for myself, I am doing my best to bear the burden of the purple which has been imposed on me, with as little detriment to the welfare of my soul as possible. But I must own to you that I am very frightened and in much danger, for I now possess a rather grand and prosperous-looking suite, men who are at my beck and call to do my least bidding with alacrity and care. Besides this, my position brings with it not a few creature comforts and, though I try not to give my heart to them, still, there they are. I am afraid, then, lest it be deservedly said to me, *Recepisti mercedem tuam.* So, having no counsellor and not knowing what to do, I commend myself entirely to God's intimate friends that they may take me with them, who am unworthy of their company, to the "everlasting dwelling-places" which by my own efforts I could never reach. I have, indeed, a good will and firm purpose not to offend God, not to enrich nor aggrandize my relatives, not to aim at higher dignities but rather to fly from their approach with all my power, not to give scandal in anything, and to say Mass every day as I have always done. But I know well that this is not enough.

The thought of renouncing the purple is constantly in my mind, but how I am to do it I cannot see. I feel that my efforts

---

[1] This letter is one of forty-nine from Bellarmine to Carminata which still lie unedited in Roman archives. Though he could find only one cardinal in the list of Saints, St Robert discovered several who had been beatified and wrote out a catalogue of them in his own hand, that he might pray to them daily. Of the twenty-seven Jesuits who are canonized saints and the hundreds who have been beatified, Bellarmine himself is the only one who wore a mitre or a cardinal's hat. The Monreale of the text is a city near Palermo.

would be unavailing and that men would say it was only
another of my poses. Nor am I sure that the renunciation would
be pleasing to God, seeing that it was by his will that I was
forced to accept the dignity. To introduce novelties into my
way of living by reducing the number of my suite or adopting
a simple style in dress would give the impression that I was
ambitious to initiate reforms which the most austere and
upright cardinals have neither counselled nor adopted. St
Antoninus, for instance, teaches in his treatise *De Statu Cardin-
alium* that a certain degree of splendour is necessary, if the
dignity of this sacred order is to receive its due meed of respect
from the world at large. I am trying as hard as ever I can to
keep *my* splendour and dignity as modest as may be. Among
those of my colleagues who are neither extravagant nor showy
but follow a middle course that has, however, its own elegance
and distinction, I hold the least elegant and distinguished place.
Indeed, within the limits of decorum and decency, I am just
not shabby.

My reason for putting these matters before you, dear Father,
is that you, as the guide and master of my soul, may admonish
me if in anything I should do wrong, and that thus, by your
means, I may be converted to wiser counsels. I will now give
you some exact details. There are ten gentlemen in my suite,
to perform various higher duties. Most of the ten have two
servants each, but some have only one. Besides these, I have
fourteen servants for ordinary house and stable work, so the
sum total of the domestics does not exceed thirty. I told each
of them privately when I engaged them that, according to the
law of my house, swearing, impurity, or any other serious sin
entailed instant dismissal. Each week I call them together and
exhort them as earnestly as I can to lead good lives and to
perform their religious duties. I continue to say Office at the
canonical times as of old, and have not given up the practice
of fasting on Wednesdays and Fridays which I adopted in the
past.

I try never to send away a poor man disconsolate or empty-
handed but, as I am poor myself, I can only give little sums at a
time. If ever I become rich, then I shall be lavish with my alms,
according to the counsel of Tobias. Goodness knows, it is not
the desire to hoard which prevents me from giving much to

each petitioner, for I never had the slightest love of money or property. As for austerities, I am afraid I am not given to hair-shirts, sleeping on the ground, a bread-and-water diet, etc., for as I am now hastening towards my sixtieth year and my health is all but broken, I doubt whether I could support such hardships for long. Still, if ever a spiritual and prudent man should recommend them, I think, unless my self-love is playing me a trick, I would be quite ready to take them up. At first I decided to have only one carriage, but I soon discovered that a second was necessary for the conveyance of my suite, without whom it is not permitted to attend the papal services and consistories. I could, of course, get a lift from my friends on the way to these functions, but the return journey was the trouble. My friends' coaches were not available then, so if I had not a second carriage of my own the gentlemen-in-waiting would have been obliged to go home on foot, and that would not have been correct. The furniture of my house is as simple and plain as possible, and I did not allow my arms to be embroidered on the tapestries or couches in the vestibule, though it is the usual custom to have them put on. All the chairs except four are plain leather-covered ones. The four are in velvet, but are only produced when we have visits from cardinals, royal ambassadors, and other great people. The rest of the furniture is very ordinary stuff indeed, which nobody could call valuable. I wear no silk at all, and have nothing grander than plain, cheap wool in my wardrobe.

I am writing thus to you that you may relieve my doubts with your wise counsel, and tell me plainly what I ought to do. You are my intimate friend and that is why I open my heart to you, but I would not like others to be told what I have said. The Pope wanted me to accept the bishopric of my native place, Montepulciano, but only on condition that I should not leave Rome. I did not accept his terms as I know how dangerous it is to be an absentee bishop. If, however, he would permit me to reside in the diocese I would not be so reluctant, because it seems to me that the episcopal office is more spiritual, more religious, more fruitful of good, and more secure, than that of the cardinalate alone, which though sacred has much that is secular about it. I am not forgetting the difficulties and dangers involved in the care of souls but, when God calls, it is not for us to cry safety first. Obedience is, without doubt, the safest state, for, as St Francis says, in obedience there is profit and in prelacy peril. But our choice should fall rather on that way of life which is most pleasing to God and at the same time least dangerous for our souls. Forgive the length of my letter and pray for me, Father. I shall be anxiously awaiting your good advice, and I beg you with all my heart to pull me with you to Heaven, somehow, even though I be reluctant.

The thirty to thirty-five retainers seem to have shocked the honest Carminata and drew from Bellarmine the following reply:

Experience proves that it is impossible to do with less. Cardinal Borromeo, a great despiser of worldly pomp, has forty-five of them, fifteen more than myself, and other cardinals who are accounted very modest in their establishments have more than sixty or seventy. The great ones keep over a hundred. Every day I am obliged to attend various congregations as well as papal services and functions, and to all these I have to go in my robes and with a suite. It is not always possible to collect friends to accompany one, so the only course is to keep eight or ten gentlemen for the purpose. Besides, thirty persons are barely sufficient to cope with all the housework and incessant ceremonial at home, as the rest discover to their cost when any one of them falls ill. Would to God I could live quietly with but a single companion. I hope soon to see you again and then your Reverence can give me all the advice I need and desire. Help me meantime with your prayers.

A year later, October 1600, Carminata had finished his term of office. It was intended that he should then devote himself entirely to mission work but he had fallen ill, and the thought of his age made him very depressed. St Robert wrote to comfort him:

According to my calculations, your Reverence is not more than sixty-four and that number of years does not make you too old for the pulpit. St Augustine preached up to the age of seventy-six, and here in Rome you will find men over seventy who have accepted bishoprics, a dignity which includes, *de jure*, the obligation of preaching. Others who have turned the biblical three score and ten would not be afraid of accepting the papacy. I very much envy you the post you will hold two months hence, because you will be able to put aside every other care and devote yourself to prayer and the ministry of the word. Every day I see more and more the good I have lost without hope of recovery. Would, at least, that I could assure myself that all this is by the call and not merely by the permission of God, for I entered upon it solely out of obedience and under pain of mortal sin in case I refused. But on the other hand, I fear lest it be a mere permission of God, because I do not see how I can render any very signal service to the Church in this state. I am convinced, for example, that in many matters we ought to go to the very roots to reform abuses, but my views meet with no sympathy. Pray, commend me to God that he may cause me to do his holy will, or call me quickly to himself.

In the first year of his cardinalate, St Robert was invited by the authorities of the Roman College to give an exhortation on the life of Ignatius Loyola in their church, on the anniversary of his death, July 31. It was to be for Jesuits only, behind locked doors, but Robert asked them to invite also Cardinal Baronius to the family festival, as he could not himself well do so, because it would look as if he were inviting him to the exhortation. Writing to Carminata about the affair, he said:

Here is a fresh bit of news for you. The Congregation of Rites has set up an Apostolic Commission to examine witnesses on the life and miracles of our Blessed Father Ignatius. So we have made the first step on the way to his canonization, and I can tell you it cost me no small labour, for I have addressed the cardinals of the Congregation several times. All the same, the favour is more owing to Cardinals Aldobrandini and Baronius than to myself. You will have heard from others what was done on the anniversary day of our Father, and how your Reverence's friend made a little sermon in the church to our brethren, behind closed doors; how Cardinal Baronius kissed the ground at our Father's tomb several times; how he then, all at once, mounted a ladder and fastened a beautiful picture of our Blessed Father over the tomb, together with two boards bearing ex-votos; how on the following day in a sermon in the church of the Vallicella he made some allusions to our Father,

calling him always Blessed Ignatius; and last of all, how in the
Congregation of Rites, two days later, he defended what he
had done with great success, declaring that his action was
entirely spontaneous and that our fathers had not said a single
word to him. Really this good Cardinal is just as much one of
the Society as any of us. Pray God for him and still more for
me, whose need is the greater.

Another of Robert's correspondents was the Bishop of Verdun,
Prince Eric of Lorraine, a very pleasant figure to meet among the
rather pompous dignitaries of that epoch. He was young, noble,
and wealthy, but his one desire was to renounce his mitre and
become a monk. The Roman authorities, however, hardened their
hearts against all his entreaties to be set free, and Eric in his sorrow
turned to Bellarmine for consolation. The answer he received
was as follows:

Most Illustrious and Right Reverend Lord,
    I was brought by one post two of your letters entrusting me
with two affairs and telling me at the same time of the wish of
your holy soul to come to Rome to lay aside your pastoral
charge, and to put your salvation in security. As to the business
matters I will do all in my power, but that, I fear, is not much,
because many other people who will not easily waive their
rights will have something to say. It is wonderful the number
of difficulties that arise when there is a question of money.
But as to your holy desire of taking wings like a dove and
flying to a place of sweet tranquillity, I will tell your Lordship
what occurs to my mind. I consider that no more lasting peace
nor truer security of salvation can be found than in fulfilling
with entire devotion of heart the holy will of God. I have always
loved particularly those words of our Lord: "Father, let this
chalice pass from me; nevertheless, not my will but thine be
done". We have been bought at a great price, so, like purchased
slaves, we owe our Lord simple, unquestioning obedience. As
long as our consciences assure us that we have not sought, nor
desired, nor chosen a higher place, that at the present moment
we have no liking for the world's honours and would willingly
lay them aside if we could, as long as conscience tells us this,
I do not see why we ought not to acquiesce in God's will which

has been made known to us clearly by the command of his Vicar. A bishop's burden is a heavy one and full of cares and danger, nor perhaps is the dignity of a cardinal less burdensome and dangerous. If it has pleased him who made us and redeemed us to call us into these straits and perils, who are we to question his wisdom? He who loved us and laid down his life for us deigned to say to Peter, and through him to every pastor, "If you love me, feed my sheep". Who then, except one who loved not God but himself, would dare to answer our Lord, "I will not feed thy sheep, lest I lose my soul"? The true lover of God would say with the Apostle, "I could wish that I myself were accursed and cut off from Christ for the sake of my brethren", rather than not bear the burden which the love of God has laid on him. But there can be no danger of salvation where charity reigns for, though we fail in many things through ignorance or human frailty, yet charity covers a multitude of sins.

My dearest Lord, if there were any hope that with God's good pleasure and the blessing of his Vicar you could come to the quiet of religious life and I could return to it, we should undoubtedly do so with the heartiest will in the world. But there is not the faintest hope, and that is why I have written what I have written. I wanted to tell you, whose holy soul I see to be tortured by the weight of your charge, what I am always telling myself.

If business should bring you to Rome, it would be a great treat not only for myself but for Cardinal Baronius and many others as well. However, if we cannot have the pleasure of your company, I know that we shall not lack the solace and help of your prayers.

St Robert might be described as having been the factotum of the Holy See. He was a member, not only of all the Roman Congregations, but also of such commissions as those for the revision of the Martyrology and the second nocturns of the Breviary, on which he worked under the presidency of Cardinal Baronius. As far back as 1584, he wrote a memorandum, *De reformatione Martyrologii Romani*, at the request of Cardinal Laurio, and eight years later a similar document in which he showed a refreshing independence of judgment. Thus, he advised a certain healthy scepticism about Greek Menologies, "because the Greeks are far too ready to admit and worship saints", and he deprecated the inclusion in the Martyrology of men whose only title appeared to be their known presence at some ancient council. "What has this to do with sanctity?" he pertinently asked. A dryly humorous modern professor of Church history, when asked by his students why saints appeared to abound everywhere in Wales at one time and so few afterwards, answered that probably the title saint in early days about corresponded to the title "Mister" in later times. St Robert also objected to the addition of so many saints from the Italian Calendar. "Spaniards, Frenchmen, Germans, and peoples of other nations will have just cause for complaint that, while we want them to venerate our saints, we are not willing to venerate theirs." In the Breviary lessons, he brought his heavy guns to bear on the legend of St James's apostolate in Spain, on the more fantastic one of St Denis the Areopagite in France, and he wished that the whole office of St Catherine of Alexandria, whom he had celebrated in Latin verse during his schooldays, should be taken in its entirety from the common of virgins. Vested interests proved too strong and Baronius's caution too great, so St James still evangelizes Spain in the Breviary, the Areopagite still remains the apostle of Paris and St Catherine still confounds the pagan philosophers. But St Robert made one contribution to the Divine Office which will not readily be discarded, the simple and beautiful hymn for the feast of St Mary Magdalene.

During the summer of the year 1601 Bellarmine wrote, at the earnest request of Pope Clement VIII, a document of three thousand words "On the Primary Duty of the Sovereign Pontiff". Clement assured him that he wanted to be told the plain, unvarnished truth and he certainly got it. If the Pope took care to appoint the right kind of bishops, then he would be fulfilling his primary duty, but if he chose unfit candidates or if he neglected to keep them up to the mark, then God would demand at his hands the souls that might be lost through his carelessness. "This consideration", wrote the Cardinal, frightens me so much that there is no one in the world I pity more than the Pope. . . . What St John Chrysostom wrote so feelingly about bishops, namely that only a few of them would be saved because of the extreme difficulty of giving a good account of the souls committed to their care, certainly applies much more to the occupants of St Peter's Throne. Nor might we flatter ourselves with talk of a good conscience or a right intention, since St Paul says, *Nihil mihi conscius sum, sed non in hoc justificatus sum*, and St James strikes terror into us with that dreadful verse, "Whoever keeps the whole law but fails in one point has become guilty of all of it".

To this the Pope, who was a very good man though sadly addicted to nepotism, replied that the thought affrighted him also, but he found consolation in the fact that after all he could only choose *men*, and that even our Lord, after a whole night in prayer, had chosen Judas. Bellarmine then proceeds to develop six points, the first of which was the long vacancies in episcopal sees. After quoting St Leo, Innocent III, and St Gregory, he says: "It is difficult to explain in a few words the harm which these widowed churches suffer, the vices into which the shepherdless flocks run headlong, the wilderness which the vineyard becomes that has no husbandman to tend it". Clement owns that he has been at fault and is still at fault in this respect but urges the difficulty of finding suitable subjects.

Second point—the promotion of bishops not possessing the necessary qualifications. Churches ought to be provided with good men, not men with good churches. . . . The Council of Trent declares in plain words that all those who are in any way responsible for the appointments of bishops commit mortal sin if they do not choose the men whom they consider best fitted for the office and most likely to be of good service. . . . I confess that I have been terrified when, two or three times in consistories, I have seen persons promoted to cardinalatial sees, who from their advanced age, or bad health, or lack of episcopal virtues, were such as could scarcely be considered useful or fit at all to have the charge of souls. But custom demands, you may say, that these churches be given to the cardinal priests, in order of seniority, whether they possess the necessary qualifications or not. I do not think that custom would ever persuade us to entrust our bodies to aged physicians, if through senility or any other cause they were less capable of doing us good. If we take such precautions when our perishable bodily health is at stake, why will we not take them for the sake of immortal souls? I pass over the fact that nowadays many are ambitious of the episcopal dignity or, rather, openly ask for and demand it, not knowing, as our Lord says, what they ask.

The Pope accepted those strictures in the best possible spirit. "This matter causes us constant anxiety", he wrote, "because if we refuse the dignity to all who ask for it or are proposed by others, we do not know how we are going to fill the vacant sees, especially the poorer ones. If your Lordship has any suggestion to make in this connection, we should be very glad to hear and make use of it."

Third point—the absence of bishops from their dioceses. What is the good of electing a suitable man if he is never to be at home? The Council of Trent declares that by divine precept bishops must know their flocks, preach the Word of God to them, and feed them by the administration of the sacraments and the example of all good works. . . . Moreover, the same Council lays it down that cardinals who are ordinaries outside Rome must reside personally in their dioceses.

Clement's comment on this is a rueful one: "We admit that we have sinned, inasmuch as we have been too easy in giving bishops leave to come to Rome. Once in Rome it is almost impossible to get them out again." Bellarmine continues:

I see such great desolation in the churches of Italy now as perhaps has not been witnessed for many a year. Residence seems to be accounted binding neither by divine nor human law. In the first place, there are at the present day eleven non-resident cardinals who are bishops of sees. Then there are many bishops who act as apostolic nuncios, and some of these have not seen their dioceses for several years. Others, again, have neglected the care of the souls committed to them in order to play at being civil magistrates, though by what reasons they justify themselves I confess I cannot imagine. Finally, there are some who have left their sheep in the wilderness, and are wasting their time uselessly in Rome or spending it on business that could be done quite well by others. I admit, of course, that some bishops are excused from residence by obedience, and I am not denying the Supreme Pontiff power to grant such exemptions for good reasons and a limited period. But I do not know whether it is pleasing to God that so large a number of bishops should be absent for so long a time and with such detriment to their flocks. If those bishops who are always in their dioceses, working might and main for the good of souls to the exclusion of every other occupation, yet find it difficult to carry out all the duties of their office, as St Augustine tells us was his own experience and as is plain from the Apology of St Gregory Nazianzen, the Dialogue of St John Chrysostom on the Priesthood, and the pastoral admonition of St Gregory, if this be so, are they not labouring under a serious delusion who think that they can fulfil their episcopal obligations while far away from their flocks and engrossed in other business?

The fourth abuse against which the Cardinal inveighs is "ecclesiastical polygamy", or as we should say, pluralism. St Thomas and the Council of Trent are his two great weapons, but he appears to have been a little too free with his strictures, for the only pluralism he could point to was that of six cardinals who possess, in addition to their titular see, a second one "in ordinary". That he should have argued so strongly against even this very mild departure from the strictest principles shows how deeply he had the welfare of souls at heart.

Fifth point—too great leniency in permitting the transfer of bishops from one diocese to another. According to the canons and the custom of the early Church, the translation of bishops ought not to be allowed except for reasons of necessity or when they would be more useful in a new sphere. Dioceses were not instituted for the advantage of bishops but bishops for dioceses. The practice is also contrary to the example of the saints. Thus St Gregory the Great never changed nor permitted the change of a single bishop, and though, as St Bernard informs us,

G

St Malachy was forced to leave his small diocese for the metropolitan see of Armagh, yet he would only go on the express condition that when he had settled the business confided to him in his new office, he should be permitted to return to his former diocese. John, Bishop of Rochester, the cardinal and martyr, was often asked by his king to accept a wealthier see, but would never consent to desert his first church though it was one of the poorest. Finally, the practice is unreasonable, because a bishop is wedded to his church by a spiritual tie stronger than any carnal one, and such a tie ought not easily to be dissolved. Indeed, *can* it be dissolved except by God or the Vicar of God declaring his Master's will? And who will believe that it is God's will to pronounce such a divorce, when the only reasons for it are some temporal honour or gain, especially when it cannot be done without harm to souls, as experience teaches us? Bishops can scarcely love dioceses which they hope soon to desert for richer pastures. . .

The sixth and last point is the resignation of the episcopal charge without a legitimate excuse. If there is a strong tie between a bishop and his diocese, a tie almost too close to be dissolved, as the canons teach, how is it that we see it broken with such ease every day? Some men resign their sees but keep the revenues, like a man who should divorce his wife and yet hold tight to her dowry. Others, when they have grown rich on their episcopal revenues, give up the charge that they may devote themselves to yet more lucrative employments, or renounce it in favour of their relatives, that under such a pretence they may still keep possession of the sanctuary of God. There are men, too, who prefer to be mere *referendarii* or clerics at the court of Rome, rather than high priests away from it, and finally we hear such excuses offered for resignation as the unhealthiness of the climate, the poverty of the diocese, or the indocility of the people. God knows whether these are legitimate grounds and whether the bishops who urge them are seeking what is their own or what is Jesus Christ's.

These are the points, Holy Father, which I considered it my bounden duty to represent to your Holiness for the relief of my conscience. They are written out of the sincerity of my heart, so I beg you most earnestly, with all reverence and submission, to read them with a favourable eye.

Pope Clement's final comment on the document is heroically meek:

The few hurried answers we have set down here are not given *ad excusandas excusationes in peccatis* but that your Lordship may look with an eye of compassion on the difficulties which have entangled us and brought us into such trouble. For we avow that not only in these matters but in many others too, nay, in everything, we have sinned, and in nothing have we done or are we doing our duty. Beseech Almighty God, then, that he would either help us by his divine and most efficacious grace, or, as we should prefer, that he would free us from this mortal coil [*mortali vinculo*] and put another in our place who would worthily fulfil the duties of his office.

The Cardinal's correspondence at this period shows how much a part of him were the counsels he gave. Having heard promising reports of the virtue and deserts of a certain Polish priest, he immediately set to work with the greatest energy to have this good man promoted to a vacant see. After the event he wrote thus to the bishop-elect:

I know that the diocese to which you are now called is very large and full of difficulties. I cannot bring myself to do other than compassionate you sincerely and beseech God that he would deign to supply you with strength to equal the burden. I offer you no congratulations at present, conscious, as I am, rather of the additional dangers and labours which have fallen to you, than of your increase of honours and wealth. Hereafter will be the time for congratulations, when the Prince of Pastors comes with an imperishable crown and says to you, "Well done!"

Count John of Reitberg, who had restored Catholicism in eastern Friesland, received the following letter in the year 1602:

Most Illustrious Count, Your communication, which reached me at the beginning of this year, caused me the greatest joy. There is no news I receive more greedily than that which tells me of a revival of the Catholic faith in a place where it was completely dead. I thank God, therefore, that he has deigned

to elect your Highness to bring about a beginning of salvation
in your country—a land that seemed lost forever—and thus to
make our souls brim over with spiritual joy. For I can distinguish in your Highness the solid grounds of an unfeigned faith,
of a thorough love of God, and what is rarely found in princes,
of a deep humility, so that I confidently hope to see my Illustrious Lord John not merely Count, as he is in fact, but a sort of
second Apostle of East Friesland. That is a glory far exceeding
any regal or imperial renown. As regards affairs at Court here,
the Supreme Pontiff will himself write to the Emperor and the
Nuncio. I, too, shall write to the latter because he is a very
intimate friend of mine, and will be sure to take to heart whatever is suggested to him in your name. I beg God our Lord to
give you and your noble lady, daily, more and more of his
Holy Spirit, and to kindle his flame so strongly in your hearts
that no force of the winds and rains of earthly persecutions may
ever be able to extinguish it. I pray your Highness to believe
me completely at your service. If you should need my assistance
in any way, write with the greatest freedom and you will
always find either what you ask or the most entire good will on
my part.

The next two letters show the Cardinal in one of his common
rôles, defending a man who has been treated with gross injustice.
A canon of Breslau named Bonaventure Han had been elected
bishop of the city by the unanimous vote of the cathedral chapter.
Another canon named Paul Adalbert intrigued against him and,
having ingratiated himself with the Emperor Rudolph, succeeded
in diverting the coveted mitre to his own head. Paul died just a
year after his nomination by the Court and then another imperial
protégé was chosen over the head of Han, the rightful bishop.
This holy and persecuted ecclesiastic fell into dire poverty and
had even to leave the city, owing to the opposition in high places.
It was at this crisis that Bellarmine came into his life:

I did not answer your second letter at once, because I wished
to have some definite news to give you. I have spoken to his
Holiness and to everyone who had any influence in the matter,
and that often and very warmly. At last it has been arranged
that you are to have a pension of 3,000 ducats from the see of

Breslau. As to obtaining the provostship for you, the Pope at first gave me great hopes, but the influence of others, whose requests it was not easy to refuse, won the day. I know how easily contented you are, but still I may say boldly that the loss of considerable wealth and dignity is not something to be greatly deplored, as we know well that their possession involves greater danger of losing eternal life. Good-bye. Continue to love me as you do, and in your prayers commend the salvation of 'my soul to God.

Bellarmine's next step was to write to the Bishop of Breslau:

Right Reverend and Illustrious Lord, Bonaventure Han, once bishop-elect of Breslau, for the sake of peace and in the spirit of obedience waived his rights, as your Lordship well knows, and was thus brought to such straits as to lack the very necessaries of life. No tie bound me to him save that of Christian charity, but that charity moves my heart and afflicts me as if I were a sharer in his misery. . . . Therefore I beg and beseech your Lordship to deign to succour this unfortunate man, to have pity on him from your heart, and to fulfil the wishes of the Sovereign Pontiff. I shall count this among the greatest favours ever done me, and should there ever be occasion I will repay you gratefully when I learn that Bonaventure's consolation has been owing to the kindness of your Lordship's heart. Good-bye, and remember me in your holy prayers.

At this same period the Archbishop of Mainz received a letter from the Cardinal begging him too, to come to the aid of people in distress:

I hear every day that there are plenty of courageous non-Catholics in Germany who would willingly return to the bosom of Holy Mother Church if they could only hope to find friends who would help them in their temporal needs. Our Holy Father, Pope Clement, spends not a little money on this good work, as I have myself witnessed, but he cannot single-handed succour all who apply to him daily. I have no doubt but that your Lordship and the other Catholic princes of Germany are most anxious to see heretics, and especially distinguished heretics, return to the Church. Nevertheless the ardent desire I have to help Germany by every means in my power urges and almost compels me to seize the opportunity provided by this letter, of commending to your kindness the temporal needs of those who, wearied with the road of perdition, are hastening to enter their native land. Your friendship is very dear to me, and be assured that if ever you need my assistance in any way in Rome, it is always at your disposal.

CHAPTER VII

THE CONTROVERSY ABOUT EFFICACIOUS GRACE

T HE closing decades of the fateful sixteenth century and the opening one of its hardly less decisive successor were marked on the theological front by very lively exchanges between a number of schools of thought within the Catholic Church on the subject of divine grace, the same exceedingly difficult and in part completely mysterious matter which, through erroneous interpretations, had earlier brought about the Protestant revolt in both its Lutheran and Calvinistic forms. St Robert Bellarmine became heavily involved in the Church's family disputes, as well, of course, as on the wider front of Catholic and Protestant strife, but the question at issue, the reconciliation of free will with the doctrine of efficacious grace, which infallibly brings about the consent of the will, is much too technically theological for deep discussion in these unlearned pages. Robert's refutation of Michel de Bay's theories which led eventually to Jansenism, during his years as a young professor at Louvain, was briefly described at an earlier stage of this book. But the trouble with Michel de Bay, chancellor of Louvain, pursued him to Rome and brought upon his eminent grey hairs a very cataract of huge letters from his holy and highly attractive disciple, Father Leonard Leys, Latinized into Lessius. Lessius had taken up the contest with the Baianists, already twice condemned in Rome, at the point where Bellarmine had left off, and entered into the battle of Israel with the joy of a warrior born. For forty-five years of his sixty-nine, he suffered without remission from a prostrating and incurable physical malady, but took advantage even of this to become widely versed in medical lore and to publish a book entitled *Hygiasticon*, dealing with the way to keep healthy. Indeed, his own atrocious health seemed to act as a kind of spur to greater labours in the service of God, which resulted in a whole array of splendid treatises on moral theology, Scripture, dogma and philosophy. Besides being a profound thinker, Lessius was also of a genially practical turn and made himself a serviceable chair out of logs of wood destined for the flames. In his spiritual life, he had reached the stage where he seemed to be able to remain in unbroken communion with God, no matter how busy with his pen, nor how distracted by long journeys, undertaken gladly, in spite of his dreadful health, for the good of the Society of Jesus which, like his idol Bellarmine, he so dearly loved. His favourite aspiration is known to have been, "O my Jesus, I long for you a thousand times over. When will you come?"

Though of a profoundly mystical bent, as his ascetical works prove, Lessius, no more than Teresa of Jesus, was deterred from donning armour when the interests of God seemed at stake. He fought the Louvain and Douay Baianists up hill and down dale, for, like their offspring the Jansenists, they would not submit honestly to the Church's ruling and resorted to all sorts of subterfuges to maintain their orthodoxy. It is significant that one of the ablest of Michel de Bay's lieutenants was Dr Jan Janson, who subsequently became the tutor and friend of Cornelius Jansen and the Abbé de Saint-Cyran, the two corner-stones of Jansenism. The Baianists, again like the Jansenists, were first-rate propagandists and made things exceeding hot for Lessius and his brethren in Belgium. In 1588, the Jesuit professor gave Bellarmine, who answered his every letter and supported him with all his might in Rome, a brief account of his anxieties:

> I doubt whether Catholics were ever so zealous in opposition to heretics as are the Louvain and Douai theologians against us. . . . Unless the Holy See intervenes, it is all over with the reputation of our Society in this part of the world. Throughout the whole country we are defamed as heretics, even by the rustics and artisans, and every day some new and more horrible rumour is spread about us. . . .

The Baianists had chosen their moment well, for at that time the great, imperious Sixtus V, a Franciscan himself, seemed determined to change in disastrous ways the constitutions which

St Ignatius Loyola had written, almost one might say in his heart's blood, for the Society of Jesus. It was the same Ignatius whose directives inspired his sons to rally shoulder to shoulder in defence of the freedom of the human will in all its operations, even under the action of divine grace. During his seven years as a poor student living on alms at the University of Paris, Ignatius witnessed with anxious thought the first efforts of the Lutherans and Calvinists to capture the Catholic soul of France and, inspired by the decrees of the Council of Sens, held at Paris in 1528 while he was there, wrote then or subsequently his own "Rules for thinking with the Church", which he embodied in his Spiritual Exercises. The seventeenth and penultimate of these rules runs as follows: "We ought not to speak of or to insist on the doctrine of grace so strongly as to give rise to that pernicious teaching that takes away free will. Therefore, we may treat of faith and grace, as far as we may with the help of God for the greater glory of his Divine Majesty; but not in such a way, especially in these dangerous times of ours, that works or free will receive any detriment or come to be accounted for nothing."

Those were marching orders for the Jesuits and explain why, at this time of crisis, their theologians, Bellarmine and Lessius among the foremost, strove with all their power to show how the will's freedom remains intact even under the impulsion of efficacious grace, an article of Catholic faith fiercely attacked by Lutherans, Calvinists, Baianists and Jansenists alike. To clarify the whole issue and to assist his hard-pressed brethren in the Low Countries, Robert Bellarmine drafted a long report, *De Controversia Lovaniensi*, for presentation to Cardinal Madruzzo, Prefect of the Inquisition. It is an elaborate defence of Lessius's doctrine as being the traditional teaching of Catholic theology, particularly expounded in the works of St Thomas Aquinas. In the event, the Holy See peremptorily silenced the Baianist campaigners in Flanders whose tactics gave an unholy joy to the Protestant leaders. But the thunder of the captains and the shouting died away in that quarter only to break out again much more violently on the hot plains of Old Castile. The leader of the battle line this time was the most eminent theologian of the University of

GX

Salamanca, Domingo Bañez, who had sat under the phenomenal Melchor Cano, and imbibed from him not only admirable theological methods, but also it would seem, a rooted antipathy to the newly founded Society of Jesus. In spite of all that the Holy See and his own Dominican superiors could do to put a curb on him, Cano persisted down to the day of his death in 1560 in regarding the Spiritual Exercises of St Ignatius, solemnly approved by the Pope in 1548, and many times since, as a little book loaded with heresies, and the Jesuits themselves as spawn of the devil, sent for the destruction, not only of all good theology, but of all good Christian living. Domingo Bañez was not so immoderate, but he believed and openly maintained that Jesuit theology was definitely a "bad thing" to be fought ruthlessly as destructive of the great synthesis of St Thomas. Bañez is deservedly remembered and honoured as perhaps the most effective of all the defenders and directors of St Teresa of Jesus. He was very severe with her, as he was with most people whom he encountered, but the Jesuits, themselves not wholly unesteemed by Teresa, came off worst of all. The trouble began in 1582, when a Jesuit, in the innocence of his heart, defended in a public disputation at Salamanca some hypothetical theses about the freedom of our Lord's human will during his Passion. Bañez attacked his conclusions with a good deal of animus and succeeded in having them censured by the Spanish Inquisition. But that was merely a curtain-raiser for the big drama to come. Portugal at this time had been annexed to Spain by the strong-arm methods of King Philip II. At the University of Evora in Portugal, the holder of the first chair of theology was a Spanish Jesuit, Luis Molina, a slight, unimpressive figure of a man whose name, largely owing to the contrivances of Domingo Bañez, was destined to ring down the centuries.

Molina, who was endowed with an extraordinarily subtle genius but only a very lumbering Latin style to convey its findings, had been wrestling for thirty years with the deep problems of grace, free will and predestination. By the year 1588 he had his bomb of a book ready for the press, bearing the title, *Concordia liberi arbitrii cum gratiae donis*—"The concord or harmony of free will with the gifts of grace". It is a piquant circumstance that this badly written but profound book, which was to rouse such a controversial storm as had never before swept through the dignified seclusion of the Catholic schools, should have begun in its title with the pleasant pacific word "harmony". Bañez knew or suspected that his own publicized views on the reconciliation of efficacious grace with the freedom of the human will would come under heavy fire in the book, and it is really evidence of his regard for Molina's power as a theologian that he did everything possible to have the publication of his work prohibited. But the Portuguese Dominicans were not to be stampeded by their Spanish confrère, however illustrious, and, delegated as censors by the Inquisition of their country, gave the book a rousing and most honourable send-off. Then the real fun began, at least for us at our vantage-point four hundred years afterwards.

The first act of the serio-comic drama was projected by Bañez at Salamanca in the shape of a widely advertised disputation on the subject of religious vows, in which it would be shown that simple vows do not constitute men or women true religious at all. As the majority of Jesuits took and take only simple, though lifelong, vows, the conclusion would be obvious. The upstart Society of Jesus was not a true religious order. In his eagerness to get even with Molina, if not on theological then on canonical grounds, Bañez seems to have been unaware of a bull issued by Pope Gregory XIII only five years earlier in which it was explicitly laid down that the simple vows of Jesuits did constitute them religious in the full sense of the word. The Fathers at Salamanca reacted vigorously. Hearing of the forthcoming disputation only five days before it was due to take place, they determined to appeal to the apostolic nuncio in Madrid. But normally it required three days riding to reach Madrid and another three days for the return journey. The weather at that time, December, 1587, was anything but normal for Castile. It rained torrentially. However, the Jesuits would try their best. They hastily acquired the services of a very gallant courier, contacted other of their houses on the route to have relays of horses ready for him and, no doubt, fell to their prayers. The courier, by headlong riding day and night through the pelting rain, galloped up to their residence in Salamanca covered in mud from head to foot and utterly exhausted, but bearing triumphantly the nuncio's ban on the disputation, just five hours before it was due to open. That courier deserves to rank with Paul Revere and other heroes on horseback.

As a fighter Bañez met his match in the quiet and retiring Molina, who surprisingly proved a very lion in defence, and even carried the war into the opposing camp by tramping twice over the weary three hundred and twenty-five miles between Evora and Madrid in order to present in person an apologia for himself and Francisco Suarez, the other Jesuit theologian under attack, as well as a denunciation of Bañez and his enthusiastic lieutenant, the Mercedarian Zumel, to the Madrid Inquisition. There followed a war of pamphlets, of disputations, of ferocious anti-Jesuit sermons by a local Savonarola named Alonzo de Avendaño. From being a contention between a few Dominicans and a few Jesuits, the affair gradually swelled into a head-on collision between the two orders and began to worry both the Spanish hierarchy and the Spanish King who had recently borne with such admirable fortitude the defeat of his "invincible" Armada and desired more than anything in life unity and harmony among his people. One cannot help feeling that if Bañez and Molina had each possessed a glimmering of a sense of humour things need never have come to such a pass. It might be safely wagered that Bañez never laughed or wept over the *Celestina*, that marvellous adumbration of Shakespeare's *Romeo and Juliet*, though the action of the play took place entirely in his own Salamanca, and it is an equally safe bet that Molina never relaxed over one of the delightful comedies and farces of Gil Vicente, so popular then in Portugal. The two rivals were excellent and devout men, but somehow not entirely human.

In April, 1594 the apostolic nuncio to Spain wrote to Cardinal Aldobrandini, the all-powerful nephew and secretary of state of Pope Clement VIII, asking for the intervention of the Holy See. Philip II also wrote requesting that something should be done to put an end to the controversy which was confusing the minds of his subjects. The Grand Inquisitor sent in a similar plea, as did other bishops, and Cardinal de Castro, who addressed his letter directly to the Pope. After giving a résumé of the two rival systems concerning grace and free will, the Cardinal continued in the following not excessively impartial vein:

This, then, is how the Dominicans treat the teaching of the Jesuits. In their public discourses and lectures they qualify it as erroneous, and warn the people to avoid its defenders as men tainted with heresy. . . . As their authority is very great in Spain, the Jesuits have become suspects and are reckoned as people of no account. The two parties struggle before the tribunals of the Inquisition and the nuncio, the Jesuits endeavouring to have their own opinion declared orthodox and that of their adversaries condemned as destructive of free will. . . . Such, Holy Father, is the state of affairs. In my opinion it is full of danger, for two religious orders of great renown are in conflict over the gravest of questions, a question that bears on the integrity of the faith. And this battle is carried on in public, in sermons and lectures. All sorts of people are mixed up in it, both learned and ignorant, some siding with the Jesuits, and others holding their teaching to be suspect. Those who keep neutral are torn with anxiety, asking themselves on which side is the truth. The most serious aspect of the matter, however, is this. When the conflict comes to the knowledge of the faithful living in heretical countries, as it is bound to do, they are certain to be troubled and discouraged, learning that the Jesuit theory, in which they had put all their confidence, is regarded as erroneous by a religious order of great and universal authority. The heretics, on the other hand, will triumph and be able to laugh at the Catholics, seeing that the doctrine of those whom they regard as their most redoubtable adversaries is condemned by their own co-religionists as opposed to the faith. It is to you, Most Holy Father, that it belongs to prevent these evils, by prescribing according to an authentic interpretation of the canon of Trent what must be held as true in this matter. Then these two orders, which at the present day suffer themselves and make the faithful suffer by their discords, will, by their common submission to the decisions of your Holiness, re-enter the ways of peace, to the great advantage of everybody.

In accordance with the wishes of those eminent petitioners, Cardinal Aldobrandini bade the nuncio in Madrid announce that the whole affair had been taken over by the supreme tribunal of the Church. The superiors of both orders were to draw up complete statements of their respective cases and, pending a decision, were to forbid, by the Pope's express command, all further discussion, private as well as public, of the matter in dispute. Superiors and subjects alike were threatened with the severest penalties for any infraction of this ruling. There was then a lull for a time and even an attempt at reconciliation by both parties, but in the early months of 1597 the theologians who believed that the truth lay with Bañez in the controversy drew up, in accordance with the Pope's wishes, a statement and defence of their position, presented to the Holy Father in June. As suited the direct and vigorous methods in vogue during that epoch, the defence largely took the shape of a frontal attack on Molina's position. This was all right except for a less polite turn of language here and there, as when Suarez is called *sophisticus argumentator* and Molina is described as "led by the spirit of pride". What the authors of the Memorial wanted appears from the following reference to the *Concordia*:

> Prostrate at the feet of your Holiness, we humbly beg that if the book be found pernicious you would condemn it. . . . There is manifestly great danger in delay, as we who live in Spain know from daily experience. Young theologians, who in a spirit of youthful rivalry embrace these new and curious opinions in a matter so difficult to understand, will afterwards tolerate, only with great reluctance, the true and ancient method of reconciling grace with free will.

Robert Bellarmine, who had meantime been busily engaged in preparing his third folio volume for the press, now comes back into the picture. As he occupied at this time the post of papal theologian, the Holy Father bade him examine and report on the document presented by the disciples of Bañez. His report is very long but deserves brief consideration on two grounds. It gives in reasonably simple terms some idea of what the whole troublesome controversy was about, and it shows the dispassionate spirit of this dedicated Jesuit who never hesitated to allow Bañez his due or to criticize the theories of Molina, embraced with enthusiasm, but not much discrimination, by his friend Lessius. Seven questions are dealt with, the first being that of efficacious grace. On this matter, Bellarmine says, there are three opinions. Some scholastics taught that actual grace owed its efficacy to the consent of the will, and Molina seems to agree with them in the *Concordia*. If a man is willing to co-operate with the sufficient grace he receives, he thereby turns it into efficacious grace. Consequently, these authors hold that if two men are given the same grace it may happen that one will be converted and the other not. They argue thus because they consider that free will and the real sufficiency of sufficient grace cannot be saved in any other way. "This opinion seems to me to be false and therefore rightly reprehended in the censure of the Dominicans." According to the second view, not only does the efficacy of grace in no way depend on the consent of the will but that consent is physically and intrinsically determined by grace, physically in the sense that it works its effects by its own nature, *physis*. The Dominicans teach this opinion because they think it was what St Thomas Aquinas held, and that the true efficacy of grace cannot be defended on any other hypothesis:

It seems to me to be no less false and dangerous than the first opinion; for to begin with, it destroys sufficient grace as the other does efficacious grace. . . ; then, it appears to contradict the Council of Trent (Sess. VI, cap. v, can. 4). . . . Thirdly, this opinion does not seem to save free will nor can it be distinguished from the formulae used by the modern heretics. . . . I do not, however, dare to condemn it absolutely, as I know it is defended by great men. But I would be very glad to hear the voice and decision of the Holy See on these matters.

Before proceeding to his next section, St Robert comments on some propositions which the followers of Bañez had severely censured in the *Concordia*. The first is about two men endowed with equal graces. Molina apparently held that if they were confronted with the same temptation, one of them might resist by the sole power of his free will, and the other be overcome. The

rival theologians contended that this statement was erroneous
and contrary to Scripture and the Fathers:

> Though it appears false and badly worded I do not think
> that it should be condemned as erroneous in the sense in which
> the author understands it. . . . St Augustine speaks exactly like
> Molina (*De civ. Dei*, 1, xii, c. vi) . . ., and as we are accustomed
> to explain the holy Doctor's words in a favourable sense, lest
> they should appear to conflict with many others of his passages,
> so, too, can we put a good construction on Molina's words. . . .
> By the phrase, *ex sola libertate*, he does not exclude prevenient
> and concomitant grace but only a new prevenient grace . . .
> given to the man who resists and not to the other.

Another of Molina's propositions ran as follows: it might
happen that a man with more and greater graces than his fellow
should be damned, while that other, owing to his correspondence
with the lesser graces given him, should be saved:

> This statement seems to be false, unless carefully explained,
> for, speaking absolutely, the man who is saved received the
> greater grace, inasmuch as it was efficacious. Furthermore, the
> fact that he was ready to co-operate ought not, I think, to be
> attributed to his free will alone but also to the circumstance
> that the grace given him was congruous. Explained in this
> sense, or with reference only to God's external helps such as
> preaching and miracles, the proposition is absolutely certain
> from the Gospels. The Jews were not converted by all the
> words and miracles of our Lord, and the Ninevites were
> converted by a single sermon of Jonah without any miracles
> at all. . . . The objections which the Dominicans offer seem to
> me to be practically worthless.

The word "congruous" in that passage refers to the theory by
which St Robert himself, Suarez and the majority of Jesuit
theologians defended the freedom of the will under the influence
of grace. Grace, Bellarmine maintained, does not consist only in
the interior movement and excitation of the will but also in
the circumstances accompanying its bestowal. If the same help or
grace is accorded to two persons with the result that one of them

believes or resists temptation while the other does not, this is due to the fact that the person who believes received the impulse of grace in the manner, the place and the time which God saw were suited or congruous to his dispositions and would infallibly lead to acceptance.

The fourth proposition of Molina censured by his critics is that the distinction between efficacious and inefficacious grace is based on the consent of the will, because it is the consent or the refusal of consent which renders the grace efficacious or inefficacious. St Robert commented as follows:

> This statement seems to me utterly false and entirely opposed to the teaching of St Augustine. I should not, however, dare to condemn it as Pelagian, as the censors do, because there is no express text of Scripture or decree of the Church declaring the contrary. The passages urged by the Dominicans would easily be refuted by Molina, for they are not to the point. . . . Besides, this view was held by many of the Scholastic theologians whom the Church has not condemned, and I myself heard the learned Cardinal Toledo teach it in Rome. Finally, the opinion has already been examined and passed three times by the Spanish Inquisition, notwithstanding the censor's objections.

The slogans of the unhappily contending Dominicans and Jesuits were respectively the two strange Latin expressions, *Praemotio physica* and *Scientia media*. Here one closes one's eyes and plunges, hoping to come up alive. By the first expression, Bañez and subsequently all, or nearly all, Dominican theologians, meant that God moves the free human will to action by an antecedent divine impulse which of its own very nature, and not at all owing to circumstances of time, place or persons and their dispositions foreseen by God, brings about the will's free consent. At the present time, the distinguished Dominican theologian Père Garrigou-Lagrange maintains this theory as strongly as Domingo Bañez ever did, but St Robert Bellarmine who was deeply attached to the Dominican Order would have none of it, at least in the sphere of grace. He confessed that he could not see how free will came out unscathed in the theory, nor how God, according to it, would not be the cause of men's sins as well as of their virtuous actions. He also denied that it was taught by St Thomas, as Bañez claimed. *Scientia media* is a knowledge attributed to God by Molina and the Jesuits generally, as it were midway between the two traditional forms of divine knowledge taught by all Catholic theologians. These two forms are *scientia simplicis intelligentiae* and *scientia visionis*. By the former God knows whatever is possible; by the latter, whatever comes into being. Molina and many other Jesuits maintained that by *scientia media* God knows what choices or decisions a free agent would make in any conceivable set of circumstances. Molina put his own theory for once in concrete terms by saying that God is like a prince who gives horses to those he foresees will ride them to the destination he has in view. Obviously this knowledge does not destroy the freedom of the horsemen. As for the "intermediate knowledge", it was such Molina would contend that our Lord used when he declared to the unbelieving Jews that the pagans of Tyre and Sidon would have done penance in sackcloth and ashes, had they been privileged to witness the miracles wrought by him in Corozain and Bethsaida (Matt. xi. 21 sq.). It has to be said for the very able theologians of both parties that when they use such terms as God's foreseeing or predetermining they know perfectly well that there is no before or after in the knowledge of God. They are the unwilling victims of language which is immersed in time and can be used of God only analogically. To speak grandly, the sequences which Bañez, Molina, Suarez and Bellarmine had in view were not temporal but ontological.

We may now breathe more freely again and turn to matters less abstruse if not less contentious, in which Robert Bellarmine became involved. Bañez, who was utterly sincere, grew restless under the law of silence imposed on him from Rome and in October, 1597, appealed directly to Clement VIII to lift it for himself and his brethren. He gave six reasons in his lengthy petition why the law of silence should have been imposed on the Jesuits alone. As before, the Pope very fairly turned over the new document to Bellarmine for his comment, which proved to be not a little incisive. Bañez contended that the law was directed against innovations in theology such as the Jesuits were prone to, whereas the sons of St Dominic held the ancient doctrine taught in the Church since the time of St Augustine. While the law remained in force, they were in a manner deprived of their immemorial possession of this doctrine. The Jesuits, on the other hand, knowing that the law put them on an equality with the defenders of the venerable teaching of St Augustine and St Thomas, were striving with all their might to delay the sentence of the Holy See. Meantime, the new theories tended to be regarded by the faithful with as much respect as the ancient doctrine of the Church. St Robert commented on those arguments in the following forthright style:

This first reason appears plainly derogatory to the Pope, for it equivalently says that his command was both unjust and dangerous. . . . The authors of the Memorial coolly assume that they alone possess the ancient doctrine. But this is the very point in dispute. . . . The question is not whether St Augustine, St Leo, and the Council of Orange are to be followed. All the fathers of the Society, including Molina himself, profess to follow them, and if printed books are made the test, it will be found that the Jesuits, to say the least, are not behind the Dominicans in their anxiety to have ancient authorities at the back of all their arguments. The real question is whether God's physical predetermination of the human will is, or is not, in accordance with the Scriptures, the Councils and the Fathers. The Jesuits contend that it is not, and consequently is a new theory. As the matter is still *sub judice*, the authors of the Memorial show a good deal of impudence by talking as if it had been decided, and as if the fathers of the Society, whom they invariably style innovators, had already been condemned. What else is this but to anticipate the judgment of the Holy See and chant triumphal odes before obtaining the victory? Besides, they admit in this first reason that so many fathers, universities, prelates, and bishops, have been called as witnesses by each party that two years would scarcely suffice to read the evidence. Why, then, are they so ready to account the doctrine of the Society new when by their own confession multitudes of patristic testimonies are alleged on its behalf? As for their charge that the Jesuits are trying to delay a decision, I can only

say that I know for certain that the contrary is the truth. . . .
The Pope knows this better than anybody, and it is very strange
that they should endeavour by their flat affirmations to call his
judgment in question.

For his second argument Bañez cited the maxim of jurispru-
dence that it is safer to permit scandal than to let the truth be
abandoned. It was for this reason that St Paul withstood St Peter
to his face, and for the same reason he and the other true disciples
of St Thomas have felt obliged to complain to his Holiness that
they should be compelled to keep silence while new and curious
doctrines about grace were being openly disseminated. It was the
Jesuits' liking for innovations that had precipitated the present
tempest. The Dominicans had no need to commemorate the
many signal marks of esteem which the Church had shown for
the teaching of St Thomas Aquinas. But the Jesuits, their juniors
in the Lord's vineyard, laughed at St Thomas and none of them
considered himself a perfect theologian until he had invented and
taught theories totally opposed to St Thomas's teaching. Bañez
at this point gave some trivial specimens of Jesuit novelties that
had nothing to do with the controversy on grace, and concluded
with the following words, which must have brought a glint into
Bellarmine's eye: "Robert Bellarmine of the same Society, a
man otherwise pious and learned, denies that images are to be
adored in the manner taught by St Thomas". The accused
commented as follows:

It has pleased the authors of the Memorial to have a hit at
Robert Bellarmine before concluding, because he does not use
St Thomas's language about the worship due to images. But
Robert Bellarmine's answer is that he does not speak like St
Thomas because St Thomas does not speak like the Popes and
the oecumenical Councils. St Thomas had not been able to
examine the testimonies of the Popes and Councils, as it was
only after his death that they were either committed to writing,
or published if written much earlier. If he had seen them, he
would certainly have expressed himself differently, for he was a
most exact observer of ecclesiastical regulations. . . . So, too,
if he had witnessed the Church's public celebration of the feast

of the Immaculate Conception, he would probably have inclined to an opinion which he saw the greater part of the Church maintain. The Dominican Fathers ought not, then, to be so aggrieved if, with the majority of Catholics, we abandon the great Doctor's teaching on a few points.

The state of the question is this. In the second General Council of Nicaea it was expressly defined that "the images of Christ are to be venerated and adored in a becoming manner but not with the adoration of *latria*, which is to be paid to God alone". Again, in the acts of the same Council we find these words: "Let them show honourable reverence to images but not, according to our faith, true *latreutic* worship which belongs to the Divine Nature alone . . .". St John Damascene, at the same period, frequently repeated in his sermons that images were to be worshipped, but not *cultu latriae*. . . . A little later, the eighth General Council under Adrian II approved and confirmed the decrees of Nicaea, teaching that "the same kind of honour is due to images of Christ as is shown to the book of the Gospels and the sacred vessels". This was the doctrine of the Church about the year 800 A.D., when the iconoclast heresy was rampant. During the early times of the schoolmen, however, that is, after the year 1100 A.D., the acts of the aforesaid Councils, the letters of Pope Adrian, and the sermons of St John Damascene, were hidden away in archives, only to be discovered and published in the present century. The consequence of their disappearance from view in the Middle Ages was that Alexander of Hales began to teach that images of Christ should be adored *cultu latriae*, because Christ who is God is so adored. Thus was a novelty, unheard of in former ages, introduced into the Church; and because there were no plain ecclesiastical pronouncements to be adduced to the contrary, some theologians, including St Thomas, who was a disciple of Alexander of Hales, admitted the new opinion, though not a few cried out against it.

In our own day, when the iconoclast heresy came to life again, the Council of Trent, which embraced the doctrine of St Thomas willingly in other matters, did not think it well to imitate his manner of speaking about this matter. In its twenty-fifth session it avoided not only the word *latria* but the word *adoratio* also. . . . This, then, is the reason why Bellarmine did not adopt St Thomas's style. He thought it better to speak as Popes Gregory and Adrian and the General Councils of Nicaea and Trent had done. . . . Why, then, do the Friars Preacher take him to task, unless their aim be to stir up enmity against him, and through him against his order? But no matter. With the help of God we shall try to fulfil his counsel: "Pray for those who persecute and calumniate you".

It would be wearisome to follow Bañez and Bellarmine further in their paper debate, so we may conclude with St Robert's suggestions to Clement VIII as to the best way of ending the controversy, written at the same time as the answers to Bañez, in the last months of 1597:

It does not seem that the present dissensions can be healed by a decision on the theories in dispute, for the matter with which they deal is a most serious and important one that would require many years and protracted investigations for its elucidation, especially as both parties have dealt with it in book after book. Besides, it is not possible easily to convict either party of manifest error since both admit the authority of the Councils of Orange and Trent, and each alleges on its own behalf at least apparent testimonies from St Augustine and St Thomas. Further, it is difficult to believe that the Holy See could be induced to fix a charge of error in doctrine on a whole religious order and on entire universities. Now, according to my information, the University of Salamanca favours the Dominicans to a certain extent, while the University of Alcalá is almost completely on the side of the Jesuits. Therefore it is vain to hope for an end of the controversy by a definite decision on the points in dispute. It seems to me, then, with due deference to better judgments, that the dissensions and scandals could be stopped, that both parties could be satisfied, the security of doctrine maintained, and the Holy See relieved of great trouble and uneasiness, if the Pope would deign to issue an edict to the following effect: First, he would seriously and paternally exhort the contending parties to be mindful of brotherly charity in their mutual relations, to avoid dangerous teaching, and to turn their literary weapons against the enemies of the

Church alone. Secondly, he might forbid each order in virtue of holy obedience, or if it be thought well under pain of excommunication, to qualify the teaching of the other as temerarious or erroneous, much less heretical, in lectures, disputations, sermons, or even in public or private conversation. Each party however, would be permitted to refute the opinions of which it did not approve, by solid arguments. In this manner all opportunity for unseemly quarrelling would be removed.

A few months after the reception of Bellarmine's comments and suggestions, Clement VIII decided to relax the law of silence for both parties but, instead of accepting St Robert's other wise views which after seven fruitless years of heated discussion *had* to be accepted under another Pope, he appointed a commission of seven men, none of them Dominicans or Jesuits, to examine and report on Molina's *Concordia*. This was really evading the issue, as Molina was only one of many Jesuits involved, including Bellarmine himself, who did not agree with all the *Concordia's* elaborate conclusions. The commission accomplished their task with extraordinary rapidity. The Spanish inquisitorial censors of Molina's book had taken three years over their work, but a little more than three months sufficed for the Romans. "We are of opinion," they pronounced, "that in the interest of the Catholic religion, the book entitled *Concordia*, etc., by Luis Molina, and the doctrine contained therein, ought to be prohibited." Meantime, by March 28, 1598, a "big wooden box covered with tarpaulin" had arrived in Rome, containing all the reports, censures, memorials, and other documents bearing on the controversy, which the Pope had ordered to be collected and forwarded from Spain. Clement had shown surprise and annoyance that the commission should have taken their labours so lightly and, feeling that they could not possibly have given the matter the consideration it deserved, he bade them go over the ground again, using the contents of the big wooden box as a help to their judgments.

Eight months later, November, 1598, they reported that they were of the same opinion as before and that the book ought to be condemned. Obviously they had not studied the enormous mass

of papers in the box, for it would have taken eight years rather
than eight months to weigh them seriously. It is possible, then,
that the Jesuits had had good reason to complain, as they did, of
unfair treatment. Molina himself addressed a huge letter to the
Pope, in which he said some plain things about Bañez, and
professed himself willing to come personally to Rome, broken
by age and infirmity though he was, to defend his honour and the
truth.

Soon, the news spread like wild-fire throughout the length and
breadth of Spain that the case had gone against the Jesuits, and
that the condemnation of the *Concordia* by the Pope was only a
matter of time. Profoundly afflicted by those rumours, the Jesuit
fathers addressed letters to various persons in high station,
imploring them to intercede for their Society. The new King of
Spain, Philip III, wrote directly to the Holy Father on their behalf,
and so did the Empress Maria of Austria, and her son, the Archduke Albert, who had originally licensed the incriminated book.
Those and many other influential appeals outweighed in the
Pope's judgment the report of his hasty commission, and decided
him to adopt an entirely new plan. On January 1, 1599, it was
arranged that picked theologians from each of the contending
parties should expound and discuss their respective theories in the
presence of Cardinal Madruzzo, the Prefect of the Inquisition.

After Bellarmine's elevation to the cardinalate at the beginning
of March, 1599, he was nominated together with the Dominican
Cardinal de Ascoli to assist the harassed president in the conduct
of the debates. In spite of the efforts of all three to keep the
debaters to the point, those gentlemen continued to talk at cross
purposes, so that the conferences degenerated into a mere occasion
for mutual recriminations. To add to the trouble, two further
memorials were drafted by the rival schools in June, which,
when published, says a historian, resounded through Rome like
explosions of dynamite. The unhappy Pope, whose own sympathies leaned to the party of Bañez, tried to extricate himself
from the maze by having recourse again to the seven men who
had already twice condemned Molina. They condemned him a
third time in the summer of 1600, but only twenty of the proposi-

tions now, instead of the sixty-one and forty-two of the previous occasions. Once more, news spread, even as far as Chile and Peru, that the Jesuits were doomed. In Spain it was widely rumoured that Molina, who was on his death-bed at the time, had been burned in effigy in the streets of Rome. It was not true, and may well have been a misinterpretation of the grim fact that Giordano Bruno had been burned alive for heresy that year in the Campo dei Fiori, surely one of Clement VIII's most lamentable blunders. He might have allowed the unhappy man to linger on in the prison of the Roman Inquisition, where he had been already for seven years and fairly reasonably treated, rather than make a gratuitous gift of him to the atheists and anti-clericals of future ages.[1]

On one occasion in the year 1601, Cardinal del Monte, who himself afterwards reported the story, had the following interesting little conversation with Cardinal Bellarmine:

---

[1] Bruno, a runaway Dominican friar, had long ceased to believe in Christianity before he was imprisoned by the Roman Inquisition. His cosmological opinions, borrowed anyhow from Cardinal Nicholas of Cusa, were never questioned. To make him a martyr of science, as some have done, is merely silly, as he never engaged in any kind of scientific activity. Pope Clement VIII kept him confined for seven years, always in the hope of winning him back to the Church and to the order he had abandoned. He was well treated by the Inquisition, given a comfortable room, all the writing materials he requested, and a change of towels, bed and personal linen twice a week. He was allowed out of papal funds a pension of four crowns a month, which enabled him to order whatever food he liked (Angelo Mercati: *Il sommario del Processo di Giordano Bruno*. In, *Studi e Teste*, 101, 1942, pp. 126 sqq.). Four crowns amounted to forty *giulii*, and Fynes Moryson, the English traveller, recorded in his *Itinerary* that he lived in much comfort in Siena at this very time on ten *giulii* a month, all found. Frederick Copleston, s.j., whose great *History of Philosophy* is a liberal education in itself, devotes five pages to Bruno (vol. iii, 1953, pp. 258-63), relieves him of the charge of pantheism towards which his philosophy tended, and regards him as one of the leading and most influential thinkers of the Renaissance. Among many distinguished men sent to visit Bruno was St Robert Bellarmine, who succeeded in winning him back to his lost faith, except on one secondary neo-Platonic question. But he was an excessively proud and unstable character and soon relapsed into his anti-Christian attitude. It was then that Clement VIII, a humane and merciful man, whose spiritual director had been St Philip Neri, decided to let the law take its course, a tragic blunder on his part.

> *Del Monte:* I believe his Holiness is going to issue a definition
> on this matter of efficacious grace.
> *Bellarmine:* His Holiness will do no such thing.
> *Del Monte:* Why are you so sure, my Lord? The Pope, you
> must admit, has the power to define the question, and I
> know that his mind is made up to define it.
> *Bellarmine:* Yes, he has the power, but he will not exercise it.
> *Del Monte:* How on earth do you make that out?
> *Bellarmine:* Because he will die before he gets the opportunity.

Bellarmine had an interview with the Pope on November 8,
1601, of which he gave an account to Aquaviva the following day.
Clement had shown himself particularly friendly to the Society,
he said, "so profiting of this benevolence, I handed him a document I had composed ... which, if my sins do not stand in the way,
may be of some use to us. As his Holiness remarked to me that he
had read in St Augustine: *Solus Deus operatur in nobis velle*, I
propose to send him this evening another document explaining
those words."

Clement's friendliness did not last long, to judge by the huge
letter which St Robert addressed to him some weeks later. "Most
Holy Father," it begins, "With all humility and reverence I beg
that you would deign to read this letter, and then burn it, as I
do not wish it to be seen by any eyes but yours." Having thus
introduced himself, he immediately embarks on a long closely-
reasoned discussion of certain passages in St Augustine. Those
passages dealt with the eminently respectable but far too optimistic
British lay theologian Pelagius and his opinions on grace. The
point was, what had Augustine considered to be the views of
Pelagius on the question? Some writers strove to show that,
judging by that Saint's account of him, Pelagius must have held
opinions very similar to those championed by the Society of Jesus.
The texts and arguments by means of which Bellarmine shatters
this contention are too abstruse for reproduction here, but the
remainder of the letter, though long, is worth giving for the
light which it sheds on his character:

And now that I have once begun to speak to my Lord, I beg

your Holiness to deliver the Church from the scandal of these quarrels as soon as possible, to restore concord between the two orders, and to deprive the heretic of his gaiety at our expense. If I, the creature and faithful servant of your Holiness, may be permitted to say what I think, I beg you to consider whether the way you have chosen for deciding this controversy may not prove a long and laborious one for you. Your holy predecessors did not rely chiefly on study and reasoning in their endeavours to penetrate the profundities of dogma. They sought to discover what was the common opinion of the Church and, above all, of her bishops and doctors, for which reason the popes from the time of St Peter have availed themselves of the help of councils, in order to determine the truths of the faith. I may say further that many popes, without fatiguing themselves in study, have happily condemned errors not a few, with the assistance of councils and universities, while others who studied much have brought both themselves and the Church into considerable difficulties. Pope Leo X, for example, condemned the Lutheran heresy without burying himself in books. It was enough for him to approve the censures passed by the Catholic universities, Cologne, Louvain, and others. . .

John XXII is an example of the opposite kind. He was convinced that the souls of the Blessed do not enjoy the vision of the divine essence and, thinking that this was what St Augustine taught, tried hard to establish it. Knowing that the University of Paris was opposed to the view, he refused to submit it to the judgment of a council or of learned academies, and spent his time diligently searching for passages of St Augustine in support of it. Villano records that he used to give ecclesiastical benefices to those who brought him such testimonies, the result of his zeal being that few had the courage to speak freely to him about the matter, and thus he slammed the door of truth in his own face. However, during his eighteen years' reign he did not attain his desire, because the divine protection which watches over the Holy See did not permit him to define a matter which was contrary to the truth. . .

Your Holiness knows, too, the danger in which Sixtus V, of blessed memory, placed both himself and the Church by his decision to revise the Bible according to his private lights. I, certainly, do not know if the Church ever ran a greater danger. Most Holy Father, I am not recalling those instances in order to turn you from study and investigation, but to convince you that such a way out would take far too long and only result in grave harm to the faith. You say that the question appertains to the faith, but if that be so it is everybody's concern, according to the dictum of Pope Nicholas. Therefore it should be discussed in the full light of day, and not secretly, with a mere handful of advisers. Of course all Catholics are in duty bound to believe and obey when your Holiness issues a decree, even though you alone be responsible for it. Still, such action on your part would inevitably lead to murmurs and protests from the various sections of the Church and the universities, who would complain that their views on the matter had been entirely ignored. That, at least, was not the customary, beaten track followed by our fathers, from which your Holiness is not wont to stray. As, notwithstanding your studious labours, it is fitting that the question should be discussed in public, either in an episcopal synod or a congregation of learned men from various universities, it would have been better if this course had been adopted earlier, and it is well to adopt it now at once, without waiting until you have finished reading all you had intended to read. There is no necessity for your Holiness to put yourself to such trouble, for you have already seen and read enough.

In conclusion, I beg your Holiness, for the love you bear to God and the Church and the holy hatred you have of dissension and heresy, that you would commend this affair to the Almighty and firmly resolve to extinguish the present conflagration. It might, in the first place, be allayed by temporizing and imposing silence on both parties to the dispute. The other method would be to convoke an episcopal synod or, should you so prefer, to call to Rome delegates from all the Catholic universities. If this does not meet with your approval, the points of disagreement might at least be put before the doctors in writing, as well as the arguments which have already been offered on both sides. After such public inquiry and investigation, your Holiness might decide the question as God should inspire you.

Meantime, however, I beg you with all my heart to stop the mouths of those who assert that your mind is already made up, that your sympathies lean decidedly to one party in the dispute, and that you listen only with reluctance to what the other party has to say. Were that true, nobody would dare to express his real convictions about the controversy. For my part, I confess that I had thought of retiring from the struggle and refusing to discuss the question with anyone in the future as soon as I was informed of certain harsh remarks that your Holiness had made about *scientia media*, a theory which is commonly taught in the schools as being consonant with the Scriptures, the Fathers, and plain logic. If I, your Holiness's devoted servant, who have spent more than thirty years in the study of these matters, lost heart and thought of withdrawing through fear of giving you offence, what will not other men do? Your great prudence and wisdom will know the remedy. Your most humble and devoted servant, Robert Cardinal Bellarmine.

At the beginning of the year 1602, the Pope, appalled by the size of the dossier upon which he was expected to base his decision and, perhaps, influenced to some extent by Bellarmine's letter, finally made up his mind to have the whole question thrashed out orally in his presence. That was the origin of the celebrated *Congregatio de Auxiliis*. Bellarmine did not take part in its meetings during the first years because the Pope had appointed him Archbishop of Capua on the death of the former occupant of that see, who had not resided in it for thirty years. Some writers, including the good historian Ludwig von Pastor, have surmised that the Pope had seized the opportunity to remove from Rome a too candid critic of his policies, but Bellarmine himself entertained no such suspicions and departed joyfully for Capua within a week of his consecration by the Holy Father.

As soon as the Cardinal was well out of the way, a Spanish adherent of Bañez tried by every means in his power to procure the condemnation of the *Controversies* as containing propositions contrary to the Council of Orange and savouring of Pelagianism. Other men of the same theological persuasion endeavoured, on the contrary, personally or through their friends, to show that Bellarmine was opposed to Molina, and thus his authority continued to be invoked on both sides, to the confusion of everybody.

The Cardinal's agent in Rome kept him informed about the illegitimate use that was being made of his name and drew from him the following avowal:

> The fathers of the Society who defend Molina do not contend that all his views are true, but only that they are not Pelagian. It is a great impertinence for anyone to say that the opinion of the fathers is heretical. As for what I have written myself on the matter, the assertion that I go against St Augustine or St Thomas could only come from people who had read neither of those doctors, or who understood nothing of what was said. Leaving aside the question of *praedeterminatio physica*, which is not being discussed in the congregations taking place just now in the presence of his Holiness, the Dominican fathers constantly bring forward my books as evidence against Molina on the other matters that engage their attention at the moment. Indeed, the Pope himself has told me several times that the Dominicans consider me to be their ally. It is not true that Father General begged me to be favourable to the Society. In fine, I care very little what anybody says, and your Reverence should not worry either. The truth will at last prevail and every good Christian is bound to embrace it, whether it be found on the side of the Dominicans or on the side of the Jesuits. Meantime, while the Pope has pronounced no decision, those who charge either party with heresy are guilty of the greatest rashness. Our Holy Father has the assistance of the Divine Spirit, and besides, he is naturally very prudent. Consequently we may rest assured that whatever sentence he may issue will be true, just, and helpful to religion.

As the months went by and the clamour grew, St Robert was missed more and more by the moderate men of all parties. Some of them begged him to return at once, Baronius, for instance, writing thus: "I long to have you in Rome again in order to be able to pour into your ear the story of a heart that is drowned in a sea of troubles". The Jesuits, of course, felt the loss of their great advocate more keenly than anybody. Bañez was still aggressively active in Spain, and in Rome events shaped more ominously every day for the cause of Molina. That sorely-tried man had gone to his rest in October, 1600, before the meetings of the *Congregatio de Auxiliis* had begun. When he was sent to Madrid to occupy the chair of moral theology at the Jesuit college there, he carried his manuscripts in an old corn sack, "as if they were so much rubbish to be thrown into a river". Just before his death the superior of the house asked him what were his wishes with regard to those fruits of his genius. "Let the Society do with them whatever it likes," he answered, and then he passed out of the storm into peace. Just four years later Bañez followed him to the grave. "Shortly before he died," wrote the Jesuit provincial of Castile to Aquaviva, "he spoke of the Society in friendly terms, saying that he had always wished our fathers well, and that if he had waged war against them in the controversy *de Auxiliis*, it was only because he considered his own opinion to be the truth."

In December, 1604, when the Molinists were at the nadir of their fortunes, they found a powerful ally in Bellarmine's friend, Cardinal du Perron, who was a convert from Calvinism and so well versed in the problems connected with grace and free will. He had come to Rome on a mission from King Henry IV and spoke to the Pope with as much frankness as St Robert himself could have used: "If your Holiness forbids as erroneous the Jesuit method of reconciling grace and free will," he said, "all the Calvinists and Lutherans of France and Germany will applaud your sentence, and see in it a formal approbation of their own teaching on human freedom". Bellarmine was greatly relieved to hear of du Perron's attitude in the controversy. Answering a letter from that learned friend on February 10, 1605, the Cardinal said:

I render heartfelt thanks to God for having brought you to Rome while the dispute *de Auxiliis* is in progress. Though I have myself several times made plain to the Holy Father how closely the theory of physical predetermination approximates to Calvinism and how much it is disliked by the majority of the Catholic universities, especially those in direct conflict with the heretics, the other party in the dispute have procured that full confidence should not be placed in me because I am a Jesuit and consequently an interested person. To your Lordship, however, no exception can possibly be taken, as everybody knows that you are better qualified than any other man to express an opinion on this controversy, and that you have no interest at heart but the truth and the Catholic faith. God has sent you, then, that the passions of many other people and their rivalry with the Jesuits may not obscure the truth, in a matter of such moment.

Between the years 1602 and 1605 there were sixty-eight sessions of the new *Congregatio de Auxiliis* and thirty-seven full-dress debates, but what Pope Clement himself thought or intended at the end of them all will never be known, for he died very devoutly on March 5, 1605, without having decided anything, just as St Robert Bellarmine had declared so confidently four years earlier, another instance of his uncanny power of divining the future. After the few weeks' reign of Leo XI, Cardinal Borghese, who had been closely connected with the *de Auxiliis* question throughout, was elected Pope, and took the name of Paul V. Bellarmine had been summoned to Rome for the conclaves, and he remained there at Pope Paul's urgent request. When, in September, the meetings of the Congregation were resumed, both he and his friend du Perron took their places as assessors, to the great joy of the Jesuits. The affair dragged on wearily and indecisively for another two years, a wordy warfare that only exacerbated feelings and made a genuine reconciliation of the contending parties less a possibility than ever. The accounts of what happened during this period are vague in the extreme, and largely a matter of conjecture. All that is known for certain is that Paul V called a special meeting of the cardinals concerned with the controversy on August 28, 1607, the feast of St Augustine. Each of the eight assembled was then asked for his opinion as to the best way of ending the long dispute, the Pope himself writing down their answers. Cardinal de Ascoli, a Dominican, was the only one who voted for the condemnation of Molina; two showed themselves favourable to the theories of Bañez without, however, censuring the opposed doctrine; three remained quite neutral considering that the question should be further discussed; and du Perron, while strongly supporting Molina, suggested that the best plan would be to postpone a decision *sine die*, in the hope that, by the mercy of God, the two parties might eventually come to terms. Bellarmine's vote was an echo of his attitude throughout the controversy, and the ultimate decree of the Pope allowing each party to retain and teach its own views, but strictly forbidding them to qualify those of the other party as temerarious or, still less, heretical, was framed exactly on the lines proposed by St Robert to Clement VIII ten years earlier. Though Pope Paul declared that he would decide the issue at an opportune time he never found such an occasion during his long pontificate nor has any of his successors down to the present day.

All that the opposition of twenty years had succeeded in doing to Molina's *Concordia* was to render the name of its author immortal, and secure for him a distinguished place in the company of those who have discoursed with greatest power and penetration on the things of God. Remembering this, it is scarcely a matter for surprise that some of the Spanish Jesuits or, at any rate, their friends should have lost their heads and posted bills on the walls of Salamanca decorated with two flaming, jubilant words: MOLINA VICTOR! In Villagarcia, a port on the north-west Atlantic coast of Spain, a bull-fight was organized to celebrate the occasion and at other colleges there were masques and fireworks in abundance. As soon as Aquaviva heard of those provocative festivities, he issued stern letters of disapproval and suspended some of the rectors who had connived at them. Thus ended the great controversy on grace in a schoolboys' holiday, and there was a fitness in the fireworks greater than was realized when they flashed in the darkness of Villagarcia centuries ago. For what are the best and profoundest of man's speculations on God's methods and purposes but a momentary flare in a night of impenetrable mystery—a night in which faith can discern stars, but which neither *scientia media* nor *praemotio physica* can turn into day. When all is said, both Dominicans and Jesuits, and everybody else for that matter, are left with the words of St Paul on their

H

lips as the final comment of reason and revelation on their theories:
"Oh, the depth of the riches of the wisdom and of the knowledge
of God! How incomprehensible are his judgments and how
unsearchable his ways!" (Rom. xi. 33).[1]

---

[1] This is not to say that the mystery of human wills, genuinely free, yet
utterly dependent on God for their operation, ought to have been left alone
by the theologians and the solution awaited in Heaven, as Cardinal Cajetan
appears to have suggested. Every problem in which God is concerned ends in
mystery, and the difficulty facing the theologian is not to admit this but to
admit it too soon. It was in that spirit that Robert Bellarmine rejected the great
Cajetan's defeatism. "Although this problem [the harmony of free choice and
divine providence] is obscure and very abstruse, as Cajetan rightly warned, still
an effort ought to be made to bring some light even to obscure matters"—
tamen conandum est rebus etiam obscuris aliquod lumen adferre (Bellarmine, *De gratia
et libero arbitrio*, lib. iv, cap. 14). Bellarmine's *tamen conandum* "became with
Molina a battle cry against a world in which it was strangely difficult to defend
human liberty". An admirable and discriminating discussion of Molina's
theories is to be found in "Molina and Human Liberty", an essay contributed
by Professor Anton Pegis to the collection, *Jesuit Thinkers of the Renaissance*,
published by Marquette University Press, Milwaukee, in 1939. A splendid
modern critical edition of Molina's epoch-making *Concordia*, edited by Johannes
Rabeneck, was published at Madrid in 1953.

CHAPTER VIII

A SHEPHERD OF SOULS

IN the *Annales Ecclesiastici* of his friend Baronius, Bellarmine is
honourably but strangely mentioned under the year 968. The
reason why he was thus relegated to the Dark Ages is of
interest as showing how obsessed the Oratorian Cardinal was
with thoughts of the companion so soon to be wrested from his
side. The April of 1602 saw the Annalist engaged on the Pontificate of John XIII. Capua came into the story, because that was the
Pope who had raised it to the dignity of an archiepiscopal see.
As he wrote the name, the Oratorian's heart took control of his
history, and he continued in the following style:

> At the present moment while we write of these affairs, this
> same Church of Capua has acquired a new and most glorious
> title to renown, which must not be passed over in silence. The
> see being vacant owing to the death of Caesar Costa its arch-
> bishop, who was formerly my professor of civil law in Rome,
> his Holiness Pope Clement VIII chose for the government of
> the celebrated diocese Cardinal Robert Bellarmine, a most
> learned and religious man whose virtues are famed throughout
> the whole Christian world.

The Capua to which Bellarmine went, nineteen miles north of
Naples, was not the lotus-land that had enervated Hannibal and
his Carthaginians. That ancient city had been completely destroyed
by the Saracens in A.D. 840, but refounded close to the original
site sixteen years later and heavily fortified. The Cardinal was
given a rapturous reception by his new flock, for his reputation
as a saintly man had gone before him, and Italians, however
imperfect their own lives, dearly love to be within reach of a
saint. It is a part of their compelling realism.

The day following Bellarmine's arrival was a Sunday, and the
feast of the patron of the archdiocese, St Stephen. It was known

as "Garland Sunday" when all the girls and women wore garlands
in their hair and the whole city went green as by magic. Capua,
congested at the best of times, was invaded by the people of the
towns and villages around, who crowded by common accord
towards the cathedral where their new pastor was to celebrate
his first pontifical Mass. The Pope had granted a plenary indulgence to all who attended it, which was a crowning attraction.
So great was the press that the cathedral canons could not get to
their stalls at all, or even into the church, and a splendid procession
which had been planned to parade through the city at the end of
Mass could not get out and had to be abandoned. "A day never
to be forgotten" was how a Capuan chronicler who was present
described that feast of St Stephen in 1602.

Many years after Robert Bellarmine's departure from Capua,
an eminent French archbishop begged him earnestly for a
character sketch of an ideal pastor of souls, that he might engrave
it in his memory. The embarrassed Cardinal answered:

> I neither know how to comply with your request nor how to
> deny it. It is a very noble request, but since I failed to become a
> holy archbishop myself, in spite of the utmost endeavours,
> how am I to show others the way to success? Still, since your
> Lordship presses me to tell you at least the methods I followed
> in my attempts to become a good shepherd to my people while
> I was archbishop in the ancient and famous city of Capua, I may
> say that they were these: I turned my eyes and my mind to the
> lives of the best and worthiest bishops of whom history has
> record. They became, as it were, my mirror, in which was the
> pattern that I must copy and become like, with the divine
> assistance. Accordingly, I always kept the lives of saintly
> bishops near my hand, and some volume of Surius lay open on
> my table the whole year through. . . . This is the best counsel
> I could give your Lordship. If you will turn your eyes to those
> mirrors and endeavour to copy what you see reflected in them,
> you will undoubtedly become a holy archbishop.

Sermons at any time except during Advent and Lent were
something wholly new in the city, but this archbishop who was
also a very famous Cardinal preached to his flock unfailingly

every Sunday and feast day during his three years in Capua, Lent only excepted, when he provided special preachers. During the week it was his custom to repair to the outlying towns and villages, and even hamlets, to instruct the simple people very lovingly in the truths of the faith. Michaele Monaco, a man of culture who regularly attended St Robert's sermons in the cathedral, left the following account of them in his book, *Sanctuarium Capuanum*:

During the first year he explained the Epistles of St Paul which are read at Mass, during the second year, the Gospels of the Sundays, and during the third, the Sermon on the Mount. Every syllable was directed to the one end of sanctifying his hearers. The great doctor sometimes spoke on very abstruse matters, but he had a wonderful way of making them easy to grasp. I used often to be astounded, observing how he was able to expound in plain, homely language things that other men can hardly express even in the technical terms of the schools. Like a most loving shepherd, he would many a time admonish his sheep, but the reprehension always came clothed in sweetness. He had no threats nor hard words for anybody. Rather did he beg them to hate sin and turn to the love of virtue, with a mournful countenance as though he were asking for an alms.

So meek and kind of heart was the Cardinal that some over-zealous people took scandal at his mildness, and complained that he did not punish offences. Rumour of the complaints reached his ears, but being meek he did not become angry. All he did was to defend his forbearance against the wrath of the zealots, which was during a sermon he preached on the feast of St Gregory Nazianzen. The feast that year fell on a Sunday, and the Cardinal, with a certain pleasing dexterity, made his panegyric of the Saint into an apology for his own way of acting.

First, he expounded the Gospel, *Vos estis sal terrae*, and showed how all that was said in it applied to St Gregory Nazianzen. Then he told his flock that he had ever cherished a great devotion towards this Saint, explaining that he had been moved to venerate and love him chiefly because he had discovered a certain resemblance between the circumstances of

Gregory's life and those of his own. His words were as follows:
"Gregory was a religious, I am a Jesuit; he was a bishop and I,
though unworthy, have been chosen for the same office; he
was a writer on theology, and I have also written some books
in defence of the Church; he composed a splendid poem on
virginity and I, when young and fond of poetry, devoted my
very first verses to the same subject; finally, Gregory's meekness and clemency of heart were accounted criminal negligence
by some people, and I hear that there are not a few who complain about me on the ground that I do not punish offenders.

"But how am I to punish offences of which I have not been
notified? And supposing that they have been denounced to me,
would you have me to impose penalties when, after diligent
inquiry, I find that the case was not at all as it was represented?
Again, is vindictive punishment the only kind with which you
will be satisfied? It is true that the pains and penalties decreed
by secular magistrates are primarily vindictive, but it is the
duty of bishops to punish with a view to the improvement of
the offender. We have the example of Ambrose, Augustine,
our Nazianzen, and other holy bishops, to guide us in the
matter. Consequently, it is my purpose to inflict only such
penalties as I may hope and trust will bring about the conversion, lasting improvement, and salvation of sinful souls."
That was what our meek Bishop said in his sermon.

The meek bishop showed himself a different man when he
spoke of the gambling to which his flock were heavily addicted.
He thundered against it, detailing the murders, suicides, brawls
and blasphemies to which the vice led, and took practical steps
to have the gambling dens closed by the civil authorities. During
his investigations the Archbishop discovered that one of his own
impecunious canons was in the habit of visiting the houses of
gentlemen who gambled privately, not to stake anything, but in
hopes of picking up some small present such as a pair of gloves,
occasionally. The Archbishop made a bargain with the offender:
"Whenever you are tempted to go to those houses in future,
come to my house instead, and I promise to give you each time
just such a present as you might have been hoping to obtain from
the gamblers".

A workman engaged on renovations at the cathedral which St Robert had set on foot stole a valuable piece of porphyry and sold it to one of the canons named Carresio for a single ducat, alleging that it had been given to him by some men who were digging on the site of the ancient church of St Peter in old Capua. The cheapness of the price asked made Carresio suspicious that the stone had been taken from the cathedral, and on investigation so it proved. The stonemason was cited before the Archbishop, who gravely admonished him on the wickedness of stealing, especially from a church. "Then," wrote Carresio who was present, "the Archbishop knowing him to be a poor man gave him with his own hands a huge quantity of coppers, which the culprit himself told me afterwards amounted to ten ducats. He then made him promise never to steal again and, as I learned subsequently, settled a sum of six ducats a month on this man, who had stolen his piece of porphyry." Once the Archbishop had to admonish a priest for some extravagant language in a sermon. Telling the story to a friend, he added, "then to sweeten the medicine I sent him a present of some trout".

In flagrant defiance of the decrees of the Council of Trent, only ten of Bellarmine's forty diocesan canons were priests, the others, subdeacons at the most, having been intruded into the chapter by family influence and intrigue. The Archbishop got rid of them all, and made the bestowal of benefices depend entirely on sheer merit and probity of character. He kept a list of all his priests by him, with notes and comments constantly expanded, as he learned to know them better, on the character, attainments and virtue of each priest. No benefice involving the care of souls was ever bestowed except by competition to discover the worthiest candidate. St Robert made a point of assisting at the examinations, with six of his canons, all men of known theological ability, in attendance. He had no seminary of his own, and was accordingly all the more exigent in his requirements from those who put themselves forward for the priesthood. He had learned of the frauds that used to be practised to create fictitious titles for ordination and of the wretched poverty into which many of the ill-educated and morally unfitted clergy had fallen in consequence, some of them even resorting to banditry for a livelihood. All this he reformed in the brief space of three years by tireless exertions, which left little bitterness because so permeated with charity and compassion.

That good observer of the Archbishop's activities, Michaele Monaco, tells of some unfair taxation imposed on the clergy of Capua which fell very heavily on poorer priests, and of the method his Lordship used to relieve them without antagonizing the civil authorities. He went to the town hall, asked to see the documents in which the tax was assessed, and then and there paid the entire sum out of his own resources. The authorities saw the point and abolished the tax.

Bellarmine was technically an abbot, as well as archbishop, for he had been endowed by the Pope with the abbey of St Benedict in Capua, no longer occupied by monks, that he might have its revenues as a means to his support. It appears to have been his principal means and enabled him to indulge freely in his charitable courses, as well as in the renovation of his cathedral and other churches which had fallen into disrepair. He had a real passion for the beauty of God's house, and in the Louvain sermons of his youth had denounced in strong terms priests who neglected to keep everything used in the service of the altar spotlessly clean and, as far as their means allowed, of the best quality. He discovered that a church in the large town of Teano was being used as a barn. This he completely restored and furnished, appointing a good priest in charge whose salary he paid himself. In the contiguous town of Sessa he found a church dependent on his own abbey of St Benedict with a priest in charge who had to live in lodgings and on a miserable annual stipend of forty Neapolitan ducats. Writing to his own deputy abbot in Capua, he said, "I have now instructed the priest to take possession of a house near the church, with a little garden attached, which belongs by right to him and not to the abbots of St Benedict's, though they have long claimed it. In order that he may feel sure in his tenancy, and not merely while I happen to be abbot, I am going to obtain a brief from the Holy See, transferring the residence once and for all to the priests who serve that church."

The devout and stately performance of the sacred liturgy was one of St Robert Bellarmine's chief ambitions. On Sundays and festivals he sang the entire office in choir with his canons, while on the other days of the year he always took his part at least in Matins and Lauds, though he had already said them privately in his room. It was no part of his strict duty to attend, but there were three reasons, he said, which determined him to do so. The first was to make sure by his presence that the office was recited becomingly, the second was to promote the use of the Gregorian chant, and the third was to earn a little extra money for his poor. The cathedral was bitterly cold in winter, and to cold weather he had been from childhood peculiarly sensitive. His fingers used to swell up and become livid, but for all that he was in his place each morning without any of the gloves or wraps with which his canons defended their extremities. Nor would he ever go near the *scaldini*, or little pans of charcoal, to which the others resorted when they were nearly frozen. To encourage himself in fidelity to a practice that cost him so much, he drew up a list of saintly bishops who had been accustomed to sing office in choir, among the eleven whom he found being two Irishmen, St Malachy and St Laurence O'Toole. The lives of those great servants of God were his constant reading and meditation.

His scrupulous care for seemliness and exactitude in all the functions of the Church was evident not only at Capua but throughout his life. Many years later in Rome, he discovered that his brother Jesuits there were not carrying out the prescriptions of the *Ceremoniale* as accurately as he would have liked. They were addicted to *Missae Cantatae* in place of High Masses proper with three ministers. Finding that the gentle hints which he gave to the fathers concerned bore no fruit, he addressed the following letter to the General of the Society of Jesus at the time, Mutius Vitelleschi:

Rome, May 28, 1617

As the Corpus Christi procession is to take place soon, and as, according to report, it will be larger and more solemn than ever this year, it seemed to me an opportune moment to set down in writing the reasons why deacons and subdeacons, vested in

HX

dalmatics, should officiate at the solemn Masses and take part in the processions.

1°. This is what is prescribed, without any exception being allowed, by the Ceremonial of Pope Clement VIII and the Ritual of Pope Paul V. That being so, I do not see what right our Society has to adopt a contrary practice, in the view of all Rome.

2°. The rite is observed in the churches of the entire Catholic world, in cathedral, collegiate, parish, and conventual churches, no matter to what religious order they may belong. How, then, is our Society to be permitted to act differently, especially since we use the Roman Missal, Breviary, and Ritual, and since we profess to follow in everything the directions of the Holy Apostolic See?

3°. It does not look well to see the priest at Masses on solemn occasions taking the deacon's place in singing the Gospel and the *Ite Missa est*. This is done, outside our Society, only by country priests who are not in a position to do otherwise.

4°. Important prelates often speak about this novelty and fad of our Society, and I never know what to say in reply.

5°. The Society has no constitution nor rule directing us to dispense with deacons and subdeacons. It is nothing more than a local custom. I myself, when in Flanders, have sung Mass with deacon and sub-deacon, and I have acted as sub-deacon when the provincial was celebrant.

To all these reasons it might be answered that the Society is an active order engaged in external work of a more important kind, and consequently its members have not the time to learn all the ceremonies of High Mass. There are two ways of meeting such a plea. First, the ceremonies are neither so numerous nor so difficult that they could not be learned in half an hour. This I know by experience, as I have sung many pontifical Masses myself in the Pope's chapel, and also in Capua. The fathers and brothers might learn the ceremonies during a single recreation, if they were coached by someone who knew them well. This might even be a more useful way of spending the time than discussing the gossip of Rome.

In the second place, if it be found too difficult to learn such a number of ceremonies, why not give up singing Masses and be content with saying Low ones? There is nothing incompatible between a solemn procession and a Low Mass, as may be seen from the example of the Pope on the feast of Corpus Christi. In truth, it is much better not to celebrate solemn Masses at all than to celebrate them unrubrically.

That is what I had to suggest to your Paternity, and I beg you to put the case and the reasons I have given you before your assistants. Afterwards, you will be able to act as God shall inspire you. I will not trouble you any more with this subject, on which I have spoken often enough already at the risk of being a burden to you. I send your Paternity my affectionate greetings, praying that God may grant you the fullest realization of your holy desires, and begging you to remember me in his presence.

Far more than the beautifying of his cathedral, the Archbishop had at heart the renewal of fervour in some religious communities that had lost their primitive spirit. One of these, the Benedictine Convent of San Giovanni in Capua, had as a punishment for indiscipline been forbidden by the authorities in Rome to receive any more novices. At the time of Bellarmine's coming to the city, the number of the nuns had dwindled to six. Being in great distress, they begged him most earnestly to do what he could for them with the cardinals of the Congregation of the Reform. These six survivors were good women, and their trouble was by itself a sufficient argument to bring the Archbishop to their side. He immediately dispatched the diplomatic Guidotti to Rome with letters to all concerned, and told him not to come back until he had obtained a favourable answer. Signor Pietro's task was by no means easy, as the Congregation had formed a very bad impression of the convent, but they allowed that novices might be received as soon as the buildings had been adapted to the rule, because previously it was the rule that had been adapted to the buildings. Bellarmine at once set to work. He completely isolated the convent by purchasing houses which had been erected close to it, and then began the interior renovations necessary, such as installing grilles and turning certain comfortable suites of rooms into dormitories. That done, and much money spent in the doing, he gave his attention to the constitutions, and brought two nuns from the strict convent at Sorrento to introduce at St John's the reforms he considered necessary. So tactfully and kindlily did he manage the whole delicate business that the two visitors whom he had put in charge were able to testify within eight months that the fervour of the community needed a curb rather than a spur. In less than half that time twenty-two novices had received the habit.

Not very long after, these good ladies began to wax a little haughty in prosperity, and thus drew on their heads from the Archbishop a strong letter of admonition. The nuns apparently declined to receive any girls who were not of noble birth and, though Bellarmine was quite willing to admit the reasonableness of taking such a point into consideration, he would not agree that it was the only or the most important point:

My Very Dear Sisters in Christ,
  Religious life cannot co-exist with the spirit of the world, nor can it be ruled by it, but by the Spirit of God alone. The spirit of the world makes account of nobility and wealth, but the Spirit of God esteems virtue and holiness of life above everything else. And so we see that Christ our Lord did not exclude from his company either fishermen or artisans. Indeed, St Paul says that he did not choose many noble or powerful ones, and St James adds that he elected men poor in substance but rich in faith and virtue. The Church, guided by the Spirit of God, has never excluded any person from holy orders, canonries, bishoprics, the cardinalate, nor even the papal office, by reason of low birth. St Augustine, in one of his letters, says that it would be intolerable in the Church of God to prefer a noble to a plebeian, if the plebeian should happen to be the better or more learned man of the two. Nor has any sainted founder excluded persons of low birth from his order, provided they be otherwise fitted for God's service, excepting only the military orders. St Augustine, in the rule that he wrote for his nuns, expressly lays it down that those who had been of good social standing in the world must never dare to contemn others whose condition had been lowly, as they were all the affianced of the same Lord.
  Now, taking this for granted, I thought that the nuns of San

Giovanni would have really laid aside the spirit of the world, and have gone out from it not less in body than in soul. Often when writing to the holy Congregation in Rome have I praised you as such, and for this reason, too, I ventured to leave you the right of refusing or accepting postulants, having first warned you to have an eye to the common interests of the convent, to the virtues and good qualities of the individuals, and not to make any distinction between high and low.

But I have since seen to my great disgust that you pay no attention to anything except good birth, thus proving that you have still within you the spirit of the world and have not learned the humility of your heavenly Spouse. Of another thing I am very sure, too, and it is that, if perchance to punish our sins God should call to Paradise the two reverend mothers who are now your superiors and you had authority to elect an abbess, you would rather have a faulty one of good birth than a saint were she low-born. And yet you know very well that it was nuns of gentle birth who caused the ruin of your convent as well as of St Mary's, whereas that of the Gesù, where women of the working-classes enter, has kept up a better reputation.

If the Blessed Virgin were on earth and wanted to become a nun, she would never be able to get into your convent, being a carpenter's wife, but the nuns of the Gesù would take her without any difficulty. This will show you in what favour you will be with the Queen of Heaven and her divine Son, if you persist in such a spirit of worldly vanity. Now I am quite determined that the Convent of St John must either continue in the true religious spirit, the spirit of humility and charity, or that it must revert to its old status and cease to receive novices. While saying this, however, I do not mean to disapprove of your accepting a larger proportion of ladies than others among you, provided that the candidates are otherwise equally suitable. It is quite reasonable, too, that, in the elections to the various offices, regard should be had to family and birth when other qualities are found to be evenly distributed. But allowing all that, I cannot and ought not to tolerate that anyone should be excluded from receiving the habit, or from profession, or from any position of dignity, merely because of the accident of her birth.

If sometimes in noble convents girls of less distinguished

extraction are received because they bring a very large dowry, why cannot you receive a person who, though lowly by birth, has been endowed by God with singular virtue and prudence? Such a one was my countrywoman, the glorious virgin, St Agnes of Montepulciano, who, though of very humble condition, was not only received and chosen prioress when quite young, but was of greater use, and did more honour to her house than any number of grand ladies. We must not try to impose our ideas on the Holy Ghost, debarring him from calling to his service those whom he pleases.

Besides this grand convent of San Giovanni there was another in the town, of Franciscan nuns, so poor that in order to live at all each sister had to go begging on her own account. The Archbishop took great trouble with their affairs, calling meetings of prominent citizens, appealing to wealthy individuals, and allowing the municipal authorities no peace until they had promised to assist. In addition, he gave a hundred ducats out of his own private funds, on which there were so many calls, and undertook the entire support of one nun. More, he said, he could not do just then because "overwhelmed by a great multitude of poor people". Their spiritual needs were, naturally, his primary care but, knowing very well that starved bodies often meant starved souls, he was always most solicitous about the circumstances of the men and women with whom he had to deal. The scapegraces who went to him for help so confidently were sure of getting a hot meal before a warm exhortation, and if they were not scapegraces they got the meal or the money without any exhortation at all.

Owing to the apathy or incompetence of priests and prelates, religious ignorance was widespread at this time in Southern Italy and gave Bellarmine deep concern. He reserved to himself the instruction of children and illiterate adults at the cathedral each Sunday. He visited every parish and hamlet in his extensive diocese each year, preached and gave his favourite catechetical instructions, and himself said the parochial Mass in all the places. In many village churches he found wooden pyxes, copper chalices and vestments so tattered and torn that even tramps would not have been very grateful for them as a gift. All these articles were replaced at his expense. He refused to accept a single penny from the people he was visiting or from their priests, and even brought his own meagre rations of food from Capua.

It was during those tours of visitation that the Archbishop wrote the only work to come from his pen during those three years —a short exposition of the Creed. This he had printed and distributed among the parochial clergy, with instructions to read one article of it aloud to the people every Sunday and festival day. The following lines to his old friend Father Carminata explain why it was that he had given up writing:

Your letter of November 12 has reached me and, as always, has given me the greatest comfort. If only you yourself could come, then would my satisfaction be complete. I have so many things to tell you that are difficult to talk about in a letter.

I am very well, by the goodness of God, but all the same I am only a feeble old workman, with sixty winters on my head, a workman called at the eleventh hour to tend this vineyard, which looks only too like a jungle. Consequently, I am in a hurry to get done all that I possibly can while God gives me life and health, for these cannot last very long.

I have with me two very good and fervent fathers of our Society. They travel about the diocese continually, preaching, hearing confessions, and teaching Christian doctrine. Their labours are bearing splendid fruit, and this is due in large measure to the fact that they accept nothing from the people. They know that I will provide them with all they need.

Just at the moment, I have no important news to tell your Reverence. Before leaving Rome I had begun to write a commentary on the Psalms, and had reached Psalm xxxiv. Here, I have no time to go on with that work. From morning to night, my diocese requires all my attention. Only during the night itself have I an opportunity for real prayer, and for reading something to aid me with my sermons. Perhaps I should say for meditating and writing my sermons, as I now read next to nothing.

Even requests to refute heretical attacks on the Church failed to "draw" him, requests that had always found him so ready in the past. There were other Jesuits besides himself in the world, he said, and they might take a turn. He had his people to think about and they required all his thought.

Bellarmine's revenues from his various benefices looked very well on paper, amounting as they did to as much as 12,000 ducats a year. That was nearly £6,000, yet he never had more than a few pounds for current expenses in his house, because all that was not spent on the churches of the diocese went month by month to the poor. A letter from him to Cardinal d'Este is among the Egerton MSS. in the British Museum, expressing regret that he is unable to employ a servant recommended by d'Este because he has not enough money to pay the man's wages. In modern English money, he must have disbursed on the poor annually at least £3,000. He particularly prized the "choir stipends" which he earned by assiduous attendance at the divine office with his canons. His share amounted to about 200 ducats a year, and it gave him peculiar satisfaction to earn them for the needy. "This money," he would say to Guidotti, when he brought it to him each month, "must not appear in your books. It is my private wages and I want to distribute it with my own hand."

The Archbishop kept a list of many respectable but poor families in Capua who were ashamed to ask for assistance. To these he sent in great secrecy a substantial sum each month. He also paid the fees and living expenses of poor students attending the university in Naples. The Theatines in Capua received fifty ducats from him every month to distribute in their own quarter, and there were many other societies or individuals who acted as his almoners without the world guessing the secret. Still it was not always possible for him to keep in the background because his charity constrained him to go personally on its errands. The sick in the hospitals and the slums were like so many magnets to his heart. Hardly a day passed that he did not set out for the bedside of some sufferer, to see that he had proper medical attention, to bring him some fruit or wine or flowers, to hear his confession and give him the spiritual strength which he knew so well how to impart. The acts of his beatification are crowded with references to these journeys of mercy.

A parish priest of Capua had been summoned on one occasion to the bedside of a dying man. All the thoughts of the poor sufferer were so concentrated on the future of three grown-up daughters, whom he was leaving behind without a friend or relative to protect them, that the priest was unable to get his confession or to turn his mind to God. In much distress, this good man hurried off to tell the Archbishop the sad story. Bellarmine returned with him at once to the patient's bedside and, bending over him, said: "In the past, you were the father of these girls; in the future they will find a father in me. I solemnly promise you that I will provide for them and act by them as you would wish to have done yourself." The dying man's face lit up at these words, whereupon the Archbishop himself heard his confession, gave him the last sacraments, and sent him to eternity in perfect peace. After the funeral, he found a home for his charges with a respectable family in the town, arranged for their marriages in due course, and gave each of them a dowry of nearly three hundred pounds. He provided many other poor deserving girls with the dowries they needed to get married and himself often performed the ceremony.

In later life St Robert wrote at the request of some bishops a small book which gave his views among other things on "The way to act in dealing with Secular Princes for the Protection of Ecclesiastical Liberties". The following is a brief excerpt from the book:

It is very difficult to defend the Church's liberties without incurring the wrath of princes, and it is very difficult to be remiss in their defence without incurring the wrath of God. Two pieces of advice occur to me in connection with this thorny problem. The first is that we should not take any step rashly and without having asked for the opinion of others. If there are none whose judgment we trust within reach, we ought to write for counsel, if time allows, to discreet and competent persons. The second piece of advice is that we should live in such a way as to convince princes and their ministers that we are not seeking to pick quarrels with them, but that in our defence of the Church's liberties we are moved only by

the fear of God and zeal for his glory. Moreover, our way of
life ought to make it plain to these men that we are anxious for
their friendship and esteem it highly. Indeed, we should strive
diligently by our good offices and services to preserve and
strengthen our friendship with them.

In the various processes of Bellarmine's beatification, which
extended over three centuries owing to the determined opposition
of Gallicans, Jansenists and champions of the divine right of kings,
twelve witnesses testified on oath that during his tenure of
office in Capua he never once fell foul of the civil authorities,
which was held to be "an exceedingly rare and singular achieve-
ment". The Spanish authorities in Naples were notoriously
jealous of the ecclesiastical administration. It was the easiest thing
in the world to rouse them, yet Bellarmine not only kept the
peace but kept their friendship. Nor was this the result of mere
deference on his part. He disliked litigation, but he was quite
prepared to go to law if the rights of his see could not be vindi-
cated in any other way. Some properties belonging to it had been
quietly annexed by certain powerful Capuan families, and for
these he fought in the courts as sturdily as any unsanctified plaintiff
might have done. *Caesaris Caesari* was his motto, but he did not
forget the other half of the divine counsel. His uncle Marcello
had been threatened with death by officials of Charles V if he
dared to remove the Council, of which he was president, from
Trent to some other city outside their jurisdiction, and had
laughed at the threat. That laugh was always ringing in the ears of
Marcello's nephew.

The Spanish functionaries were in the habit of sending *hortatorie*,
or admonitions, to the bishops in the Kingdom of Naples. Speaking of these documents, Guidotti relates the following incident
in his dealings with Bellarmine:

He told me once that the *hortatorie* usually take this form:
Monsignor, we have heard this or that report about you. We
beg your Lordship to consider the matter and to desist from
your present course as you value the favour of our Lord, the
King. They have never sent *me* such a *hortatoria*, he continued,

and if they did I would write them the following answer: "Sir, I have read your Excellency's note. It surprises me greatly that you should interfere in matters that do not concern you, as you are not an ecclesiastical superior. Accordingly, I beg you to remember that you will have to give an account of your actions to God, who is much more your master than is the King. Nor do you know how soon you will be summoned to render this account. Wherefore, I pray you to desist from your present course as you value the grace of God, our Lord."

Another piece of counsel in St Robert's little book for bishops is on "Dealing with Relatives". It opens very bluntly: "Inordinate love of relatives and kindred seems to be a vice common to all churchmen". The remedy for this evil is then proposed, namely the strict and rigid observance of the rule laid down by the Council of Trent that the goods of the Church are on no account to be used for the enrichment of relatives, but only for the relief of their poverty, should they happen to be poor. That was the line of conduct followed by the two great bishops of early times, Ambrose and Augustine, for they treated their relatives, in this respect, exactly as they treated other poor people, giving alms "not so much to enrich them but that they might not suffer dire need or be less needy". Those words from the life of St Augustine by Possidius were deeply engraved in Robert Bellarmine's memory, and are the clue to all his methods of dealing with the claims that came so insistently from Montepulciano. He was sincerely devoted to the interests of his family, so much so that various "promoters of the faith" in the several processes of his beatification used his family *pietas* as a weapon against him, in default of more damaging weapons. But there were distinct limits to his family interests.

One of the most persistent of the Cardinal's suppliants was his brother Thomas, who could point to fourteen children as so many arguments in favour of his claims. He was not satisfied with the sums that came to him from Capua and even lectured Robert on the duty of being more generous to one's kith and kin. Let him imitate that holy disciple of St Philip, Cardinal Tarugi, who was not given to counting the coppers when he opened his purse to his friends. On May 30, 1603, he received the following answer:

> If what I have written about not wishing to enrich my rela-
> tives is displeasing to you, it is proof that you would not mind
> seeing me lost in hell, provided you were well off in this world.
> Read the first chapter *de Reformatione* in the last Session of the
> Council of Trent. . . . If some have followed another course,
> that is their affair. The holy canons are my law, not the example
> of other men. . . . God will help you, provided you do his holy
> will, nor will I be wanting in whatever is just and right accord-
> ing to my conscience.

Strong as it was, that letter by no means daunted the "*molto
magnifico fratello*", so on November 20 of the same year Robert
was obliged to write again:

> I have read what you say about the duty of affording assist-
> ance to relatives and, as far as this means helping them in their
> poverty, I quite agree with you. The real difficulty is to know
> how much ought to be given, for if the Church's goods are to
> be dispensed on relatives at all, they must be given only as alms,
> *non ut fiant ditiores sed ut minus indigeant*. . . . If, as you say,
> Cardinal Tarugi is liberal towards his kinfolk, that is because
> he is not a religious under vows, as I am, and besides he has
> private means, which I have not. My income may be larger
> than his at present, but there are far more calls on it than he has
> to bear. He has no church to support, whereas I must spend
> huge sums on the upkeep of mine. Moreover there are count-
> less numbers of poor people in these parts, and I know that the
> ecclesiastical revenues of any particular place must be spent on
> the church and the poor of that place.

After Thomas, the member of the family who caused the
Cardinal most anxiety was Camilla, the sister who had been his
special confidante and playmate when they were children together.
She had married a man named Bartolomeo or Bartoletto Burratti, and Bartoletto seems to have been a thoroughly improvident
husband. Nothing ever went right with the poor fellow. His
oxen die, and a distressful letter is immediately posted to Capua,
begging for the price of a new beast; the police are on his track
for rent and taxes which he has not paid, so would the Archbishop

kindly come to the rescue. That long-suffering brother-in-law
wrote to him as follows on August 3, 1603: "I would like you to
make your need known to my brother. Though my income is
small and there are many calls on my purse, I will do all that I
possibly can to pay off your debts." Besides saving Bartoletto's
and Camilla's furniture from seizure by bailiffs, Robert granted
the pair a monthly pension of five silver crowns, or fifty *giulii*,
an adequate sum, as we know from Fynes Moryson's experience
in Siena.

In view of this, it is no wonder that the Cardinal should have
attributed the distress at the Casa Burratti to *"il mal governo"*.
Nor were they and brother Thomas the only relatives who
considered him their legitimate prey. After a careful study of the
documents, one temperate biographer came to the following
conclusion:

> The twenty-two years of [Bellarmine's] life as a cardinal were
> twenty-two years of lively conflict with his relatives. Never
> once was there peace or truce, because the principles that led
> them to beg and him to refuse were too insuperably opposed,
> his answer being that he was not rich in order to enrich his
> family, and that he would never deviate by a hair's breadth
> from his principle of granting them alms only to the extent
> necessary to keep them from actual want, according to their
> state. . .
> Infinite must have been the patience needed to deal with the
> continual stream of worrying letters from families in Monte-
> pulciano, related to him distantly or nearly, by blood or by
> marriage. They reached him every day, full of demands,
> prayers, tales of distress, arguments, and supplications, yea,
> sometimes of curses and abuse, vented on him by enraged or
> desperate persons. He was accused of inhumanity, of preferring
> to lavish his charity on strangers rather than on his own kindred,
> on rogues and blackguards rather than on gentlemen of his own
> country and his own blood. But neither the abuse nor the
> flattery ever made him abandon his principles in the slightest
> measure, for he cared not whether his people were pleased or
> angry with him, his only anxiety being to avoid doing that
> which he knew ought not to be done.

At Christmas time of the year 1603 Bellarmine wrote to the Pope, Clement VIII, sending him the season's greetings. The Pope replied with real affection but said that he would have received Robert's greetings with "still greater pleasure had you put aside your somewhat courtier-like style and mentioned the failings which you had noticed in us during this year, reminding us and teaching us how we might next year remedy them, make amends for them, and serve the Divine Majesty better than we have done so far". Robert, whose heart was as simple as a child's, took the Pope's words in all seriousness and, when the Christmas of the year 1604 came round, was careful to give the advice and reminders for which he had been asked:

Most Holy Father,

Last year your Holiness deigned to reply to a letter of mine in which I had wished you all the blessings of Christmas. With your wonted kindness, you gave me a loving, paternal admonition, saying that my letter savoured somewhat of the court, and that it would have been more welcome had I given you some good advice. Now that Christmas and New Year's Day have come round again, while praying with all my heart that they may bring you the fullest measure of happiness, I would remind your Holiness, in obedience to your wishes, of one matter that seems to me to be of great importance for the service of God.

Accordingly, with the courage which you have yourself given me, I beg you when appointing bishops not to regard a talent for preaching as the least necessary quality in the candidates. Your Holiness knows better than anybody that the first bishops of the Church kept themselves free from temporal cares, saying: "It is not desirable that we should forsake the word of God and serve at tables. Therefore, brethren, select from among you seven men of good reputation that we may put them in charge of this work. But we will devote ourselves to prayer and to the ministry of the word." It was thus that they had seen Christ, the Bishop of all bishops, do, and the holy bishops who came after them, almost to a man, have spoken according to their example. So too, quite recently, did Cardinal Borromeo of blessed memory, a man about whom it might be said with reason that his like was not to be found in our days. He was asked again and again to propose Monsignor N. for a bishopric to his Holiness, Pope Gregory XIII, but he could never be persuaded to do so because, as he said, the person in question had no talent for preaching, and preaching was the principal duty of a bishop, according to the Council of Trent.

This is evident, too, from the ceremony of consecration, in which the book of the Gospels is placed on the shoulders of the bishop-elect to show that the chief burden of his office is to preach the Gospel. Afterwards the book is placed in his hands, with the words, *Accipe Evangelium, et vade praedicare populo tibi commisso*.

What I say on this matter is not of such importance for great cities where there are always plenty of excellent preachers, as it is for the huge number of small cities in the country. If the bishop does not preach in these, nobody preaches, and so the little places become like fields that never get any rain, or on which the rain falls only during one month in the year, that month being the season of Lent. Even then, the preachers that come to them are for the most part men who take wages, and look rather to the good of their pockets than to the good of the people.

And now, since a bishop cannot preach in his diocese if he does not live in it, I beg your Holiness to lay great stress on this most important point. Last year, you sent many bishops away from Rome to their dioceses, an action deserving of all praise. Similarly, it would now be a most holy undertaking on your part if you were to clear Naples of its episcopal visitors. The bishops of this Kingdom go there on the slightest pretext and, once established in the city, they seem to find it impossible to return home. Your Holiness will pardon me if my expostulation goes too far, because it is charity that drives me to say what I am saying.

I have by me a letter written at his last hour by that most learned and saintly man Father Pedro Soto. It was addressed to Pope Pius IV, and its principal piece of advice to that Pontiff was that he should compel bishops to keep residence in the strictest manner. As cardinals who are made bishops do not usually live in their dioceses, he further counselled that such men should not receive episcopal consecration, but be given benefices of some other kind, and then he added the following words as his opinion of what would happen to the Pope if he neglected to take the course pointed out to him: *Non dubito Sanctitatem Vestram ultimam damnationem in Divino Judicio incursuram.*

The other Soto, namely Domingo,[1] has written clearly in the tenth book of his treatise, *De Justitia et Jure*, that a cardinal who is a bishop commits no sin if, through continued residence in his diocese, he never sets eyes on Rome, but that he unquestionably sins if, through staying in Rome, he never sets eyes on his church. If these great doctors do not excuse cardinals from residence that they may serve the universal Church by keeping in close touch with its Supreme Head, what would they think of the lesser services of other prelates, considered as a pretext for non-residence?

I must not importune your Holiness any further, but it was your kindness and zeal for the honour of God that carried away my pen.

In October, 1604, St Robert entered on his sixty-third year, which, as being the grand climacteric, was reckoned in those days the most perilous time of life. Accordingly he made his will, constituting as his heir "his dearest Spouse the Cathedral of Capua, or rather its holy patrons, Stephen and Agatha". On becoming a cardinal, he had at first determined not to make a will at all, for he was a professed religious, and of such St Augustine had said: "One of Christ's poor servants does not make a will because he has nothing to bequeath". Finding himself in possession of the rich endowments of Capua, however, he began to fear that should he die intestate his property might not go to the poor, and consequently he applied to the Pope for leave to make a will "for pious purposes only".

The grand climacteric, instead of seeing him into his grave, was to see him back in Rome. Soon after his arrival in Capua, he had devoted his spare moments to finding out the names and dates of his predecessors in the see. These he then arranged in chronological order, "from St Priscus, the disciple of St Peter, down to

[1] Those two famous Dominican theologians were always special favourites and authorities with Bellarmine.

his own day". After writing the name of the last archbishop, Caesar Costa, and noting that he had ruled the diocese for thirty years, something moved him to make a final entry, which ran: *Robertus Bellarminus sedit annis tribus*—"Robert Bellarmine held the see for three years". Pope Clement died on March 5, 1605, and Bellarmine was then summoned to his first conclave. He had long felt strangely certain about the date of the Pope's death. On his appointment as archbishop, his gentlemen-in-waiting had become very depressed at the thought of moving from Rome to dull, provincial Capua, and he had rallied them saying: "Cheer up, we shall be there only for something under three years".

Giuseppe Vignanesi, that important member of the Cardinal's household, was always very curious about his master's predictions. Many years after their time together in Capua he begged him one day to obtain a certain favour for him from Pope Paul V. That was in 1619 when Bellarmine was very ill and, in the doctor's opinion, near the end of his pilgrimage. Great, then, was Vignanesi's astonishment to hear him answer confidently: "It will be time enough for us to treat of this matter when another Pope is reigning". "He said these words with such assurance," Vignanesi testified, "that I felt eaten up with curiosity to know how and why he was so certain. Taking my courage in my hands, I said to him: 'Your Lordship predicted the death of Pope Sixtus while you were in France, that of Pope Clement while in Capua, and now that of Pope Paul. How do you do it?' At this question, he laughed, though he was in great pain, and answered: 'Oh well, I'll tell you. All the Popes either think themselves, or other people think for them, that they will reign such and such a number of years. Now what I do is to take away a third of that number, and thus I hit the mark.'"

Bellarmine's first conclave began immediately after his arrival in Rome, and he must have found the new experience a strange contrast to the peaceful spiritual activities in which he had been directly absorbed. Politics seemed to have control of the issues, for the great question mooted was not who was the best man to feed and foster the flock of Christ, but who was the man who would be most acceptable to the King of France or the King of

Spain. The cardinals were divided roughly into two parties, one, mainly French in sympathies, owing allegiance to Pietro Aldo-brandini, the powerful nephew of the late Pope; the other, strongly Spanish, a kind of coalition whose chief bond was hostility to his influence. Owing to the determined opposition of this latter body, it was recognized that, though Aldobrandini was the foremost figure in the conclave, he had personally no chance of being elected, and Baronius was in consequence put forward as the candidate of his party. Bellarmine refused to give his unqualified adhesion to any group, but as soon as the candidature of Baronius was made known, he took up his cause with great enthusiasm.

Curiously enough, after the first scrutiny St Robert himself was found to be at the head of the poll, with Baronius two votes behind. A relative majority at such an early stage of the proceedings is not usually of much significance, but it was significant enough to frighten the Jesuit cardinal. Something was said in a previous chapter about his views on the duties and responsibilities of the Supreme Pontiff. No man who sincerely held such views could possibly want to be elected pope, however high might be his opinion of himself. From a thousand indications it is plain enough that Bellarmine was not inclined to overrate his own virtue or administrative capacity, and consequently it was very natural that he should not merely have had no desire to wear the triple crown, but that he should have been genuinely terrified at the mere thought of such a burden being laid upon him. That he was terrified is proved not so much by his public actions as by his letters to intimate friends like Carminata, and the prayers that he was heard to utter when he thought that there was nobody near.

After the first ballot, he was noticed by the other cardinals and the officials of the conclave to have become very gruff and unapproachable in manner. They noticed it because it was so unusual in him. He moped in his cell or said his rosary in some out-of-the-way place and, if anyone approached, he used to slink off down another corridor so as to avoid him. When he did speak to his friends, it was to harp on the fact that he came of a

very long-lived race. He had drawn up a list of his ancestors who
were in the running to be centenarians and this he used to produce,
as much as to say, if you make me pope you may very easily have
more of me than you bargained for. His constant private prayer,
during those days, was, by his own admission, *A papatu libera me
Domine*—"From the papacy, deliver me, O Lord"!

Pietro Guidotti did not at all approve of his master's strange
behaviour. With an eye to their own prospects, he and the
Cardinal's other attendants naturally wanted him to keep in the
limelight, to be affable to the electors and, above all, to cultivate
Aldobrandini. "I tried," says Guidotti, "to get him to pay a visit
of courtesy to that cardinal, but his answer was: 'I see your
point. You wish to have me elected to the papacy. Well, I may
tell you that if the only act required of me in order to become
pope were to walk out of the room, I would not so much as rise
from my chair'."

It is unnecessary to follow in detail the intrigues and sudden
changes of the conclave, as Bellarmine, through his own tactics
and for other reasons, soon fell into the background. On April 1,
Cardinal Alexander de' Medici was unanimously elected by the
method known as "adoration", a result due in good measure to
the efforts of Baronius. He took the name of Leo XI, and he was
dead within a month. On April 29, two days after that tragedy,
St Robert wrote to Carminata:

> *Quis novit sensum Domini, aut quis consiliarius ejus fuit?* A Pope
> was elected who, as you have heard, was a very good man,
> a friend of our Society, and full of intentions so excellent that
> if he could only have carried them into effect he would have
> proved himself a model shepherd of souls. I know this for certain
> because, on Palm Sunday, he chose to unveil his heart to me in
> a general confession, as he expressed it, not of sins but of good
> resolutions. On April 27 he died. Who can unriddle these
> judgments of God?
>
> Here we are, then, once more preparing to enter the con-
> clave, and we need prayers more than ever because I do not see
> in the whole sacred college one who possesses the qualities
> which you describe in your letter. What is worse, the electors

make no effort to find such a person. It seems to me a very serious thing that, when the Vicar of God is to be chosen, they should cast their votes, not for one who knows the will of God, one versed in the Sacred Scriptures, but rather for one who knows the will of Justinian, and is versed in the authorities of the law. They look out for a good temporal ruler, not for a holy bishop who would really occupy himself with the salvation of souls. I, for my part, will do my best to give my vote to the worthiest man. The rest is in the hand of providence for, after all, the care of the Church is more the business of God than ours.

Part of the duties of the Spanish embassy in Rome was to keep a careful watch on the conduct of the cardinals. Six months before the death of Pope Clement, a conference of the officials was held to discuss the question of his successor, and among the names mentioned were those of Baronius and Bellarmine. The comment of King Philip's representatives is interesting:

> Baronius is reputed to be a man of no consequence except in the writing of history books. As regards capacity for government, Bellarmine's reputation stands no higher. He is not versed in Spanish affairs, and the fact of his having been a Jesuit is against him.

At some date, also prior to the death of Clement, the Spanish ambassador himself addressed a memorial to his master "on those Cardinals to whom it might be well for his Majesty to assign pensions". Here again St Robert is mentioned:

> Bellarmine, who was taken by his Holiness from the Society of Jesus, is a good man and learned in theology, but not of much practical ability (*de poca sustancia in agibilibus*). He is known to be the mere creature of the Pope and would scruple to accept a bribe. Being a native of Montepulciano, he is a vassal of the Duke of Florence. . .

The next note in the series, which was written immediately before the second conclave, show that the diplomatists were puzzled what to think about the Jesuit cardinal:

> Bellarmine of Montepulciano is a learned man and a good

Christian, for which reason many desire to see him promoted.
... The chief obstacle to his candidature is that he belongs to the
Society of Jesus, and has given his attention to study rather than
to affairs of government. His great goodness, his learning, and
his virtue render him worthy of the tiara, but his rectitude and
candour are such that he would not hesitate to oppose any
prince whatever, if he considered that the good of the Church
required him to do so.

The cardinals who were working in the interest of Spain also
sent reports and advice to his Catholic Majesty. "Bellarmine,"
wrote Cardinal Borgia, "deserves to be elected for his goodness,
but his great rectitude and integrity of character are against him."
"The only real obstacle to his promotion," added Cardinal
Zapata, "is that he is a Jesuit, and might show too much favour to
his order." When King Philip had read and carefully considered
those various letters and dispatches he came to the conclusion
that it would be better not to give St Robert any Spanish assistance. Taking his pen, he scrawled in huge characters on the margin
of the document: *Bellarmino, que se le deje correr su suerte*—"Let
Bellarmine be left to his fate". His Majesty's ministers explained
in detail what the Spanish workers in Rome were to understand
by leaving St Robert to his fate:

> If the conclave shows an inclination to declare for him, he is
> not to be opposed, because he is regarded as a very learned and
> virtuous man. His virtue and learning, however, would raise
> doubts and apprehensions about him in the minds of princes,
> as he professes to act in accordance with his convictions. His
> being a Jesuit would not do any more harm than if he were a
> member of some other religious order, except in so much as it is
> the way of Jesuits to be dependent on their Society.

So far, then, as Spain was concerned Bellarmine was to be
neither helped nor hindered. In a list of likely candidates which
was transmitted at this time to the new King of Spain, Philip III,
who succeeded his father in September, 1598, four cardinals were
described as being for Spain, five for France, three for Venice,
and three for no country in particular. To these was added a

mysterious fifth class, under the rubric *per la conscienza*, and in it were the names of Bellarmine and Baronius. The holy old Oratorian devoted all his energies to obtaining the return of his Jesuit friend, and in the early stages of the second conclave it looked as if his efforts were going to be crowned with success. "On May 11, Bellarmine was all the cry", wrote one of the officials at the Spanish embassy. As soon as he became aware of the activities of his Oratorian friend, he went and implored him most earnestly to desist. "If picking up a straw from the ground would make me Pope," he said, "the straw would remain where it was."

The persistent efforts of Baronius and the strength of his party frightened the forces hostile to Bellarmine into strenuous activity. It has to be remembered that the controversy on efficacious grace was as yet undecided, and many men thought, very reasonably, that the promotion of a Jesuit at such a time would be highly inopportune. St Robert, to his intense relief, soon fell out of the running, but he and Baronius were appalled when Cardinal Aldobrandini and his party declared for a certain Cardinal Tosco who bore a shady reputation as a churchman, whatever his practical ability. Baronius declared openly and solemnly that were Tosco elected he would be the last to do him the usual reverence, because he was unworthy of the office. Owing to his recognized sanctity the Oratorian cardinal wielded much influence in the conclave and, after a stormy interlude, worsted the efforts of Aldobrandini and the Spanish and French cardinals who, for political reasons, favoured Tosco. After a final critical struggle on the night of May 16, Cardinal Borghese was acclaimed Pope, to the enormous relief of Bellarmine and Baronius who knew him well and greatly esteemed him. He took the name of Paul V. When all was over the French ambassador to Venice wrote to a friend: "Having learned the particularities of the conclave from Cardinals de Joyeuse and du Perron, one is forced to admit that it is the Holy Ghost who makes popes". What particularly delighted Bellarmine was that the new Pope enjoyed robust health and was only fifty-two years of age, thus giving promise of a long and fruitful pontificate. Nevertheless there was a prediction going round that he would be dead by September of that same year, 1605. Mgr Luigi Aragazzi, Bellarmine's chaplain at the conclave, mentioned the rumour to him. "Do not believe it," he answered, "for he will have a long reign." When the chaplain asked how long, the Cardinal answered confidently, "Sixteen years, he will reign sixteen years". Paul V died in 1621.

In mid-August, 1605, St Robert wrote as follows to his old friend Father Carminata:

As you know, I have at various times consulted with Father General and others of the Society, and with several holy persons, as to whether I should not return to Capua, a course which seemed to promise greater quiet for myself, more profit to souls, and a better example to my neighbour. But one day, when I was with the Pope and had told him that I was resolved, as soon as the weather grew cooler, to return and reside in Capua, his Holiness made this formal statement to me: "We desire above all things that you remain in Rome, because we require you at our side".

On hearing this I replied: "Holy Father, I am bound to pay obedience to your every sign, yet I beg you to consider that residence in my see is still more necessary. There are numbers of cardinals in Rome and, if some were to go away, the court would not suffer, but in Capua there is only one archbishop, and if he does not reside his diocese will suffer greatly. If, then, your Holiness is determined that I shall stay in Rome, you must look after my church." When I had finished, the Pope answered, "I repeat that I want you above all things to stay in Rome, for though there are numbers of cardinals, there are few like yourself, so it will be well for you to think about renouncing your see."

I then told him that I would think about it. Afterwards I proposed to him some names, and several days later, when the question had been thoroughly considered, it was resolved to give the bishopric of Capua to Monsignor Antonio Gaetano, a man of sufficient learning, of virtuous life and quiet disposition, of noble birth, and one who was on good terms with the officers of the crown. So you see that God, who by his Vicar gave me the charge, has now by his Vicar taken it away from

me, and the whole time I have been in Rome I have prayed God
for one thing only, and that was to know his holy will, as my
sole desire is to fulfil it.

The Cardinal imparted to his friend at the end of the letter a
piece of good news which shows that his gifts of precognition
were strictly limited. "It is that the Grand Duke of Moscow is
now a Catholic. Two of the fathers of the Society are with him,
so a great gate is open for the conquest of all that immense
Empire."

As St Robert had no money of his own, the Pope proposed
that he should retain the revenues of Capua and pay his successor,
who was sufficiently well provided, an annual pension of a
thousand *scudi*. His immediate answer was that it would be a
strange thing for a man to divorce his wife and yet keep her
dowry. Paul, however, was determined that, as he was the cause
of the Archbishop's resignation, he should not suffer through his
ready obedience to his wishes. In a brief of September 1, whose
enormous length belied its name, he arranged that Gaetano should
pay him a pension of about two thousand *scudi* a year, to be
derived from various benefices in the archdiocese. A short time
later the Cardinal sought an audience with the Pope and persuaded
him to reduce the amount. His business manager Giuseppe
Vignanesi was present at the interview and recorded part of the
dialogue:

Pope Paul: Every other cardinal at his first audience has asked
    for some favour; you only ask to give away what you already
    possess.
Bellarmine: Holy Father, I was born a poor gentleman. I have
    been brought up and have lived as a poor religious, and now
    I am quite content to spend and end my days as a poor
    cardinal. I have quite as much as I want, nor shall I ever
    trouble your Holiness by asking for anything for myself.

His revenues came to him, or rather were supposed to come,
from several unexpected quarters. By an arrangement of Clement
VIII the Bishops of Strongoli and Gubbio were each to pay him
two hundred and the Bishop of Pienza five hundred *scudi* a year.

As the former prelates were poor men like himself, he refused ever to touch a penny of their money. With his Lordship of Pienza it was different. That gentleman complained loudly at having to pay five hundred *scudi* out of his scanty means but, all the while, he was rigidly exacting two hundred *scudi* from the very poor Bishop of Montepeloso, a see which he had previously governed. Bellarmine knew this, and told him that he would have pleasure in remitting the five hundred when he learned that he, in his turn, had cancelled his claim to the two hundred. The pleasure was very soon his.

Among the many people in Capua who were sorely troubled at the prospect of losing their Archbishop were the nuns of San Giovanni, for they had loved him dearly, admonitions and all. To these ladies he wrote an affectionate farewell on August 30:

Dear Reverend Mother and Sisters,

You ought not to grieve at my resignation, because your new bishop is so holy that he will be able to make up for my shortcomings, and also because, in the place of one father, you will now have two who will compete with one another in doing you any service that lies in their power. I, for my part, offer you my help whenever you need it, for, though I left Capua at the Pope's command to be at his service and disposal at all hours, I have not lost my affection for the people of Capua nor my interest in them. You, in particular, are dear to me, and you will find that this is so whenever you need my assistance. Remember to pray for me, and also for your new pastor that the Lord may give him grace faithfully to serve his divine Majesty and the souls in his keeping. With this I send you a thousand blessings.

Your father and brother, CARDINAL BELLARMINE.

One hope expressed in this letter was not destined to be fulfilled. Archbishop Gaetano scarcely ever resided in his diocese, his whole time being occupied in nunciatures at the different Catholic courts. This was a life-long sorrow to Bellarmine, and years after, on April 10, 1618, he wrote expressing it to the absentee, who was then at Madrid:

Forgive me if I make known to you the grief I feel at seeing a church so dear to me separated for so many years from its pastor. Never seeing him, it is unable to follow his lead, never hearing him, it cannot obey his voice, though our Lord says of the good shepherd, *ante eas vadit et oves eum sequuntur et audiunt vocem ejus.* When you were in Bohemia as nuncio to the Emperor, I often begged the Pope to recall you and to restore you to your Spouse, and I used to remind him that a husband when separated from his wife can neither have any more children nor bring up properly those God has already given him.

CHAPTER IX

TROUBLE WITH THE REPUBLIC OF VENICE

TO St Robert it was compensation for many sorrows that so good a Pope as Paul V had the Church's destinies in his hands. We know the high standards of probity and prudence which he demanded in one to whom that tremendous commission might fittingly be entrusted, yet, even judged by those, he was able to apply to the new Pope the words of the *Iste Confessor*, in the version then current:

> *Qui pius, prudens, humilis, pudicus,*
> *Sobrius, castus fuit, et quietus.*

One reason for this enthusiasm was that the Pope had commanded all cardinals who were in possession of bishoprics to reside in their dioceses or to provide and finance coadjutors, failing which they must resign from their sees.

Not all the acts of Pope Paul, however, were as pleasing to Bellarmine as that one. Canon law had always been the new Pope's favourite study, and lawyer-like he was inclined to insist somewhat rigidly on the observance of all that was to be found in the code. The question of ecclesiastical immunities, and particularly of the *privilegium fori* by which clerics, even in civil or criminal cases, were exempted from the jurisdiction of the secular courts, was a dangerous one to air in that age of transition, when the secular state, Catholic to the core though it might be, was beginning to feel its power and to be impatient of all outside interference. Pope Paul brought this thorny question to the front without the slightest misgiving, before he had been a year on the throne. His predecessor, Clement VIII, who was more of a statesman, had again and again turned a blind eye on the uncanonical behaviour of civil rulers, and had shown particular restraint and patience in his dealings with the haughty Republic of Venice. As the papal fief of Ferrara abutted on the territory of the Republic, there were continual disputes about boundaries and other matters.

The Venetian senators had decided, as a measure of national
defence, to deflect the course of the river Po by means of a great
canal, and had entered into an agreement with the Ferrarese
authorities, whose interests were closely involved. In 1602 they
violated the terms that had been accepted, and naturally received
a remonstance from the papal nuncio. Their answer was to send
troops and galleys up the river, whereupon the Cardinal of San
Clemente strongly advised the Pope to mobilize his own forces
and teach the provocative signori that they could not defy him
with impunity. The reply given to the Cardinal is recorded by
Canaye, the French ambassador in Venice: "His Holiness having
hitherto maintained the peace of Christendom has no wish to
start trouble at the end of his pontificate and it is his intention
to let the affair settle itself quietly".

At this same time, the Venetian Senate passed a law forbidding
any subjects of the state to give more than a thousand ducats to
the convents in which their daughters might become nuns.
Pope Clement replied by forbidding all the orders for women on
Venetian territory to receive novices until the law was revoked,
but at the same time bade his nuncio inform the government that,
if they would leave the matter in his hands, he would issue instructions of exactly the same import as their law. Considering that
Venice had been the very first state to accept the decrees of the
Council of Trent in which the Pope's jurisdiction over all matters
affecting clergy and religious was so strongly and clearly affirmed,
the conduct of Clement VIII must surely be reckoned moderate
and forbearing in a very remarkable degree. The French ambassador, whose feelings towards the Republic were altogether
friendly, even felt that the senators were trading on the good-will
of the Holy Father, and surmised that under a *pape plus brusque*
there might be serious trouble.

The *pape plus brusque* appeared in the person of Paul V. One
of the first of his public acts was to excommunicate a recalcitrant
minister at Naples, a move, du Perron informs us with much
satisfaction, that made the Spaniards *extrémement irritez et estonnez*.
Spain put in its place, the Pope turned his attention to Venice.
Things there had been going steadily from bad to worse. One

after another, the traditional privileges and exemptions of the clergy had been violated or entirely abolished. Indeed, anti-clericalism had become a fixed habit of the proud aristocracy of wealth who ruled the state, for in their campaign against the immunities which their forefathers had accepted and embodied in the law, they showed not the slightest disposition to meet the ecclesiastical authorities half-way. The decrees of Trent were dis-regarded, and clergy and church property were treated as it suited the state to treat them, without any respect being paid to rights that were, at least, deeply rooted in history. For the better part of a year, Pope Paul contented himself with remonstrances and paternal admonitions. Several avenues of peace or compromise were explored, but the Republic refused to make a single con-cession. During all this time, the man who nerved the Senate to resist and defy the demands and threats of Rome was Paolo Sarpi, the clever, scheming, enigmatic Servite friar, celebrated in England for his prejudiced and ironical *History of the Council of Trent*. He had been the procurator of his order in Rome while Bellarmine was delivering his controversial lectures there. The two men had often met, and the Jesuit appears to have been attracted by the brilliantly gifted Servant of Mary.[1] At the time, nothing indicated that they would one day be brought together in a duel that should have all Europe as onlookers. Sarpi longed to be made a bishop, but he was too erratic mentally and too much of a *vagabundus* as a religious to please the ecclesiastical

---

[1] Bellarmine's friendly feeling towards Sarpi was alleged as an argument against his beatification, in 1713, by no less a person than Prosper Lambertini, later the great Pope Benedict XIV. The answer of the Cardinal's defenders was to remind the court of St Augustine's kindly dealings with Pelagius, and of the friendly visits of St Francis de Sales to Theodore Beza. Bellarmine's titular church as cardinal, Santa Maria in Via, was in the charge of the Servites. The historian Lord Acton, who was not celebrated for his addiction to papal policies, pronounced a very severe judgment on Fra Paolo: "It is now certain he despised the doctrines [of the Christian faith] which he taught, and scoffed at the mysteries which it was his office to celebrate . . ; the most consummate tactician in modern polemics, a sceptic and an absolutist at heart, who sought to compass his evil ends in Church and State alike by assailing the authority of the Holy See" (*Essays on Church and State.* Edited by Douglas Woodruff, London, 1952, p. 255).

authorities. His repeated failures to obtain the coveted mitre, notwithstanding the warm testimonials of his country's government, rankled and bred in his none too humble heart a bitter antipathy to the Holy See. The troubles of 1605 and 1606 gave him his opportunity for revenge.

The quarrel between Venice and the Pope is only a chapter in the long, troubled history of the relations between Church and State. Men being made as they are, churchmen and statesmen alike, conflicts between the two powers were inevitable. In the particular case of Venice, it might be said with some justice that there were faults or errors of judgment on both sides. The Venetian Senate was undoubtedly a haughty, worldly-wise, money-loving oligarchy, adept at giving fair names to nasty realities and knowing well how to play the bully under the mask of injured innocence. Whatever justification they may have been able to plead for their anticlerical policy, their methods of carrying it out were extremely provocative. The Pope, on the other hand, was definitely wanting in the diplomatic caution and shrewdness of his predecessor, Clement VIII. The world had moved on since the time of Innocent III and measures salutary and effective in the troubled conditions of the Middle Ages would hardly prove opportune in the secularist atmosphere of post-Reformation Europe.

Yet it was to such measures that Paul, a stickler for the letter of the law, proceeded. In a consistory held during the middle of April, 1606, he informed the cardinals that it was his intention to issue a bull of excommunication against the Doge and Senate of Venice, and to lay the whole city under an interdict if, after due time for consideration, the government refused to abrogate its obnoxious laws and hand over to the ecclesiastical courts two priests who had been thrown into the state prisons. The day after the consistory, du Perron, who had diplomatically absented himself on the plea of illness, wrote to tell Henry IV that, with the exception of the two Venetian cardinals, the sacred college had unanimously approved the Holy Father's design. This does not seem to be quite accurate, for a year later, when peace had been restored, and the Venetian ambassador, Contarini, had been welcomed back to Rome with every mark of honour, he wrote informing his government that, though the cardinals were still reluctant to admit that they might have been a little hasty or injudicious, there was one exception:

Bellarmine was the only one of the number who appeared anxious to apologize. He showed marvellous courtesy to me and said that he wished to confide two things to me for his own satisfaction. The first of these was that he understood it had been divulged that he had counselled the Pope to publish the Monitory against the Republic. This report, he said, was not true, for though the Pope is wont to consult him in cases of conscience or religion, he had never spoken to him on this subject, nor did he know anything thereof until his Holiness gave account of his resolve in the consistory. . . . Had the decision been communicated to him, his opinion would indubitably have differed from that which was adopted.

At the beginning of May, 1606, just a day before the expiry of the three weeks and three days allowed by the Pope in his bull, the streets and public buildings of Venice were placarded with the following notice:

Leonardo Donato, by the grace of God Doge of Venice, to the most Reverend Patriarchs, Archbishops, and Bishops of our Seigniory of Venice, and to all Vicars, Priors, Rectors, parochial Ministers, and other ecclesiastical Persons, greeting.

It having come to our knowledge that by order of the most Holy Father, Pope Paul V, a certain brief was published and posted in Rome, on April 17 last, fulminated against us, our Senate, and Seigniory, and addressed to you in formal terms; . . . and seeing that the said brief has been published against all reason, and in opposition to the teaching of Scripture and the holy Fathers; that it prejudices the liberty of our Senate and the sovereign authority given to it by God; that it troubles the peaceable dominion which God has given us over the property, the honour, and the lives of our subjects; and that it causes great scandal to the whole world; we do not hesitate to declare that the said brief is not only unjust and unfair, but that it is null and void and of no effect whatever; that it is entirely without grounds in law; and that it has been fulminated in defiance of all right and of the common legal formalities. . . .

Such, we are certain, it will be considered by you, by our other subjects, and by the whole world. Accordingly, we feel assured that you will go on as heretofore with your pastoral duties, and with the divine services, which, by our care and diligence, flourish in this our Seigniory as nowhere else in the world.

It is our firm resolution always to live, like our predecessors from the foundation of this City, in the holy and apostolic Catholic Faith, under the guidance of the Holy Roman See . . . which we pray God our Lord to inspire with the knowledge of the nullity of the brief, of all its other acts against us, and of the justice of our cause. . .

> Given at our Ducal Palace, May 6, 1606.

The studied moderation and pious tone of that interesting document were intended to catch the sympathy of the watching world. The Doge and Senators knew very well that France would not move against them, for Venice had been the first Catholic state in Europe to acknowledge the rights of Henry of Navarre, who was then on the French throne. England was only too anxious to help them, and Spain did not feel too enthusiastic about the new Pope. Consequently, they were in a very strong position and proceeded to take full advantage of it. All priests and religious who, in accordance with the terms of the interdict, refused to say Mass or administer the sacraments, were invited to take the road to exile. Only the Jesuits, Capuchins, and Theatines were brave enough to stand up to the omnipotent Council of Ten. Galileo, the astronomer, was in Venice at the time, probably on a visit to his friend Fra Paolo. On May 11, 1606—that is, the very day the interdict came into force—he wrote as follows to his brother Michelangelo:

At two o'clock last night, the Jesuit Fathers were placed on board two ships to be transported beyond the confines of the State. They walked to the ships, each with a crucifix hanging round his neck, and a lighted candle in his hand. Yesterday, after dinner, they were locked up in their house, and two policemen were put on guard at the door to prevent anybody from entering or leaving the convent. I believe they are also to be expelled from Padua and the rest of the Venetian dominions, to the great regret and sorrow of many women who are devoted to them.

The *molte donne loro devote* of this letter has a touch of Sarpi's sarcasm in it. Fra Paolo hated the Jesuits as he hated nothing else in the world, but many indications justify the belief that the aim of his work in life was something bigger than the destruction of their Society. In 1611, four years after the withdrawal of the interdict, he wrote that it was essential to ruin the Jesuits, for to ruin them was to ruin Rome and, Rome destroyed, *religion in Venice would reform itself*.[1] During the interdict, he was in correspondence with several of the most influential heretics of the day. To Count du Plessis-Mornay he wrote: "Our main object is to prevent the Republic from yielding a tittle of its rights, and to win greater liberty for it. We urge the reading of the Bible, we commend the merits of Christ, we make a laughing-stock of the Pope." More than once in his letters he described the Pope, Luther-like, as "the harlot". When the Calvinist scholar, Isaac Casaubon, had read a bundle of tracts from the Servite's pen, he wrote to congratulate him, and prophesied gleefully that Venice would soon be another Geneva. Fra Paolo was a brilliant pamphleteer and his *History of the Council of Trent*, first published in London, is written in a vivid attractive style which the Jesuit, Pallavicini, could not emulate in his much more sober and accurate history of the Council, now superseded by the great work of Mgr Jedin, still in progress.

Fra Paolo was given rooms at the Doge's palace, and a liberal salary. Each morning, he went to work from the Servite convent in company with his trusty colleague, Fra Fulgenzio, a man whom the Protestant physician Asselineau judged, after hearing him preach, to be "another Melanchthon or Luther". The two Servites proved themselves a model pair of civil servants, and gave the Republic excellent value for the ducats it showered upon them. In a short time, they enlisted the services of five other theologians, one being the vicar-general of Venice, and the rest religious of

[1] Letter of July 5, 1611, in Fontanini's *Storia Arcana di F. Paolo.*

JX

various orders. Then the seven, captained by Sarpi, began a war of pamphlets and small treatises against the Pope and his interdict to which, at the Holy Father's express command, Cardinal Bellarmine was required to reply. All the pamphlets and booklets were written in Italian and answered by Bellarmine in the same language.

The first tract to engage him was by a Franciscan who argued temperately that "secular princes, and the Pope himself in so far as he is a secular prince, derive their power immediately from God". Bellarmine criticized this theory of the divine right of doges and kings in the following terms:

> Turning to the word "immediately", we observe that it may be understood in two different ways. First, it may mean that princes, in so far as they are superiors, have immediate authority from God to command their subjects, that is, the duty of obedience is imposed by God immediately. Understood in this way, the proposition is perfectly true and no Catholic every denied it. . .
>
> Secondly, the word may mean that secular princes have immediately from God this or that people as their subjects, the Most Christian King, for instance, having the French, his Catholic Majesty having the Spaniards, and the Republic of Venice having the Venetians. . . . This proposition is patently false, and the author himself is obliged to confess as much in his book, for he says that the power of princes may be acquired in any of four ways, by election, heredity, donation, or conquest in a just war, all of which titles are certainly not divine but human. Consequently, if by one of them a man obtains possession of power over this or that people, such power does not come immediately from God. . . . Should someone ask the Most Christian King by what right he holds the throne of France, he would not answer that it was by divine right,[1] but through hereditary succession, and if a similar question were put to the Doge of Venice, he would not reply that his seigniory

---

[1] Henry IV might not have answered so himself, but plenty of his subjects, both Catholic and Protestant, would at this time have been ready and eager to do it for him.

had come to him straight from God, but rather through the election of the people.

Herein lies the great difference between the ecclesiastical power of the Pope and the political power of secular princes. The Pope's right to command all Christians is not based only on the general ordinance of God, in virtue of which obedience is due to every legitimate superior, but also on the fact that God has given him immediately all Christians as his subjects; for though the Pope is elected by the cardinals, it is not the cardinals but God who gives him his power. . . . One evident proof of this is that he cannot remove from his jurisdiction any province or city or single person. He cannot be a true pope without being at the same time the superior of all Christians, and this because the title by which he holds his power is divine.

Kings and secular princes, on the other hand, may lose their subjects entirely or in part. They can even themselves alienate one of their cities or provinces, and place it under the control of another prince in such a way that they shall no longer have any authority over it, this being possible because the title by which they hold their power is human and not divine; but no one can diminish or take away the power of the Supreme Pontiff, not the college of cardinals nor a general council, nor the pope himself, because papal authority comes immediately from God, and is not subject to the control of any created will. It is the contrary that we see in the case of secular princes, for their power often suffers curtailment, either at the hands of their subjects or at those of greater princes. Sometimes, too, monarchical states transform themselves into free republics, and free republics into monarchical states, all of which is possible only because the power in these cases is not immediately from God but from man.

The historical instances adduced by St Robert in support of ecclesiastical immunities may not always be above criticism, but neither, assuredly, are those of his adversaries, and he undoubtedly had on his side what they had not, namely the logic of a long tradition which, whatever its genesis, was the plain doctrine of the Tridentine decrees that had been accepted by the Venetian senate. Venice was a republic, and it was the boast of the citizens that their doge was simply an elected official like the prime ministers of modern states. In the struggle of 1606 Sarpi and his friends found that the constitutional limitations on the power of their ruler were a hindrance. The absolute claim of the Pope could be met effectively only by opposing to it a claim on the part of the doge equally absolute, and this, in defiance of their country's history, the theologians proceeded to urge. Bellarmine's embarrassing answer was to mention the name of Marino Faliero, the celebrated doge and military commander who had been decapitated by order of the senate in 1355 for plotting to make himself a dictator.

The second work that evoked a reply from the Cardinal during the same year, 1606, was a reissue of two small tracts on the question of excommunication that had been written by John Gerson, the famous chancellor of the University of Paris at the time of the Council of Constance. These reprints were furnished with a preface in which their teaching was turned to account against Pope Paul. The book bore no date or name, and the author of the preface pretended that he was writing from Paris. Bellarmine immediately unmasked the deception by announcing that the Roman authorities were aware that the preface, the printing, and everything else had been done in Venice but, though he knew that the man responsible was Fra Paolo himself, he forbore to mention him by name. Gerson's two tracts had been chosen because of their author's reputation for learning and holiness, and because of his theory that a general council is superior to the pope. It was a clever ruse, but Bellarmine pointed out that it was a most unfair use to make of a good man's name:

No one can deny that John Gerson was a doctor of much learning and piety, but the unhappy times in which he lived must be remembered, for it was the long duration of the Great Schism of the West that caused him, as well as some others of his age, to think poorly of the authority of the Apostolic See. Hoping that by means of a general council the Great Schism might be brought to an end, he thought it would help if he were greatly to exalt the authority of councils and, on the other hand, greatly to depreciate the authority of the pope. It was through his efforts in these directions that he fell into errors plainly against Holy Scripture and the common teaching of theologians who flourished both before and after his age. Consequently, his authority in questions touching the power of the pope is of no account, and a host of safer writers might be cited, whose opinion on the matter of excommunications is different from his.

Fra Paolo soon had ready an answer of 55,000 words to the criticism of his Gersonian enterprise. He was an able, if not too scrupulous debater, and one of his aims was to make Bellarmine appear self-contradictory. St Robert replied without delay. "Thanks be to God", wrote the Saint in reply, "that my works were printed in Venice, for the Venetians can now see for themselves what I teach about clerical immunities." He has often been charged by his critics with a kind of theological opportunism, yet the views on political authority, papal jurisdiction, and ecclesiastical immunities expressed by him while the Venetian trouble was at its climax, were identical in every respect with the views which he had taught daily to his students, thirty years earlier, within the peaceful precincts of the Roman College. All his conclusions stood rooted in age-old traditions, and it is small blame to him that he should have stood up for them sturdily against the irreverent, cynical criticism of a priest and religious who had gone over to the camp of the enemy. The conclusion of his reply to Sarpi was an appeal to the Venetians to renounce their false guides and return to their obedience:

It only remains for me now to turn to the Most Serene Republic and put before it a consideration which more than anything else in the world deserves to be taken into account. I do so with confidence because my heart tells me that I have ever been deeply concerned for the glory, exaltation, and true happiness of so ancient and noble a Republic. What I would say, then, to its people is that, calling to mind the religion and piety of their ancestors, and how God requited them with prosperity on land and sea, and preserved their liberties for a longer time than those of any other republic on earth, they should now use every means to preserve that same religion and not permit it to be stolen from them by men whose one object appears to be its ruin.

Think who those are who today give you counsel, and you will find that they are not the strictest religious, nor the best priests, nor the most famous theologians of the Church. Remember that it was men such as the men to whom I refer who turned Germany upside down. Study the signs, and you will see the end at which they aim. Fra Paolo speaks not once but twice, and in exaggerated terms, about abuses in the Church for the reform of which the world has long been waiting in vain. What does he mean by these words? One thing I know and that is that the favourite catchwords of our modern heretics are the abuses of the Roman Church. Do we not hear them moan every day that they had hoped for reform from the Council of Trent, but that they were deceived? If you enquire a little further, you will discover that the abuses in question are the Sacrifice of the Mass, the celibacy of the clergy, the vows of religious, the fast of Lent, the invocation of the saints, the veneration of images, and other such things, which they have abolished or desire to abolish.

Do not tell me that the theologians of Venice are not thinking of abuses such as these. Men do not set down all their thoughts in tracts. In England, there was at first no thought of these things. It is quite enough that your theologians should lament that while the present abuses in the Roman Church continue, men cannot save their souls, for such was exactly the lament of the heretics. When Fra Paolo tells you that the alleged abuses are a positive hindrance to your salvation, that they have endured for many centuries, and that there is still no sign of their disappearance, what do his words mean but that in the Roman Church as it is today it is impossible for a man to save his soul?

Further, is it not the aim of Fra Paolo and the other theologians who write in Venice to reduce and confine the Church's activity to a pure and simple ministry of teaching the word of God, and of administering the sacraments? Fra Paolo says as much in express terms on page 56 of his *Apologia*. And what else but this was the aim of modern heretics? . . . Fra Paolo tells you that many provinces and kingdoms have separated from the Roman Church for no other reason but that the popes had begun to meddle in their temporal concerns. The meaning of his words and the nature of the temporal concerns of which he speaks are nicely explained by the subsequent history of the provinces and kingdoms that separated from the Church, for the only liberty that was left to the clergy within their borders was freedom to preach sermons. The secular princes became the patrons of church livings and the final judges of all matters appertaining to religion, a state of affairs unheard of in past centuries. It is to this state that Fra Paolo would like to reduce Venice. Perhaps it was his hope and dream about the matter that inspired him to have our Lord engraved on his front page, pointing to the globe and saying, *Regnum meum non est de hoc mundo.* ... True, his Kingdom is not of this world in the sense that he derives his authority from the world, or governs according to the rules of worldly prudence, but nevertheless, in the words of Holy Writ, *Data est ei omnis potestas in coelo et in terra; est Princeps regum terrae, et Rex regum et Dominus dominantium.*

His vicar on earth has no desire to meddle in the temporal affairs of seculars, and such meddling, to use Fra Paolo's expression, was not the real cause but a false pretext used by heretics to justify their secession from the Church of God. The pope's only desire is to safeguard the power entrusted to him by God for the government of the Church and for the guidance of his sons, among whom are all Christian princes, to their heavenly country. Should they, then, stray from the way of salvation by abusing their authority or endeavouring to usurp authority that does not belong to them, it is his right and his will, in virtue of his Apostolical office, to admonish them of their duty and to punish them if they do not obey. . .

Finally, I would ask you to consider why it is that the theologians of Venice should have thought it well to omit the usual protestation of all Catholic writers since the Lutheran heresy, that they submit their works to the judgment and censure of the Holy Roman Church or the Supreme Pontiff. They say, indeed, that they submit their tracts to the decision of Holy Mother Church, which cannot err, but why do they so carefully omit the adjective Roman? This again is not a good sign, and I cannot desist from warning you to beware of the tactics of these new pilots of your Most Serene Republic, for should they succeed, which God forbid, in making shipwreck of its faith, it would not be very strange if they were also to destroy its temporal glory and prosperity, which are so closely connected with that faith.

I pray the divine goodness with all the fervour of my heart that by the intercession of the most Blessed Queen of Angels and the glorious Evangelist St Mark, the power and craft of the devil may not prevail, and that a door may not be opened in your midst for the entrance of heresies that would bring about the ultimate ruin of your ancient and noble Republic.

It would be tedious to give further details of the wordy warfare in which Bellarmine had become unwillingly engaged. To the grievous disappointment of Sarpi and of Sir Henry Wotton, the English ambassador in Venice, peace was restored through the good offices of Henry IV of France, who employed Cardinals de Joyeuse and du Perron to carry through the delicate negotiations. Interdicts are still part of the Church's spiritual armoury, and reasonably so, because they are nothing but a withholding from her contumacious children, until they repent, of her spiritual treasures, the Mass, the sacraments, Christian burial. It is known that Sarpi practically never said Mass, in the efficacy of which he appears to have lost all belief, until the interdict came into force, when he never missed a morning. Mass said in that spirit of defiance is nothing but a blasphemous mockery, as that unbeliever in a religious habit must have known perfectly well. Interdicts are still occasionally launched against individuals, and St Pius X put the censure on a small, obstreperous Italian town, but no sovereign state has been subjected to such a measure since the days of Pope Paul V. The story may fitly close with the following brief letter of Bellarmine to the Doge, Leonardo Donato, written on December 5, 1611:

Most Serene Prince,

I received the letters of your Highness with all reverence from the hands of that noble and most worthy Senator, Tommáso Contarini, whom you have appointed as your ambassador in ordinary to our Holy Father, Pope Paul V. Signor Contarini made known to me the great good-will of your Highness in my regard, and I, in turn, made plain to him the eager desire I harbour to be of service to your Highness and your glorious Republic, should I ever be given the opportunity. Meanwhile I pray God long to preserve your Highness, and to protect, strengthen, and extend the power of your Seigniory of Venice, for the glory of his holy name, and for the defence of the Catholic faith by land and sea.

CHAPTER X

THE CARDINAL VERSUS THE KING OF
ENGLAND

S T ROBERT BELLARMINE, by nature so peaceable
and friendly, seemed destined never to be out of the battle-
line. As Queen Elizabeth I of England drew towards her
end, childless, and secretive as to her successor, Rome and all the
European courts began to look towards James VI, King of
Scotland, the Calvinist-bred son of the Catholic queen whom
Elizabeth had permitted by her tergiversation to be judicially
murdered. King James needed, or thought he needed, Catholic
neutrality and benevolence in order to secure the coveted throne
of England. Danger threatened from Spain where Father Robert
Persons of the Society of Jesus was busily promoting the candidature of an infanta directly descended from John of Gaunt.
But other Jesuits, including Bellarmine, hoped to find in King
James another Henry of Navarre. The son of a staunchly Catholic
mother and baptized a Catholic himself, he had married a wife
strongly inclined towards Catholicism, and hated with all his
heart the bitterly anti-Roman Kirk. In the year 1600 a Scottish
gentleman named Edward Drummond came to Rome, ostensibly
to gain the Jubilee, but bringing with him letters signed by the
King, for Pope Clement VIII and various cardinals, including
Bellarmine. Bellarmine answered at once with a very long
courteous letter detailing many reasons why his Majesty of Scotland should return to the faith of all his ancestors. "If your
Majesty should draw nearer to the Catholic faith," he concluded,
"there will be nothing however difficult which you may not
promise yourselves from the Sovereign Pontiff and from me."

St Robert's keen interest in the conversion of the Scottish
King went with him to Capua where he studied with liveliest
attention James's *Basilikon Doron*, in a Latin version published in
London in 1604 and transmitted to him from Rome. That

pedantically titled book, meaning Royal or Kingly Gift, was written for the instruction of the author's son and heir, Prince Henry, and set forth in the plainest terms James's theory of the divine right of kings, which he had excogitated under the influence of the French political theorist Bodin, and in direct opposition to the hated Kirk with its democratic nonsense and claim to complete freedom from state control. James's tutor during the fifteen years of his boyhood had been George Buchanan, late of the University of Paris, who dedicated to his royal pupil his treatise, *De Jure Regni apud Scotos*, and therein taught him that monarchs reign by the will and for the good of the people, that it is the people who make the laws for the king to administer and himself obey, that if he breaks the contract with his people, contained in his coronation oath, they have the right to depose him and even to put him to death. James reacted violently against such anarchic doctrines and began to hate Buchanan as much as he hated the Presbyterian elders.

It is impossible not to feel a certain sympathy for the unhappy boy-king over whose most impressionable years had lain the grim shadow of John Knox. The tyranny of the Kirk compelled him to learn the arts of dissimulation till they became almost a second nature and deceived everybody, including himself. As against the Kirk and Buchanan, he maintained in the *Basilikon Doron* that kings were accountable to God alone, that all law and constitutional forms were mere concessions of their wills, and that the whole duty of a Christian was active obedience in the case of every morally lawful royal command and patient endurance of whatever penalties the king might choose to inflict for refusal to obey commands judged by the subject to be contrary to the law of God. Bodin and other continental advocates of absolutism had regarded the power and claim of the pope as the principal enemy to be combated in their arguments, but King James's theory of divine right was not in origin anti-papal. It was anti-Kirk and anti-Buchanan, and took on a thoroughly Protestant flavour only at a later time under the exigencies of controversy.

Robert Bellarmine was disappointed to find an undercurrent of veiled hostility to the Catholic Church already apparent in his edition of the *Basilikon Doron*. But it was not very pronounced and he continued to hope and pray that James, like Henry of Navarre, would shed his Calvinism and become a genuine Catholic. Thus brooding over the enigmatic book during his rare moments of freedom from his pastoral duties in Capua, he decided at last, as was the intention of those who had sent him the book, to address a friendly remonstrance to King James, ruler of England as well as Scotland since the death of Queen Elizabeth in March, 1603. He would write a *Hieratikon Doron* or "Priestly Gift" in exchange for the Royal Gift of his Majesty. This he proceeded to do, but his lively little book remained in manuscript, owing to untoward developments in England, and was not given the light of print until 1913. It is of consequence only because it reveals St Robert's profound concern for the restoration of the faith in England, his grief over the sufferings of the Catholics, and some of his delusions, surrendered only very reluctantly, about the character of King James. He regarded Mary Queen of Scots as definitely a martyr for the faith and, being a man who had dearly loved his own mother, thought quite erroneously that James might be moved by appeals to the memory of his mother. Mary is always turning up in his arguments, and Elizabeth her gaoler is painted as a very Jezebel of iniquity, which she certainly was not. Robert was fair enough to delete his strictures on Elizabeth's private morals in a subsequent revision of his manuscript. He is deferential and truly courteous to James throughout and begs this "glorious and prudent King" to take in good part the criticisms he ventures to offer of some blemishes in his otherwise admirable book.

The first criticism concerns the King's assumption of the title "Defender of the Faith", still to be found on every coin of the English realm:

> Nobody is ignorant that this title was given by Pope Leo X to Henry VIII in recompense for that monarch's book on the Seven Sacraments against Luther and other innovators of the age. Consequently, if it be asked what the word "faith" in the title signifies, there is plainly no other answer but that it signifies the faith held by him who gave the title, professed by

him who received it, and defended in the book on account of which it was bestowed. The man who dignified the king of England with that most honourable title was either the Vicar of Christ, as we Catholics believe, or Antichrist, as Protestants and Calvinists maintain. If he be the Vicar of Christ, why does not the defender of Christ's faith hear, acknowledge and venerate him? If, on the other hand, he be Antichrist, why does a Christian Prince glory in a title coming from such a source? Why, in a word, does he carry about the mark of the Beast?

St Robert finished his manuscript in Rome. By that time, 1605, all the bright hopes which the Catholics of England and Robert himself had entertained at the accession of Mary Stuart's son two years earlier were in black eclipse. King James personally did not favour persecution on religious grounds and might, if he could have put in practice his mystique of divine right, have given the Catholics some relief. But Elizabeth's dour parliament, and her brilliant, rabidly anti-Catholic ministers, were there to see that he maintained the savage laws against the recusants. Indeed, they introduced a new and shocking element of tyranny into the old laws, which Queen Elizabeth, to her honour, would not have tolerated, by forcing the Catholics under penalty of crippling fines not only to attend the Protestant religious services but to receive the Protestant sacrament. That was to outrage conscience in a way never attempted in any other country. Robert Bellarmine rightly guessed that this monstrous measure was not of King James's devising but, after news of the Gunpowder Plot, which Robert Cecil, son of Elizabeth's chief minister, Lord Burghley, so cleverly exploited, had reached Rome, Bellarmine gave up hope of James's conversion and finished his manuscript with the following appeal to his clemency:

If these reasons of mine do not move your Majesty to acknowledge the Catholic Church and embrace the faith of your mother and all your ancestors, may they at least obtain a little peace for those of your subjects who profess that faith. Grant this much to the honour of your parents and the memory of your forefathers that their religion may not be entirely driven out of their kingdom, now that you are its King. Do not consent, Sir, that the golden opinion which all men had of your clemency and kindness when you were King of Scotland alone, should now in some men's opinion be deservedly eclipsed, nor that you who were held for the meekest of kings, should now, where Catholics are concerned, be esteemed the most unkind. This I say, having read not without a keen sense of sorrow, the laws and decrees against Catholics, passed by you in your recent parliaments. I have seen, too, some of those venerable priests whom your laws have driven into exile, and the sight has created such a general feeling of horror that scarcely anyone can persuade himself that you are responsible —you, the most humane and learned of kings and the son of a Catholic father and mother.

Nevertheless, we do you justice, and are not ignorant that these measures proceed rather from the evil counsels of your advisers than from your own head and heart. Of a surety, it will in no way profit your reputation, your honour, your personal safety, nor the peace and tranquillity of your kingdom, that so many thousands of Catholics who welcomed you so gladly as their King, and hoped so much from the goodness of your heart, should now be subjected to persecution for that Catholic faith which flourished so many centuries in your native island. We heard not long since, and, as was natural, with the greatest sorrow and indignation, of the dreadful danger in which your Majesty's life had been placed through the conspiracy of some of your subjects. While rejoicing that, by the providence of God, you were spared, we would advise your Majesty in all sincerity that there is no safer nor easier protection against such perils than the love and good-will of your people.

After finishing his *Hieratikon Doron* in Rome and putting it to sleep indefinitely in the Jesuit archives, Cardinal Bellarmine hoped that he had done with King James and all other controversial personages for good, and would be allowed to spend the evening of his life in the ordinary routine work of the Roman congregations, as well as in peaceful preparation for death. He was sixty-five and very weary of fighting in the trenches so many years when, in 1607, Pope Paul V condemned for a second time the new Oath of Allegiance imposed by the English Parliament "for the better trial how his Majesty's subjects stand affected in point of their loyalty and due observance". The Oath was an integral part of an "Act for the better discovery and repressing of Popish Recusants". This measure was intended to suffocate Catholicism in England by the imposition of exorbitant fines on all who refused to do violence to their conscience by regular attendance at Protestant services and reception of the Protestant Eucharist. Husbands and wives not married in a Protestant church and by a Protestant minister were each to be deprived of all interest in the lands or property of the other. Children smuggled abroad for education by Catholic parents were deprived of all rights to inherit from the same parents who were themselves mulcted in a fine of a hundred pounds for each such offence, equivalent to a fine of at least a thousand pounds in modern money. It has been estimated that James I acquired for his personal fortune the equivalent of a quarter of a million pounds in modern values, from fines on the Catholics. The worst feature of all this brutal legislation was the award of a third or a half of the fine to those who denounced Catholics for a breach of the law, thus turning England into a land of spies, pursuivants, and other covetous Judases. The new Oath of Allegiance was part and parcel of the general penal laws and has to be judged in their context.

The Oath, which appears to have had the astute ecclesiastical diplomatist, Richard Bancroft, at the time Bishop of London, for its principal author, though King James himself studied and revised Bancroft's draft, is a clever blend of perfectly legitimate declarations with others at least highly debatable. The paragraph which caused the greatest trouble to Catholic consciences was this: "And I do further swear, that I do from my heart abhor, detest and abjure, as impious and heretical, this damnable doctrine and position that princes which be excommunicated or deprived by the Pope may be deposed or murdered by their subjects, or any other whatsoever". Rivers of ink have been expended in defending the lawfulness for Catholics of solemnly swearing those few words, or in stigmatizing them as utterly unacceptable. The debate continues, but for our Catholic forefathers it was not academic. It was a matter of life or death, for the Pope had twice solemnly condemned the Oath and forbidden any Catholic to take it. The historian Ranke, dealing with English affairs, considered that by the Oath of Allegiance "the supremacy of King James would be practically acknowledged and the connection of the English Catholics with the Papacy dissolved".

When the Oath became law in 1606, it had the effect, intended by its framers, of widening the division that already existed between a group of secular priests and the Jesuits on the English mission. George Blackwell, a secular, appointed archpriest or general superior of all secular missionaries in England, was alleged to be a tool of the Jesuits. Blackwell had at first been determinedly opposed to the Oath, but for reasons unknown soon veered round completely, and was with difficulty restrained by his advisers from issuing instructions to the Catholics of England that the Oath might safely be taken. This stand he maintained even after the Brief of Pope Paul V condemning the Oath had been placed in his hands, and obstinately refused to make it known to his Catholic flock. The spies of Robert Cecil, recently created Earl of Salisbury by the King, and nicknamed by him "Little Beagle" because so gifted at nosing out conspiracies and traitors, real or imaginary, soon captured a copy of the Brief. James became enraged on reading it and ordered the immediate arrest of Blackwell. He was taken with all his papers to Lambeth Palace and there browbeaten into renewal of his approbation of the Oath, as well as into taking it himself and writing a letter to the English clergy engaging them to follow his example and to urge their Catholic charges to do the same. Bancroft caused this letter to be printed and widely distributed throughout England. But the Pope's Brief had also been widely distributed, and the majority of the priests, both secular and regular, chose staunchly to obey the Pope, in spite of their immediate superior's defection. Blackwell was lodged in the Clink Prison and gave himself the airs of a true confessor of the faith, though the whole thing was a pretence and he became in fact the King's pensioner, with a comfortable room, good food and other amenities.

When news of the Archpriest's defection reached Rome, it was felt that someone of authority who had known him in the past should write a friendly admonition and endeavour to win him back to obedience. As had so often happened before, Cardinal Bellarmine was chosen. The original of his letter, not in his own hand but in that of some neat Roman scribe, is now in the Record Office, London, for it, like the Pope's two Briefs, was intercepted by the "Little Beagle's" splendidly efficient spies. "Reverend Sir and Brother in Christ," Robert began, "it is almost forty years since we did see the one the other. But yet I have never been unmindful of our ancient acquaintance, neither have I ceased, seeing I could do you no other service, to commend you, labouring most painfully in the Lord's Vineyard, in my prayers to God." The Cardinal went on to tell Blackwell of the sorrow and alarm caused in Rome by his disobedience to the Holy See and maintained that the Oath of Allegiance was little else than a cleverly disguised form of the Oath of Supremacy, for refusing which Thomas More and John Fisher had so bravely died. Perhaps he was stretching a point here, but not very far, because to allow a lay person, no matter how eminent, to decide what was or was not *heretical* in Catholic belief, that being the exclusive prerogative of the Holy See, amounted in fact to a denial of the pope's spiritual supremacy. In working out his own theory of the indirect power of the pope in temporal affairs, Bellarmine had been deflected from the natural course of his argument by the recent action of St Pius V in excommunicating and deposing, as far as in him lay, Queen Elizabeth in 1570. St Robert felt obliged to take account of this revival of a doctrine commonly held in the Middle Ages, and rather ruined his theory of the indirect power by tacking on to it a direct power of deposition in cases of extreme emergency. He must have been as well aware as any man that social and political conditions had changed completely since the centuries when the Holy See slowly and laboriously created order out of the anarchy resulting from the barbarian invasions, and thus made possible the emergence of national states. The Church became the mother of Christendom and was acknowledged universally to have a direct power of control over such emperors as Henry IV and Louis of Bavaria who aimed to subject her to their ends by the policy of lay investiture of her bishops.

Christianity was saved from the creeping totalitarianism of the secular state by the resolute action of such great popes as St Gregory VII and Innocent III. To account their action as "heretical", as was done in King James's Oath of Allegiance, showed an ignorance of history naïve to the point of stupidity. The steps taken by the popes of those times were, however, emergency measures and neither they nor their theologians and preachers, except possibly a few irresponsible hotheads, claimed that the Church had received from her Founder any power in this world other than spiritual. Only when the spiritual interests of her flock were jeopardized by the encroachments of the state was she entitled normally to have recourse to measures of coercion by the inflicting of *spiritual* penalties, such as excommunication or interdict. Unhappily, a few popes of the sixteenth century, encouraged by such die-hard canonists as Bellarmine's bitter enemy, the Spaniard Peña, could not forget the prerogatives conceded to and exercised by their great predecessors, Gregory VII and Innocent III, under the totally different conditions of their times. So it happened that, disastrously for English Catholics, Pius V, saint though he was, launched his perfectly futile sentence of deposition against their heretical and oppressive Queen, and so too did the imperious Sixtus V put a volume of Bellarmine's *Controversies* on his new Index because in it he was denied direct power in temporal affairs. Those two happenings, as it were two battered, weather-beaten ships stranded on his theological shores, greatly disturbed St Robert, for he felt that he ought somehow to allow for them in the serene landscape of his own theory of indirect power. Alas, he did, and thus gave James I and all other champions of the fatal Reformation maxim *cujus regio, ejus religio*, the weapon they needed to belabour him, and by association the Jesuits, for the rest of his life.

Archpriest Blackwell answered Bellarmine's well-meant but perhaps injudicious letter with a good deal of asperity, and of course it was soon in Salisbury's hands. There can be little doubt that it was written under the direction of Blackwell's new friends and so phrased as to make him seem a martyr to the designs of Rome. In one place the letter reads as an appeal to Bellarmine's heart: "If your Amplitude's most mild disposition could but in the least part conceive the ruin of Catholic families which the refusal of this Oath would bring upon us, assuredly you would not dissent from us who by most woeful examples do find that from thence were like to proceed, not only the loss and hazard of souls, but the lamentable extirpation of the whole Catholic state amongst us all".

In this, Blackwell, or rather the agents of King James at his elbow, totally misjudged the temper of the English Catholics. The penalties for refusing the Oath were indeed dreadful, in general life imprisonment and the confiscation of all property for a second refusal by any Catholic man or woman over the age of eighteen. In the opinion of Professor McIlwain, Editor of *The Political Works of James I* (Harvard, 1918), the Oath of Allegiance was "England's answer to the Jesuit challenge contained in Bellarmine's theory of the Pope's indirect power. . . . It marks a turning point in the history of modern politics and its effects were felt at once in every corner of the western intellectual world." That is talking very imposingly but not very accurately. The Oath resulted from the Gunpowder Plot, engineered by a small group of fourteen desperadoes, many of whom, including the ringleader Catesby, under suspicion of anti-state activities for years before the Plot, had only the most tenuous connection with the Catholic Church. The whole purpose of the Oath was to create the impression that the Catholics in general, and above all the Jesuits, were disloyal by virtue of their Catholicism and therefore needing to be controlled by such a measure as the Oath. Never was a more insulting and affronting measure conceived. The Catholics as a whole, in spite of the defection of their leader Blackwell who was quickly deposed from his office by the Pope, rejected the Oath with scorn. As the classic historian of King James's reign, S. R. Gardiner, put it, "men who would have been satisfied to allow the deposing power to be buried in the folios of theologians, and who would never have thought of allowing it to have any practical influence on their actions, were put upon their mettle as soon as they were required to renounce it".

La Boderie, the acutely observant French ambassador in

London, informed his master Henry IV, who had set the first and
only genuine example of toleration in that starkly intolerant age
by his Edict of Nantes, that immediately after the proclamation of
the Oath of Allegiance,

> the poor Catholics were still incredibly numerous, and resolved
> for the greater part in a way almost past belief, to suffer every-
> thing rather than give up their religion. . . . Many Catholics
> are making ready to go into exile, and among them some so
> old that I think they are seeking foreign shores merely to find
> there a peaceful grave. It is an admirable thing to see the large
> numbers who are in no wise frightened by all the penalties.
> I could not have believed that so much fervour and zeal were
> still to be found in our religion. . . . So far are these Catholics
> from losing heart under the persecution that they seem to
> derive new strength and courage from it, and instead of
> Catholics who were known to be such renouncing their faith,
> others who were not known declare themselves openly every
> day.

Most noteworthy is the large number of priests, condemned to
death for their priesthood alone, who were offered their lives
and sometimes even their freedom at the foot of the scaffold, if
they would only take the Oath of Allegiance. The first to be
offered his life on this condition was the secular priest Robert
Drury who refused the Oath as against his conscience and was
hanged, drawn and quartered at Tyburn on February 26, 1606-7,
at the age of thirty-nine. He was followed to heaven the following
year by Matthew Flathers, also a secular priest, condemned for
his priesthood at York but, like Drury, offered his life if he would
take the new Oath of Allegiance. He refused and was executed
with extreme barbarity. The same year, 1608, Thomas Garnet, a
Jesuit priest and nephew or near-kinsman of Father Henry
Garnet, that true martyr of the seal of confession whom St
Robert Bellarmine so greatly loved, was indicted at the old
Bailey and condemned to death for his priesthood. His is a very
explicit case, as among the great throng assembled at Tyburn to
see him die was the Earl of Exeter, a member of the Privy

Council, "who endeavoured to persuade the confessor to save his life by taking the Oath, alleging that several priests had taken it, and that many more looked upon it as a disputable matter in which faith was not concerned: why therefore should he be so stiff, and not rather embrace the offer of the King's clemency, by conforming as others had done? Father Thomas replied: 'My Lord, if the case be so doubtful and disputable, how can I in conscience swear to what is doubtful as if it were certain? No, I will not take the Oath, though I might have a thousand lives. . . . This new oath is so worded as to contain things quite foreign to allegiance, to which in my opinion no Catholic can with a safe conscience swear.' " In 1610 Roger Cadwallador, a secular priest of Herefordshire and one of the most genial and attractive of the martyrs, was condemned to death for his priesthood but, as usual, offered his life if he would take the Oath of Allegiance. At the foot of the scaffold, "he protested that he acknowledged and held his Majesty that now is to be the true and lawful king of this realm and other his dominions, and that he was very willing to swear to him all true allegiance . . ., whereupon some gentlemen present applauded this his protestation wishing him to proceed forward to the rest of the Oath. 'No,' said the martyr, 'there is a secret poison in the sequel.' " George Nappier, an Oxford man and secular priest, was hanged, drawn and quartered in his native city in the same year. "They insisted upon his taking the Oath of Allegiance as set forth in the Act of Parliament, and upon this condition promised him his life should be saved. But this he refused. Then they persuaded him to peruse Mr Blackwell's treatise of the lawfulness of this oath. Mr Nappier took the book and gave it a reading, but some few days after sent it back, and told Mr Vice-Chancellor that he still continued in his former resolution—the Oath of Allegiance, as it stood worded, he would not take."

All eighteen priests who were condemned solely for their priesthood in the reign of James I were offered their lives and sometimes even their freedom if they would but take the King's Oath. They chose rather to die a dreadful and degrading death.

Meantime, at Lambeth, the farce of Blackwell's examination

had been played out in full. In 1607 a volume of 170 pages was published in London by the King's printer, Robert Barker, bearing the full-page title: *A Large Examination taken at Lambeth, according to his Majesty's Direction, point by point, of M. George Blackwell, upon Occasion of a certaine Answere of his, without the Privitie of the State, to a letter lately sent to him from Cardinall Bellarmine, blaming him for taking the Oath of Allegiance. Together with the Cardinall's letter and M. Blackwell's said Answere unto it. Also M. Blackwell's Letter to the Romish Catholicks in England, as well Ecclesiasticall as Lay.* The most brazen touch in all that verbiage was the phrase "without the Privitie of the State", seeing that the State had stage-managed the whole affair, with the ready compliance of Blackwell its pensioner. The State, of course, was James I, who once informed his dutiful Parliament that "as to dispute what God may doe is blasphemie, so is it sedition in subjects to dispute what a King may doe in the height of his power".[1] Bellarmine's letter to Blackwell riled his Majesty to such an extent that he was not content to let Blackwell's trumped-up answer suffice, but must needs enter the lists himself to deal with the effrontery of the Cardinal. On February 14, 1608, Robert Barker issued a small volume quaintly entitled, *Triplici Nodo, Triplex Cuneus*, meaning, in so far as it meant anything, "A Threefold Wedge for a Threefolk Knot" (in wood). The subtitle explained that the threefold knot consisted of the "Two Breves of Pope Paulus Quintus and the late Letter of Cardinall Bellarmine to G. Blackwell, the Archpriest". No author's name was printed, but the royal arms engraved on the back of the title page and the general style of the book were a sufficient indication of its distinguished parentage. Besides, a few days after publication copies of the little book were presented to each of the foreign ambassadors in London for transmission to their respective sovereigns. The book first presents the King as the pattern of a loving and most tolerant monarch. Then the two Briefs of Pope Paul are reproduced and "the wordes of his thunder" subjected to vigorous, highly disrespectful criticism. But the author wastes

[1] *Political Works*, ed. McIlwain, p. 307.

little time over this part of his task, and soon dismisses the Pope
to introduce Bellarmine in the following fashion:

It is not sufficient to ratifie the last yeeres Brieve by a new
one come forth this yeere: but (that not onely every yeere, but
every moneth may produce a new monster) the great and
famous Writer of the Controversies, the late un-Jesuited
Cardinall Bellarmine, must adde his talent to this good worke,
by blowing the bellowes of sedition and sharpening the spur to
rebellion, by sending such a Letter of his to the Arch-priest
here, as it is a wonder how passion and an ambitious desire of
maintaining that Monarchie should charme the wits of so
famously learned a man. . . . And now that I am to enter into
the fielde against him by refuting his Letter, I must first use this
protestation; That no desire of vaine glory by matching with so
learned a man, maketh mee to undertake this taske; but onely
the care and conscience I have, that such smooth Circes charmes
and guilded pilles, as full of exterior eloquence as of inward
untrueths, may not have that publique passage through the
world without an answere.

I must here desire the world to wonder with me at the
committing of so grosse an errour by so learned a man that hee
should have pained himselfe to have set downe so elaborate a
letter, for the refutation of a quite mistaken question. For it
appeareth that our English Fugitives, of whose inward societee
with him hee so greatly vaunteth, have so fast hammered in
his head the Oath of Supremacie, which hath ever bene so
great a scarre unto them, as he thinking by his letter to have
refuted the last Oath, hath in place thereof onely payd the
Oath of Supremacie, which was most in his head. . . . For as
the Oath of Supremacie was devised for putting a difference
between Papists and them of our Profession; so was the Oath,
which he would seeme to impugne, ordained for making a
difference between the civilly obedient Papists and the perverse
disciples of the Powder-Treason.

This last point is the burden of all the King's arguments. The
Oaths of Supremacy and of Allegiance were as different as chalk
from cheese and Bellarmine had mixed them up. The Queen's
Oath did indeed deny the Pope any spiritual jurisdiction over her

subjects, but the King's Oath left that question out altogether, and demanded, with the backing of Scripture and councils, that purely civil obedience which every king has an incontestable right to demand. So far the royal author is temperate and reasonable but Bellarmine's statement that no pope in history had ever commanded that any prince, though a heretic, a pagan, a persecutor, should be murdered or did approve of the deed when done by any other, and followed up with the question: "Why, I pray you, doth only the King of England fear that which none of all the other Princes in Christendom either doeth fear, or ever did fear?", made James exceedingly angry, abusive and reckless in his retort:

> I know not with what face he can set so stout a deniall upon it against his owne knowledge; . . . let us turne our eyes upon our owne time, and therein remember what a Panegyrike oration was made by the Pope, in praise and approbation of the Frier that murthered King Henry the third of France. . . . How neere it scaped that the said Frier was not canonized for that glorious acte, is better knowen to Bellarmine and his followers, than to us here. . . . What difference there is, betweene the killing or allowing the slaughter of Kings and stirring up and approbation of practises to kil them, I remit to Bellarmine's owne judgment. . . . And howsoever the Pope will seeme to cleare himselfe of any allowance of the Powder-treason; yet can it not be denied that his principall ministers here, and his chief *Mancipia* the Jesuites, were the plaine practisers thereof; for which the principall of them hath died confessing it, and others have fled the countrey for the crime; yea, some of them gone into Italy: yet neither these nor Baldwine in the Low-countreys were ever called to account for it by the Pope: much lesse punished for medling in so scandalous and enormous businesse. And now what needes so great wonder and exclamation, that "onely the King of England feareth"?

The sum and substance of James's conviction is in his final words: "Christ is no more contrary to Belial, light to darkness, and heaven to hell, than Bellarmine's estimation of Kings is to God's". Brave words, yet despite its unmannerly language and less than regal insinuations, the *Apology* was genuinely learned, and would not have been a discredit to the best scholar on the Anglican bench of bishops. The Old and New Testaments were used with skill, and the arguments employed by court theologians ever since the great struggles between the Papacy and the Empire were again urged forcibly. The writings of the Fathers of the Church, the documents of the Councils, the edicts of kings and emperors, all have their place in the argument.

As soon as the *Apology* was brought to the notice of the Pope, he and his advisers began to consider whether in view of its wide diffusion and skilful presentation of the anti-papal case an answer should not be provided. The King of France, fearing with good reason that were the feelings of his English Majesty ruffled his Catholic subjects would be made to pay, urged strongly through his ambassador in Rome that silence would be the best and safest course. Assuredly he was right, but the Pope came to a different conclusion, and ordered the reluctant Bellarmine to reply. As King James had chosen to remain anonymous the Cardinal felt entitled to do likewise, and accordingly borrowed the name of his chaplain, Matteo Torti, a circumstance that was to prove a godsend to facetious Anglican controversialists later on, because Torti means tortured or twisted. St Robert must have worked rapidly, as his book of 156 pages appeared in print at Cologne within a matter of months: *Reply of Matthew Torti, Priest and Theologian, to the book entitled Triplici Nodo Triplex Cuneus, or an Apology for the Oath of Allegiance*. It is in Latin throughout. "We shall easily prove," it begins, "that in this oath there is question not solely of civil obedience but of the Catholic Faith, and this in the first place from the royal edict in which the formula of the oath is contained and prescribed. The title of that edict is: *For the detecting and repression of Papists*. Why was not the title, *For the detecting and repression of rebels*? It should have been, but for the fact that the purpose on account of which the oath was formulated was not the detection of men refusing civil obedience, that is to say rebels, but for the detection of those who deny the spiritual supremacy of the King and confess the spiritual supremacy of the Supreme Pontiff, that is to say Catholics, whom you call Papists."

K

Having made that point, surely a good one, Bellarmine went on to argue that the Oath of Allegiance was in fact and aim only a cleverly disguised form of the Oath of Supremacy. The purpose of both in the last resort was to secure for the civil ruler a perfectly free hand in his management of his subjects. James was careful not to say so in as many words, but his denial of the Pope's right to interfere under any circumstances was little less than an assertion of his own supreme jurisdiction, both civil and spiritual, over his Catholic as well as his Protestant subjects.

So far St Robert has argued well, but his strenuous defence of the deposing power as still inherent in the Pope's jurisdiction, though only employable in cases of extreme emergency, is not quite so much to our modern taste. Even a pope as little inclined to liberalism in his later days as Pius IX entirely rejected it. It was the other Pius, the Fifth, who made Robert mistakenly think that he had an obligation to find a place for it, if only on the very outskirts of his perfectly valid theory of the indirect power. However, the challenge had come from King James and his advisers, all of whom must have known perfectly well after the utter failure of St Pius V's anachronistic effort that his Majesty stood not in the remotest danger of a similar attempt on the part of Paul V, made wise as that pope had been by the stand of even a Catholic power against his interdict. Yet James deliberately made denial of the deposing power as *heretical* a condition of citizenship in England. Unless he wished to imply that the Holy See was in some way behind the Gunpowder Plot, there was no reason for dragging the Pope into his Oath at all.

In his reply, Bellarmine pointed out that to oblige a Catholic to swear that the doctrine of the deposing power was heretical came to the same thing as making him swear that a whole succession of medieval popes, saints and theologians had been heretics.

James had shown himself greatly aggrieved that the Pope and the Cardinal had expressed doubts about his tolerant intentions in their letters. After offering a little grudging incense at the shrine of the "late Queene of famous memorie who never punished any Papist for religion", the King had turned to the more congenial task of praising his own regime, and this is what he said about it:

Whatsoever was the [Queen's] just and merciful government over the Papists in her time, the King's Government over them since hath so far exceeded hers, in mercy and clemency, as not only the Papists themselves grew to that height of pride in confidence of his mildnesse, as they did assuredly promise themselves equalitie with other of his subjects in all things; but even a number of the best and faithfullest of his said subjects were cast in greate feare and amazement of his course and proceedings.

The proceedings are then described one by one, the last being, in the King's words, the "gracious proclamation whereby all priests that were at liberty and not taken, might go out of the country by such a day". However, this was only a selection out of many golden deeds and the modest monarch concludes: "Time and paper will faile me to make enumeration of all the benefits and favours bestowed in generall and particular upon Papists: in recounting whereof, every scrape of my pen would serve but for a blot of the Pope's ingratitude and injustice in meting [the King] with so hard a measure for the same".

To this rather disingenuous remonstrance the Cardinal's answer was a neat and exact summary, under fourteen heads, of the penal legislation of the year 1606. Having set this out, he continues:

Here, then, we behold that incredible clemency of the King towards Catholics, the memory of which causes him to denounce the ingratitude of the Pope for having written that he was afflicted by the news of what the Catholics had to endure for the sake of their faith. . . . If civil obedience was all that his Majesty desired to secure, why does he still keep the Archpriest, and others who have taken his Oath, in the prisons of London?...

As for the gracious proclamation whereby all priests who were not actually in chains might go out of the country by such a day, what astonishing kindness it was to allow men to go into exile whom his Majesty could not catch, try he never so

long and hard! And if exile seems a mercy to the writer of this
Apology, one may wonder what sweet names he has for the
rack and rope.

If the author urges that the penal measures were an immediate
and necessary result of the Gunpowder Plot, I may remind him
that before ever there was a plot, and in the very first year of
the King's reign, his first Parliament confirmed and considerably augmented the persecution laws of Queen Elizabeth. Nor
can it be said that it was the sentence of excommunication
launched by Pope Pius V against that Queen that had angered
her into issuing such edicts, for in the first year of her reign
also, that is, nine years before Pius V became Pope, a second
refusal to take the oath of ecclesiastical supremacy excogitated
by her father, Henry VIII, was made punishable by death. . . .
From the way the author of this Apology talks, he would seem
to be under the delusion that we had never read a word about
English affairs.

The King descended to very unkingly abuse from time to time,
as when he waxed scornful about Thomas More's "very fleshly
cause of martyrdom" and John Fisher's "dayly ambitious expectation of the cardinal's hat". But Henry Garnet is the chief target of
his rather artificial rage. He is set down as a ringleader among the
"caitife monsters" who had plotted to blow his Majesty to pieces,
which his Majesty knew perfectly well was an enormous concocted lie. As for Paul V, "if the Devil had studied a thousand
yeeres", he could not have worked more mischief than his
Holiness. With all his hectoring, there was something likeable
about James, a boyish exuberance and addiction to showing off
which had very little real malice in it. The only things rather
difficult to forgive him are his constant vicious and malicious
references to Father Henry Garnet. Perhaps he was trying to
stifle a reproachful conscience for having let that saintly and
innocent man be butchered. Cardinal Bellarmine ignored his
sallies, but revealed one deadly fact which it might have been
more charitable, as well as more circumspect, to omit in the
circumstances. The discussion at the moment turned on two
briefs which Pope Clement VIII had addressed to the English

Catholics in the first year of the new century. James argued with heat that those briefs were meant expressly to exclude his chances of succeeding Queen Elizabeth. Bellarmine answered that they were not:

On the contrary, they were drafted rather in favour of the King of Scotland, because they consisted of an exhortation to the Catholics to promote, as far as in them lay, the succession of an upright and orthodox monarch, and the envoys of that King had given good reasons for believing that their master was such a one, and not at all averse from embracing the Catholic Faith. This hope received a striking confirmation when the King himself addressed extremely kind letters to the Pope, and to Cardinals Aldobrandini and Bellarmine, in which he begged, among other things, that some Scotsman might be raised to the purple, to act as his representative at the Court of Rome.

These few innocent-looking words were a terrible riposte to James's lofty professions of indifference to Roman opinion, and very soon his Puritan enemies would be shouting them from one end of England to the other. The Presbyterian minister, Mr James Melvill, who was much in favour with the King though they differed so profoundly in their views on Church government, recorded in his diary, September, 1608, that Bellarmine's book as a whole "did trouble the King at the heart", and that the reference to his Majesty's letters to Rome "not only galled the King but moved much the Counsell and whole estaite". Vigorous steps were immediately taken at the English court to repair the damage done by the Cardinal's criticism and disclosure. Further sale of the King's *Apology* was strictly prohibited and orders were issued to buy back as many as possible of the copies that had gone into circulation. Four court bishops, of whom the "devout Andrewes" was one, then set to work to revise the text, while James himself renounced the world, the flesh, and the devil, that he might devote all his energies to the composition of a magnificent preface for a new edition. Bishop Andrewes, who was given the hard task of suggesting ideas and corrections to the King, found "that he had Penelope's web to weave, for what he finished at night his Majesty undid in the morning". When at last the work came from the press, more alterations were seen to be necessary, and the unfortunate Robert Barker, the printer, was committed to prison for having allowed some copies to get into circulation before this operation was completed. By February 6, 1609, the definitive version was in the printer's hands, but James would not budge from London until he had seen it through the press. The woods of Windsor in their spring-time glory called to him in vain. His unfortunate courtiers swore under their breath and consigned all theologians indiscriminately to the devil, but not until the month of May, when Barker issued the first copies of the hated book, did they get their release. The title of the new edition ran thus: *An Apologie for the Oath of Allegiance: First set foorth without a name: and now acknowledged by the Author, the Right High and Mightie Prince, James, by the Grace of God, King of Great Britaine, France and Ireland; Defender of the Faith, etc.: Together with a Premonition of his Majesties to all most Mightie Monarches, Kings, Free Princes and States of Christendome.*

The Premonition is addressed to Emperor Rudolph II and to all Right High and Mighty Kings and Right Excellent free Princes and States of Christendom who are exhorted to wake while there is still time and not to suffer the strings of their authority as lieutenants and vicegerents of God to be cut one by one. James explains to his august readers why he first wrote anonymously: "I thought it not comely for one of my place to put my name to bookes concerning scholastic Disputations, whose calling it is to set forth Decrees in the Imperative Moode. . . . I was never the man, I confesse, that could think a Cardinall a meete match for a King, especially having many hundred thousands of my subjects of as good birth as he. As for his Cardinalship, I know not how to ranke or value it, it being indeed onely a new Papall erection tolerated by the sleeping connivance of our Predecessors."

The Premonition is very long-winded and all in the same angry, aggrieved tone. James does not seem to have credited his fellow monarchs with much intelligence, as when, having complained of Bellarmine's unmannerliness, he goes on to speak of the matter of the Cardinal's book:

It well fits indeed the manner thereof. . . . So doeth he, upon that ground of *Pasce oves meas*, give the Pope so ample a power over Kings, to throne or dethrone them at his pleasure as I doubt not but in your owne Honors ye will resent you of such indignities. . . . I am none of the Pope's flocke, but yee are in the Pope's folde; and you, that great Pastour may leade as sheepe to the slaughter, when it shall please him. . .

And because I have in my booke (by citing a place in his *Controversies*) discovered him to be a small friend to Kings, hee is much commoved; . . . because, I say, citing this place of his in my booke, I tell with admiration that he freeth all Churchmen from any subjection to Kings, even those that are their borne-subjects, hee is angry with this phrase and sayth it is an addition for breeding envie unto him. But whose hatred did he feare in this? Was it not yours? Who have interest, but Kings, in the withdrawing of due subjection from Kings? And when the greatest monarchs amongst you will remember that almost the third part of your subjects and of your Territories is Churchmen and Church-livings; I hope yee will then consider and weigh what a feather he puls out of your wings, when he denudeth you of so many subjects and their possessions, in the Popes favour: nay, what bryers and thornes are left within the heart of your Dominions, when so populous and potent a partie shall have their birth, education and livelyhood in your Countries and yet owne you no subjection, nor acknowledge you for their Soveraines?

After all that ludicrously false history, the King felt that some strong declaration against Rome might help to kill in the public mind the suspicion that had been instilled into it by Torti's allegation about the letters to Pope Clement and the two cardinals, so before concluding his Premonition he wandered off into a long dissertation that aimed at proving the Pope to be antichrist, which the French ambassador described as "the silliest that had ever been written on such a subject". Then he returns to Bellarmine, but only to dismiss him contemptuously:

As for the particular answering of his booke it is both unnecessary and uncomely for me to make a Reply. . . . Uncomely it must needs be (in my opinion) for a King to fall in altercation with a Cardinall, at least with one no more nobly descended then hee is; unnecessary because (as I have alreadie told you) my booke is never yet answered. . . . And therefore having resolved not to paine myself with making a reply, I have thought good to content myself with the reprinting of my Apologie; having, in a manner, corrected nothing but the Copiers or Printers faults therein.

The King concludes his Premonition by telling Protestant rulers that they must stick together to promote "the spirituall libertie of the Gospel, and not suffer this incroching Babylonian Monarch to winne still further ground". Finally, the Catholic princes are addressed:

As for you (my loving Brethren and Cosins) whom it hath not yet pleased God to illuminate with the light of his Trueth, I can but humbly pray with Elizeus, that it would please God to open your eyes. . . . But leaving this to God, his mercifull providence in his due time, I have good reason to remember you to maintaine the ancient liberties of your Crownes and Commonwealths, not suffering any under God to set himselfe up above you. . . . I end, with my earnest prayers to the Almightie for your prosperities, and that after your happie temporall Raignes in earth, ye may live and raigne in Heaven with him for ever.

In spite of his high and mighty language, King James was in many respects a modest and timid person who did not over-estimate his own gifts as a controversialist. At all events, he decided that his *Apology* was too small a book and, perhaps, too rhetorical, to impress learned men. Some larger and more imposing craft must sail from the press in its wake to give it countenance. For this purpose of confuting Bellarmine on a larger scale, the King turned to the one man then living in England who most resembled Bellarmine in knowledge and piety, Lancelot Andrewes, Bishop of Chichester. The *Preces Privatae* which this good man compiled from the Scriptures, the

Missal, the Greek liturgies and the medieval *Hours of the Blessed Virgin*, for his own use would have delighted St Robert had he known of them, for they bear in many places a close resemblance to his own little book, *The Mind's Ascent to God by a Ladder of Created Things*. Both works are penetrated with the spirit of the *Benedicite*, but Andrewes was a more acute observer of nature than Bellarmine and much less impeded by the shadow of Aristotle. Throughout the *Preces*, too, runs such a deep spirit of penitence as informs the whole of Bellarmine's *De Gemitu Columbae*, the Mourning of the Dove, or the Value of contrite Tears. Andrewes wrote the *Preces* in Latin, Greek and occasionally Hebrew, because they were intended for no eyes but his own and, in fact, were not published until some years after his death. The best English translation of the first Greek part of the work was made by John Henry Newman in 1840, as the seventy-eighth of the *Tracts for the Times*. It has long been a spiritual classic of Anglicanism, but Catholics also use the *Preces*, for there is nothing in them alien or disturbing, only a most beautifully articulated method of growing nearer to God in constant prayer.

What a strange contradictory world it is that set those two men, Andrewes and Bellarmine, so much alike in the very texture of their minds and hearts, at loggerheads. Bellarmine found the controversy with King James totally against the grain, and Andrewes against his will and inclination found himself the chief controversialist of the English Church. But he was not allowed to perform his distasteful task at his own pace and in peace. On November 11, 1608, a private gentleman, John Chamberlain, wrote from London to his friend Sir Dudley Carleton in France: "I thank you for your Remonstrance of the French Clergy, which will give me occasion perhaps to visit the good Bishop of Chichester, though I doubt he be not at leisure for any bye matters, the King doth so hasten and spur him on in this business of Bellarmine's, which he were likely to perform very well (as I hear by them that can judge) if he might take his own time, and not be troubled nor entangled with arguments intruded to him continually by the King". This letter from the *State Papers Domestic* in the Record Office, London, may well be the explana-

KX

tion of passages in Andrewes' large volume (nearly five hundred pages) which are utterly unlike anything to be expected from the gentle and truly devout Bishop's pen. The worst of these concern Father Henry Garnet and I, for one, refuse to believe that Andrewes was responsible for them. Bellarmine had described Garnet as being, of his own certain knowledge, "a man of profound learning and incomparable sanctity". In Andrewes' book we are told of Garnet's speech that "it smacks more of Bacchus than Apollo", and as for the man's sanctity, "it is only too well known that he was often drunk". The author of the *Preces Privatae* never wrote those words. They were intruded by his master in his immitigable animus against the innocent man he had sent to a terrible death. Nor is it credible that such a saintly man as Andrewes deliberately falsified the text of a letter of Garnet's, published in his pages, in order to make his alleged knowledge of and connivance at the Gunpowder Plot more apparent. Andrewes, who had an extremely sensitive conscience which he examined daily with all the rigour of St Ignatius Loyola, could not have stooped to such a base action as that. But King James could and, as is well known, often did. And he had his "Little Beagle", the hunchback with no conscience whatever, to help him along. What follows is a good example of their procedures.

Nothing touched King James more nearly than Bellarmine's revelation of his dealings with Pope Clement VIII and with himself, while he was still in Scotland, angling for the crown of England. He had attained his ambition, but Bellarmine's disclosure in 1608 of his earlier friendly attitude to the Catholic Church became a real thorn in his flesh, especially with so many pestilent Puritans and other radical sectaries sprouting all the time to take gleeful advantage of it. Probably counselled by Lord Salisbury, his invaluable "Little Beagle", he determined to brazen the matter out and deny that he had ever sent or dreamed of sending a personal message to the Pope or to Bellarmine. Lord Balmerino, who as Sir James Elphinstone had been his chief secretary in Scotland, was summoned forthwith and charged with having surreptitiously passed the letters in among other papers awaiting the King's signature. The door of the room in which the blustering interview took place was left open, and in the apartment beyond witnesses were concealed who could hear all that went on. Balmerino, the story goes, fell on his knees and acknowledged that he had drawn up the letter to the Pope. Moreover, he is supposed to have testified that the King could not have known what was in the unlucky documents, as he had signed them hastily, with the impatient barking of the staghounds in his ears. After scoring this initial victory James placed the whole affair in the hands of his Privy Council, sending them at the same time elaborate instructions as to how they were to proceed. "Though ye were born strangers to the country where this was done," he told them in his own hand, "yet are ye no strangers to the King thereof; and ye know, if the King of Scotland prove a knave, the King of England can never be an honest man. Work so, therefore, in this, as having interest in your King's reputation." That hint was plain enough, but there were plainer to come. "I remit to you and all honest men," he wrote to Salisbury, "to think upon all ways that may be for clearing of my honesty in it, which I had the more need to do, considering his treachery. I only pray you to think that never thing in this world touched me nearlier than this doth."

The Privy Council put a very cleverly written confession of their own devising before the unfortunate Scottish peer, and bade him sign it without more ado. Considering the means of persuasion at the Council's disposal, resistance was hopeless from the start, so Balmerino did as he was told. The next act of the judicial farce took place at St Andrews, whither Balmerino was sent for his trial. The verdict was a foregone conclusion, but "the doome after his convictione", says the contemporary Presbyterian historian David Calderwood, "was delayed till the King's farther pleasure were known, and then it was pronounced in the Tolbooth of Edinburgh, that he should be beheaded quartered and demaimed like a Traitour, and his members set up in publick places". Whatever his responsibility in the matter, James had no intention of letting the sentence be executed. In the following October Calderwood reported that he sent a warrant giving Balmerino "libertie of free ward in Falkland, and a mile about, he finding caution not to escape under the pain of fourtie thousand pounds. Yet he, fearing the worst, or taking deeply to heart the great disgrace and ignominie, under which he was laying, ended his days in displeasure not long after." Before he died, however, he committed to paper a very different account of the whole affair from that contained in his extorted confession. It is interesting to know that that confession was originally intended to be part of the King's answer to Bellarmine, but his Majesty, fearful probably of some other compromising trumps which the Cardinal might have in reserve, thought it best to pass the matter over in silence at the time.

James's caution may very well have been due to a letter now reposing quietly in the British Museum (Add. MS. 37021, f.25). It is dated from Dalkeith, July 31, 1601, and addressed to Cardinal Borghese, then protector of the Scottish nation at Rome, and subsequently Pope Paul V. It is signed by James's Queen, Anne of Denmark, but expressly claims to have been written on the authority of James himself, in answer to letters received by him from Pope Clement VIII. The King, wrote Queen Anne, could not personally reply to the most welcome letter of his Holiness because of the danger of his answer falling into the hands of Queen Elizabeth, but had given her authority to do so in his name to Cardinal Borghese. "By the grace of the Holy Spirit," her letter continues, "we are coming to life again from the darkness of heresy into the light of Catholic truth, and we have committed to this our nuncio and procurator [the Sir Edward Drummond of Bellarmine's letter to King James in 1600] the charge of professing the Catholic faith in our name before the Holy Apostolic See." Queen Anne next explains how difficult it is to get letters to and from Rome without their interception by the agents of the Queen of England:

> Having reason to fear the fate that befell our forebears, we are obliged to proceed cautiously and slowly. . . . Our nuncio will signify in our name what we most need for an increase of the harvest, and we look to your Illustrious Lordship, for whom his Serene Majesty the King has conceived the warmest feelings, to obtain with diligent care all that we desire from His Holiness our Lord Pope, so that this Kingdom, recovering from the

wretched calamities of our times, may happily return to that faith which none of its ancestors has hitherto relinquished. We make willing offering of ourselves to endure for this end all evil chances and even the danger of losing both our lives and our thrones.

Your Illustrious and Most Reverend Lordship's Dutiful,
Anna R.

King James's *Apology* for the Oath of Allegiance and its prancing Premonition got a very poor reception in Catholic countries, and in Venice caused a diplomatic uproar through the indiscretions of the English representative, the bitterly anti-Catholic Sir Harry Wotton, a crony of Fra Paolo Sarpi. Later on the filibustering champion of Bellarmine against King James, Gaspar Schopp, damaged Wotton badly in the royal estimation by revealing to the world the quip which Sir Henry had written in the album of a gentleman in Augsburg, to wit that "an ambassador is an honest man sent to lie abroad for the good of his country". Naturally Rome headed the opposition to James's little book. It was at once put on the Index and forbidden under pain of excommunication reserved to the Holy See.

The unfortunate Cardinal Bellarmine, sick and tired though he was of such controversies, received peremptory orders from the Pope to answer the King's book, though the wisest political authority in Europe, Henry IV of France, had most earnestly deprecated any renewal of the warfare. It was the dogdays in Rome, and St Robert's room at the Vatican lay defenceless under the blistering sun. Some Vatican officials referred to his room as purgatory, and others as hell. In the autumn of the year 1609, Bartholomew Zanetti of Rome issued the book which had literally been written in the sweat of its author's brow: *Apology of Robert Bellarmine, Cardinal of the Holy Roman Church, for his Answer to the book of James, King of Great Britain*. In this volume of 160 pages, the Cardinal answers effectively the various derisive arguments of the King against Catholic dogmas and, at least in one place, perhaps due to the heat, returns his Majesty scorn for scorn: "With reference to the fair green meadow that is in

Purgatory, let the King inquire of that noble English doctor, the Venerable Bede, from whom I borrowed the story, whether there be a river running through it. However, it matters little what Purgatory is like to people who do not believe in it. 'Tis plain enough their curiosity should be about Hell, as that is the only place left for them." The passage in the *Controversies* was about Limbo, not Purgatory, and James had asked Bellarmine facetiously in his book whether a river ran through Bede's fair green meadow, "that in case I come there I may have hawking upon it".

The Cardinal's knowledge of history was extensive, if not always accurate, and he used it to some purpose in his book. He had hinted in his pseudonymous reply to the King that in spite of his Majesty's professed loathing for Puritans, he had himself signed a Puritan or Presbyterian confession of faith in 1581, condemning episcopal government and establishing the jurisdiction of the Kirk. This charge made the King furious, and with some reason, because St Robert, right on the main point, omitted to mention through ignorance of the fact, that James was only fifteen at the time and under the complete domination of the Kirk Sessions and presbyteries. "It is no wonder," he retorted, "that Bellarmine takes the Puritans' part, since Jesuits are nothing but Puritan-Papists." This is a reference to Bellarmine's teaching in the *Controversies*, which is the common teaching of theologians, that bishops do not derive their jurisdiction directly from God but have it mediated to them by the Holy See.

Robert, sweltering in his oven, must have breathed a heavy sigh when he came to the trashy pages of the King, laboriously trying to establish that the Pope was Antichrist. He had given fifty thousand words of his *Controversies* to this weary business of which the Protestant athletes were so fond. Still, he did not refuse to follow his critic on to that arid ground where never a blade of common sense was known to grow. Finally, he takes up once more the defence of the persecuted English Catholics. "I do constantly maintain," wrote the King, "that no man, either in my time or in the late Queene's, ever died here for his conscience. For let him be never so devout a Papist, his life is in no danger by the Law if he break not out into some outward act against the words of the Law." Bellarmine answered:

> In deciding whether a man is a martyr, it matters little whether he was killed because he professed the Catholic faith, or because he broke the Law which commanded him to renounce the same. It was an old trick of the pagan Roman Emperors to make a law against the Christian Religion, and then murder men, not intolerantly on account of religion, of course, but for offending the majesty of the constitution. As for the priests and popish churchmen who are forbidden to return to their home country of England under pain of treason, on account, as the King alleges, of their manifold plottings and conspiracies— that story, too, has its parallels in the past. The pagan Emperors used to allege similar charges against the early Christians, imputing to them all manner of public crimes. Nero burnt down a large part of Rome and then burnt the Christians for doing it.

James's uneasy conscience had endeavoured to blacken the name of Father Henry Garnet, "that straw saint[1] who was so publicly and solemnly convicted and executed upon his own so clear, unforced, and often repeated confession of his knowledge and concealing of that horrible treason", the Gunpowder Plot. Bellarmine, who had been Henry Garnet's spiritual director and confessor in Rome twenty years earlier, and had learned to love him dearly, made the following protestation:

> Let the King urge and argue as much as he likes, yet will I tell him what an important personage who is not a priest, nor a Jesuit, nor a pupil of the seminaries, swore solemnly before me here in Rome; namely that he was present at Garnet's execution, and heard the Father say clearly, just as he was about to die, that he had had no knowledge of the treason except what was given to him under the seal of confession. And I for one can easily believe it, since he was my intimate friend during many years. No one knew better than I what an absolutely upright man he was; no one was in a better position to

[1] A reference to the well-known story of the ear of corn, bedewed by a drop of the martyr's blood, on which Father Garnet's features were said to be represented.

appreciate the perfect purity of life which crowned his great gifts of intellect and learning.

The doctrine of the sacramental seal was "damnable" in the eyes of King James, but he knew enough about it to be able to urge that Garnet ought to have given some warning of the plot, even if, according to his Jesuit theology, the plotters' identity had to be carefully concealed. "I would ask the King," Bellarmine replied, "whether, if Father Garnet had warned him that his life was in danger from the machinations of traitors, he would have forborne out of respect for the seal of confession to demand their names. Certain it is that one holding such views as he does about the sacrament would instead have ordered the Father to be clapped into chains and subjected to the most terrible tortures until he revealed everything."

A leading Catholic authority on the theology of the relations between Church and State has summarized excellently the problem as it confronted the English Catholics in the reign of King James I:

> The denial of the papal right of deposition, required of Catholics in the Oath of Allegiance, could not in the concrete be made by them, because it meant in effect the denial of the spiritual sovereignty in itself and in its necessary reach into the temporal order; furthermore, in the concrete it meant stigmatizing as a usurpation the right that the Church had claimed and exercised throughout the whole medieval period. The situation was indeed tragic for the Christian conscience. Catholics had really been manoeuvred into a false position; they were compelled to rally to the defence of an outpost that in 1606 could have been well abandoned, because its defence was part of an ancient war, long since concluded. However, its abandonment in the circumstances of 1606 would have meant in effect the surrender of the fort itself.[1]

Father Courtney Murray considers that Bellarmine's defence of the distinction of the two powers, spiritual and secular, "was

[1] That passage is from a magisterial article, "Bellarmine on the Indirect Power", by John Courtney Murray, in the immensely rewarding American periodical, *Theological Studies*, for December, 1948.

brilliant and effective". He gave it a newly luminous statement by his emphasis on the purely spiritual power of the Church. "In this respect he effected a doctrinal advance within the Church herself, by finally disposing of the confusions and exaggerations" of those who claimed direct temporal power for the Holy See. Also, in his effective statement of the primacy of the spiritual power, "he did a service not only to the Church but to the spiritual freedom of mankind, in that he set a stern barrier to the tyrannical pretensions of royal absolutism".

But unfortunately Bellarmine "in the zeal of controversial argument confused the absolute and permanent with the relative and contingent". He rightly defended the action of some medieval Popes in deposing tyrannical emperors, but he failed to recognize that what the Church then did "was to step into a political vacuum, created by the absence of a political institution able to constrain the monarch to obedience to law". But the deposing power was only a makeshift and transitional institution made necessary by a temporary defect in the political order. "If the Pope did not depose the ruler grown tyrannical or unjust or heretical or useless, there was no other way to get rid of him." Political institutions were then in an adolescent stage and needed the tutelage which only the Church could and did give, *jure divino*. But the civil order did not remain adolescent. It grew into statehood "as a society in its own right, with its own institutions to direct and correct its action". Robert Bellarmine failed to take account of this development and tended to think in terms of a unitary Christendom which had once prevailed and would, by the mercy of God, return when the Church's dissident children discovered the error of their ways and rejoined her fold. It was a dream, beautiful but unreal, and part of it seemed to him to be the power of the Pope, as a last resort, to rid a people of a ruler unfit to govern by his tyranny or his oppression of the Church. He failed to see that the right of deposition claimed and exercised by St Gregory VII and Innocent IV was entirely relative to the immaturity of political institutions at their time, and not an absolute power resident for all time in the Holy See. So the "indirect power" which St Robert did not invent but systematized finely, became peripherally for him a

"direct power", only to be used, however, in cases of extremest
urgency. Undoubtedly, the action of St Pius V in regard to Queen
Elizabeth pushed him into this error, and James I's Oath of
Allegiance confirmed him in it.

Bellarmine had taught his views and had committed them to
print in his *Controversies* long before James I expounded his theory
of the divine right of kings or devised his Oath of Allegiance.
The French Calvinists had been staunch supporters of the "democratic" doctrine that princes ruled only by the consent of their
peoples, until suddenly their worshipped leader, Henry of
Navarre, became heir to the crown of France. Then, with almost
ludicrous haste, they reversed course and declared themselves
ardent champions of divine right. The League, on the other hand,
had been vociferous defenders of the same divine right until the
same Henry of Navarre and his claim turned them into fierce
"democrats". Finally, both parties reached agreement that kings
rule by divine right when Henry of Navarre became King Henry
IV, and promulgated the Edict of Nantes. Bellarmine's name was
often mentioned with love or with loathing during those see-
saws of opinion, but he took no notice until a Scottish Catholic
layman named William Barclay, who taught law with distinction
at Catholic universities in France, rose to challenge him.

In the year 1600 Barclay published in Paris a book defending in
set form and excellent learning the theory of the divine right of
kings. The Cardinal read it but let it pass. King James in Scotland
read it and was enthralled by it. No sooner did he succeed to the
throne of England than he warmly invited Barclay to enter his
service. Barclay honourably declined and employed his leisure
hours at the University of Angers excogitating a second book in
confirmation of his first. He died in 1608 before he could get it
out, but his son John published it in London the following year
and so won the special favour of King James. It was written in
Latin and bore the title, *On the Power of the Pope, an Inquiry
concerning the Existence and Extent of his Dominion over Secular
Princes*. The title bears a resemblance to that chapter of Horre-
bow's *Natural History of Iceland* which Dr Johnson boasted to
Boswell that he could repeat by heart—Chapter 72, *Concerning*

snakes: "There are no snakes to be met with throughout the whole island". What Barclay meant was that the Pope had no dominion over secular princes. Robert Bellarmine was Barclay's target all through, and he was urged from all sides to reply, as the book, very ably written, came from a Catholic pen and was therefore calculated to do all the more harm. He did not want to reply and Pope Paul V did not want him to either. There had been more than enough wordy warfare already, and the Catholics of France, always so sensitive about the *Franchises et Libertés de l'Église Gallicane*, would probably be antagonized by anything he might say. However, in a weak moment the troubled Cardinal gave way to the ardent but unwise advisers. His book, an octavo of 276 pages, appeared in 1610 under the title, *A Treatise on the Power of the Supreme Pontiff in Temporal Affairs*.

A personal note very unusual in Bellarmine's books runs through this one, as in the Epilogue:

> When I stand before the tribunal of the Supreme Judge, as I shall soon have to do, I think I shall be able to plead with a good conscience that neither enmity nor a desire to curry favour has ever inspired my pen. I have written down what I judged to be the truth, what I learned from the Church, and what many wise and holy men had written before me. Nor was it of my own sweet will that I engaged in this combat, but because I was attacked by a man of whom I had no knowledge, and so compelled, in my old age, to defend what I wrote when I was young. If, according to my most earnest desire, I have acquitted myself becomingly, I offer my humblest thanks to God who holds us all, as well as our arguments, in the hollow of his hand. But if on the contrary I be found wanting through human weakness, in any or many respects, I crave forgiveness from him who is meek and kind and full of mercy to all who call upon his name.

St Robert's own misgivings about the book and the Pope's reluctance to sanction it were abundantly justified. There was nothing not already in the *Controversies*, except a few flings at Barclay senior whom the Cardinal thought to be still alive. But appearing in a form which all who ran might read, at any rate, all who knew Latin, and at that critical time immediately after the assassination of Henry IV by the crazy ex-friar Ravaillac, it provided all the minimizers of papal jurisdiction in France, chiefly the Sorbonne and the legal fraternity known as the *Parlement*, with exactly the weapon they needed. In November, 1610, Bellarmine's thesis on the indirect power of the Pope was solemnly condemned at a session of the *Parlement* as "a false and detestable proposition which tended to the subversion of sovereign powers ordained by God, to the rebellion of subjects against their princes, to the instigation of attempts upon their persons and states and to the disturbance of public order and tranquillity". That *arrêt* or sentence was printed and posted all over Paris. The papal nuncio to France, Cardinal Ubaldini, who regarded Bellarmine as the "Athanasius and Augustine of the age", was so indignant that he asked the Regent, Marie de Medici, for his papers and determined to quit the country. The threat roused the Regent and her Council to issue an *arrêt* of their own, stringently forbidding the *Parlement* to meddle in affairs of state, and requiring them immediately to suspend their judgment on Bellarmine and his book. This *arrêt* was also posted at Paris and wherever else the denunciation had been made public. At Bourges it was proclaimed not only by posters and handbills, but also by the town crier to the sound of trumpets on the public square.

St Francis de Sales, who so much admired Cardinal Bellarmine, wrote to his friend Bénigne Milletot in 1611: "No, I have not found to my taste certain writings of a saintly and most excellent prelate in which he touches on the indirect power of the Pope over princes. Whether his theory is right or wrong is not for me to decide, but only that at the present time when we have so many external enemies, I think it behoves us not to cause any stirs within the body of the Church. The poor mother hen which shelters us like chicks under her wings has, goodness knows, trouble enough to defend us from the kite, without us straining her by pecking at one another." That was well said, but, all the same, Bellarmine's book, haunted though it was by that last enchanter of the Middle Ages, St Pius V, did help to check for a while the victorious progress of Gallicanism. At the meeting of the States General in

1614, an oath of allegiance was suggested almost identical with the English one, which the deputies wanted imposed on all ecclesiastics and magistrates. In a powerful harangue to the assembly, Cardinal du Perron said that the proposed oath resembled the mermaid mentioned by Horace: "It has the head of a beautiful woman, to wit, the pretext of loyalty to sovereigns; but its tail is the tail of a fish, for it has swum over to us from England". The speech made a profound impression and nerved Marie de Medici to forbid absolutely all further debate on the oath.

John Barclay, who, though a Catholic, Jesuit-educated, and grand-nephew of the eminent and saintly Father Edmund Hay, was responsible more than anybody for Bellarmine's troubles by the publication in London of his father's unprovoked attack on the Cardinal, basked for a time in the favour of King James, and the Little Beagle, then Lord Treasurer. That was no wonder, for he wrote of Lord Salisbury, keeper of the bawbees, that "the wisdom of Burleigh bore the like proportion to that of his son, as the waters of the Thames do to the ocean". To pleasure his royal and noble patrons, he wrote and published in London a spirited but scurrilous book: *The Piety of John Barclay, or a public Vindication of his Father William Barclay, against Robert Bellarmine's Treatise on the Power of the Pope in Temporals*. Fortune, however, for John proved a fickle jade. For some reason, perhaps because he would not go the whole way and declare himself a Protestant, he fell out of favour at court. He may even have been threatened. Anyhow, he felt unsafe in London and nervously inquired whether he might have permission to reside in Rome. Pope Paul, always kindly, not only invited him to come, but settled on him a pension for life. It is pleasant to record that he and Cardinal Bellarmine soon became good friends. Having found security, John turned to the cultivation of tulips and, in his leisure moments from that exacting occupation, produced an *Admonition to Sectaries*, with a dedication to Bellarmine in which he wrote: "As a chief part of my happiness and good fortune here in Rome, I reckon the friendship of my dear patron Cardinal Bellarmine. Who is there who, without sorrow and regret, could find himself in opposition to so great a captain of Christ; or have merited the displeasure of one endowed with so many virtues of heart and gifts of mind? Just as he is the admiration of all men alive now, so will future ages never cease to venerate his memory." John could pour out such compliments by the bushel and they may not mean very much, but the whole incident does tell us something about St Robert Bellarmine.

Writing to the Spanish ambassador in London, Count Gondomar, on December 16, 1618, St Robert said: "Our friend Barclay is quite well and is very much liked by the Pope and his whole court. As your Excellency foretold to him, he is as dear to me as if he were my well loved child. He often comes to visit me and to consult me about his affairs." The two friends died within a month of each other in 1621.

One last name has to be mentioned in connection with the controversies of those days, that of Roger Widdrington, which appears on no less than ten volumes in Latin or English, all in defence of King James's Oath of Allegiance. The first of the series was issued in 1611 and entitled *Apologia Cardinalis Bellarmini pro jure Principum*. The title-page bore the Jesuit seal and the imprint Cosmopoli, which had first appeared on Blessed Edmund Campion's *Ten Reasons*. There never was any such place as Cosmopolis, any more than there was an island called Utopia. Campion invented it to confuse the pursuivants, and it is now common knowledge that the *Decem Rationes* was printed at Father Persons' secret press, first set up at East Ham and later removed to Stonor Park, near Henley. Why did this Roger Widdrington seek so carefully to cover his tracks? Because, though he gave himself out for a Catholic, his book charging Cardinal Bellarmine with gross inconsistency is known from a letter of the King's printer to have been produced in London by special command of his Majesty, "purposely to enlarge and nourish the contentions between the Jesuits and secular priests, to make Popery appear the more odious". It was suspected by many Catholics at the time, and by some firmly believed, that Roger Widdrington was an alias, most unfairly purloined from a staunch Catholic squire in Northumberland, to conceal the identity of Thomas Preston, superior of the Cassinese Benedictines on the English mission. That suspicion and conviction has now been established once and for all as the sad truth.[1]

Thomas Preston took the Oath of Allegiance, and became the special protégé of George Abbott, Archbishop of Canterbury. It would have ruined the considerable influence which he wielded with his fellow Catholics had this become known, so an elaborate front was prepared behind which he could pursue his pro-government activities fruitfully. He was committed to the Clink as Blackwell, the fallen Archpriest, had been, and assumed all the airs of a persecuted confessor of the faith in the Blackwell manner. The truth is that they both lived at the Clink in considerable comfort, at government expense. He, and presumably Blackwell also, was allowed a personal valet, was given all the books he desired, and could come and go as he fancied from his suite in the Clink. All his ten volumes, with their various foreign imprints, were in fact published by the King's printer in London. The King required only one concession from his faithful servant, which was not to exercise his priestly functions outside the Clink. To this Preston readily agreed, showing the sort of confessor he was. Despite condemnation by Rome and the constant efforts of true Benedictines to bring him to his senses, he felt too well off under the patronage of King James, which was continued by Charles I, and died in 1640, still unreconciled with the Church. Owing to the extremely clever façade arranged for him by the Archbishop of Canterbury and Lord Salisbury, he was enabled to cause "a grave decline of concord and steadfastness among the Catholics". God provided two great Benedictines to balance the account, Blessed John Roberts who, after ten years of heroic missionary work, was apprehended, condemned to death for his priesthood, and hanged at Tyburn on December 10, 1610, together with a secular priest, Blessed Thomas Somers *alias* Wilson. Both were offered their lives if they would take the new Oath of Allegiance and both steadfastly refused. The other Benedictine was the celebrated mystical writer, Father Augustine

---

[1] In a brilliant article by William Webb, s.j., contributed to *Biographical Studies*, a subsidiary of the Catholic Record Society, volume 2, No. 3, 1954, under the title, "Thomas Preston, alias Roger Widdrington".

Baker, who came to England as Preston's subject just before the issue of the first papal brief condemning King James's new Oath. The brief was expected at any moment and Father Augustine was strongly advised to take the Oath at once before its condemnation. It seems highly likely that his own superior, Preston, was among those who urged him, but Father Baker rejected the specious advice. Though Preston continued to be his superior for another seven years, he never again mentioned his name in any connection.

As for Robert Bellarmine, he replied to Preston's first "Widdrington" book, apparently without any suspicion of its real authorship, though that was already being rumoured in Rome. His *Examen* was printed, but he did not permit its publication, and its very existence was forgotten until 1913, when the indefatigable research worker X. M. Le Bachelet, s.j., discovered the Cardinal's original manuscript and published it in his *Auctarium Bellarminianum*. That was the end of all St Robert's controversies, and we might feel kindly towards the memory of the strange Preston that he unwittingly brought it about.

CHAPTER XI

THE APOSTOLATE OF THE POST

THE next phase in Cardinal Bellarmine's busy life is very much more attractive than his long involvement in the disputations of his fiercely argumentative age. He was not by nature built for the controversies that were forced upon him, political as well as theological, and he stumbled sometimes under the heavy burden which the popes and his own profound love of the Church laid on his shoulders. When the burden was at last removed, the real heart of the man appeared in the thousands of letters which he wrote in his own flowing but small and not easily readable hand to princes, bishops, heads of religious orders, missionaries, troubled people of every kind. One who had been in the Cardinal's service for seventeen years testified that during all that time he had never known him to take the afternoon siesta which in Rome is almost a necessity of life during the hot summer months. After his long formal prayers, which were so little formal, and his interviews with a constant stream of visitors, he would give himself up body and soul to the task of dealing with his enormous correspondence, working away at it through suffocating heat or freezing cold, in sickness as well as in health. Thousands of those letters still exist in manuscript and have never been published. He never had a secretary, considering such a convenience too much of a luxury for a man dedicated to poverty. It is a real mystery how he managed, seeing that after his return to Rome in 1605 he was appointed a member of nearly all the Roman congregations. During his later years, he was prefect of four congregations, including the Holy Office, and all his work for those bodies was done so conscientiously that a colleague, Cardinal del Monte, dean of the sacred college, was able to write after St Robert's death: "Often enough the whole Congregation of Rites, which numbered upwards of fourteen cardinals, abandoned or changed decisions that had been reached by common agreement, solely out of respect for the learning and authority of this one man".

After his own Jesuits, who needed quite a deal of defending from his pen, there were no men to whom Bellarmine felt more drawn than those who looked to St Francis of Assisi as their father, whether Friars Minor or Capuchins. They had recourse to him constantly and about all sorts of affairs, now proposing cases of conscience or difficult doctrinal or liturgical questions for solution, now asking him to obtain various privileges for them, to help them with the publication of books or to intervene personally in the settlement of some dispute. One petition that reached him in May, 1608, was signed by no fewer than thirty-six Capuchins. In the last year of his life, Robert received a signal of distress from the Friars Minor. A learned Dominican named Abraham Bzovius published in 1616 a thirteenth volume of the *Annales Ecclesiastici* which Baronius had left incomplete. In this volume, under the year 1294, there appeared a heading on "The Death and Praises of John the Scot". Now, the praises lavished on Duns Scotus were, to say the least, equivocal, and the religious brethren of the great Franciscan doctor resented the Dominican's remarks intensely. One of them, a holy but hasty Irishman named Hugh Mac-Caghwell, subsequently appointed Archbishop of Armagh, was so much roused that he sent to printers in Antwerp a book with the terrific title: "An Apologia for John Duns Scotus, the Subtle Doctor, against the Insults, Calumnies and Injuries with which Father Abraham Bzovius, O.P., oblivious to all Modesty, has over- whelmed and outraged him in his utterly false annals". This fiery retort exasperated the Dominicans in their turn and they succeeded in procuring a decree of the Index against the assailant of Bzovius. Bellarmine at the time, less than nine months before his death, was prefect of the Congregation of the Index and to him the distressed Franciscans had recourse. He managed somehow, without offending either party, to have the decree against Mac- Caghwell's book rescinded. The pugnacious Friar Hugh then returned to the charge and published at Paris an *Apologia* for his *Apologia*, in which, with characteristic "devilment", he called Duns Scotus the prince of all theologians, and paid a warm tribute to Robert Bellarmine, then dead, for having delivered him from the toils of the Dominicans.

The Dominicans and the Jesuits were not always exactly the best of friends, but one Jesuit at least kept his place permanently in the affections of the more venerable order. In 1714, nearly a hundred years after Bellarmine's death, Anthony Cloche, Master General of the Dominicans, addressed the following lines to Pope Clement XI as a persuasive to the Cardinal's beatification:

> The note of sanctity, which is characteristic of the Catholic Church alone, shone resplendently in these latter days in the Servant of God, Robert Bellarmine, of the Society of Jesus, Cardinal of the Holy Roman Church. Dissimilar virtues were united so harmoniously in his soul that his candour was in no way diminished by his prudence, nor the nobility of mind, which came of his high breeding, by the spirit of religious poverty which he assiduously cultivated. He was both grave and gay, indefatigable in study and devoted to piety. During his life as a Jesuit he showed tireless zeal in the performance of every duty, unremitting diligence in the pursuit of knowledge, and the greatest readiness for every office of charity and kindness; nor was there ever an undertaking or project of his that had not the glory of God or the good of his neighbour for its end...
>
> As a cardinal he was known to everybody and venerated by all for the singular modesty, frugality, and religious austerity of his life, as well as for his noble contempt for earthly riches and his immense charity to the poor, for whose sake he stinted himself that he might have the more power to give. These virtues, however, were not the greatest in his soul. The crown of his sanctity was his burning love of Holy Church, a love with which he was so consumed that his heart held nothing more dear than the Church's glory. Nothing did he defend with such valorous eagerness as her traditional teaching, and nothing did he desire so much to promote as the holiness of each and every one of her children.

Bellarmine was on terms of such close friendship with the Discalced Carmelites and so keenly devoted to their interests, especially the canonization of St Teresa of Jesus, that a rumour began to circulate in 1616 according to which he had once

assured a saintly member of the order that were he beginning life
again, he would be a Carmelite and not a Jesuit. When this tale
was brought to his notice, he laughed and said that when he
joined the Jesuits in 1560 the Carmelite reform had not yet even
begun and, anyhow, the tendency of his feet to swell would
have barred him from joining the Discalced St John of the Cross.
The General of the Discalced Carmelites petitioned Pope Clement
XI for the Cardinal's beatification and, referring to his intimate
relations with the Carmelite community of Santa Maria della
Scala, said: "Were we to be silent the pillars and marbles of our
convent would cry aloud and proclaim our family tradition of
the many examples of outstanding virtue with which the Venerable Servant of God adorned this our home".

The Augustinians of Venice sent Robert a large basket of
truffles in token of their regard, as did the Dominicans other
dainties. In his letter of warm thanks for the truffles, he said
"I did not dare to accept them for myself, as religious are not
allowed to accept anything unless it comes as a present to the whole
community, so I sent them on to our Father General, who has
now sent them back to me in the name of the whole Society of
Jesus". Perhaps, he then allowed himself a truffle or two with his
horrible regular diet of garlic and chicory, the fare of the very
poor.

Bellarmine was also in close touch with the numerous families
of St Benedict. The zealous Abbot of Fulda, Dom Balthasar von
Dermbach, was an energetic promoter of the Catholic revival in
Germany, but his own chapter became tainted with heresy and
expelled him in 1576. For twenty-five years he pleaded his cause
and that of his great monastery in the imperial courts, Bellarmine
all the time following the negotiations with anxious interest.
When the controversy *de Auxiliis* was at its most critical stage in
March 1602 the Cardinal wrote as follows to the sorely tried
Abbot:

> Your Lordship would find it difficult to believe me were
> to explain to you the full measure of my distress at seeing an
> affair of such importance and such moment to religion held up

by so many obstacles and delays. The only way in which I have power to help is by exhorting and imploring those who have charge of the negotiations. This I have done again and again and there is no fear that I shall grow weary in the future of constantly urging the matter by word of mouth and in writing. I am sending your Lordship a copy of the letter which I am posting to the Apostolic Nuncio. The very first time that a favourable opportunity presents itself I shall earnestly beg the Holy Father to use his authority to bring so just a cause to a speedy conclusion.

Five months later the Emperor decided the case in favour of the Abbot, who wrote immediately to tell his benefactor the good news. Bellarmine answered as follows on October 10, 1602:

The joy and delight which your Lordship's letter gave me were in proportion to the despair which was beginning to creep over me of ever seeing a happy end to your most righteous cause. It was beginning to look as if it might go on for ever. . . . Now it remains for your Lordship to apply yourself with all your might in your pastoral solicitude to the reformation of that diocese, to collect your scattered flock and, driving out the wolves, to make up by increased vigilance for the time which the injustice of your adversaries forced you in a manner to waste in litigation.

I pray to God with all my heart that as he has given your Lordship the opportunity of gathering the most sweet fruit of daily patience on earth, so he would grant to both of us to find in Heaven the crown of our pastoral office and labours. Let us go on loving each other, and let us pray for each other that we may save our souls.

Two other Benedictine abbeys turned to Bellarmine for help in difficulties and were not disappointed. The schemes for the restoration of the Benedictine order in England met with the Cardinal's warmest sympathy. He knew Dom Sigebert Buckley, the only surviving Benedictine who had been professed at Westminster Abbey before the Tudor spoliation. In 1607 Dom Sigebert, then nearly ninety, aggregated to the old English Congregation two or three young Cassinese monks, and thus passed on the succession unbroken. In this he had the zealous assistance, to give him his due, of Father Thomas Preston, alias Widdrington. Bellarmine was in correspondence with Father Jones, or as he was known in religion, Dom Leander of St Martin, who held the post of vicar-general of the Anglo-Spanish Congregation, and aided him in the controversy with the English Cassinese monks under Thomas Preston.

In June, 1616, when he was nearly seventy-four years of age, Bellarmine's devotion to St Benedict, the Father not only of Western monasticism, but of Western civilization, led him, though not in good health, to make a pilgrimage to Subiaco where Benedict had lived as a hermit before founding the monastery of Monte Cassino. All went well until he came close to the great Abbey where the monks had provided a horse to take him up the steep mountain path. He had not ridden for some time and may have been awkward in mounting. Anyhow, the animal bolted, flinging him violently to the ground. No bones were broken, but the Cardinal's left arm was badly crushed, and the shock to his system such that at first his monastic hosts, who nursed him devotedly, did not think that he would survive. The kindly monks brought him back to Rome in a litter and there he had to spend another month in bed where he kept up his practices of devotion in detail, despite the head-shaking of the doctors. So eager was he to say Mass again that he petitioned the Pope to let him elevate the sacred Host with his right arm only, as the left after several weeks was still out of action. He had transacted a great deal of business in the various congregations for the zealous Archbishop of Gnesen in Poland and wrote to him as soon as he could hold a pen: "I have two of your Grace's letters on my conscience. The first I was unable to answer because it found me lying in bed, suffering greatly owing to a fall from a horse. As I am an ancient of seventy-four, I thought that owing to the accident, I should have gone to God, but it pleased his Divine Majesty so to break the fall that, without killing me, it might serve as an opportunity for patience and as a penance for my sins. Now, that I am suffering only in my left arm, I thought that I must no longer delay answering a letter so full of love and kindness." Nearly all his letters concluded as did this one with a promise of further help: "If there is anything more that I can do, you will always find me completely at your disposal".

In March, 1606, Pope Paul V had nominated Bellarmine cardinal protector of the order of Celestines who then had a hundred houses in Italy and many others in France. They were founded in the thirteenth century by Pietro Morone, himself a Benedictine priest who had been permitted to live a completely eremetical life in the wild mountains of the Abruzzi. Attracted by the rumour of his sanctity, men pursued him into his successive retreats until he was compelled to organize them as a society of hermits under his jurisdiction. Then, though utterly unfitted by his simplicity and lack of education, he found himself most unwillingly on the Throne of the Fisherman as Pope Celestine V, from which, after five months of bewilderment and misery, he solemnly resigned. This was the "great refusal" which caused Dante the Ghibelline to put the poor old hermit in his *Inferno* with the cowards. The Church reversed that judgment and canonized Pietro Morone under his papal name of Celestine while Dante was still alive.

Within a few weeks of his appointment as protector of the widespread family of Celestine Benedictines, Cardinal Bellarmine obtained a bull from the Pope confirming their various privileges and expressly declaring that the jurisdiction of the abbot-general extended over all the monasteries, as well those of France as those of Italy. A certain amount of rivalry and tension had developed between the monks of the two countries, and these their new protector set himself with tact and sympathy to remove or lessen as much as possible. He showed so much kindness and obvious devotion to their interests that he gradually won the devotion of all the monks who rallied to his support in his efforts to restore discipline and deepen the spiritual life of the monasteries. To one of the provincial superiors he wrote: "With all my heart I commend to you peace and union, but above everything a most strict observance of the holy and wise rule of our most blessed Father St Benedict. This was indeed the stair by which our blessed Father ascended to Heaven, and by which St Celestine also ascended. We, too, shall surely reach the same goal if we are their faithful imitators."

Cardinal Bellarmine took a prominent part in the revision of the Benedictine Breviary under Paul V and in securing its acceptance by the Celestine monasteries, though the French brethren at first demurred for the following reasons:

> Are we to be expected to leave our own saints in the lurch in order to venerate other people's saints? The translation of the relics of Blessed Benedict [to France] is an event scorned and denied by the monks of Monte Cassino and other Italian Benedictines, but as the bones of our holy Father are here in our midst in the territory of Orleans to prove it, we, together with all the monks on this side of the Alps, as well as nearly all cathedral churches, celebrate the feast of the translation with a solemn octave in the July of each year. . . . We are sending your Lordship our Breviary, then, that you may examine it, make up your mind about it, and tell us freely whether you think we may be allowed to retain it in the future.

A year later the new Breviary was accepted by the French monasteries also, through St Robert's tact in dealing with national susceptibilities.

In May, 1612, Bellarmine, then close on his three score years and ten, made the long and toilsome journey to the head house of the Celestine congregation on the slopes of Monte Morone, near Sulmona, in order to preside at the triennial chapter of the monks. He was in bad health at the time, but did not miss a single function, and gave the monks an address each morning before business began. To his immense joy, reforms which he had been tirelessly advocating for six years, concerning the training of novices, the better provision for philosophical and theological studies and, above all, the adoption of the practice of mental prayer by the monks, in addition to their choir duties, were decreed at this meeting for the Italian provinces. Immediately afterwards he wrote to the French provincial, telling of what had been done:

> I was anxious to make known all this to your Reverence

that you might consider, with the other fathers at our next chapter, whether it would not be a good thing if you were to make similar regulations about the novices and students, as well as about the practice of mental prayer. In this way your province, which is proud of its reform and observance, would make sure of not being found in any respect inferior to the Italian provinces, but would rather rival them in goodness, just as I most earnestly desire that the Italian provinces may emulate the French province in many other matters pertaining to the strict observance of the rule.

Bellarmine worked unweariedly in the interest of the Celestines up to the time of his death. The French provincial, who had been contending with dissensions among his own monks, wrote to express his indebtedness from Amiens on April 8, 1619: "Truly if we had not had your Lordship for our protector we should have been lost. May God bless you for your most vigilant care of us. All that you have done and endured for love of us will be kept in faithful memory that the fruit of your labours may not perish through carelessness on our part. God alone can reward you as you deserve, for our debt to you is too great for us ever to hope to repay it."

Among Bellarmine's innumerable correspondents was the new Archpriest of England, George Birkhead, who had attended St Robert's lectures in Rome and was well aware of his deep sympathy for the persecuted Catholics. Birkhead was strongly persuaded that the appointment of a bishop or bishops to reside in England would greatly relieve the calamitous situation in that country. In his first letter, after alluding to the harm that was being done by Roger Widdrington's *Apologia* and begging Bellarmine to refute it, he continued:

If we had bishops, as is the case everywhere else throughout the Church, this evil of bad books written by persons who pretend to be Catholics might be more easily put down. As, however, for nearly fifty years we have been entirely deprived of so necessary a help and have lived without any settled order, we cannot be surprised to see a thousand troubles of this kind rising in our midst. We who are every day stricken by the

enemy's missiles and see so close at hand the evils of our time
are endeavouring by every means in our power and by most
earnest entreaties to do away with such a calamitous state of
affairs by having bishops set over us. . .

We do not fear to entrust to your Illustrious Lordship this
most just demand of ours, imploring you earnestly that by the
mercy of God you may be pleased to further efficaciously with
his Holiness a matter so necessary for the good of our most
afflicted Church. Of a truth the heretics spare no endeavour to
root out the Catholic faith from men's minds, and what
reasonable person will blame us if, notwithstanding a most
grievous persecution, we do all we can to oppose those most
ferocious and cunning enemies, by asking to have our forces
better organized so that we may endeavour to keep the precious
jewel of faith unharmed in spite of pursuivants and Parliament?

Your Lordship sees how confidently we deal with you and
how much we trust to your kindness. I personally have special
reasons for doing so because I know that I am bound to you by
the strong tie of gratitude, as a scholar to his old master. More
than thirty years back I attended your lectures in Rome, and I
owe to God and to you what little learning I have acquired.

Birkhead had long been writing to his agent in Rome, Mr
Thomas Fitzherbert, who on the death of his wife had become a
secular priest in 1602, always urging the appointment of bishops
for England. The correspondence between the two men was
discovered by a fortunate accident in 1946, and edited for the
Catholic Record Society by Leo Hicks, s.j. Those letters have
put an end to much bad and prejudiced history, for they prove that
Father Robert Persons, the chief bogyman of the small but
ruthless and government-aided faction of secular priests known as
the "Appellants", had for many years, dating from the appointment of Blackwell as Archpriest by Clement VIII, been one of the
warmest advocates of an English hierarchy, the very cause which
the Appellants accused him loudly of hindering. In 1608, two
years before his death, Persons was still doing all in his power to
persuade the Pope and the cardinals of the Inquisition to whom all
English matters were referred. The Pope and those cardinals
who included Bellarmine, realized perfectly well how useful

bishops would be in England, but hesitated to appoint them because of the disunion among the English clergy caused by the Appellant faction, with the Protestant bishop of London's active backing. Thomas Fitzherbert was himself of opinion that, "seeing it must be done sooner or later", bishops should be appointed there and then in 1608, when the persecution of the Catholics was at its worst, for they could suffer no further extremity by such a measure. Still, the cardinals were not convinced, and a letter of Birkhead himself to the vice-protector of England, Cardinal del Bufalo, in June, 1608, did little to reassure them. He said that he was unable to perform anything worthy of his office owing to the severity of the persecution: "We dare not creep forth day or night from the lairs in which we are forced to lurk like so many rats and mice: we are surrounded by so many false brethren that we are never safe, or sure as to whom we can trust. . . . I deplore our conditions; for hemmed in as we are by so many perils, never shall we be able to carry out or fulfil the tasks that are laid upon us."[1] Yet, later in the same letter Birkhead petitions for bishops who would surely have run greater dangers and have undergone worse frustrations than himself.

Several letters passed between Birkhead and Bellarmine, but the Cardinal, though invariably courteous and truly sympathetic, was unable to hold out much hope for the hierarchy which the Archpriest so greatly desired. "Your Lordship seems ever ready," wrote that harassed man on January 10, 1613, "to go to the Pope and to treat with him on our affairs." It was true, for no country occupied more of Bellarmine's prayers and solicitude than England.

In 1609 affairs of a very different complexion became the Cardinal's concern. The pugnacious Gaspar Schopp, an *enfant terrible* with a mordant pen much feared by the plotting English emissaries in Madrid and Paris, brought Bellarmine a letter from the Archduke Ferdinand of Styria, who was elected Holy Roman Emperor ten years later. This man in his fervent zeal for the Catholic cause was intent on organizing a great Catholic league

---

[1] Catholic Record Society, vol. 41 (1948), edited by L. Hicks, s.j., p. 90, n. 9.

by which he hoped to save the faith of the German people and the integrity of the Empire from the Protestant and revolutionary agencies that threatened both. Europe, in fact, was tuning up for the terrible calamity of the Thirty Years War.[1] His appeal for Bellarmine's influence on behalf of the League received an immediate answer:

Mr Gaspar Schopp brought me your letter on September 2 and told me a good deal about the tremendous disturbances in Germany on the religious question. I thank your Highness deeply for addressing yourself to me who am bound by so many titles of affection to your noble House. My one great grief is that I have not sufficient influence to secure the favour you mention, though my respect for your Highness would lead me to do almost anything to obtain it, especially as it is for a cause so closely bound up with the welfare of Germany and the entire Catholic Church.

As a beginning, at least, I went straight off to the Pope and most earnestly commended the whole affair to him, urging him at the same time to forestall and ward off such great dangers by every means in his power, and in his prudence to find a remedy for all these impending evils. He listened to me most willingly, telling me that he had the cause deeply at heart and that he was quite ready to give his very life for the salvation of so many souls. God grant that his deeds may answer to his words. Meantime we shall see what plan his Holiness will adopt, and if it is referred to a committee of cardinals of which I, as generally happens, am nominated a member, I shall not fail in the duty and devotion which I owe to your Highness and the noble House of Austria.

In due course the Catholic League came into being under the leadership of Maximilian the Great, Duke of Bavaria, its purpose being to withstand the Protestant Coalition or Evangelical Union,

[1] The following is a pronouncement about the results eventually achieved by Ferdinand's League: "When every allowance has been made, the dispassionate inquirer, however badly he may think of the religious system by which Protestantism was superseded in the territories [the Austrian dominions], can hardly do otherwise than rejoice at the defeat of the political system of the men by whom Protestantism was in the main supported" (S. R. Gardiner, *History of England*, vol. iii, p. 263).

captained by Frederick, the Elector Palatine, son-in-law of King James of England. In August, 1609, the three archiepiscopal Electors of Mainz, Cologne and Trier addressed a joint supplication to Bellarmine to engage his interest on behalf of the Catholic princes. Their letter did not reach him till March 12, 1610, which accounts for his answer being dated March 14 of that year:

The Reverend Count Frederick of Hohenzollern delivered to me your letter of August 31 last year on March 12. From it and from the lips of your envoys I learned not only the danger to which religion is exposed but also the zeal and diligence of your Illustrious Lordships in maintaining the interests of Catholicism. The envoys will inform you what you in turn may expect from the Apostolic See and the Sovereign Pontiff. Out of my littleness, I thank God from my heart that in such perilous times, he has fired the minds of so many illustrious princes to unite in a league, not only advantageous, but almost necessary for religion. If you all stand by it, I have not the slightest doubt but that God will be with you and by his almighty hand will prosperously further your efforts.

Meanwhile, both by my prayers to him and by my counsel and exhortations to our Holy Father, the Pope, I will aid the common cause with all my power. May God confirm what he has begun in you and, as he has given you the resolution to act, so may he help to bring your plans to complete success, to the glory of his holy name.

The head of the League, Duke Maximilian, also had a letter posted to him on the same day:

Julius Caesar Crivelli brought me your Serene Highness's letter on March 12, and laid before me the commission with which you had entrusted him on behalf of the common cause of the Church, now in such danger in Germany. A few days earlier, he had entrusted to me another affair which directly concerned your Highness. I have done all in my power to further it, and was given the opportunity because the Pope expressly asked for my views about the matter. . .

Your Highness may rest assured that I shall do all that I possibly can and with the greatest good will in the world, by advice to the Holy Father, by prayer to Almighty God, and by a grant of money too if the Pope thinks well. Though my revenues are very small indeed, still it will be the greatest pleasure to me to give, like Tobias, a little out of my little. May God preserve your Highness many years for the defence of the Church and the increase of your own merits.

In the seditious and unruly land of Bohemia where the Thirty Years War began in 1618, Cardinal Bellarmine had one good nobleman on whom to pin his hopes. He had been in correspondence with this man, George Drugeth von Homonay, for several years, transacting business for him in Rome and acting as his unofficial spiritual director. He counselled him to read and choose for the pattern of his conduct the life of St Elzear, Count of Ariano in the Kingdom of Naples (died 1323), as told in the *Lives of the Saints* by the Carthusan Surius. Elzear was French, a fact much disliked by his Italian vassals, who rebelled against him. For three years this most winningly attractive saint opposed against the rebels no other arms than those of meekness and patience. His cousin, the Prince of Taranto, lost patience with such methods. "Let me deal with these people for you," said he one day to Elzear. "I will hang up half a thousand, and make the rest as pliant as a glove. It is fit to be a lamb among the good, but with the wicked you must play the lion." St Elzear replied: "It is no great matter for a lion to tear lambs, but for a lamb to pull a lion to pieces is a different matter". He carried on as a lamb and completely won over his vassals without hanging a single one. This beautiful character wrote to his devoted wife when away from home: "You want to hear often of me, dearest Delphina. Go then and visit our loving Lord Jesus in the Blessed Sacrament and enter in spirit into his sacred heart. You will always find me there."

It is amusing to find that Robert Bellarmine, who greatly loved St Elzear, sided heartily with the Prince of Taranto in the question of lambs and lions. Thus, he wrote to his friend the Bohemian Count in 1617 on the very eve of the insurrection that touched off the Thirty Years War: "God aiding you, may you fight might and main against the enemies of the Church and enjoy a glorious victory". When the zealous Archduke Ferdinand was elected Emperor, the somewhat unlamblike Robert could not wait till the end of his annual retreat at the Jesuit novitiate before giving expression to his joy at the news. His lyrical letter went off on September 14, 1619:

My heart bounded with delight within me when I heard of your happy election as the head of the Holy Roman Empire, and my joy was all the greater because it was clear that the providence of God, for the good of the Holy Catholic Church, had broken down and scattered every unseen obstacle which the devils of hell could throw in your way and every visible difficulty which heretics and false Christians could raise up against you.

To the great God, to his only-begotten Son, Jesus Christ our Redeemer, and to the whole Court of Heaven, be glory and praise evermore. May the King of Heaven grant your Imperial Majesty a long life, and complete victory over all your enemies. . . . To everyone of us, the humble servants of your Majesty, it would be the greatest of pleasures to see you crowned here at Rome by the Sovereign Pontiff, who holds on earth the place of his Divine Majesty, the King of kings. . . . There is not one of us but would gladly give his life for your sake, for all recognize you as the Father of your country and the defender and steadfast champion of our holy faith. I must say no more for fear I should weary your Majesty, but pray remember that I shall ever be your most faithful and humble servant with all my heart.

That the old Cardinal's enthusiasm about Ferdinand was not without solid grounds may be seen from the following estimate:

He [Ferdinand] knew of but one fountain of justice and order —the Church of Rome. To a life-long struggle against that which was in his eyes the root of all evil, Ferdinand devoted himself by a pilgrimage to Loreto. Yet it would be wrong to speak of him as an ordinary persecutor. He never put himself forward as a general extirpator of heresy. He never displayed any personal animosity against heretics. His own nature was kindly and forgiving, and he was, by disposition, inclined to peace. . . . In maintaining his position he was as fearless as he was incapable of doubt. When called upon to face a raging multitude, he would be as calm as if he were standing in the midst of a circle of devoted friends.[1]

During the first or Palatine period of the Thirty Years War, which was all of the struggle that Bellarmine lived to see, his hero of heroes was the brave and chivalrous captain of the Catholic League, Maximilian of Bavaria. The lawless Protestant aristocracy of Bohemia had chosen Frederick the Elector Palatine king of the country in August, 1619, instead of its rightful sovereign Emperor Ferdinand, and the Elector had been rash enough to accept the fateful crown. Before Duke Maximilian took the field against the usurper, Bellarmine wrote to counsel and encourage him in an enterprise that vitally concerned the welfare of the Catholic cause:

> The letter from your Highness rejoiced my soul. As from the first beginning of the Lutheran heresy the House of Bavaria held high the banner of Catholicism, and as its sovereigns have been the only ones, if I mistake not, who have kept their territories free from the dreadful contagion of false doctrine, so now with God's help that same noble House will not only preserve its own dominions but, at the head of the Catholic League, will deliver many other lands from the plague of heresy. Even though the gates of hell be opened wide and the kingdoms of Bohemia and Hungary be confident in their united strength of their ability to overthrow Jerusalem, the Holy City, it is not difficult for the Lord of Hosts to shield his servants from all danger.
>
> One thing, however, is necessary above all others, and that is that the soldiers of Christ should have the honour of God and the safety of the Church as their single aim. Before taking the field they should have their sins washed away by confession and their souls strengthened by Holy Communion. . .
>
> I beg the great, good God from my heart to direct and to protect your Serene Highness and the other Catholic princes and to grant you a glorious victory over the enemies of the faith.

Duke Maximilian was evidently deeply attached to the old

[1]Gardiner, *History of England*, vol. iii, pp. 268-9.

Cardinal whom he had never seen, and answered his letter from the battlefield. In Bellarmine's next communication he refers as he had often done before to the Protestant John George of Saxony, a gallant soldier, and bluff, hearty person, famous for his potations, who had thrown in his lot with the Catholic princes:

Most Serene Prince and Ever Victorious General,
    I was exceedingly delighted with the good news which your Highness deigned to write to me. I hear that the whole of a vast province has been subdued in so short a time that your Highness might well cry, *Veni, vidi, vici*. I am in good hopes that we shall soon be able to apply to Bohemia the words spoken by the holy and valiant King of Israel: "I will pursue after my enemies and overtake them: and I will not turn again until they are consumed. I will break them, and they shall not be able to stand: they shall fall under my feet."
    One great desire I cherish is to see the Duke of Saxony return to the true faith, now that he is leagued with so many Catholic and religious Princes, vigorously supporting the most Christian Emperor and fighting against the heretical and forsworn Bohemians. I hear on good authority that he does not hate the Sovereign Pontiff as do other Protestants, and that he is fond of the company of that excellent and most prudent man, the Prince Bishop of Würzburg and Bamberg. Would that in reward for his benevolence the Holy Ghost might bestow upon him the gift of the true faith! . . .
    If I could but soon hear of these two things, the complete pacification of the Holy Roman Empire and the conversion of the Duke of Saxony, then would I, who am an old man of almost eighty years, gladly sing my *Nunc dimittis*.

On October 8, 1620, Duke Maximilian won an overwhelming victory in the famous battle of the White Hill, Prague. Within a week Bellarmine was writing his congratulations:

    Your Highness does me too great an honour by your frequent letters. Not only do they honour me, but they also afford keen pleasure to many to whom I show them. All are very solicitous about the issue of the War, and it is a great delight to them in their anxiety to hear read the letters of a great Prince whose news, they can be sure, is not rumour but the truth. Some

LX

people, I may say, write to tell us, not what has taken place, but what they would like to have taken place and which they seem to believe as if it were accurate in every detail.

But passing over such gossip, I must tell you that I have the greatest pity for the soldiers and pray for them every day. Though I was never a soldier myself I have very often seen war at close quarters and witnessed the hardships of those who do the fighting. As a boy in Italy, a young man in Belgium, and a grown man in France, I have seen the dying slaughtered in cold blood, and have myself tasted the torments of siege and starvation. I will not say anything about the many crimes and iniquities which I have either beheld committed with my own eyes, or have heard of from others, by men who died shortly after in battle and found themselves in hell before they had begun to think of preparing for their judgment. It is such happenings as these that make me respect and venerate those religious generals and commanders who teach their men by word and example how to shed the blood of the enemy without offence to God, and who inspire them to lay down their own lives for the cause of justice and religion.[1]

St Bernard, writing to the Templars, praises such conduct marvellously, "Go forward, soldiers", he says, "go forward with intrepid courage and drive back the enemies of the Cross of Christ, certain that neither death nor life can separate you from the love of God which is in Christ Jesus, and repeating to yourselves in every danger: Whether we live or whether we die, we are the Lord's. How glorious is the conqueror's return from battle, how blessed are the martyrs who do not return! Rejoice, brave soldier, if you survive and conquer in the Lord, but rejoice and glory still more if you die and are joined to the Lord. Life, indeed, is fruitful and victory a splendid thing, but death by sacred right is to be preferred to both, for if blessed

[1] "Like Ferdinand, Maximilian was a man of deep and sincere piety... But unlike Ferdinand, he had the statesman's capacity for holding the thread of complicated affairs in the grasp of a strong intellect... He was never in a hurry; but when the time for action came it was certain to be found that everything had been done that human ingenuity could devise to secure success... His people were happy and contented under his rule. He had the best-filled treasury and the best-appointed army in Germany. The general at the head of his forces, the Walloon Tilly, was one of the ablest commanders in Europe" (Gardiner, *History of England*, vol. iii, pp. 317-8).

are those who die in the Lord, are they not to be accounted more blessed far who die for the Lord?" This and much more did St Bernard write about the war of the Christians against the infidels, but it is all quite applicable to a war of Catholics against heretics.

The class of men with whom Bellarmine had most frequent dealings were the Catholic bishops in various part of the world. His high conception of their office and his thorough appreciation of the difficulties with which they were so frequently confronted had bred in his soul the warmest sympathy with them, and an eager desire to help them in any way within his power. In the year 1610 the Bishop of Verdun, Prince Eric of Lorraine, whom he greatly loved, resigned his see in order to enter a monastery. His nephew, Charles of Lorraine, was nominated his successor but, as he was only eighteen years old, it was arranged that he should not be consecrated nor exercise episcopal functions until he was thirty. Charles does not seem to have been much impressed, at first, by the dignity for which he was destined, and went off to have a gay time in Paris. However, both Francis de Sales and Bellarmine were soon on his track, and their exhortations bore such fruit that like his uncle he became a model bishop, and after some years of zealous work in his diocese resigned in order to satisfy his hunger for self-effacement in a religious community. Charles was a lovable young fellow, and Bellarmine, to whom he looked as to a father, reciprocated his affection. When he had to lecture him he did it with much gentleness, feeling all the time that he was dealing with a spirited character in which there were immense capacities for good. The following letter of May 14, 1611, must have made gay Charles thoughtful:

What your Lordship so holily promises me in your letter is just exactly what I myself promised the Pope a long time ago, sure as I was of your gifts and goodness. That we may not be put to shame when the Prince of Pastors appears to demand an account of the flocks committed to our care, it is necessary in the first place that your Lordship should apply yourself with all earnestness to the study of sacred theology. Then the next thing necessary is that you should teach others with tireless zeal all that you have learned, and feed and rule your people by example as well as by word.

As I quoted the example of St Louis, Bishop of Toulouse, to the Holy Father in order to persuade him to confirm your appointment in spite of your being so young, it is only right that your Lordship should fix your eyes on this Saint and endeavour to imitate one whose youth was at once so thoroughly austere and so mature.[1] Or if you prefer examples nearer to our own time, look at Saint Charles Borromeo, who was made Archbishop of Milan at the age of twenty-two, and who, wise "above old men", has glorified the whole Church with the marvellous splendour of his sanctity. Or again, if you prefer to take a model nearer home, there is Blessed Peter of Luxembourg, who, when he was named Bishop of Metz, though only a boy of fifteen, bore himself so well as to deserve that God should glorify him after his death by miracles.

Your Lordship will forgive me if I seem overbold in my exhortations and admonitions, for I must confess to you that it was not without fear and trembling that I advised the Pope to place over a diocese one so young as yourself, though otherwise you are of such excellent character and ability. Many and great are the perils that hang over young men who are set in high positions of trust and honour. Your Lordship will then, I am sure, take in good part all that I have ventured to write to you, as it proceeds from the well-meaning heart of one most eagerly anxious for your salvation and eternal glory. If you think that I can be of service to you in any way, command me freely.

Cardinal Bellarmine's zeal for the Catholic cause brought him

---

[1] This St Louis was born in Provence and of royal blood through both his parents. His father, Charles II, King of Naples and Sicily, suffered defeat at the hands of the King of Aragon, and Louis had to spend seven hard years as a hostage in Barcelona, where he made a vow to join the Franciscans, thus renouncing the crown of Naples. Pope Boniface VIII peremptorily ordered him after ordination to accept the bishopric of Toulouse, though he was only twenty-three. St Robert Bellarmine modelled his life as a bishop on this marvellous youth, and St Aloysius (Luigi, Louis) Gonzaga was named after him. It appears that Aloysius borrowed the habit of never looking any woman, not even his mother, in the eyes from his extremely austere but cheerful and lovable patron, who died in 1297, aged twenty-three years and six months. St Aloysius died at twenty-three years and eight months.

in 1609 into close connection with the new Prince Bishop of
Bamberg, Godfrey von Aschhausen, who in virtue of his position
became one of the seven imperial electors. For many years
previously, the see, which was counted one of the most important
in Germany, had been held by a man entirely unworthy of his
trust, for not only was his life a scandal but everyone knew that
he had decided leanings to Lutheranism. After his death in 1609,
von Aschhausen, who was then provost of the cathedral of
Würzburg, was elected as his successor and wrote immediately
to tell Bellarmine the news. The answer he received was as
follows:

> *A Domino factum est istud, et est mirabile in oculis nostris.* The
> news of Your Lordship's election has given joy to the entire
> City of God. We had long wept over the oppression of the
> diocese of Bamberg and begged God for the succour which we
> could not ourselves provide. Our merciful Lord has granted
> our desires in fuller measure than we had asked or could have
> hoped for, and it only remains now for him who has begun
> the good work in you to perfect it, to give glory to the see of
> Bamberg through your labours in this present time that in the
> Day of the Lord you may receive from the Prince of Pastors a
> crown that will never fade.
>
> As to the hastening of the business with which you have
> entrusted me and the remission or reduction of the expenses,
> I have treated very earnestly with our Holy Father, Paul V,
> and with the heads of the Sacred College about these matters.
> The Sovereign Pontiff promised me quick dispatch, and this
> very day he has fulfilled his promise in the consistory. What is
> to happen about the reduction or remission of the charges I am
> not quite certain, but this much I can assure you that I used every
> possible means of persuasion of which I could think in order to
> bring about a decision favourable to your Lordship. My very
> heartiest good wishes to you, and if you think there is anything
> else I can do for you I am entirely at your disposal.

The Cardinal took the new bishop to his heart completely and
did everything in his power to help him with the hard task of
reform which had been given him. Letters passed between them

constantly, the following being one which Bellarmine wrote shortly after Bishop Godfrey's appointment:

Most Illustrious Prince and Right Reverend Lord,

What I did in the matter of the provostship was a keen pleasure for me, but it was not of such importance as to call for a letter of thanks and so to give an excellent Bishop the labour of writing when he has much more weighty business to engage his attention. Still, as you have written, nothing could be more agreeable to me than to write in reply to one whom I regard as a man sent by God. I have never had the pleasure of meeting Godfrey, Prince Bishop of Bamberg, but as I know him well by his deeds, I love and revere him ardently, and I ever pray God, who put you, at so opportune a moment, over a see that was fast falling into ruin, to keep you safe and sound for many years, to direct and protect you, and at last, when full of days and merits, to place upon your head an imperishable crown of glory.

It is not necessary for me to offer my services for they are already entirely and irrevocably at your Lordship's disposal. Good-bye, and remember me in your prayers.

Knowing the Cardinal's word to be his bond, Godfrey turned to him for advice and help again and again. He was never disappointed, and the most charming friendship developed between those two apostolic men who, as St Robert lamented, had not yet had the joy of seeing each other face to face. Up to the day when he took to his bed never to rise again, Bellarmine was nearly always engaged transacting business for his innumerable episcopal friends in Germany, Poland, Belgium, France, Switzerland, Portugal, Italy and various missionary countries. No task they could give him to do was ever found too long or too tedious. Indeed, he showed himself quite greedy of employment in their service and nearly all his letters to them ended with such sentences as: "If it is in my power to do you any service here in Rome you have a right in charity to command me; I shall most diligently take care of any commission or business commended to me in your name; if I can do anything for your Most Reverend Lordship here you have but to let me know by one of your representatives or by letter, and I shall, with the best will in the world, see to it".

St Francis de Sales was Bellarmine's ideal of a pastor of souls, and St Francis, on his side, had long since recognized in the Cardinal the greatest gift of God to his Church in that age. On July 10, 1616, Francis wrote from Annecy to tell his friend that he had founded in that city and in Lyons two congregations of unmarried ladies and widows, who, though they were not enclosed and did not take solemn vows, yet practised all the virtues of the religious life. The Archbishop of Lyons had considered that it would be advisable to give these ladies the standing of real nuns by providing them with a rule and introducing solemn vows and enclosure. St Francis had taken the advice and was anxious to obtain the approbation of the Holy See for his plans. Continuing, he tells Bellarmine, after alluding to "the wondrous, sweet readiness to obey" of his two communities, that the ladies had a few special customs which they did not want to surrender:

They have just three special practices of piety to which they are particularly attached. . . . These do not seem to my way of thinking to be incompatible with enclosure or the religious state, and according to those well acquainted with French affairs they seem to help on piety rather than to diminish it. The first [exemption which they hoped for] is that they should not be bound to recite the clerical or Great Office, but merely the Little Office of the ever Blessed Virgin. The reason of this wish on their part is because in their congregation elderly women are very often received who scarcely ever or never could learn the Great Office with all its rubrics.

Besides, they are accustomed to say the short Office of the Blessed Virgin with great distinctness as to voice, accentuation, and pauses, a thing they could never do if they had to recite a longer office. This is the more deserving of consideration because, of all the women in the world, there are none who pronounce Latin worse than do the French, so they would be utterly unable to observe the laws of accents, quantities, and right pronunciation, if the Lessons and Psalms were constantly to be changing. It is, indeed, lamentable to find in most con-

vents such ignorance of pronunciation as sometimes causes even
devout persons to smile, while it scandalizes and provokes to
mirth people of irreligious minds and those tainted with heresy.

The next practice for which St Francis wants Bellarmine to
obtain the sanction of the Pope is that of allowing widows in
secular dress to live within the convent walls. The Saint pleads
very earnestly on behalf of this custom because, as he puts it,
"in this country men so worry even pious widows with their
attentions that however much they may want to do so, it is almost
impossible for them to live according to the spirit of true widow-
hood". Finally, Francis would very much like to obtain the
Pope's approval for the admission of married ladies to the
convents that they might pass some days in retreat. The very long
letter then ends as follows: "Most eminent Cardinal, it is to your
intercession alone that I have recourse. You are in fact the only
member of that august apostolic college whom I have the honour
of knowing. You are moreover thoroughly conversant with our
affairs on this side of the Alps and therefore able to bring home to
others that the progress of God's service must be procured, here
in one way and there in a different way, according to the differences of customs and countries. Finally, as guarantee of your
sympathy with devout souls, I have by me your last-born and so
lovable Benjamin. It leaves me with no doubts at all."

Bellarmine's "last-born and lovable Benjamin" was probably
the little spiritual treatise which appeared in 1615 under the title,
De Ascensione Mentis in Deum. Its author appears to have been
perplexed by the question of the "virgins and widows", as there
were certain legal technicalities to be observed in the transaction
of such business, and St Francis had not made the necessary
arrangements:

Very Reverend and Honoured Lord,
      Though perchance your Lordship is known to few in Rome
your many and great virtues have been thoroughly well known
by me for a very long time. And not to me only but to our
Holy Father is also known your Reverend Lordship's pastoral
zeal and charity towards your flock.

As to the business of the unmarried ladies and widows which you have entrusted to me, I am completely at a loss to know what to do because, as far as I am aware, no official advocate has been appointed to undertake the legal part of the matter. Then again, I feel quite certain that you will never obtain the confirmation of the two communities as a true religious order while the three conditions you mention remain. Nevertheless, I am most willing to further your Lordship's plan by every means in my power, if in compliance with the regulations someone will appear and register an official supplication on your behalf. I have not been visited by anyone so far, and I am at a loss to know to whom I may entrust the present letter.

Meantime, however, I will tell your Lordship the kind of advice I would myself follow if the affair were mine. I would let well alone and keep these ladies in the state in which they now are; for there were nuns in the Church, both in the East and the West, before the time of Boniface VIII . . . who were not so enclosed in convents that they could not go out when necessary. Your Lordship knows that simple vows are just as binding before God and of just as much merit as solemn ones. It was Pope Boniface who introduced by an ecclesiastical law both solemn vows and enclosure. Even at the present day we have here in Rome a flourishing convent for ladies of noble birth, founded by St Frances, in which there are neither solemn vows nor enclosure. If then, in your country, unmarried persons and widows lead such holy lives without being enclosed or professed and at the same time can be of such service to people in the world, I do not see why this mode of life need be changed. Such is my opinion but I willingly submit it to better judgments.

While I was engaged in writing to your Lordship, I received a second letter from you about the Avignon business. I will use my utmost endeavours on your behalf. Good-bye now, your Lordship, and remember me in your holy prayers.

Canon law has always been extremely rigid in the matter of nuns, and Paul V was a notoriously conservative canon lawyer. In consequence the Visitation, which by its very name proclaimed the original purpose of its beloved Founder at least partially, for with him contemplation always came first, was turned into a strictly enclosed religious order, entirely precluded from visiting the poor or the sick. Somewhat earlier, St Angela Merici's original conception for her Ursulines foundered on the same rock of enclosure, and so, under Pope Paul's successor, Urban VIII, did Mary Ward's gallant attempt to get nuns out and about. St Vincent de Paul alone skirted the rock by adopting a modified version of Bellarmine's advice to St Francis de Sales.

In 1607, Robert Ubaldini, the *maestro di camera* of Paul V, had been appointed to the see of Bellarmine's native town, Montepulciano. The two Roberts were great friends, so when Ubaldini, who was a zealous and conscientious man, was ordered to France to act as papal nuncio at the court of Henry IV, he begged Bellarmine to undertake the administration of his diocese in his absence. The Cardinal agreed willingly, as such work had far greater attractions for him than the official business, often of a secular nature, to which he had almost daily to devote his attention, but he stipulated that he was not to be put under an obligation of justice but only of charity, in the fulfilment of his new charge.

The reason why he laid down this condition and even insisted on its being mentioned in the brief of his appointment was because he knew that he would not be permitted to reside permanently in the diocese. He firmly intended to go there as often as possible, and was looking forward to some of the apostolic joy of his Capuan days, but he reckoned without Pope Paul. When, after all had been arranged, he hinted to the Pope that Montepulciano ought to have an early visit from its administrator, he was met, to his dismay, with a polite but definite refusal. If he wished to go to his native town for rest or change, Paul told him, he was most welcome to do so, but he must not go there to work. Hearing these words, the Cardinal began to lament that he had accepted the trust at all. However, it was too late to draw back, so he vowed that he would at least try to do through others what he was prevented from doing in person.

Then began a period of tremendous activity. The city on the hill which had given him birth and nurture was in the Cardinal's thoughts from morning to night. He hunted round Rome until he found a man whom he could thoroughly trust, and him he then dispatched to investigate and bring back with speed a full and careful account of the state of affairs in the diocese. After the report had been studied and prayed over most earnestly, a work of reformation and renovation was started in Montepulciano comparable to that which had been carried through in Capua. Each parish priest was sent a copy of the Cardinal's smaller *Catechism* and *Explanation of the Creed*, with strict injunctions to hold classes in Christian doctrine every Sunday. The clergy in general received constant, lovingly-worded exhortations to zeal and diligence in God's service, the discipline of the many religious houses was carefully regulated and strengthened, and the spiritual life of the diocese as a whole was stimulated into new fervour.

No man is a prophet in his own country. "The Cardinal", wrote his vicar-general, "met with opposition which was an exceedingly sore trial to his patience and goodness of heart. . . . Every wise scheme which he sought to put into operation was thwarted and criticized by malcontents, and he was kept in continual trouble during the whole four years of his administration." His efforts to increase the slender endowments of the diocesan chapter were so much resented by a few meddlesome laymen that they lodged a charge against the Cardinal with the nuncio in Florence, and enlisted the influence of the Grand Duke's ministers on their side. Bellarmine was then compelled to write to the Dowager Grand Duchess, Christina of Lorraine, to beg for her intercession.

That, however, was only one incident in the story. The clergy, too, caused the Cardinal much anxiety, for some fierce quarrelling went on among them. He had to write to their superior to beg him to moderate his language, as this good man was reported to have angrily told a colleague in the course of a heated argument that "he had better shut up if he didn't want to burst". The other man thereupon so far forgot himself as to spit in the archpriest's face. Bellarmine wrote to inform him that he had incurred excommunication by such an outrage, but his letter was treated with contempt by the culprit. A second letter followed, the last section of which runs as follows:

You say at the close of your letter that you will claim from
God the reward of your good deeds, and leave your revenge in
his hands. In the same place you protest your innocence and
express a wish that God may take vengeance on me for having
judged you wrongfully. I may say in answer that you need not
wait so long for the vengeance you desire, for you can demand
it from the Pope or from the Sacred Congregation of Bishops,
by appealing to them against my sentence. I shall not take it ill
if my sentence be reversed, though I must warn you that I
believe it would only be confirmed to your still greater dis-
comfiture.

As to what you write with regard to the evil deeds of the
archpriest, I answer that they have either not happened during
my term of office or have not been made known to me. When
they are proved to me juridically, I shall not fear to look any
man in the face.

This is what occurs to me at present. As soon as you think
well to write to me acknowledging your sin and asking for
forgiveness, you will find me ready to grant you not that favour
only but many others besides.

Shortly after the dispatch of that letter, certain clerics came to
Rome on a legitimate appeal about some matter that concerned
the municipal authorities of Montepulciano. The civil courts of
the town had then ordered the arrest of their relatives, and so drew
upon themselves a strong expostulation from the much-tried
Cardinal. He reminded the officials implicated that they had
incurred the censures of the Church, but finding that he was
unable to enforce his demands and feeling that it was his duty not
to give way, he at last placed his resignation in the hands of the
Pope on October 14, 1611. A little while earlier, his brother
Thomas had pressed him to come and spend a month or two at
his house, assuring him that his good work for the city made all
the people want to "put a crown upon his head". The Cardinal's
sad answer was that there was no need for him to go there to
receive such an honour, for Montepulciano had crowned him
already—with thorns.

To compensate for his failure with his native town which he
dearly loved, and honoured on the title-pages of his famous books,

Cardinal Bellarmine achieved complete success in his dealings with a far more illustrious place, the very ancient city of Lucca, at the time an independent republic. Lucca had already contributed more than its fair quota of recruits to the Lutheran and Calvinist camps, some of them very distinguished people. The Lucchesi valued the presence in their midst of a colony of German silk-weavers, Lutheran in belief, but the Bishop of Lucca, Alessandro Guidiccioni, regarded those foreigners as an abiding source of infection for his flock. He made strenuous efforts to have the Inquisition set up in the republic, a course so much resented by the senators that, in 1605, they declared him an enemy of the state and suspect of treason. Paul V, made wise by his experience with Venice, refused to take action and, indeed, kept the obstinate Guidiccioni, who would not resign even when offered a see with equivalent revenues, almost a prisoner in Rome for thirteen years. Then, in 1618, he was allowed to return to a part of his diocese outside the bounds of the Republic. The senators dispatched an embassy to Rome to protest against even this small concession, and their envoy, Lorenzo Bonvisi, called upon Cardinal Bellarmine to see whether he could enlist his support for Lucca. Though seventy-seven years old at the time, St Robert eagerly seized the chance to settle the long dispute and dealt with the suspicious senators, who after all were good if decidedly anticlerical Catholics, so tactfully that by common accord they appointed him arbitrator between themselves and the Bishop, and agreed to abide by his decision. Many were the interviews which he then had with Guidiccioni and many the letters, among the longest he ever wrote, which he addressed to the Senate of Lucca. The upshot of his efforts was that the Bishop re-entered Lucca amid great pomp and public rejoicings on November 8, 1619, and continued to rule his diocese in perfect peace with the civil authorities until his death in 1637.

CHAPTER XII

GALILEO'S FIRST MISFORTUNES

IT was Cardinal Bellarmine's hard lot in the last years of his
harassed existence, when he so greatly longed for a remission
of the daily drudgery that he might have undistracted union
with God, to become entangled in the affairs of the portentous
Galileo. He must have been aware that a wind of change was
blowing in the world about him, that many men, Bishop Grosse-
teste, Friar Roger Bacon, Bishop Oresme of Lisieux, Cardinal
Nicholas of Cusa, had already seriously questioned the validity
of Aristotle's *Physics* and astronomy and that among friends of his
own there were not a few disposed to accept the heliocentric
theory of the heavens propounded by the Polish Canon Copernicus. The Canon's treatise *On the Revolutions of the Celestial Orbs*
had appeared in print in 1543 when Robert was a year old,[1] but
the general thesis of the book had become known long before,
for it was scouted as the anti-biblical notion of a fool by Martin
Luther in his *Table Talk* and received with respectful attention by
Pope Clement VII and his cardinals in 1533. A learned Austrian
named Albrecht Widmanstadt had been invited to lecture to
them on the subject in the Vatican Gardens, and an inscription
on the former buildings of the papal observatory there records
that the Pope awarded Widmanstadt a "precious codex" for his
pains. The codex still exists in a Munich library, ancient but hardly
precious, except that it bears on its title-page an attestation
written and signed by Widmanstadt, who had become chancellor
of Lower Austria, that it had been given to him by Clement VII
for his lecture on the Copernican astronomy. Plainly, in those

[1] As did also a book revolutionary in another sphere, the *De Fabrica Humani
Corporis* by the Belgian Andreas Vesalius who was appointed surgeon to
Emperor Charles V at Madrid the following year. Vesalius died on a pilgrimage
to Jerusalem.

days there was no disposition to reject heliocentrism out of hand as opposed to Scripture.

In 1536, when Paul III had succeeded to the papal throne, Cardinal Schönberg, Archbishop of Capua, a German, wrote a warmly worded letter to Copernicus in his northern retreat of Ermland, then appertaining to the Polish crown, begging him most earnestly to communicate his discoveries to the learned world. Schönberg, who died the following year, had been given the red hat by the new Pope, and was one of the "reform" cardinals who sponsored the famous *Consilium de emendanda Ecclesia* that anticipated much of the later legislation of the Council of Trent. He was close to the Pope, and it may well have been at the Holy Father's instance that he wrote to the dilatory canon of Frauenberg. Copernicus so much prized the letter that he had it printed in his epoch-making book when, six years later, at the persistent entreaty of the Catholic Bishop Giese of Ermland, he allowed his enthusiastic young disciple Rheticus, an Austrian who had embraced Lutheranism, to copy his manuscript and have the work printed and published in Germany. Rheticus found a Lutheran publisher in Nuremberg ready to undertake the difficult task, though the book was dedicated to Pope Paul III.

At that time the leading Lutheran authority in Nuremberg was Andreas Osiander, who strongly upheld heliocentrism and had been in friendly correspondence with Copernicus. As Rheticus had been called to Leipzig, he entrusted to Osiander the task of seeing the book of *The Revolutions* through the press. Osiander wanted it to be a success, but he knew well that the twin stars of Wittenberg, Luther and Melanchthon, with whom he had had theological quarrels, were strongly, even violently, opposed to the new astronomy. He therefore composed an unsigned preface or introduction to the book in which it was stated, as though by Copernicus himself, that the heliocentric theory put forward was a mere hypothesis to explain the heavenly movements in a simpler fashion than the cumbrous Ptolemaic system, but not claiming any greater reality. That was carrying diplomacy beyond decent limits, for Osiander knew perfectly well that Copernicus, who then lay dying in Frauenberg, regarded heliocentrism not as hypothesis, but as physical fact. More than sixty years later, the attractive genius Johannes Kepler discovered that Osiander was the author of the preface, written to spare himself thunderbolts from Wittenberg, and Galileo, with his usual flair, divined independently that the preface was bogus, but the fraud did not become generally known until the nineteenth century, though there is an obvious discrepancy between the genuine dedication of the book to Pope Paul III and the intruded piece.

Pope Paul, of course, received a copy of the very expensive book, and so probably did a few other friends of Copernicus in Rome, but it may well be doubted whether the Pope or any other read much beyond Osiander's clever piece of forgery. *The Revolutions* was altogether too technical for any but skilled mathematicians to follow, and besides there was in it a reassuring dependence on Ptolemaic epicycles for those who might have been alarmed by the central thesis that the earth revolved round the sun. Copernicus retained even the Pythagorean notions borrowed from them and from Plato by Aristotle, that the earth, moon, planets and stars must move in circles because that was the only perfect form of locomotion. That was mythology rather than science and it maintained its sway until Kepler hit almost by accident on the true explanation of the erratic behaviour of the planet Mars, its progressions and retrogressions, namely that its orbit was not circular but elliptical, with the sun in one of the foci. Even Galileo stood by Aristotle on this point and treated very shabbily the generous if wayward Kepler who had sent him his book establishing the true Martian orbit.

Presumably some attention must have been given to Copernicus and his book in learned Italian circles. His name was familiar in Rome, where he had lectured in the jubilee year 1500, and was consulted on the reform of the calendar by the fifth Lateran Council in 1512, but the minds of even highly intelligent men had become so much imbued with the views of Aristotle on the mechanism of the heavens that they could not shake themselves free from his solid transparent crystal spheres carrying the moon, the planets, the sun and the fixed stars in their circumferences and all set in motion by a ninth crystal sphere, the *primum mobile* or first mover which carried no heavenly bodies. Beyond lay the Tenth Heaven or Empyrean, the abode of God and his saints, without position or movement or duration, but eternal and infinite. In the second century A.D. Ptolemy of Alexandria resurrected the ingenious device of the Greek Hipparchus called epicycles, that is, circles whose centres move along the circumference of other larger circles called deferents, in order to keep the errant planets within the bounds of the only perfect form of motion, and by so doing he saved not only the appearances but also Aristotle's sacred crystal spheres. According to the Master of Those Who Know the universe consists of two distinct worlds, the superlunary and the sublunary. In the superlunary world are the moon itself, the five known planets, the sun, and the fixed stars, all imperishable and undergoing no change except that of local motion in perfect circles. The sublunary world, that is to say the spherical earth, is at rest in the centre of the universe and round it lie the layers, concentric and spherical, of water, air and fire. This is the world of generation and decay, in fact, the dustbin of the cosmos. The superlunary world, from the moon outwards, is composed of a fifth element, an imperishable *aether*, incapable of any change other than change of place in circular movement. How could intelligent men for eighteen hundred years accept this *a priori*, unproved and unprovable, scheme of things as the truth? There were several reasons. It answered well enough to their daily experience. The earth certainly seemed at rest, and any man who sat up late enough on a clear night could see for himself the majestic wheeling of the heavens. The Scriptures, the revealed word of God, seemed to be permeated through and through with the same idea, though the sacred writers had never heard of Aristotle. The Fathers of the Church did not so much believe the geocentric theory as take it for granted. Ptolemy's elaboration of Aristotle did in fact account for the celestial phenomena well enough, and by it eclipses could be predicted and ships guided to their destinations with reasonable accuracy. The one serious argument against Ptolemy was the complication of his system, but as no one until Copernicus had suggested a simpler explanation based on mathematical calculations, the swarming epicycles did not seem too heavy a burden on the mind. If comets appeared, travelling in plainly non-circular orbits, they could be explained as some sort of sublunary exhalations. In fact that is what Galileo himself came to think them. Except as signs and portents, they were of no consequence.[1] Such was the vision of the universe pervading the whole of Dante's *Divine Comedy*, which Robert Bellarmine knew and loved so well. Indeed, such was all western men's vision if they thought about the matter at all, until the star-struck champion of Copernicus, Galileo, came to rouse them from their Ptolemaic slumbers.

Galileo was a great optimist and appears to have thought that he could shake and overthrow Aristotle's pillared heavens by brilliant argument. But a medieval Yorkshire man named John Holywood stood in his path and defied him. This man, known to fame as Joannes de Sacrobosco, Low Latin for Holywood, taught mathematics and astronomy at the University of Paris when St Thomas Aquinas was a student there. He won great renown and his book called *The Sphere*, Ptolemaic to the last epicycle, became the astronomical bible of the schools right on into the seventeenth century. Printed for the first time in 1472, *The Sphere* went into forty new editions, excluding innumerable commentaries, by the year 1647. During the same period, the life-work of poor Copernicus, in which lay explicitly the revolution and diurnal motion of the earth, and implicitly, a mighty revolution in human thought, was reprinted exactly twice. In 1570 when he was thirty-two the Jesuit Christopher Clavius, who had mathematics in his blood, wrote a commentary on Sacrobosco's *Sphere* in which he directly combated the Copernican theory, on mathematical grounds. Clavius and Bellarmine had been students together at the Roman College and remained life-long friends. It was to this expert that St Robert turned for advice when rumours of Galileo's discoveries reached Rome.

[1] But Tycho Brahe had established by observation of the comet of 1577 that it lay far beyond the moon in the superlunary world. This at a stroke abolished the theory of solid, transparent crystal spheres and the supposed immutability of the heavens.

Galileo paid his first visit to Rome in 1587 at the age of twenty-three, and on that occasion made the acquaintance of Clavius whose friendship he retained until the end of the Jesuit professor's life in 1612. On his return to his native city of Pisa, he was appointed to the chair of mathematics at the university where he had made his first studies and earned the nickname of "the Wrangler" owing to his choleric and disputatious temper. A wrangler he remained to the day of his death. At Pisa, and subsequently at the University of Padua in the serritory of the Venetian Republic, he taught his students the traditional astronomy of Ptolemy, though he assured Kepler that he had by then become a confirmed Copernican. It is very likely that he had, but it was not until the year 1604 that he made his first attack on the Aristotelians whose bread and butter depended on the maintenance of the traditional astronomy. A new star, or rather an obscure star already there, suddenly flared up to extraordinary brilliance in the October sky of 1604 and then gradually faded to its former dimness. It was the sign that Galileo needed, for it proved that the immutable heavens of Aristotle had changed dramatically. Tycho Brahe, the aristocratic and wealthy Danish observer, and Johannes Kepler, poor as any church mouse, had long before studied those so-called new stars which suddenly flamed in the sky and then slowly faded, but they had no desire to make them an issue with the Aristotelians. Galileo, like Goliath, a battler from his youth, seized on the *nova* of 1604 as a weapon of war.

A few years later, a far more deadly weapon came into the restless genius's hands in the shape of the instrument subsequently called the telescope, which he did not invent but improved immensely. He presented a fine specimen to the Doge and Senators of Venice, who were so much impressed that they doubled his salary. He remained at Padua as principal professor of mathematics for eighteen years, and lived there in concubinage with a Venetian woman named Marina Gamba who bore him two daughters and a son. Both daughters became nuns and were their father's great joy and comfort in his old age. While at Padua in the year 1609, Galileo turned his "spyglass", as he then called it, on the moon, the Milky Way, various other nebulae and the

planet Jupiter. On the moon he discovered mountains and huge
chasms just like those on the earth, thus disproving once and for
all that the earth's satellite was composed of the immutable fifth
element and without a spot or wrinkle. In the constellation of
Orion, the telescope revealed more than five hundred new stars,
and instead of the Pleiades being seven sisters, they appeared as a
large family of some forty stars. The Milky Way, supposed for so
long to be merely a denser part of the aether reflecting the light of
stars or sun, revealed itself in the telescope to be a collection of
innumerable stars grouped in clusters, and the same applied to the
other nebulae. But the greatest thrill of all came to the watching
genius when in January and February, 1610, four planets, "never
seen from the creation of the world", swam into his ken, four of
the twelve moons of Jupiter. He thought at first that they must
be fixed stars, but, patiently watching night after cold night, he
discovered their relationship to Jupiter. Never again could it be
said that all known planets revolved round a stationary earth, for
the new planets revolved round the mighty Jupiter and provided
an example of Copernicanism in miniature.

All those shattering discoveries the Astronomer of Padua
consigned to a brief book, hardly more than a large pamphlet,
and set forth with admirable sketches and diagrams drawn by
himself. He wrote in Latin for the sake of learned men outside
Italy and called the little book *Siderius Nuncius*, meaning the
Starry Messenger or else Message from the Stars. It was published
at Venice in 1610 and dedicated to the Grand Duke of Tuscany,
Cosimo II de' Medici, whom Galileo had coached in mathematics and in whose honour he named the newly discovered
moons of Jupiter the Medicean planets. He had long been angling
for an invitation to Florence as chief mathematician and philosopher to the Grand Duke, as he had tired of his light teaching
duties in Padua and wanted to be entirely free for research. Only
four months after the appearance of the *Starry Messenger*, he was
given his heart's desire, and at the same time appointed chief
mathematician of the University of Pisa, without any obligation
to reside or teach in that city. He had already parted from the
mother of his children in Padua, for their irregular union did not

bring either of them contentment and she sensibly married a man of her own class who was not a genius. Galileo kept to the end his bachelor status, did everything in his power for his three children, and almost beggared himself in his efforts to help other relatives who sponged on him mercilessly. This generosity was one of the most attractive features of his very complex character.

The Doge and other authorities in Venice regarded Galileo's departure from Padua as an act of black ingratitude. His best friend in the Republic, a diplomat named Sagredo whom he was to immortalize, respected his intentions but warned him that in departing from the free atmosphere of Padua he might easily incur opposition to his open sympathy for Copernicanism as declared in the *Starry Messenger*. Mr Stillman Drake and other recent historians of science adopt the views of Sagredo, but appear to forget that Giordano Bruno had been delivered by the Inquisition of Venice, without the slightest opposition of the civil government, to the Inquisition of Rome.[1]

The reception given to the *Starry Messenger* was variously enthusiastic, cautious, or absolutely hostile. Kepler, always generous, though Galileo would not let him have the use of one of his telescopes and ignored his epoch-making book, the *Astronomia Nova*, in which lay hidden the true explanation of planetary movements, acclaimed the new discoveries from the first and so did a number of Galileo's pupils, especially the Cassinese Benedictine, Benedetto Castelli. Clavius was one of the cautious people, thinking not altogether unreasonably that some imperfection in Galileo's primitive telescope or the fatigue produced by his long observations might account for the alleged phenomena. But shortly afterwards the Roman College acquired possession of a fairly good instrument, and then Clavius saw for himself that Jupiter's moons were not merely Galileo's imagina-

[1] Stillman Drake, *Discoveries and Opinions of Galileo*, New York, 1957, p. 72. This admirable book contains partial translations of all Galileo's works published during Cardinal Bellarmine's lifetime, and also of the famous *Assayer*, demolishing a Roman Jesuit, published in 1623, two years after Bellarmine's death. Mr Drake furnishes excellent introductions and notes to the various translations, which make joyous reading. Besides being a genius as a scientist Galileo was also a genius as a controversialist and pamphleteer.

tion. He immediately wrote to that gentleman, expressing his delight at being able to confirm the discovery, and Galileo replied in the friendliest terms, giving his latest observations of the "circumjovial planets", as Kepler had named Jupiter's moons. The Jesuits in Florence had been shown those objects by their discoverer and pleased him by introducing the moons into their sermons and lectures. But this did not in the least mean that Clavius and his brethren had been won over to Copernicanism.

It is often forgotten that those men were first and foremost religious, vowed to the sanctification of their own souls and, as a result of that, apostles dedicated to the promotion of the greater glory of God by striving to bring about, aided by divine grace, the supernatural salvation of their fellow men. As religious under solemn vows, they could not then, no more than they can now, be pure scientists in the sense of making science the predominant interest of their lives. That is the reason why they could never produce scientists of the calibre and detachment of Galileo, no more than they could produce great poets, except as it were by accident in the case of Gerard Manley Hopkins. They were not founded to promote science, poetry, music or anything else, except in so far as such pursuits might advance the glory of God and the sanctification of their own and other men's souls. Consequently, though the mathematicians of the Roman College were delighted by Galileo's discoveries, they were very far from sharing his optimism about the imminent triumph of heliocentrism. The traditional mould of human thinking could be suddenly broken only with danger to spiritual interests far exceeding in importance any concern for strict scientific truth. Tycho Brahe, possibly the most persistent and accurate observer and recorder of celestial motions that ever lived, by long study of whose tables Kepler discovered his three laws, was, like Kepler, a good Lutheran, and rejected Copernicanism as opposed to the Scriptures. He maintained the earth stationary at the centre of the cosmos, but made the five known planets revolve round the sun which, carrying the planets, revolved round the earth. This was merely the revival in completer form of the system proposed by Heracleides of Pontus in the fourth century B.C., and the Jesuits adopted it as a half-way house to the Copernicanism which they believed could not be reconciled with the Scriptures.

After the publication of the *Starry Messenger* and its enthusiastic reception by Kepler, Galileo condescended to wrote to that worthy, who was Mathematician to the Emperor, Rudolph II. This was the first of the only two letters he wrote directly to Kepler during his life, and the second was separated from it by an interval of thirteen years. In the letter of 1610, he regaled the German genius with stories of the reactions of the Aristotelian stalwarts to his discoveries: "How you would laugh if you heard what things the first philosopher of the faculty of Pisa brought against me in the presence of the Grand Duke, for he tried, now with logical arguments, now with magical adjurations, to tear down and argue the new planets out of the heavens". Meantime, Galileo's telescope, though not powerful enough to reveal Saturn's rings, composed of countless tiny moonlets, and still less its nine moons, yet did show the planet as a very strange object, apparently flanked by two stationary satellites, as Kepler had taken to calling the planet's attendant moons. Far more important, though, was Galileo's discovery of the phases of Venus which seemed to him to clinch the argument for Copernicanism. He communicated these startling revelations to the Jesuit mathematicians of the Roman College, who verified them with their own telescope but were not at all prepared to jump to Galileo's heliocentric conclusion. Tycho Brahe's system provided satisfactorily for Venus, without it being necessary to push the earth around and raise difficulties for the theologians.

In January, 1611, Galileo, then in his exalted post at Florence, decided to visit Rome again to rescue the college of cardinals once and for all from the thraldom of Aristotle and Ptolemy. That this was the principal purpose of his visit is revealed by his own avowal and by the collection of telescopes in his baggage. He arrived in Rome on March 29 and the following day turned his steps towards the Roman College where he had discussions with Father Clavius and some other professors who had been engaged in observation of the Medicean planets continuously for two months. "We have compared notes," he informed a friend on April 1, "and have found that our experiences tally in every respect."

On this occasion Galileo was received in a long private audience by Pope Paul V who assured him of his unalterable good will. Federigo Cesi, son of the powerful Duke of Aquasparta, a young enthusiast for the study of philosophy, science and mathematics, had founded a society for the promotion of those subjects which he called the *Accademia dei Lincei*, the Academy of the Lynx-eyed. At first it consisted of only four members, himself and three friends, and was frowned upon by his autocratic father, who considered the pursuit of science sheer folly and waste of time. But Federigo persisted and won the adherence to his Academy of a renowned person named Giambattista Porta. That made five members until Galileo was elected the sixth in April, 1611, after which the Academy grew greatly in size and influence. London's Royal Society which had similar aims and methods was not established until several years later. The importance of the Academy, membership of which Galileo greatly prized, lay in the fact that in those days, as contrasted with our times, universities had become hidebound in conservatism, with a vested interest in maintaining the accepted views. The academies, of which several sprang up in imitation of the Lincean or for other purposes, offered an alternative to enterprising men and so promoted the advancement of knowledge. Federigo Cesi, the pioneer of academies, was an intimate of Robert Bellarmine and wrote after his death "of the happy memory of Signor Cardinal Bellarmine, my very good patron, who bore me particular affection".[1]

Cesi and Cardinal Farnese both gave banquets in honour of the man of the hour, who when the feasting and toasting were over produced his newly named telescopes and invited Bellarmine,

[1] This was in 1628, two years before Cesi's own death: Favaro, *Opere di Galileo*, Edizione nazionale, vol. xiii, pp. 429-30. This great work was completed in twenty volumes in 1909, after nineteen years labour. Professor Favaro acknowledged that he received great help in his enterprise "thanks to the high and enlightened wisdom of Pope Leo XIII". Favaro was an enthusiastic "Galilean", but reserved his slings and arrows for the enemy in separate studies, distinct from his magnificent editing. He died in 1922, on which occasion Pope Pius XI sent his family a letter of affectionate sympathy. He was not a Catholic.

among other distinguished guests, to view Jupiter's moons and other phenomena for himself. That what he saw gave him food for thought is evident from the following inquiry which the Cardinal addressed to Father Clavius and his colleagues at the Roman College on April 19, 1611:

Very Reverend Fathers,

I know that your Reverences have heard of these new astronomical discoveries which an eminent mathematician has made by means of an instrument called a *cannone* or ocular tube. I myself by means of the same instrument have seen some very wonderful things concerning the moon and Venus, and I would be grateful if you would favour me with your honest opinion on the following matters:

1°. Whether you confirm the report that there are multitudes of fixed stars invisible to the naked eye, and especially whether the Milky Way and the nebulae are to be regarded as collections of very small stars.

2°. Whether it is true that Saturn is not a simple star but three stars joined together.

3°. Whether it is a fact that Venus changes its shape, increasing and diminishing like the moon.

4°. Whether the moon really has a rough and unequal surface.

5°. Whether it is true that four movable stars revolve round Jupiter, each with a different movement from that of the others, but all the movements being exceedingly swift.

I am anxious to have some definite information about these matters, because I hear conflicting opinions expressed with regard to them. As your Reverences are skilled in the science of mathematics you will easily be able to tell me whether these new discoveries are well-founded, or whether they may not be a mere illusion. If you like you can write your answer on this same sheet.

Your Reverences' brother in Christ,
ROBERT CARDINAL BELLARMINE.

The professors' reply was in the following terms:

We give our answer on this sheet, as your Lordship bade us,

M

and we do so in the same order in which you proposed the questions.

1°. It is true that the telescope reveals a vast number of stars in the nebulae of Cancer and the Pleiades, but it is not so certain that the Milky Way consists entirely of small stars. It seems more probable that there are parts of it which are denser and more continuous, though the existence of the many small stars cannot be denied. In fact, from what is to be seen in the nebulae of Cancer and the Pleiades, it may be conjectured that in the Milky Way, also, there are probably stars in immense multitudes, which cannot be discerned because they are too small.

2°. We have observed that Saturn is not spherical in shape, as we perceive Jupiter and Mars to be, but oval, though we have not seen the two stars at the sides detached from the centre one in such a way that we might call them separate stars.

3°. It is perfectly true that Venus diminishes and increases like the moon. During our observations of it when it was the evening star and almost full, we noticed that it grew less by gradual degrees on the illuminated side, which always faces towards the sun, and at the same time became ever more crescent-shaped. As the morning star, after conjunction with the sun, we perceived that it was horned and always presented its illuminated surface to the sun. This illumination continually increases while the apparent diameter of the planet gradually diminishes.

4°. With regard to the moon, the great irregularities and inequalities of its surface cannot be denied, but Father Clavius is of opinion that these inequalities are merely apparent, being due to the fact that the lunar mass is not uniformly dense but composed of more rarefied and more solidified sections, which are the ordinary spots one sees with the naked eye. Others think that the surface of the moon is really unequal, but so far there is not sufficient evidence on this point to enable us to give a positive answer.

5°. About Jupiter. Four stars may be seen revolving round that planet with great rapidity—now, all four moving towards the east, now, all towards the west—while at times some of them move in one direction and some in the other, almost in a straight line. These objects cannot be fixed stars since their movements are far swifter and altogether different from the movements of the fixed stars. Moreover, their distance from one another and from Jupiter varies continually.

This is what we have to say in reply to your Lordship's questions and, in conclusion, we offer you our humble respects, and pray God to grant you the fullest measure of happiness.[1]

The Jesuits of the Roman College played their part in honouring Galileo by organizing a public conference at which he was installed like a king on a throne to listen to Father Odo van Maelcote, one of the signatories of the reply to Bellarmine's inquiry, pronouncing an enthusiastic discourse on the new astronomical discoveries. The students of the College had been well coached in Galileo's views and expounded them to the large assembly with a little too much gusto for the liking of the Aristotelians in the audience. "We proved clearly," wrote one of them long afterwards to his friend the great Dutch scientist Christian Huygens, "that Venus revolves round the sun, but not without murmuring from the philosophers." The murmuring was to grow in volume, in Rome as in Florence and other learned centres, with almost every day that passed until it drowned the voices of reason and responsibility, even among the cardinals. The first assailants of the discoveries reported in the *Starry Messenger* were all laymen. Martin Horky, a young German Lutheran, studying at Bologna and a protégé of Kepler, wrote a scurrilous and disgustingly personal attack on Galileo's morals, which lost him Kepler's friendship. Then a Florentine named Francésco

---

[1] Favaro, *Opere di Galileo*, vol. xi, pp. 87-88, 92-93. Galileo saw to it that the answer to Bellarmine's inquiry became widely known. It drew amusingly diverse comments. Thus, a Florentine amateur astronomer named Ludovico delle Colombe wrote to thank Father Clavius warmly for having defended an unspotted moon, while a friend of Galileo, the artist Cigolo, remarked that the old priest (Clavius was seventy-six) must have no eyes in his head. The word *colombe* means doves or pigeons and from that circumstance Galileo lumped all his Aristotelian opponents together in what he called the Pigeon-League. Colombe himself was a bit of a fool whom Aristotle would have scorned as much as did Galileo, but he was influential and persistent, and helped to rally the champions of the old views against their destroyer and his abominable telescope.

Sizzi, who was an excellent mathematician, published a silly diatribe against the moons of Jupiter. Galileo's champions like to record that this man was subsequently broken on the wheel in France for having written a violent political pamphlet against King Louis XIII. Ludovico delle Colombe published a small book significant for the future because it consisted mostly of biblical texts supposedly irreconcilable with Galileo's views. This was the first set attempt to enlist the Scriptures against the great scientist, and it came from the pen of a completely unqualified lay person.

Galileo could afford to despise such adversaries while he was being lionized in Rome. Just before his return to Florence in June, 1611, Cardinal del Monte addressed a note to the Grand Duke of Tuscany in the following terms: "During his stay here Galileo has given the greatest satisfaction. . . . I verily believe that were we living under the ancient Roman republic, a column would have been erected on the Capitol in his honour." The great man himself wrote: "Everybody is showing me wonderful kindness, especially the Jesuit Fathers". But the eight cardinals of the Holy Office, among them Bellarmine, were more reserved in their attitude to the visitor from Florence. They were not at all concerned to question Galileo's remarkable astronomical discoveries, but may well have wondered whither this extraordinary man was heading in his persistent onslaughts by voice and pen on views accepted by the generality of mankind from time immemorial. A philosopher at Padua named Cesare Cremonini had been called to account by the Inquisition of Venice for views about God and nature which were considered heretical. The cardinals in Rome knew that Galileo had been a friend of this person during his Paduan days, though, as Cremonini was an out-and-out Aristotelian, the friendship did not last. They accordingly inquired at Venice, while Galileo was being fêted in Rome, whether his name had been mentioned in the inquisitorial investigations, which in fact came to nothing owing to the opposition of the civil authorities. Some estimable champions of Galileo have read sinister meanings into the routine inquiry from Rome and have made Cardinal Bellarmine solely responsible for it, though he was not, as they imagine, prefect of the Holy Office nor head of the Roman College.

It may have been all the excitement in Rome caused by Galileo's visit that inspired St Robert to have a faulty sundial, set in one of the outer walls of his residence, mended. As appeared in his little book, *The Ascent of the Mind to God*, he was much interested in the movement of the sun. The gnomon or pin of the dial had become twisted out of position, so the Cardinal asked Father Grienberger of the Roman College to come and see whether anything could be done about it. Grienberger brought with him one of the brightest of his students in mathematics named Orazio Grassi, who was destined to be given a kind of black immortality in the most brilliant and merciless of Galileo's polemical writings, *Il Saggiatore*. Having examined the sundial the visitors told the Cardinal that it could be put right at a cost of two *giulii*. When the old man heard this, Grassi reported, his face fell and he remained silent for a moment. Then he said: "I have not the heart to spend so much on my own convenience, for two *giulii* is enough money to support some poor wretch for two days". So the sundial remained unmended, and some mendicant got the two *giulii* thus saved. It is a trifling story but, according to one system of values, it perhaps revealed a disposition more precious by far than all Galileo's fine mathematics. Galileo had little charity in him. He loved to score off people and to make them look silly, which was a frame of mind quite incomprehensible to St Robert Bellarmine.

After his return to Florence Galileo became involved with the diehard Aristotelians in a matter of physics rather than astronomy. His astronomical discoveries had convinced the Roman Jesuits that Aristotle's views on the unchangeability of the heavens, his perfect moon, and his system of crystal spheres, carrying the celestial bodies, were no longer tenable. Now, the Principal Mathematician and Philosopher to the Grand Duke of Tuscany came right down to this earth which he already firmly believed to be a planet like Venus or Saturn, though he could not prove it in a way to convince the Jesuits or anybody else. The Grand Duke liked to give public dinners to which were invited distinguished men and women. It was hot on one such occasion and ice was obviously provided, for the conversation turned on the reason why that substance floats. According to Aristotle and his sixteenth- and seventeenth-century disciples, the floating of bodies immersed in water depended on their shape. Galileo who was present had long devoted his splendid talents to this problem and maintained strongly the opinion of Archimedes that whether objects in water floated or sank depended entirely on their specific gravity, or the ratio of the weight or mass of a given volume of a substance to that of an equal volume of another substance, in this case water. Ice floats because its weight is less than an equal volume of the water in which it is immersed. Two visiting cardinals from Rome graced this particular dinner, one of whom, Maffeo Barberini, sided entirely with Galileo against the outraged Aristotelians at table. This Barberini, who formed a fast friendship with Galileo, later became Pope Urban VIII and was chiefly responsible for the great scientist's condemnation by the Roman Inquisition in 1633. Urban had some excuse, for Galileo had flagrantly presumed on his friendship and understanding by publishing his overtly Copernican *Dialogue Concerning the Two Chief World Systems* in 1632.

The Grand Duke of Tuscany was so much impressed by Galileo's brilliant argumentation that he requested him to publish his views. This he did in Italian the following spring (1612), calling his book a *Discourse on Things that Float or Move on Water*. He at once sent a presentation copy to Bellarmine and received the following reply:

Illustrious Signore,

I have received your letter and the accompanying treatise on bodies that move about or remain still when placed in water. I shall read it with much pleasure, sure as I am that it is a work worthy of so eminent an author. While thanking you most heartily for your courtesy in sending it to me, I would like to assure you that the affection you have thus shown me is fully reciprocated on my part, and you will see that this is so, if ever I get an opportunity of doing you a service. With my kindest respects and a prayer that God may grant you every blessing.[1]

As has often been seen in these pages, St Robert Bellarmine was much too candid and open-hearted a man to engage in empty compliments. He meant every word of his letter to Galileo, and proved that he did up to the hilt when that impatient genius got himself into trouble with the Roman Inquisition three years later. He felt nothing but benevolence for Galileo whose splendid talents and deep Catholic faith he fully appreciated, though he may well have been puzzled how to reconcile the discoveries of the telescope with the traditional cosmology and physics of Aristotle, which he had been taught in his youth and saw no reason to discard until the crusader from Florence made his appearance. In his *Ascent of the Mind to God*, published in 1615, the year Galileo made his third and disastrous visit to Rome, the Cardinal wrote: "We know that there were some who by the movement of the stars defined the nature of the sky as a fifth element, simple, incorruptible, and constantly moving in a circle." By the words that follow, St Robert shows clearly that he was not wedded to that tenet of the strict Aristotelians which, Tycho Brahe first, and Galileo much more thoroughly, had utterly discredited. Bellar-

---

[1] Favaro, *Le Opere di Galileo*, vol. xi, pp. 337-8. In his stimulating and engagingly enthusiastic book, *The Crime of Galileo* (Chicago University Press, 1955), Professor Giorgio de Santillana makes no reference whatever to this letter, though it was there before his eyes in the second volume of Bellarmine's life by the present author (published in 1928 and now completely revised) from which he drew practically all the information about the Cardinal in his book, and, alas, constantly, though unintentionally, "slanted" it against him in his headlong quixotism to justify Galileo under every circumstance. His portrait of Bellarmine, owing to the intrusions of his vivid imagination, is a mere caricature. The Professor learned from his hero, Galileo, to be scornful of all critics, long dead or still living, but he did not so well learn from him to keep to the point and avoid irrelevancies. It is often extremely difficult to follow his line of thought, and his animus against the Society of Jesus is so extreme as to be ludicrous. The crime of those "trained seals", the Jesuits, balancing the world-system of the Lutheran Tycho Brahe on their silly noses, was not to have embraced wholeheartedly the system of the Catholic priest Copernicus as expounded by Galileo. But on the main point, Professor de Santillana is undoubtedly right. Galileo was condemned in 1633, at least in part, on the evidence of a document forged in 1616. It was a terrible miscarriage of justice, whose echoes still linger.

mine never believed in astrology, though in his youth he had lectured on the subject as one of great contemporary interest. For him, the providence of God, not stellar influences, ruled and guided men's lives. He was no scientist, but neither was he, even in scientific matters, anybody's fool.

In reading the *Discourse on Floating Bodies*, the Cardinal may have been troubled by Galileo's mockery of his Aristotelian opponents, to whose argument he added others that they had not thought of, and then brought their whole house of cards tumbling about their heads with his own irrefutable proofs. It was the way to create even greater enmity than already existed, and he need not have resorted to such polemical methods at all. In his next important work, his *Letters on Sunspots*, which was published for him by the Lincean Academy at Rome in 1613, he kept a bridle on his unkind wit, and the book is all the pleasanter to read.[1] It is in Italian, and concerned to prove that sunspots are in or very close to the surface of that luminary and prove by their recurrence that the sun turns on its axis, as against the theory of the German Jesuit astronomer, Christopher Scheiner, who had studied the spots through his telescope and, obviously to save the immaculacy and unchangeability of the sun, maintained that the spots were in fact stars, circling round it. The Jesuit wrote under the pseudonym of Apelles and was treated with unusual courtesy by Galileo. Subsequently the two men fell out on a question of priority in discovery of the sunspots, which was childish on both sides, as sunspots had been observed with the naked eye in the time of Charlemagne, if not centuries earlier. Father Grienberger, the best of the Jesuit astronomers now that Clavius was dead, at first sided with Scheiner, who appears to have been an irascible and contentious person, but subsequently went over to Galileo's views. In his book, published at Rome under the eyes of the Pope and cardinals, Galileo for the first time pronounced unequivocably, though still somewhat vaguely, in favour of the Copernican system, not as a hypothesis but as a physical fact, and predicted its forthcoming universal triumph. As the book was in Italian, it must have been widely read, yet no cardinal or bishop nor other

[1] Drake, *Discoveries and Opinions of Galileo*, 1957, pp. 89-104.

person of any consequence in Rome raised the slightest objection.

But trouble loomed on the horizon all the same. On December 13, 1613, eight months or so after the publication of the *Letters on Sunspots*, the Grand Duke of Tuscany invited several learned men to a banquet at Pisa where the court was then staying. Among the guests was Benedetto Castelli, the Cassinese Benedictine monk who had been for years one of Galileo's closest friends and admirers. Through the First Philosopher's influence Castelli had been appointed to the chair of mathematics at Pisa University and richly deserved the honour both for his good science and his good teaching, though he was forbidden by the rector of the university to expound Copernicanism. The most that could be said against him is that he, perhaps, embraced Galileo's unproven heliocentric views with more enthusiasm than discretion.

At the dinner in Pisa talk had naturally turned on the "Medicean Planets" and other discoveries of Galileo, who was himself in bed ill at the time. The Grand Duchess Christina, mother of Cosimo II, was not entirely satisfied that the "Planets" were real and asked Professor Boscaglia, an ardent Platonist, for his opinion. He answered that the real existence of the moons of Jupiter brooked no denial, nor did any other of Galileo's discoveries but, he added privately to the Grand Duchess, the motion of the earth seemed incredible, and indeed was not possible, as the Scriptures were opposed to such an idea. At the conclusion of the dinner Madama Christina sent a messenger to recall Father Castelli who had left the palace. In her suite he found assembled the Grand Duke, his wife, an Austrian Archduchess, Professor Boscaglia, a certain Don Antonio de' Medici, and Don Paolo, a member of the powerful Orsini family. The Grand Duchess forthwith started to argue the Scriptures against the theory of the movements of the earth, but Castelli was not dismayed. As he wrote to Galileo: "I began to play the theologian with so much assurance and dignity that it would have done you good to hear me. Don Antonio assisted me . . . and I carried the discussion off like a paladin. I won over the Grand Duke and his Archduchess completely and Don Paolo contributed to my help a very apt quotation from the Scriptures. Only Madama

MX

Christina remained against me, and as for Professor Boscaglia, he never opened his mouth."

A year earlier, towards the end of 1612, while he was recuperating at the villa of his friend Filippo Salviati a few miles to the west of Florence, Galileo received word that his views had been attacked in a private discussion by a Dominican priest named Niccolo Lorini, a Florentine patrician aged seventy, much esteemed by the Grand Duke and all others who knew him. Galileo, who was hypersensitive to criticism from churchmen, at once demanded an explanation from Lorini. Lorini might well have told him to mind his own business, as the discussion was private and no affair of his. Instead, he replied very courteously, assuring the great scientist that he had not joined in any discussion on philosophical subjects, but had merely thrown in a few words at one point, in order to avoid the appearance of stupidity, to the effect that "the opinion of Ipernicus, or whatever his name is, would appear to be incompatible with the sacred Scriptures". The matter was of little consequence to him, as he had other things to do. In a letter to Prince Cesi a few weeks later, Galileo referred to Lorini in derisive terms as a clumsy idiot who had decided to detest the mobility of the earth and was so unfamiliar with the author of the doctrine that he could not even spell his name.

Benedetto Castelli's account of the discussion after the banquet in Florence in December, 1613, stung Galileo into writing his Benedictine friend a very long letter, laying down the conditions that should obtain between religion and science. It was a brilliant letter and displayed an acquaintance with the Bible and the interpretations of the Fathers of the Church, especially St Augustine's *De Genesi ad litteram*, quite extraordinary in a man whose interests lay in a very different field. Among biblical commentators of his own time whom he quoted was the Spanish Jesuit Benedict Pereira (died Rome, 1610) to the following effect: "In dealing with the doctrine of Moses we must be careful to avoid saying confidently and without reservation anything which contradicts manifest experiences and the reasoning of natural philosophy or the other sciences. Since every truth is in harmony with all other truth, the truth of Holy Writ cannot be opposed to the solid reasons and findings of human knowledge."

Throughout his great letter to Castelli and even more plainly in his subsequent revision and strengthening of it known as the *Letter to the Grand Duchess Christina*, Galileo assumes, without ever saying so explicitly, the truth of the Copernican system. He also maintains that it is not his business but that of the commentators and theologians to disprove it, by arguments as good as those then available for its establishment, by which he meant the moons of Jupiter, the phases of Venus, and the changing nature and rotation of the sun. Those discoveries had certainly wrecked and ruined Aristotle's conception of the heavens, but they still fell far short of establishing the Copernican conception. This was the crux of the whole matter. Galileo believed that he had a physical proof of the earth's rotation on its axis in the phenomenon of the tides. In that he was wholly mistaken, but even if the tides had been due to the causes which he assigned, and not to the attraction of the moon, he would still have done nothing to prove the revolution of the earth around the sun. His telescopic discoveries did certainly require a new interpretation of the heavenly appearances, but it was provided for by Tycho Brahe's system which did not involve the revolution of the earth. Galileo might have been counted a little disingenuous in his attempt to shift the burden of disproof on to the shoulders of the theologians, seeing that he had himself provided no proof that was more than a mere persuasion, and he also tried to manoeuvre the theologians into a position which they had not tried to maintain. Copernicanism, he insisted obliquely, must be accepted as physical fact, or else altogether repudiated as heresy. What the theologians maintained all along was a third position, that the heliocentric theory could freely be held and discussed as a *hypothesis*, even as a better hypothesis to explain the appearances than that of the traditional Ptolemy. But Galileo would have none of this compromise. He seemed bent on ramming Copernicanism down people's throats as established fact, when he must have known that it was not established, seeing that he was unable with the best of his telescopes to discover the slightest stellar parallax, which he felt to be necessary if the earth travelled around the sun. Also, his insistence on circular motions, like any benighted Aristotelian, rendered the movements of the planets inexplicable. Kepler had discovered the laws of planetary movement, but Galileo was too proud to accept his assistance. At the end of his letter to the Grand Duchess Christina, he attempted an explanation of the standstill of the sun and moon at the command of Joshua, maintaining that "by the aid of the Copernican system we have the literal, open and easy sense" of the statement. That is obvious nonsense, for apart from the fact that the sun itself with all its planets is speeding to an unknown destination at the rate of twelve miles a second, which naturally Galileo did not know, the stoppage of the sun's rotation would have resulted in chaos in the solar system.[1]

Notwithstanding Galileo's inadequacy as an exponent of Scripture, his *Letter to the Grand Duchess Christina* is an epoch-making document, a manifesto for the freedom of natural science to pursue its own noble aims by its own experimental methods, without let or hindrance from theologians, politicians or anybody else. "The Bible was not written to teach us astronomy", he remarked with perfect justice, and he cites the *bon mot*: "The

---

[1] Joshua x, 12-14. The texts have been a difficulty to biblical exegetes all through the centuries. But since the publication by Pius XII in 1943 of *Divino Afflante Spiritu*, there has been a great and salutary revival in Catholic biblical criticism, due largely to the Pope's sanction of the conception of "literary forms" of various kinds, poetry, epic history, legend, allegory, each with its own form of truth, in the construction of the Scriptures. Archaeology developed at an extraordinary rate since the Second World War and brought to light much new knowledge of the great pagan civilizations in the midst of which the Hebrew people grew to political maturity and were in many ways affected by the cultures of the nations around them. The Book of Joshua is now seen to be peculiarly rich in "literary forms". The difficult chapter X is "epic history". The capture of Jericho, and the battle of Gabaon as described by the sacred writer, are not history in the modern western sense of the word, but have the strictly religious design of exalting the greatness and power of Yahwe. "An ancient poem containing an incantation to the sun and the moon is first cited and then transformed into a story. The narrator thus adds to the victory of Gabaon a detail calculated to fill his hearers with admiration: The day of victory was the longest that men had ever seen" (*Introduction à la Bible*, sous la direction de A. Robert et A. Feuillet, with the *Imprimatur* of Cardinal Feltin, Archbishop of Paris, Vol. 1, Paris, 1957, pp. 392-3. The section on Joshua is by Professor J. Delorme).

intention of the Holy Ghost is to teach us how to go to Heaven, not how the heavens go". He assigns the epigram to Cardinal Baronius from whose lips he may very well have heard it on the occasion when Baronius and Bellarmine made their holiday trip to Padua and Venice in 1598.

At this point the prime villain of the story comes storming on to the scene, Fra Tommáso Caccini, of the beautiful Dominican priory of Santa Maria Novella, Florence. The Galilean praetorian guard have no epithets strong enough for this priest and he certainly deserves most of them. He was a fiery preacher, given to sensationalism, and he also indulged in intrigue. It was the good custom in Florence in those days to expound the entire Bible in church during the course of the year. On the fourth Sunday in Advent in the year 1614, which fell on December 21, the tenth chapter of the book of Joshua had been reached at Santa Maria Novella, and Fra Tommáso seized on that circumstance with avidity to denounce in unmeasured terms the Copernican views then being widely aired in Florence by Galileo's disciples. There is no evidence that the preacher was the mouthpiece of the Aristotelians. He appears to have acted entirely on his own responsibility, and it is quite certain that the notorious sermon had nothing whatever to do with Galileo's letter to Castelli of exactly a year earlier (December 21, 1613). Caccini did not even know of the existence of the letter. The silly man made a savage attack on mathematicians in general and expressed a wish that they should be banished from all Christian states as fomenters of heresy. But he had just enough sense not to mention Galileo by name. Caccini's religious brethren were shocked by his outburst and reported him to the Master General of the Dominican Order in Rome, Fra Luigi Maraffi, who promptly apologized to Galileo: "I have been extremely annoyed by this scandal caused by a member of my Order. It is my misfortune to have to answer for all the stupidities which some of the thirty or forty thousand of my brethren in religion may and actually do commit." Tommáso's brother Matteo, then an official in Rome, wrote the culprit a scathing letter, and the aged Dominican Niccolo Lorini, whom Galileo had impertinently called to account two years before, also expressed himself as very much troubled that "il buon Padre Tommáso" should have let himself go in such an intemperate fashion. Fra Tommáso seems to have been little affected by the various protests and admonitions. He was in the limelight and apparently loved it.

By this time Galileo and his adherents had cast prudence to the winds and openly championed the Copernican astronomy on every occasion that offered. And this though Prince Cesi sent urgent warnings to be cautious, as Cardinal Bellarmine, for one, had told him that he considered the heliocentric theory to be contrary to the Bible. Benedetto Castelli, who referred to Caccini and his like as "pickpockets and highway men who waylay mathematicians", had unwisely permitted copies of Galileo's great letter to him on science and religion to be made and distributed. Old Father Lorini on a visit to Pisa came upon a copy and was profoundly shocked by its contents. He had admitted to Galileo three years earlier that he knew nothing about mathematics or astronomy, and was totally uninterested in this "Ipernic or whatever his name is". Lorini appears to have been an unmitigated 'fundamentalist', though so many of his Dominican brethren were celebrated for their biblical commentaries. It is difficult to think of this somewhat obscurantist and interfering old gentleman living among the exquisite frescoes of Fra Angelico at San Marco, so redolent of love and peace. But it was from San Marco that his letter denouncing Galileo and his disciples went off to Cardinal Paolo Sfondrati, Prefect of the Holy Office at Rome, on February 7, 1615:

> All our Fathers of this devout convent of St Mark are of opinion that the letter contains many propositions which appear to be suspicious or presumptuous, as when it asserts that the language of Holy Scripture does not mean what it seems to mean; that in discussions about natural phenomena the last and lowest place ought to be given to the authority of the sacred text; that its commentators have very often erred in their interpretation; that the Holy Scriptures should not be mixed up with anything except matters of religion. . .
> When I saw that this document was in everybody's hands. . .;

that [the disciples of Galileo] were taking upon themselves to expound the Holy Scriptures according to their private lights and in a manner different from that of the common interpretation of the Fathers of the Church; that they strove to defend an opinion which appeared to be quite contrary to the sacred text; that they spoke in slighting terms of the ancient Fathers, and of St Thomas Aquinas; that they were treading under foot the entire philosophy of Aristotle which has been of such service to scholastic theology; and, in fine, that to show their cleverness they were airing and scattering broadcast in our steadfastly Catholic city a thousand saucy and irreverent surmises; when, I say, I became aware of all this, I made up my mind to acquaint your Lordship with the state of affairs, that you in your holy zeal for the faith may, in conjunction with your illustrious colleagues, provide such remedies as will appear advisable.

Galileo, suspecting that there was something in the wind, wrote shortly afterwards, on February 16, to one of his most trusted counsellors in Rome, Mgr Piero Dini:

Since these fathers and especially the man who spoke against me [at Santa Maria Novella] have, as I am told, made another move with regard to my letter [to Castelli], I thought it would be well to send your Reverence an accurate copy of it. You would oblige me very much by reading it to Father Grienberger, that excellent mathematician and my very dear friend and patron. If you consider it advisable, you might also find some opportunity of bringing it to the notice of Cardinal Bellarmine, as I am given to understand that these Dominican Fathers are proposing to apply to his Lordship, in the hopes of securing at least the condemnation of the book and teaching of Copernicus. . .

Galileo was well advised to send Dini an authentic copy of his letter, for some unknown person, but probably not Lorini himself, who was at least a gentleman, had changed two of his expressions, rendering them much more objectionable. Thus Galileo had written that the Scriptures sometimes "overshadow" their own meaning. In the copy sent to Rome by Lorini the word "overshadow" was changed to "pervert". This and the other forged word, "false", were the only two criticized by the consultor of the Holy Office to whom the letter was submitted. The letter as a whole he found quite in accord with Catholic teaching. Mgr Dini delayed his reply to Galileo until March 7 for the reasons stated in his letter, which ran as follows:

The thousand spectacles and other celebrations during these days of carnival have prevented me from finding the persons with whom I desired to have audience. However, I made up for the delay by having several copies of your letter to Father Castelli transcribed. One of these I afterwards presented to Father Grienberger, and at the same time read to him the letter which you had addressed to myself. Several other people have had copies presented to them also, and I had a long conversation with Cardinal Bellarmine about the matters you mentioned.

He assured me that since you and he had discussed the astronomical question together, he had never once heard it ventilated in any way. As to Copernicus, his Lordship said that he could not believe that his work would be forbidden, and that the worst that could happen to it would, in his opinion, be the insertion of a note stating that the theory was introduced to save the celestial appearances, or some similar expression, in the same way as epicycles had been introduced. With this reservation, he continued, you would be at liberty to speak on these matters whenever you had occasion to do so. Concerning the matters themselves, it seemed to him that the passage of Holy Scripture most opposed to the new interpretation of the celestial phenomena was the Psalmist's text, *Exultavit ut gigas ad currendam viam*, together with the words that follow, as all commentators up to the present time have understood it to imply that the sun is in motion.

I answered that the Holy Scriptures might be considered in this place as simply employing our usual form of speech, but the Cardinal said that in dealing with such a question we must not be too hasty, just as it would not be right to rush into condemnation of any one for holding the views which I had put before him. He added that if you had given any cogent reasons in your letter for those views, he would be very pleased to study them. . . . Then he told me that he intended to invite

Father Grienberger to his house that he might discuss the question with him, and this very morning I have been to visit the Father, to see if there was any further news. I found that there was nothing fresh except that Father Grienberger would have been better pleased if you had first given your proofs before beginning to speak about the Holy Scriptures. I answered him that if you had done this, you would have been taken to task for giving your own facts preference, in the discussion, to the Word of God. As for the arguments which I put forward on behalf of your views, the Father said that he doubted whether they were not more plausible than true. . .

Meantime, another devoted friend of Galileo in Rome, a young official named Giovanni Ciàmpoli, later to be secretary to Pope Urban VIII, wrote to tell him that he had had a conversation with Cardinal Barberini, the future Urban VIII, who had already given proof of his admiration for Galileo's genius, and that the Cardinal was of opinion that "the more prudent course in dealing with these matters would be to confine oneself to the reasons given by Ptolemy or Copernicus and not to employ any other except physical and mathematical arguments, as the theologians consider the exposition of the Sacred Scriptures to be their province". Three weeks later, March 21, Ciàmpoli wrote again to tell of an interview that he and Monsignor Dini had had with Cardinal del Monte:

Cardinal del Monte told us that he had discussed the question of Copernicanism at great length with Cardinal Bellarmine, and that they had concluded as follows. "If you treat of the system of Copernicus and set forth its proofs without bringing in the Scriptures, the interpretation of which is the business of qualified theologians, then you should not be opposed in any way whatever. . .

A book has recently been published at Naples, with the object of showing that the doctrine of the motion of the earth and the immobility of the sun is not opposed to the Sacred Scriptures or to the Catholic faith. This book is in great danger of falling under the suspicion of the Congregation of the Holy Office for the reason I mentioned above, namely that it drags the

Scriptures into the discussion. I will do my best to obtain a copy for you before anything happens.

The book referred to by Ciàmpoli was entitled, *A Letter*[1] *of the Reverend Father Master Paul Anthony Foscarini, Carmelite, concerning the opinion of Pythagoras and Copernicus on the motion of the Earth and the immobility of the Sun*. Foscarini had come to Rome to preach and to take on all comers in debate on the subject of his book. That was surely a provocative action, as Dini and Ciàmpoli had hinted to Galileo, but Prince Cesi and Father Castelli, who were young and ardent, thought it a marvellous piece of good luck that a distinguished Carmelite priest should have come out so openly in Galileo's favour. Galileo, to whom Cesi had sent Foscarini's book, thought so too, and determined to have done with compromise and fight for the truth of Copernicanism openly.

Foscarini, who appears to have been as lacking in prudence as the other enthusiast Castelli, sent a copy of his book to Cardinal Bellarmine and received from him the following interesting reply:

My Very Reverend Father,

It has been a pleasure to me to read the Italian letter and the Latin paper you sent me. I thank you for both the one and the other and I may tell you that I found them replete with skill and learning. As you ask for my opinion I will give it as briefly as possible because, at the moment, you will have very little time for reading and I have very little time for writing.

First. It seems to me that your Reverence and Signor Galileo would act prudently were you to content yourselves with speaking hypothetically and not absolutely, as I have always believed that Copernicus spoke. To say that on the supposition of the earth's movement and the sun's immobility all the celestial appearances are explained better than by the theory of eccentrics and epicycles, is to speak with excellent good sense and to run no risk whatever. Such a manner of speaking is enough for a mathematician. But to want to affirm that the sun, in very truth, is at the centre of the universe and only rotates on its axis without going from east to west, and that the earth is situated

[1] So called because it was addressed to the General of the Carmelites.

in the third sphere and revolves very swiftly around the sun is a very dangerous attitude and one calculated not only to annoy all scholastic philosophers and theologians but also to injure our holy faith by contradicting the Scriptures. Your Reverence has clearly shown that there are several ways of interpreting the Word of God, but you have not applied those methods to any particular passage and, had you wished to expound by the method of your choice all the texts which you have cited, I feel certain that you would have met with the very greatest difficulties.

Second. As you are aware, the Council of Trent forbids the interpretation of the Scriptures in a way contrary to the common opinion of the holy Fathers. Now if your Reverence will read, not merely the Fathers, but modern commentators on Genesis, the Psalms, Ecclesiastes, and Josue, you will discover that all agree in interpreting them literally as teaching that the sun is in the heavens and revolves round the earth with immense speed, and that the earth is very distant from the heavens, at the centre of the universe, and motionless. Consider, then, in your prudence, whether the Church can tolerate that the Scriptures should be interpreted in a manner contrary to that of the holy Fathers and of all modern commentators, both Latin and Greek. It will not do to say that this is not a matter of faith, because though it may not be a matter of faith *ex parte objecti* or as regards the subject treated, yet it is a matter of faith *ex parte dicentis*, or as regards him who enounces it. Thus he who should deny that Abraham had two sons and Jacob twelve would be just as much a heretic as a man who should deny the Virgin Birth of Christ, because it is the Holy Spirit who makes known both truths by the mouth of the Prophets and Apostles.

Third. If there were a real proof that the sun is in the centre of the universe, that the earth is in the third sphere, and that the sun does not go round the earth but the earth round the sun, then we should have to proceed with great circumspection in explaining passages of Scripture which appear to teach the contrary, and rather admit that we did not understand them than declare an opinion to be false which is proved to be true. But as for myself, I shall not believe that there are such proofs until they are shown to me. Nor is a proof that, if the sun be supposed at the centre of the universe and the earth in the third sphere, the celestial appearances are thereby explained, equivalent to a proof that the sun actually is in the centre and the earth in the third sphere. The first kind of proof might, I believe, be found, but as for the second kind, I have the very gravest doubts, and in the case of doubt we ought not to abandon the interpretation of the sacred text as given by the holy Fathers.

I may add that the man who wrote: *The sun rises and sets and returns to its place*, etc., was Solomon, who not only spoke by divine inspiration but was wise and learned, above all others, in human sciences, and in the knowledge of created things. As he had all the wisdom from God himself, it is not likely that he would have made a statement contrary to a truth, either proven or capable of proof. If you tell me that Solomon speaks according to appearances, inasmuch as though the sun seems to us to revolve, it is really the earth that does so, just as when a man is leaving the shore it looks to him as if the shore were receding from the ship, I answer that though it may appear to a voyager as if the shore were receding from the vessel on which he stands rather than the vessel from the shore, yet he knows this to be an illusion and is able to correct it because he sees clearly that it is the ship and not the shore that is in movement. But as to the sun and the earth a wise man has no need to correct his judgment, for his experience tells him plainly that the earth is standing still and that his eyes are not deceived when they report that the sun, moon, and stars are in motion.

With this I salute your Paternity affectionately and pray God to grant you all happiness.

From my house, April 12, 1615.

Your very Reverend Paternity's brother,

CARDINAL BELLARMINE.[1]

Galileo must somehow have come by the original or a copy of

---

[1] *Opere de Galileo* (Ediz. Naz.), vol. xii, pp. 171-2. Bellarmine's belief that Copernicus had spoken only hypothetically was due to Osiander's preface. Galileo divined that the preface was a fraud, but the fact did not become generally known until 1856, when Frisch published for the first time a treatise written by Kepler in 1600 which showed the real author of the preface to have been Andreas Osiander, the Lutheran leader.

Bellarmine's reply to Foscarini very shortly after it was written, for he commented on it point by point in some notes possibly intended to help the Carmelite in the revision and amplification of his book which he had returned to Naples to supervise.[1] In the notes Galileo rejects outright the Cardinal's suggestion that Copernicanism ought to be regarded as a working hypothesis, even superior to that of Ptolemy, until such time as it could be physically proved. He regards the Ptolemaic system as demonstrably false because it does not account for all the celestial phenomena, whereas, he implies, the Copernican astronomy does. This was not the case and Galileo must have known it, for Copernicus had been obliged to use eccentrics and epicycles to account for the movements of the planets, and Galileo himself had accepted the same imaginary machinery, together with Aristotle's circular movements, which was a judgment on him for having ignored the work of Kepler. He would not share his glory with Kepler or anybody else. In his great polemical work *The Assayer*, directed against the Jesuit Orazio Grassi who had published a book on comets under the pseudonym of Lothario Sarsi, Galileo wrote: "You cannot help it, Signor Sarsi, that it was granted to me alone to discover all the new phenomena in the sky and nothing to anybody else. This is the truth which neither malice nor envy can suppress". Galileo possessed wit in abundance but he seems to have been somewhat lacking in a sense of humour.

It would obviously be anachronistic and unfair to judge St Robert Bellarmine's views on Scripture and the Fathers of the Church by the standards of modern Catholic biblical criticism, especially as developed since the publication of Pope Pius XII's encyclical *Divino Afflante Spiritu*, in 1943, curiously the fourth centenary of the publication of *De Revolutionibus Orbium Caelestium*. The development of Christian doctrine has been a continuous process since the Apostolic age, as the implications of divine Revelation became clearer to the Church under the guidance of the Holy Spirit, and much is obvious now to the instructed Catholic mind which was far from plain even to so great a

[1] The substance of these notes is given in translation in Stillman Drake's *Discoveries and Opinions of Galileo*, pp. 168-170.

man as Bellarmine. But, it might be asked, how does the
Cardinal stand when judged by the standards of such highly
intelligent Catholics of his own age as Galileo himself, Foscarini,
Castelli, the Jesuit Pereira, and others? The answer must surely be,
not too well. For instance, when he says that "the Council of
Trent forbids the interpretation of the Scriptures in a way
contrary to the common opinion of the Fathers of the Church",
Galileo was able to reply with the very words of the conciliar
Fathers at the fourth session, held on April 8, 1546: "So far as I
can find," he wrote in the *Letter to the Grand Duchess Christina*,
"all that is prohibited is the 'perverting into senses contrary to
that of holy mother Church or that of the unanimous agreement
of the Fathers, matters of faith and morals pertaining to the
upbuilding (*aedificationem*) of Christian doctrine.' But the mobility
or stability of the earth or sun is neither a matter of faith nor
contrary to morals".[1] As for "the common opinion of the Fathers"
in the matter of the earth's stability, Galileo again scores heavily
against St Robert whose principles of patristic interpretation were
very superficial and not accepted by some good theologians of
his own time, e.g. the Spanish Augustinian Didacus à Stunica, in
his *Commentary on the Book of Job*, published at Toledo in 1584,
or the Jesuit Pereira *On Genesis*, or the Carmelite Foscarini
himself. Galileo cited Didacus à Stunica, whose book had freely
circulated among Catholic students for thirty-one years, much to
his purpose:

> He discourses at length upon the Copernican opinion and
> concludes that the mobility of the earth is not contrary to
> Scripture. I question the truth of the statement that the Church
> commands us to hold as matters of faith all physical conclusions
> bearing the stamp of harmonious interpretation by all the
> Fathers. Either the Fathers reflected upon this conclusion [the

[1] The words within single quotation marks are an accurate summary of the
Council's words, though Galileo adds on his own account "and those alone"
after "faith and morals" (Denzinger-Bannwart, 786). Pope Leo XIII cites the
same passage from Trent in his encyclical *Providentissimus Deus* on the study of
Scripture, November 18, 1893. Much in Galileo's *Letter* is in complete accord
with *Providentissimus Deus*.

mobility of the earth] as controversial, or they did not; if not, then they cannot have decided anything about it even in their own minds and their incognizance of it does not oblige us to accept teaching which they never imposed, even in intention. But if they had reflected upon and considered it, and if they judged it to be erroneous, then they would long ago have condemned it; and this they are not found to have done.[1]

Bellarmine's rather 'fundamentalist' views were not special to him. They were widespread at the time and, in a sense inevitable, owing to the cautionary and defensive attitude with regard to the Scriptures, forced on the Church by the Protestant revolution.

It may be doubted also whether St Robert was any more justified in counselling Galileo and his disciples to regard and speak of heliocentrism as a mathematical hypothesis which they could freely maintain as superior to the systems of Ptolemy and Tycho Brahe in explaining the observed celestial phenomena. The eminent French Catholic physicist, Pierre Duhem, went so far as to write in 1908: "Logic was on the side of Osiander, Bellarmine and Urban VIII, not on that of Kepler and Galileo; the former had grasped the exact significance of the experimental method, while the latter had been mistaken".[2] We may leave Osiander out of the argument, for he believed in the physical reality of the Copernican system as strongly as its author himself, and wrote his preface with his tongue in his cheek. But to attribute to Bellarmine and Urban VIII a grasp of scientific principles in the modern sense, while denying them to Kepler and Galileo, was surely an appalling piece of anachronism.[3] Robert Bellarmine was a lovable saint

[1] Drake, *Discoveries and Opinions of Galileo*, p. 203.

[2] *Essai sur la notion de Théorie physique de Platon à Galilée*, first published in the *Annales de philosophie chrétienne*, September 1908, pp. 587-8 and subsequently in book form. It was translated into English under the title, *The Theory of Physical Reality* (New York, 1952).

[3] Alas, thirty-two years ago the writer of these present lines was misled by Duhem's eminence as a practical scientist in thermodynamics into embracing his views as a historian of science. Thirty-two years is a long time, and one almost of necessity learns a little wisdom with greying hairs. In his exhilarating and most informative book, *The Sleepwalkers*: A History of man's changing vision of the Universe (London, 1959), Arthur Koestler, who admits to a bias against Galileo because of his scurvy treatment of Kepler, pretty well revives

and a phenomenally learned theologian, but he knew next to nothing of science in Kepler's and Galileo's understanding of the word, and perhaps cared just as little about it. He was aware, because the experts of the Roman College had so assured him, that Aristotle's unchanging heavens had been laid in ruins by the observations of Tycho Brahe, Kepler and Galileo, and that Galileo had also irreparably damaged much of Aristotle's physics as well as his astronomy. But at seventy-four and with his cast of mind, it was psychologically impossible for him to accept the revolutionary idea, which Copernicus, Kepler, and Galileo had intuitively grasped, that the solid earth under his feet was a planet in rapid motion around the sun. Indeed, in trying to explain, erroneously be it said, why the Bible speaks according to appearances, Galileo himself had written: "It is sufficiently obvious that to attribute motion to the sun and rest to the earth was necessary lest the shallow minds of the common people should become confused, obstinate and contumacious in yielding assent to the principal articles that are absolutely matters of faith".[1]

Galileo did not himself show much concern for the common, ignorant people, the "herd", as he called them, in his rather snobbish attitude to all who were not great mathematicians and experimentalists of his own type. Even if, as he suggested, they should lose their faith through being told that the earth was speeding round the sun at the rate of eighteen miles a second, still Copernicanism must be preached in season and out of season. The common man, as has often been seen in these pages, was a person very dear to the heart of Bellarmine, and he could not understand Galileo's headlong precipitancy in forcing an issue that might trouble the faith of the simple when he could so easily have kept his intuitions, as scientists do today, for debate and

---

Duhem's idea of Bellarmine's rightness and Galileo's wrongness. In the process, he makes Bellarmine General of the Jesuits and head of the Roman College, both erroneous statements. All his information about St Robert is borrowed confessedly from Professor Giorgio de Santillana, who unconfessedly borrowed it all, including its mistakes, from Brodrick's Life of Cardinal Bellarmine in two volumes, London, 1928.

[1] Letter to the Grand Duchess Christina, translated in Drake, Discoveries and Opinions of Galileo, p. 200.

quiet study among his peers. Bellarmine was surely entitled to ask for some more solid proof than the moons of Jupiter, the phases of Venus, and the spots on the sun, all of which fitted perfectly well into Tycho Brahe's system, while leaving the earth stationary. As mentioned, that was the system adopted by the Jesuit astronomers, who were neither the fools nor the "trained seals" of Professor de Santillana's imagination. They may very well have felt, they almost certainly did feel, that Tycho's system was only a half-way house to full heliocentrism, but they wanted this to be borne in on men's minds gradually, without too great a dislocation of traditional thinking. Also, they believed in waiting for the discovery of stellar parallax, which both Copernicus and Galileo knew to be necessary if heliocentrism was a fact, but which neither of them had been able to observe, and, indeed, was not observed until December 1838, when the astronomer Friedrich Bessel, after very great labour, succeeded in determining the parallax, or almost infinitesimal displacement, of the star 61 Cygni.

Galileo was perfectly justified in rejecting Cardinal Bellarmine's naïve invitation to regard the Copernican theory as a mere hypothesis to account for the face of the heavens. Besides being a great scientist, he was the first great theoretician of science, and knew in his bones that its business was to attain to the structure of reality, that hypotheses are formulated, not to save appearances, but to be verified or rejected by experiment, and also to try and bring a great unifying principle into the diversity of phenomena. By his own telescopic discoveries he had already made an enormous contribution to the unifying principle by proving that the material of the heavens, of the sun and of the moon, was no privileged fifth incorruptible essence, but the same changeable elements as those that composed the earth.[1]

[1] In his marvellous *Dialogue concerning the Two Principal Systems of the World*, which brought such troubles on his head, and on our heads too, Galileo in the person of the interlocutor Sagredo wonders why such special virtue should be attributed to the imperishable and unchanging heavens of Aristotle: "For do not these persons consider that if there should be as great a scarcity of Earth, as there is of Jewels and pretious metals, there would be no Prince but would gladly give a heap of Diamonds and Rubies, and many wedges of Gold to

It was the greatest pity that he gave a handle by his propagandist efforts and by his unconcealed scorn for the peripatetic backwoodsmen, to such mischief-making hotheads as Padre Caccini. He had a forum in the Lincean Academy, whose members would at least have listened with interest and respect to his views, propounded intelligent difficulties, and gradually, by their own prestige, have secured him a more general recognition. Scientists today do not go tub-thumping at the public forum in Hyde Park, London, or seek a hearing for their abstruse views in the columns of the popular press. They make their contributions to learned specialized journals, or ventilate them in the serene atmosphere of the Royal Society or at the meetings of the British Association for the Advancement of Science. But Galileo would not wait. He was born for battle, which is what polemics mean, and must not only state his own admirable views in a gentlemanly fashion, but visit his vitriolic contempt on all who dared to remonstrate. "Why was she in such a hurry?" asked the Dalai Lama quietly, when told by an enthusiastic English visitor to Lhasa of Miss Amy Johnson's famous solo record-breaking flight in May 1930 from Croydon to Port Darwin, Australia. Why was Galileo in such a hurry? He believed completely in the physical truth of Copernicanism and was certain that it would eventually be recognized by all mankind. But he wanted it recognized almost overnight, and thereby hangs the miserable and entirely unnecessary tale of his condemnation.

Galileo's letter to Castelli, denounced to Cardinal Sfondrati by Lorini, had been examined by the cardinals of the Holy Office who had called two witnesses supposed to be familiar with the

---

purchase only so much Earth as should suffice to plant a Gessemine in a little plot, or to set therein a China Orange, that he might see it sprout, grow up, and bring forth so goodly leaves, so odoriferous flowers, and so delicate fruit?" (Cited by F. Sherwood Taylor from Thomas Salusbury's seventeenth-century English translation of the Dialogue, in *Galileo and the Freedom of Thought*, London, 1938, pp. 123-4. This best of all books in English about Galileo is now out of print and very difficult to obtain. Watts and Company, publishers to the Rationalist Press Association, originally produced it, but seem strangely reluctant to issue it again. It was while studying the Galileo case that Mr Sherwood Taylor decided to become a Catholic. The excerpt proves that the amazingly gifted Galileo was also at heart a true poet.)

Galilean agitation in Florence. The names of the two were supplied by Caccini, who had constituted himself principal defender
of the faith against the new Copernican errors. He came to Rome
in person on another pretext, against the wishes of the Master
General of the Dominicans, Luigi Maraffi, who admired Galileo's
genius and always remained his good friend. Though not called
as a witness, Caccini eagerly volunteered his testimony, which
proved to be a tissue of contradictory nonsense. The case against
the letter to Castelli was dismissed. "So far as high officials of the
Church were concerned, the prosecution seems to have been
rather half-hearted. Bellarmine had given Foscarini a written
opinion, without asking for an official ruling, and although he
associated Galileo's views with Foscarini's in this, he had not
reported the matter to the investigating body. Yet he knew very
well that Galileo was under scrutiny. His actions suggest that truly
responsible officials did not particularly wish to see an official
ruling on the points in dispute. Officious clerics like Caccini,
however, behaved very differently."[1]

They certainly did, and it was to counteract their nefarious
activities that Galileo decided he must once more visit Rome,
where he arrived on December 7, 1615, fortified with commen-
datory letters from the Grand Duke of Tuscany. That ruler's
ambassador in Rome, Piero Guicciardini, had protested against
his coming to the Grand Duke's secretary, Curzio Picchena, a
good friend of Galileo's:

> I am told that Galileo is coming here. . . . As his views on
> science and some other matters are not to the taste of the
> consultors and cardinals of the Holy Office, Bellarmine, among
> others, has told me that while all respect is due to whatever
> arrangements have the sanction of his Serene Highness, if
> Galileo stays here any length of time he is certain to come out
> with some defence or justification of his opinions. . . . I do not
> know whether he has changed those opinions nor whether his
> temper has improved, but this I know for certain that some

[1] Drake, *Discoveries and Opinions of Galileo*, p. 217. The sobriety of Mr
Drake's tone is refreshing as compared with that of some other ardent "Gali-
leans".

Dominicans and others who are very influential with the Holy Office bear him no goodwill. This is not the place to come to dispute about the moon, nor is this the time in which to propound and defend novelties.

But Galileo himself was full of optimism, and told the same Curzio Picchena five days after his arrival at the centre of Christendom that he found the way clear to maintain and increase his reputation, and felt so satisfied that his health, recently very bad, "was improving not a little in consequence". He had the resilience of a high-spirited boy and a good dash of the same charming creature's irresponsibility. From all accounts, he took an unholy delight in baiting and exasperating the Aristotelians. Another of his many priest friends and admirers, Antonio Querengo, said in a letter of January 20, 1616, to Cardinal d'Este at Modena: "Your Lordship would enjoy Galileo's discourses immensely. . . . He turns the laugh against all his opponents . . . and answers their objections in such a way as to make them look perfectly ridiculous."[1]

The Tuscan Ambassador's next letter from Rome to the Grand Duke's secretary, Picchena, dated March 4, 1616, sums up the situation as seen by that anxious man:

Galileo sets more store by his own opinion than by the advice of his friends. Cardinal del Monte and myself (though my influence with the man is small), as well as other cardinals of the Holy Office, have endeavoured to pacify him and persuade him not to stir up this affair but, if he wished to hold his opinion, to hold it quietly, without using so much violence in his attempts to force others into holding it. We all doubt very much whether his coming here is not going to prove

[1] Up to a point they were fair game, those over-confident persons, including the eleven theological consultors of the Holy Office, who seemed never to wish to raise their eyes from the pages of Aristotle, "as if this great book of the universe had been written to be read by nobody but Aristotle, and his eyes had been destined to see for all posterity" (*Letters on Sunspots*, Drake, *Discoveries and Opinions of Galileo*, p. 127). But the Jesuit Scheiner, against whom Galileo was arguing, was not that sort of peripatetic. He had a genuinely scientific mind, though his theory of sunspots was hopelessly wrong and Galileo's, by the same token, was not completely right. Sunspots are still a problem.

prejudicial and dangerous for him. As we did not appear to him to be sufficiently enthusiastic about his plans and wishes, after having bothered and tried several cardinals with his story, he concentrated on Cardinal Orsini . . ., and on Wednesday last Orsini spoke to the Pope in a consistory on his behalf. The Pope told the Cardinal that it would be a good thing if he could persuade Galileo to abandon his opinion. Orsini made some answer or other . . ., whereupon the Pope told him that the question had been referred to the cardinals of the Holy Office...

I do not think that there is any possibility of Galileo suffering in person, because as a good and sensible man he will be ready to submit to the decision of the Church. But he gets hotly excited about these views of his, and has an extremely passionate temper, with little patience and prudence to keep it in control. It is this irritability that makes the skies of Rome very dangerous for him.[1]

The two propositions submitted to the eleven consultant theologians of the Holy Office were: 1. The sun is the centre of the world and altogether devoid of local motion. 2. The earth is not the centre of the world nor immovable, but moves as a whole, and also with a diurnal motion. Of the eleven men called to pronounce, six were Dominicans and included the Portuguese Thomas de Lemos, a brilliant theologian who earned fame in the *Congregatio de Auxiliis* by his battle-royal with the Jesuit Gregory of Valencia. The Augustinian, Gregory Coronel, a fine theologian prominent in the same dispute, was also an anti-Molinist. But the eminence in theology of those two was far surpassed by that of another of the consultants, an Irishman from Waterford bearing the unlikely name of Peter Lombard. Peter had been designated Archbishop of Armagh by Clement VIII, but, of course, was prevented by English law and police methods from ever occupying his see. His long course of studies at Louvain rendered him distinctly anti-Jesuit in his theology and he showed his bias when appointed president of the *Congregatio de Auxiliis*. He spent his life as a curialist and did notable service to the Holy See. Only one Jesuit figured in the list of eleven consultors, Benedetto

---

[1] The Orsini mentioned was very young, twenty-two, and a keen "Galilean".

Giustiniani, chiefly notable for a good commentary on the Epistles of St Paul. An odd collection of men, one might think, to pronounce on what were definitely scientific questions, and not a mathematician among them. But Pope Paul V was primarily a canon lawyer, completely uninterested in mathematics, and evidently considered the eleven adequate as a team. Neither had Cardinal Bellarmine any misgivings about them, for they were certainly adequate in the only science which he valued much, which was theology.

The verdict of the eleven was a foregone conclusion, and the delight of anti-Catholic scoffers ever since, who conveniently forget the existence of Benedetto Castelli, o.s.b., Archbishop Piero Dini, Luigi Maraffi, o.p., Mgr Ciàmpoli, and Christopher Clavius, s.j., to name but a few of the many on Galileo's side of the fence. On February 24, 1616, the report of the consultors was laid before the cardinals of the Holy Office:

> *First proposition:* The sun is the centre of the world and altogether devoid of local motion.
> *Decision:* All were agreed that this proposition was foolish and absurd philosophically, and formally heretical, inasmuch as it expressly contradicts the doctrines of Holy Scripture in many places, both according to their literal meaning, and according to the common exposition and meaning of the holy Fathers and learned theologians.
> *Second proposition:* The earth is not the centre of the world nor immovable, but moves as a whole, and also with diurnal motion.
> *Decision:* All were agreed that this proposition merited the same censure in philosophy, and that, from a theological standpoint, it was at least erroneous in the faith.

Those lamentable decisions, born of an obstinate disregard for the realities of the situation, were not accepted exactly as they stood by the cardinals, and remained secreted in the files of the Roman Inquisition until they were produced seventeen years later in the trial of Galileo under Pope Urban VIII, his former friend and protector, Maffeo Barberini. Instead, on March 5, the Congregation of the Holy Office issued a decree condemning outright Father Paolo Foscarini's *Letter*, but only suspending "until they be corrected" the *Book of the Revolutions* by Copernicus and the commentary on Job by Didacus à Stunica. The word "heretical" used by the consultors was omitted from the decree, and Galileo's name was not mentioned at all, though he was the man chiefly responsible for bringing the whole unhappy affair to a head. Piero Dini had once told him that he could write what he liked "provided he kept out of the sacristy". True, some of his sillier peripatetic foes had trespassed there furtively before him, but he made his entry to the sound of drums and trumpets.

Though he was not mentioned in the decree of March 5 nor was his Book on the Sunspots, in which he had openly declared for Copernicanism, put on the Index, he was admonished officially but privately, on February 25, to abandon the propositions censured by the theological consultors the day before. By direction of the Pope, Cardinal Bellarmine was to summon him and tell him to do so. In case he refused, the Dominican Commissary General of the Holy Office was to order him, before a notary and witnesses, "that he abstain altogether from teaching, defending, or discussing this opinion and doctrine, and that he is to be imprisoned if he remains obstinate".[1] That document would seem to point plainly to two separate occasions, one at Bellarmine's residence, and a second, in case the Cardinal had to report failure, at the Holy Office building where the Commissary would have his notary and witnesses ready.

But there is another and very strange document in the Vatican files, dated a day later, February 26, which has the appearance of a report on what took place the previous day. It runs as follows:

At the Palace [the Vatican, where by the wish of the Pope St Robert had apartments], the usual residence of the aforenamed Lord Cardinal Bellarmine, the said Galileo, having been summoned and standing before his Lordship, was, in the presence of the very Reverend Father Michael Angelo Seghiti de Lauda, of the Order of Preachers, Commissary General of the Holy Office, admonished by the Cardinal of the error of the aforesaid opinion and that he should abandon it; and immedi-

[1] Favaro, *Galileo e l'Inquisizione*, Florence, 1907, p. 61.

ately thereafter [*successive ac incontinenti*], in presence of myself, other witnesses, and the Lord Cardinal, who was still in the room, the said Commissary did enjoin upon the said Galileo, there present, and did order him (in his own name), the name of his Holiness the Pope, and the names of all the cardinals of the Congregation of the Holy Office, to relinquish altogether the opinion in question, namely that the sun is the centre of the universe and immovable and that the earth moves; nor henceforth to hold, teach, or defend it in any way, either orally or in writing. Otherwise proceedings would be taken against him in the Holy Office. The said Galileo acquiesced in this ruling and promised to obey it.

Done at Rome, in the place aforementioned, in presence of the Reverend Badino Nores from Nicosia in the Kingdom of Cyprus, and Augustino Mongardo, of the diocese of Montepulciano, both witnesses belonging to the said Lord Cardinal's household.

There has been controversy about that document, not even yet finally settled, ever since, in 1870, the German scholar Emil Wohlwill called attention to the discrepancy between it and a protocol of a meeting of the Holy Office on March 3, 1616, published for the first time that same year, 1870:

Thursday, March 3, 1616.
The Lord Cardinal Bellarmine having reported that Galileo Galilei, the mathematician, had, according to the instructions of the Sacred Congregation, been admonished to abandon the opinion he has hitherto held, to the effect that the sun is the centre of the spheres and immovable, and that the earth moves, and had acquiesced therein; and the Decree of the Congregation having been registered, by which were suspended and prohibited respectively the writings of Nicholas Copernicus *De revolutionibus orbium caelestium*, of Diego di Zuniga on the book of Job, and of Paolo Antonio Foscarini, Carmelite Friar—his Holiness ordered this edict of suspension and prohibition respectively, to be published by the Master of the Sacred Palace.

Galileo remained three months in Rome after the decision of the Holy Office was made known to him by Bellarmine. He was not in the least depressed by that decision, as he could still discuss

Copernicanism as a hypothesis with perfect freedom. He even told friends that he had won a signal victory over his malign and ignorant enemies. One friend, the Venetian diplomat Giovan Francesco Sagredo, whom he later immortalized in the great *Dialogue Concerning the Two Chief World Systems*, alas, the cause of his condemnation in 1633, wrote to him shortly after the decree of the Index: "Now that I have learned from your valued letters the particulars of the spiteful, devilish attacks on and accusations against you, and the issue of them, which entirely frustrates the purposes of your ignorant and malicious foes, I, and all the friends to whom I have communicated your letters and messages, are quite set at rest". On March 11, 1616, Galileo was closeted with Pope Paul for three quarters of an hour, "con benignissima audienza", and wrote happily about the event to the Tuscan secretary of state the following day:

> I told his Holiness the reason for my coming to Rome . . . and made known to him the malice of my persecutors and some of their calumnies against me. He answered that he was well aware of my uprightness and sincerity of mind, and when I gave evidence of being still somewhat anxious about the future, owing to my fear of being pursued with implacable hate by my enemies, he consoled me and said that I might put away all care, because I was held in so much esteem both by himself and by the whole congregation of cardinals that they would not lightly lend their ears to calumnious reports. During his life-time, he continued, I might feel quite secure, and before I took my departure he assured me several times that he bore me the greatest goodwill and was ready to show his affection and favour towards me on all occasions.[1]

But the malicious foes continued with their attacks and spread a false rumour that he had been compelled to recant and punished with a salutary penance. To stop the mouths of those calumniators he confidently applied to Cardinal Bellarmine for a statement of what had really happened at his residence. St Robert readily agreed and issued him the following certificate, which he carefully preserved for the rest of his life:

[1] Favaro, *Opere di Galileo*, n. 1189.

We, Robert, Cardinal Bellarmine, having heard that Signor
Galileo Galilei has been calumniously reported to have abjured
in our hand, and moreover to have been punished with a
salutary penance, and having been asked to make known the
truth as to this, declare that the said Signor Galileo has not
abjured in our hand, nor in the hand of anybody else here in
Rome, nor, so far as we are aware, in any place whatever, any
opinion or doctrine held by him; neither has any penance,
salutary or otherwise, been imposed upon him. All that
happened was this. The declaration made by the Holy Father
and published by the Sacred Congregation of the Index was
intimated to him, wherein it is declared that the doctrine
attributed to Copernicus that the earth moves round the sun
and that the sun is in the centre of the universe and does not
move from east to west, is contrary to the Holy Scriptures, and
therefore cannot be defended nor held.

In witness whereof we have written and subscribed these
presents with our own hand the 26th day of May, 1616.

As above, ROBERT CARDINAL BELLARMINE.[1]

That certificate, Galileo's own confident attitude, and the
protocol of the Holy Office issued on March 3, 1616, form a
powerful combined proof that he was at no time called before the
Commissary General and forbidden absolutely to hold, teach, or
defend in any way, either orally or in writing, the Copernican
views. What, then, is to be thought of the document dated
February 26 in the Vatican files and produced by the prosecution
in 1633 in proof that Galileo *had* been given an absolute injunction
by the Commissary of the Holy Office, in 1616? The modern
writers who believe this to have been the case, including unfortunately Arthur Koestler in his delightful and most learned *Sleepwalkers*, harp on the fact that the expression *successive ac incontinenti* meant, in the curial usage of the time, not right away or
without pause, but, in due course or later on, even several days
later. Koestler is highly critical of Santillana for overlooking this
distinction, but the American professor was completely justified
in passing it over, as it had no relevance to the dark truth of the
matter, which is that the document of February 26, 1616, in the

[1] Favaro, *Galileo e l'Inquisizione*, p. 68.

Vatican files is not an original text, but somebody's concoction, probably that same year, to embroil Galileo with the Inquisition, should he at any time seek to maintain Copernicanism as a physical reality.

The bogus injunction is in the same handwriting as that of neighbouring and certainly genuine documents, so the man responsible must have been some unscrupulous curial official hostile to Galileo, whom it is now impossible to identify. He succeeded beyond his wildest hopes seventeen years later, when his imaginary injunction was produced as a trump card against the unfortunate astronomer during his trial in Rome. He was taken completely by surprise, and maintained that he had never been given such an injunction. In proof, he produced Cardinal Bellarmine's certificate in 1616, and it is incomprehensible, if the Dominican Commissary Firenzuola in 1633[1] was really trying to discover the truth and not pre-determined on a verdict of guilty, that he should not have seen the complete incompatibility between the false injunction and St Robert's certificate.

However dictatorial Paul V may have been, he was humble enough to ask advice when he could not himself see a way out of a difficulty. Thus, he consulted St Francis de Sales as to how best to end the long controversy between the Dominicans and the Jesuits on the subject of efficacious grace, and followed the good advice given him. So too, he asked St Robert Bellarmine for his views on the Copernican question which had been made such a live issue by the incessant propaganda of Galileo and his disciples, and the Saint had answered him frankly that, regarded as a physical reality, he did not think it compatible with the Scriptures, though, like many other speculative theories such as Bruno's plurality of inhabited worlds, it might freely be held and discussed as a hypothesis more satisfactory than that of Ptolemy. If the old Cardinal, who was seventy-four in 1616, had studied Galileo's great *Letter to the Grand Duchess Christina*, it might have shaken his belief that the text in particular from Psalm 18 (A.V.

[1] Koestler, for good measure, turns this man into a Jesuit (p. 470). He is rather vague throughout about ecclesiastical distinctions. Both he and Santillana lump all Dominicans together as monks.

19), 5-7 did not necessarily imply that the sun was in motion around a stationary earth. But he probably had not read the *Letter*. He was too old to change the convictions of a lifetime for the sake of what he considered to be only an ingenious surmise, supported, as Father Grienberger, the expert, had informed him, by no really compelling physical proof. So he explained to Paul V, who then referred the question to the Holy Office for further light on it. That was the extent of St Robert's involvement in the case of Galileo, unfortunate indeed, but surely not enough to condemn him, as some have done, as an enemy of scientific or any other kind of human progress.[1]

[1] As for the Jesuits and their provisional adherence to the system of Tycho Brahe, for which compromise they are scorned by Professor de Santillana, it is interesting to know that even such a scientist of genius as Blaise Pascal (1623-1662) found it impossible to decide between the Ptolemaic, the Copernican and the Tychonic systems, since, as he maintained, all three agreed with the visible appearances, which they were designed to explain. "Who, then, can, without danger of error, support any one of these theories to the prejudice of the others?" (Letter to Père Noël, cited in Professor Arthur O. Lovejoy's *The Great Chain of Being*, sixth printing, Harvard University Press, 1957, p. 126). No one could call Pascal a "trained seal".

CHAPTER XIII

BELLARMINE'S LAST BOOKS

HAVING thankfully finished with Galileo, we may now give our attention to St Robert Bellarmine in the daily routine of his life, which was regulated by a divine astronomy of his own. After his return from Capua in 1605, he was permitted by the Pope to choose any part of Rome that he liked for his abode, and also was assigned modest apartments at the Vatican, which he seems to have occupied only sporadically. Up to 1608 he lived in a house near the church of Santa Maria in Trastevere. Then he changed to the Piazza Colonna on which was situated his own titular church of Santa Maria in Via. In 1611 he moved out once again and installed himself in a quarter "near the obelisk of St Malo" which was close to the Roman College. It was on his house there, a poor one, that the damaged sundial was fixed. A Jesuit priest who observed the Saint's movements gave an explanation of them to the superior of the Roman province just after the Cardinal's death:

It may be worth while to say something about Cardinal Bellarmine's intentions in coming to live near the Roman College, a house to which he was extremely attached. His idea was to be close enough to hear the community bell that so he might regulate the principal actions of his day according to the routine of the College. Moreover, he at first cherished a plan of establishing direct communication with the College either by an underground tunnel or by a bridge that he might thus be able to have recourse to the books in the library and to spend the hour of recreation with the Fathers, for such converse with his brothers in religion was one of the things which he enjoyed most and felt the loss of most keenly. He soon learned, however, that the project would involve considerable difficulties, so he abandoned it entirely, preferring to renounce his own inclinations rather than be troublesome to anybody. So delicate was his tact in this respect that he never ventured to ask or even to hint that he would like an invitation to assist at the solemn functions and festivities which took place at the Roman College, the house of the professed Fathers, or elsewhere.

According to a decree passed by the authorities of the order in 1607, each member of the Society of Jesus was to make an annual spiritual retreat of eight or ten days. From that time on St Robert, who as a cardinal was in no way bound by the decree, made it his custom to go every September or October to the Jesuit novitiate of Sant' Andrea on the Quirinal, there to give himself up to prayer and meditation. At first his retreats lasted only the prescribed time of about ten days, but afterwards he devoted an entire month to them and made annually the "long retreat" which other Jesuits are obliged to go through only twice during their religious lives. That stay among the novices each year was the only summer holiday the Cardinal allowed himself. Joseph Finali, a Vatican employee who joined the novitiate as a lay brother in 1616, gives the following details about St Robert's behaviour:

Whenever the bell rang for meals he used to come down in one of our black gowns just like any novice. . . . He was asked by the superior to give the ordinary Friday exhortations which in that novitiate are called the common exhortations to distinguish them from those given every day in private to the novices. Even the veterans of the house are present on these occasions, the subject of the addresses being the observance of rule.

The Cardinal, having mounted the pulpit in the hall, began his discourse with a digression, saying that he wished to reply to an objection that might be raised against him: "The Fathers and my brothers the novices might say to me that it is all very well to talk about the virtue of obedience when one always does just as one likes; that it is easy enough to praise poverty when one is robed in costly purple; and that one may be very severe in recommending the observance of the rule of silence who himself is engaged in perpetual conversation. But I assure you, dear Fathers and Brothers, that these robes are on me just as though they were hanging on a peg, and that I am under the same obligations as one of yourselves to observe the special prescriptions of our Institute. Like you, I am bound by each of our rules, and if I do not observe them I shall have to render a very strict account to God, an account, owing to the position in which I am placed, much stricter than you would have to give. St Thomas, the Angelic Doctor, says so clearly, and I as clearly understand him in that sense."

His Lordship came to us with only one attendant. He used to say the Hours of his Office, kneeling on the bare floor, at the exact canonical times, and often, as we noticed, with tears in his eyes. When, in order to say Matins towards dawn, he required a light, though the lamp was on a staircase a long way from his room, he would not waken his attendant or anybody else but would go and return himself as quietly as a mouse. If he wanted any book from the library, he used to fetch it with his own hands, though he had to walk the length of three corridors to do so. The master of the novices told him that he had only to mention what volumes he required and they would all be taken to his room, but he would not accept this offer because he feared that other people might need the books in the meantime.

It was suggested to him that a walk in the garden each evening would do him good. "I would like it very much", he said, "but I am afraid my presence in the garden would frighten off the novices and consequently it would not be right for me to go there." Instead he used to walk up and down a corridor.

A direct result of St Robert's retreats at Sant' Andrea was a series of devotional books that became immensely popular with both Catholics and Protestants. These little books were preceded by a much bulkier one, his largely devotional *Commentary on the Psalms*, over which he laboured off and on for the space of twelve years, mostly in the quiet night hours when everybody around him was asleep. His day belonged to the Pope, and that was the only time at his own disposal. His treatment of the Psalms was very unequal, because, as he wrote, "he did not always feel the same spiritual devotion, nor enjoy the same mental alacrity". The reason he persevered under such wearying conditions was his hope that it might help priests to recite their office with more devotion.

The huge *Commentary*, published in 1611, long enjoyed wide popularity and was reprinted thirty-three times, but has now become somewhat dated. One passage (Psalm 18. 2; A.V. 19) may be given, obviously written when the author was not too tired nor emotionally exhausted:

Day to day uttereth speech, and night to night showeth knowledge. Wonderful, indeed, is the sermon of the sun and stars declaring the glory of God. . . . This verse shows us how they declare it incessantly, for the heavens announce his glory in the day by the splendour of the sun and at night by the beauty of the stars; but as the days and nights do not endure and are succeeded by others, the Psalmist finely and poetically imagines one day at its close, when its sermon is over, passing on the text of God's glory to the following dawn, and so with each night, which, having sung its hymn of praise, passes on the music to its successor. . . . And thus, without ever a break, day and night hymn, as it were in a perpetual round, the praises of their Creator.

The first and best-known of St Robert's professedly spiritual books was written during the period at Sant' Andrea in September 1614, and published the following year by the house of Plantin in Antwerp. The title of the book was, *De Ascensione Mentis in Deum per Scalam Rerum Creaturarum*—"The ascent of the mind to God by a ladder of created things"—but the Cardinal's manuscript shows that the naming of his "Benjamin", as he liked to term the little work because he "wrote it in his old age", had been a matter of some difficulty. He had chosen fifteen steps for his ladder because he was particularly fond of the fifteen Psalms called Gradual which were supposed by St Augustine among others to have been sung by Jewish pilgrims to Jerusalem as they mounted the fifteen steps of the Temple. *Gradus* is Latin for a step. St Robert's steps are not all as evenly disposed one above another as the steps of a ladder ought to be. He found his metaphor, a traditional one, too difficult to maintain after he had mounted a little way. He tried to find a more exact title for his book but could not and so let the ladder idea stay. In his preface he explains the purpose of the book, which he had written for his private use to help his own prayer, but was persuaded to publish:

For us mortal men there would seem to be no other ladder by which to ascend to God, than the works of God. If, through a singular privilege of divine grace, some have been admitted to the secrets of Heaven by another way, they did not ascend but were caught up to hear the words which it is not given to man to speak. But that it is in every man's power by means of God's work in creation to rise to the knowledge and love of the Creator, is the teaching of the Book of Wisdom and of St Paul in his Epistle to the Romans. Reason itself sufficiently confirms this truth, since a cause may be known by its effects and an original pattern from its copies. Now all created things are effects of God's causation, and the Scriptures teach us that men and angels are not only the works of his hands but also his images.

The consideration of man is naturally the starting point, "for we are all of us both the creatures and the images of God, and nothing is nearer to us than ourselves". Man is a microcosm, an epitome of the universe, according to its causes, the four causes of Aristotle and scholasticism:

If I look for my Maker, I shall find him to be God alone; if I seek for the substance whereof he made me, I shall find nothing though I search for ever, because all that is in me is from him. Should I desire to know the form which he has given me, I shall learn that he has made me in the likeness of himself, and should I ask about the end and purpose of my being, I shall discover that the selfsame God who fashioned me in his own image out of nothing is my supreme and only good. And so I am brought to understand that my closeness to God and my need of him is such that he alone is my Creator, the source of my existence, my Father, the pattern according to which I was made, my beatitude, my all. Knowing this, how could I fail to seek him with all the eager love I possess, to think of him, to sigh and yearn for him, to long for the day when I may see and embrace him?

This introduction leads to a development in five chapters of the words *homo creatus est*, which stand at the beginning of the "First Principle and Foundation" of St Ignatius Loyola's Spiritual Exercises. When speaking in the fourth chapter of man as the

NX

image of God, St Robert introduces a theme of which echoes are to be found in nearly all his writings. True wisdom, the first gift of the Holy Ghost, was an endowment that he never tired of glorifying:

> Thy pattern, O my soul, is God himself, the infinite beauty, the light in which there is no darkness and at whose loveliness the sun and moon stand in amaze. . . . The beauty of God, thine exemplar, doth consist in wisdom and holiness, for as corporeal beauty doth result from the just proportion of the body's members and the soft, sweet colouring of the same, so in a spiritual being the light of wisdom corresponds to every hue that fascinates the eye, and the attribute of justice or righteousness, which is not any particular virtue but the substance of them all, corresponds to the fair proportion of the bodily members. Most beautiful, then, must a spirit be whose mind shines with the light of wisdom and whose will is ennobled with the fulness of perfect justice. Now God, thy pattern, O my soul, is not merely wise and just and consequently beautiful, but he is wisdom and justice itself, and consequently the very essence of all beauty. Therefore, if thou dost desire to become his true image, it behoves thee to love wisdom and justice above everything else on earth. True wisdom is to judge all things according to their highest cause, and that cause is the divine will, or the law which makes the divine will known to men. As a lover of wisdom, then, the will of the Lord thy God must be thy only concern. In whatever circumstances thou art placed thou must be deaf to what the law of the flesh may command, to what the senses may approve, to what the world may favour, to what kinsmen may urge, to what flatterers may propose; and thou must judge that to be most profitable, glorious, desirable and good in every respect, which is in conformity with the will and law of God.

Having considered the microcosm, the Cardinal turns his thoughts to the macrocosm or great world of inanimate nature, and expatiates in five chapters on the vastness, multitude, variety, power, and beauty of created things. With the third step the metaphor of the ladder becomes blurred and indeed is abandoned altogether. Instead of "going up higher", St Robert stops to examine separately the mysteries and marvels of the universe. He first directs his attention to the earth itself and finds in its stability and fruitfulness symbols of the relation of man to his Maker:

> Just as the human body cannot rest in the air however widely diffused, nor in water however deep, because its centre is not air or water but earth; so the human soul cannot rest in honours as transient as a puff of wind, nor in riches as unstable as a morass, nor in soft pleasures that pass like a ripple on a sheet of water, nor in the glow of human knowledge as deceitful as a will-o'-the-wisp. In God alone, the centre of souls and their only true place of rest, can it find its rest. . . . Therefore, if thou art wise, my soul, treat as of no account all things that pass away lest they carry thee away with them, and cling and cleave in the bond of love to him who abideth for ever.[1]

The problem of the rich and the poor, the bounden duty of almsgiving, of sharing wealth with those less well endowed, was almost an obsession of Cardinal Bellarmine. Whenever he gets a chance, even when it is not particularly relevant to his main argument, he is always sure to bring it in. Had he been a millionaire, like St Paulinus of Nola, he, too, would surely have made over his riches to the poor. Of course, he believed in the legitimacy of private property, but he thought profoundly that no man should have too much of it while others lived, even if partly through their own laziness or improvidence, on the verge of destitution. It may strictly have little to do with his *Ladder of Created Things*, but the following passage, in which he is discoursing on the gold, silver and gems produced by mother earth, reveals his constant preoccupation:

> The gold, silver, and pearls which are so much esteemed on

[1] In *The Great Chain of Being*, Professor Lovejoy comments on the apparent inconsistency in Bellarmine's conclusion here. The ladder of created things "is, after all, only another name of a progressive *contemptus mundi*" (p. 92). Lovejoy detects a touch of illusionism and acosmism in St Robert's language, but admits that it is only an extreme statement of one side of a double doctrine evident in the teaching of our Lord, the other side being the reality, goodness and beauty of created things.

earth are perishable things, but the gold and silver that gleam in the City of God are fadeless and everlasting. But if by the hands of the poor thou wilt store up in Heaven the corruptible gold and silver that are thine, which if thou art wise thou wilt surely do, then they will become incorruptible and remain in thy possession for ever. O incredulity of the sons of men! A tongue that can lie promises ten for every hundred and the repayment of the whole sum borrowed, and the lender believes. God, who cannot lie, promises to him who gives alms a hundredfold in Heaven and life eternal, but men cling in distrust to their gold and cannot easily be persuaded to believe him. . . . O unhappy man, to whom will belong those things which thou hast gathered and stored with so much labour, supposing that thieves do not steal nor the moth or rust consume them? Thine, for certain, they will not be, though they might have been thine if thou hadst transferred them by the hands of the poor to the treasury of Heaven. Thou art more wretched than the poorest of the poor, and hast great cause to weep and lament on account of the terrible calamities that will assuredly come upon thee. For the superfluous riches which thou didst hoard and suffer to become rotten when thou shouldst have given them in alms to the poor, the superfluous garments which thou didst possess and preferred to see eaten by moths rather than clothing the poor, and the gold and silver which thou didst choose to see lie in idleness rather than spent on food for the poor, all these things, I say, will bear testimony against thee in the day of judgment.

After considering the earth, St Robert devotes three steps of his ladder to the other elements of the famous four, water,[1] air, and fire, and then, in the seventh step, voyages out into space to muse on the sun, moon and stars. That done, he returns to study the human soul in the ten chapters of his eighth step. The ninth step is on the angels, and the remaining six are turned into a new ladder up which he climbs to explore the very essence and attributes of

---

[1] The fourth step, *ex consideratione aquarum ac praecipue fontium* ends thus: "Whatever good thou seest in creatures, know that it flows from God, the fountain-head of all good things, and so with St Francis learn to taste the primal source of goodness in each created object, as in a little stream that has it for its origin".

Almighty God. This concluding part is not a ladder of "created things" at all, so it is easy to understand why the Cardinal was dissatisfied with the title of his book. It had immediate and amazing success. The first translation, made but a few months after the appearance of the original Latin, was into English. Within four years, it had gone into several editions, and was being read in Italian, Spanish, Portuguese, and French. Then there followed Bohemian, Chinese, Greek, German, Russian, Polish, Illyrian, and other versions. It has been translated into German nine different times, and into French as often.

By far the best translation that has yet appeared in English was issued in 1925, from the pen of an anonymous Anglican nun. Real love and the highest competence went to the making of this admirable piece of work. Unlike other non-Catholic versions, it presents us with the Cardinal's complete and unadulterated text. He is even given his new title of "Blessed" on the cover, and his book is described as having been for more than three centuries "one of the classics of the spiritual life". In an extremely sympathetic preface to the translation, Rev. Dr. P. Waggett, whose speciality was physics, says: "Certainly those who follow for a few days the instructions of Bellarmine will find that he does not give them crutches they might dispense with, but a secret of escape from all worldliness and all despondency. He does not naturalize our prayer. He spiritualizes our daily walk."

When the book appeared in 1615, the Cardinal was seventy-three years old and very infirm. He felt certain that it would be the last of his publications. He had long planned but could never find time for an extensive commentary, literal, moral and dogmatic, on the Epistles of St Paul, but he felt in his old bones that the project had become an impossibility. The thought of dying, or, as he put it, going home, filled his mind and gave him great contentment. He passionately longed to be dissolved and be with Christ, and each new year that came and passed caused him increasing astonishment. Was he never going to die? The result of his preoccupation with the world to come was a duodecimo, numbering in English translation 260 pages, and entitled *The Eternal Happiness of the Saints*. It appeared in print in 1616, the year of Galileo's trouble in Rome. If that genius had chosen to read it, it might have done him a great deal of good, for, though a deeply believing Catholic, he was worldly-minded and far more interested in how the heavens go than in how to go to Heaven. Books on Heaven are rare, except as theological treatises, and this of Cardinal Bellarmine is certainly one of the most attractive ever written. Considering his years, his bad health and, as he wrote in the dedication of the book to Cardinal Farnese who had largely financed the building of the Gesù, "the daily occupations which engross so much of my attention that there is scarcely a moment left over for the work of writing", it is an astonishing production, permeated with the Holy Scriptures and above all with the Epistles of St Paul, as though in compensation for the large commentary he was unable to write. The ready way in which he produces apt texts from St Augustine, St Jerome, the two St Gregories of Cappadocia, and many other ecclesiastical writers, is truly impressive. He makes Heaven thoroughly desirable without ever going beyond the bounds of what God has chosen to reveal. And he can be humorous, too, in his quiet way, as when he says, "since in the Apocalypse we read of nothing but the fruit of one tree for food, and the water of a river for drink, I am afraid that some may wonder at the scantiness of the fare in Heaven, and think that more substantial meat is to be found in this land of our exile". He goes on to interpret the "river of the water of life" that springs from the fountain of life which is God, as being the wisdom of God of which the saints partake, and the tree of life, the food of the saints, is the enjoyment of a "share of the ineffable love whereby goodness itself being clearly seen can be loved, and by which God loves himself, who is infinitely good and the fountain of all goodness. . . . How great this joy will be is quite inexplicable, nor shall we know it before we have experienced it. . . . It is not said, 'May the joy of thy Lord enter into thee', but 'Enter *thou* into the joy of thy Lord', which is a proof that the joy will be greater than we can conceive. We shall enter into a great sea of divine and eternal joy, which will fill us within and without, and surround us on all sides."

St Robert's spiritual teaching is completely Ignatian, and

insists tirelessly on the necessity of effort and self-conquest. Heaven is not an open garden into which idlers may walk at will. It is a fortress to be stormed, a prize, a crown to be won by rigorous training. "Everyone that striveth for the mastery refraineth himself from all things; and they, indeed, that they may receive a corruptible crown, but we an incorruptible one." The Cardinal cites also St Paul's great passage, "Take unto you the armour of God . . .", and comments, "Dear God! how full of terror and awe-inspiring earnestness is this exhortation. . . . Twist and turn and try to escape as you will, the crown of ever-lasting bliss can never be yours unless you sweat and strive to win it with all the power and energy of your body and soul."

Robert was an exigent spiritual director. In this book on Heaven, as in each of his other five devotional books, he comes round invariably at some point or other to his two most cherished themes, the duties of the rich to the poor, and the paramount obligation of bishops to reside in their dioceses and to preach and personally administer the sacraments to their flocks. "If business seems to require that we leave our flocks, more important business, even war of the most terrible kind, compels us to stay and defend them. The trumpet of St Paul sounds in our ears: For ours is not a conflict with mere flesh and blood, but with principalities and powers, the forces that control this dark world, the spiritual hosts of evil arrayed against us in the heavenly war-fare."[1]

Each year that remained to him on earth, Cardinal Bellarmine produced a new devotional work. These were De Gemitu Columbae, sive de bono lachrymarum (1617); De Septem Verbis a Christo in Cruce prolatis (1618); Admonitio ad Episcopum Theanensem (1619); and De Arte bene Moriendi 1620). The first of those books, "The Mourning of the Dove, or the Value of Tears" is, as its

[1] The De Aeterna Felicitate Sanctorum was translated into English in 1620 by Catholics, and at four subsequent dates. In 1710, a Protestant named Jenks brought out a version of it under the odd title, Ouranography or Heaven opened. This was followed in 1722 by another Protestant rendering with a preliminary "essay on the same subject written by Mr Addison", the editor of the Spectator. Mr Addison had lain in Poets' Corner of Westminster Abbey for three years at the time.

name implies, a little treatise on the fruit of penance and compunction of heart. The Cardinal describes twelve sources of tears for the devout Catholic in as many chapters, among which were the persecutions of the Church, the laxity of life among priests, the decline in fervour of religious orders, the careless living of so many professing the Catholic name. Bellarmine did not set himself up as a *censor morum* but told in compassionate terms of abuses among the Church's children which weighed upon his own heart, and caused the enemies of the faith to blaspheme. There had been so many apostasies even in Italy: Ochino, the general of a religious order; Peter Martyr Vermigli, trusted go-between of the Popes with the Protestant leaders; Giordano Bruno, the ex-Dominican of genius; Marcantonio de Dominus, the Catholic bishop who became Dean of Windsor; Renée, Duchess of Ferrara, who smuggled a disguised Calvin into her court. Those and other defections undoubtedly created in Rome an atmosphere of "Who goes next?" and afford some explanation of Robert Bellarmine's anxiety about Galileo. The Cardinal had good reason for his devout tears, especially in his reflections on the Passion of our Lord, who seemed to have suffered and died in vain for an unheeding world. Four years after St Robert's death, a religious of the order of Minims named Hilarion de Costa produced in Paris a *Histoire ecclésiastique* of his own times, in which he spoke very warmly of Cardinal Bellarmine's spiritual books, and went on to give some information of how much they were appreciated: "A great man who is one of the most distinguished and prominent members of the *Parlement* of Paris has said that he reads *The Ascent of the Mind to God* four times every year, and that it is not inferior to the *Imitation of Christ*. Similarly, Monsignor the Bishop of Geneva, who died eighteen months ago, used never to tire of reading and praising the *Mourning of the Dove*."[1]

[1] Bellarmine himself would have been horrified by the comparison of his work to that of à Kempis. He loved the *Imitation of Christ* and cites it often in his works, but he knew it to be a work of spiritual genius, and that his own effort was on an altogether lower plane. It is true though, that St Francis de Sales very greatly appreciated the *Mourning of the Dove*. In volume II of Bellarmine's life published in English in 1928, the author gave, "for what it is worth", a story told by a witness before the Congregation of Rites to the

The little book of Bellarmine addressed to the Bishop of Teano, in the province of Capua, resulted from the earnest petition of Cardinal Fernando Taberna, who had been consecrated as a bishop and appointed to the government of a diocese in 1615. He was an earnest devout man, and wanted from St Robert a letter of advice and instructions similar to that which he had written at the request of Pope Clement VIII many years earlier. Robert had taken every precaution on that occasion that his letter should be seen by his Holiness alone but, despite his care, its contents had been quickly divulged by some prying person at the Vatican. Remembering what had happened then, he felt reluctant to act as counsellor to a prince of the Church, but a nephew of whom he was very fond, Angelo della Ciaia, provided him with a way round the difficulty when he was appointed Bishop of Teano in 1616. Uncles have an immemorial privilege of giving good advice to nephews, so Robert addressed his ostensibly to Angelo, though it was meant for Cardinal Taberna. The matter treated at greatest length is the strict duty of bishops to reside in their dioceses, "except for brief periods of absence necessitated by very urgent reasons". Absenteeism was not nearly so prevalent at this time as it had been in the past, but it was still to be found, and our Saint did not hesitate to say that "several bishops now alive" were in the gravest danger of losing their souls. He follows with a rather terrifying statement of what is required of bishops in the way of personal holiness: "If men who aspire to be bishops would but consider the perfection of sanctity and wisdom strictly required by God in those advanced to episcopal dignity, they would not be so eager in pursuit of its dread responsibilities, but would accept them with the greatest reluctance, only under

---

effect that James I King of England, once Bellarmine's arch-enemy, in his later years "practically always carried the Cardinal's *Mourning of the Dove* about with him" (pp. 259-60). This story, probably pure fable, is not included in the present complete revision of the 1928 Life. But Professor de Santillana seems to have liked it and trots it out twice in his *Crime of Galileo* (pp. 79 and 102), as ascertained history, which is odd of him. Arthur Koestler in *The Sleepwalkers* (pp. 433-4) reproduces Santillana to the letter. Brodrick's sceptical note, "for what it is worth", is swept aside altogether. It is a small point but troubling to find it in the historians of science.

compulsion and constraint". As for the revenues of a diocese, "it is certain that the bishop would sin mortally if, not content with a frugal table and modest furnishings, he fails to spend what money remains on the upkeep of his churches and the sustenance of the poor". Needless to say, those stern conclusions are supported by a formidable array of biblical and patristic texts. Occasionally St Robert would seem to have strained their meaning a little in support of his arguments. Whatever else may be said about his counsels, they were decidedly realistic and bracing, at a time when many bishops still displayed the showy manners of their Renaissance predecessors.

Another prelate, a very engaging one, who sought advice from Cardinal Bellarmine was François de Harley, Archbishop of Rouen. At the beginning of the year 1618, he addressed the following letter to St Robert:

> As I read and re-read the letter which your Lordship so kindly sent me . . . it seemed to me not so much a letter as an oracle. The more I try to carry out what you have told me so gravely and modestly, the more is the desire, or rather the fire, enkindled in my heart to practise every detail of your counsel perfectly. Now you who have lit this fire must provide it with fuel if you do not want to see it die down. . . . I beg and implore you, then, in my own name and in the name of all the prelates of Holy Church, to have the goodness to describe for us in writing your ideal of a perfect archbishop, I mean such a pastor of souls as St Ambrose or St Augustine would be, were they alive in this wretched age. . . . Many writers put before us ideal bishops in the Platonic sense of the word. Others sketch for us hermit bishops who are admirable hands at weeping but useless for governing a flock. Then there are some who think they have done a great thing by stringing together a number of passages from the Fathers, and out of this mosaic constructing a bishop, forgetful that many ways and customs, good and holy in former times, would now, especially in countries where heresy is deluding and corrupting souls, be found either ridiculous or useless.
>
> But your Lordship who knows everything, and is acquainted with the perversity of this iron age, who has been an archbishop

for three years and who has learned by experience what needs to be done, who is so full of zeal, prudence, and profound erudition, who is versed in so many affairs, who has seen France and Flanders, and knows what heresy really means, who, in fine, has such authority that your words are received as so many oracles,—your Lordship, in my opinion, is better qualified than any man alive to paint a true portrait of a holy archbishop, suited to our times.

Non dimittam te nisi benedixeris mihi! Do not deny me so just a demand, and to those golden treatises which you have published during the last three years, add this also in order to animate every prelate of the Church to fulfil his duty in a truly apostolic fashion. . . . This would be for me a great favour, nay, the greatest of favours, and not for me only but for all the bishops and archbishops in the world. I know not how to write my thanks for the exceeding kindness of your letters and for the holy advice you give me from time to time. Were I not already entirely devoted to you, I should now lay my heart at your feet. Accept, then, my continued and cordial affection, and believe me, as with all love, I kiss your hand, to be now and forever

Your Lordship's most affectionate and obliged servant,

FRANCIS, Archbishop of Rouen.

To satisfy the zealous Archbishop's desires the Cardinal sent him a manuscript copy of the *Admonitio*, which he liked so much that he felt he must share it with other bishops, his friends. One of them liked it so much that he had it printed and published in Paris, without by-your-leave to either Harley or Bellarmine. The Archbishop expressed his sorrow and indignation in a letter of September 8, 1619:

I cannot tell you how profound was my sorrow when I discovered that some friends of mine had played me false by publishing behind my back that golden manuscript you sent me. I am all the more angry because I do not know even now against whom my anger ought to be directed. I have no idea who has done me this bad turn. Forgive him, I beg you, whoever he be, for perhaps he meant well. So greedy are numbers of men to see anything that comes from your pen, that they cannot wait until you have made it ready for publication, feeling sure that nothing is written by you which is not full of merit. This little work, on which you set no store at all, they prize as a real treasure.

For myself, I am and always will be most grateful, whether you think that what you have done is enough, or set about the preparation of something still more substantial. Though you never add another word, you have written sufficient to make every prelate of Holy Church a saint. Should God give me an opportunity to be of service to any member of your order, I trust I shall make him see clearly how deeply I reverence your Lordship, and how much I am indebted to you.

The last of Bellarmine's devotional books, *The Art of Dying Well*, appeared in 1620, about nine months before he was to show by his own example how a Christian ought to die. It was translated into English almost immediately by Father Edward Coffin, the Jesuit spiritual director of the English College in Rome, that seminary of martyrs. In it the old Cardinal reiterates and emphasizes all the chief points of his spiritual teaching, the necessity of constant prayer and self-denial, of alacrity and watchfulness in God's service, of charity in speech and, above all, of generosity in the use of earthly possessions. He proves from Scripture and the Fathers that alms-giving according to one's means is not a counsel but a strict precept. Then he dilates with moving eloquence on the various blessings which wait for the generous heart, and finally considers the manner in which alms ought to be bestowed. The following passages are from the pleasant, racy old version of Father Coffin:

Let us now speak of the *manner* of bestowing almes, for that is necessary more than any other thing, that we may vertuously live and die most happily. First, it is necessary that we give almes with a most sincere intention of pleasing God and not for seeking of popular prayse. This doth Christ teach us when he saith: *When thou doest give almes, do not sound the trumpet, and let not thy left hand know what thy right hand doth...*

Agayne, our almes is to be given *readily*, and with facility, that it may not seeme to be wrung out by intreaty, nor delaied from day to day when it may presently be dispatched. . . . Abraham, the friend of God, requested the passengers that they would come to his house, and expected not to be intreated by them. . . . Neyther did Toby expect that the poore people should come unto him, but he himselfe did seeke for them.

Thirdly, it is requisite that our almes be given *cheerfully*, and not with grudging. *In everything thou givest* (saith Ecclesiasticus) *shew a cheerful countenance;* And the Apostle: *Not out of sadness or out of necessity, for our Lord doth love a cheerfull giver.*

Fourthly, it is necessary that our almes be given with *humility*, in such manner as the giver may know himselfe to receive more than he giveth, of which point thus writeth St Gregory: "It helpeth much to check the pride of the giver of almes if when he bestoweth his earthly substance he do weigh well the words of the heavenly Master, *Make you friends of the mammon of iniquity that when you shall fayle they may receive you into the everlasting tabernacles.* For if by the friendship of the poore we do gayne the eternall tabernacles, doubtless we who give are to perswade our selves that we do rather offer presents to our benefactours than bestow almes on the poore."

Fifthly, it behoveth that we give *abundantly*, according to the proportion or measure of our ability, for so did Toby, that famous alms-giver: *As thou shalt be able, so be thou pitiful to the poore; if thou have much give plentifully; if thou have but little, study how to give that little willingly.* The Apostle teacheth us that an almes is to be given as a blessing, not as covetousness. St Chrysostome addeth, not to give only but to give abundantly is to be called almes, and in the same sermon, that such as desire to be heard of God when they cry, *Have mercy on me O Lord God according to Thy great mercy,* must also have mercy on the poore according to their great almes.

Last of all, it is specially required that he who will be saved and dye well do diligently search out, eyther by his owne reading and meditation or by other devout and learned men, whether a man may keep superfluous riches without sinne, or whether such be not of necessity to be given to the poore; and further, which are to be deemed superfluous riches, which necessary; for the case may so stand that meane riches to one man may be superfluous, and great wealth to another may seeme necessary. And for that this small treatise cannot comport any

prolixe dispute of scolastical questions, I will briefly repeat
certayne passages of the Holy Scriptures, and Fathers as well
ancient as moderne, and so conclude this difficulty.

The places of the Scriptures are the sixth of S. Mathew:
You cannot serve God and mammon; the third of S. Luke: *He who
hath two coates, let him give to him that hath none, and he that hath
meat let him do the like*; and in the twelfth of the same Gospel
it is sayd to a rich man who so abounded in substance as that
he scant knew where to lay them: *Thou foole, this very night they
will take from thee thy soule*; which wordes S. Augustine doth
thus expound, that this rich man was everlastingly damned
because he reteyned superfluous wealth.

The chiefest authorityes of the ancient Fathers for this
matter are these. *St Basil:* And art thou not a theefe or robber
who esteemest that as thine owne which thou hast receaved
only to dispense and give away? *St Ambrose:* What injustice is
there if I who take not other men's goods from them do diligently keep myne owne? O impudent assertion! Dost thou
call them thine owne? It is no lesse a crime when thou art able
and wealthy to deny almes to the poore than to steale or take
away from him that hath it. *S. Hierome:* Whatsoever thou hast
more than is necessary for thy diet and apparel that bestowe,
and know that for so much thou art a debter. *S. Chrysostome:*
Dost thou possess that which is thyn owne? The goods of the
poore are committed to thy custodye whether thou possesse
them out of thyne owne just labour or by lineal descent of
inheritance. *S. Augustine:* The thinges that are superfluous to
the rich are necessary to the poore; they who possesse more than
they want possesse more than is theirs. *S. Leo:* Earthly and
corporal riches do come unto us from the bounty of God, and
therefore worthily is he to exact an account of these thinges
which he hath no more committed unto us to possesse than to
disburse and distribute. *S. Gregory*: Such are to be warned who
neyther desire other men's goods nor bestow their owne that
they attentively know that the earth of which we are all made
is common to all, and therefore in common yieldeth substance
for all; in vaine do they thinke themselves without fault who
challenge as their owne that gift of God which he hath bestowed
upon all. *S. Bernard:* The poor cry out and say, it is our goods
that you wast; it is with cruelty taken from us which you so

vainly spend. *S. Thomas of Aquine:* The things which some have more than they need are by the law of nature dew unto the maintenance of the poore. Our Lord commandeth not only the tyth or tenth part but whatsoever is superfluous to be given to the poore. Upon the fourth booke of *Sentences* [S. Thomas] affirmeth this to be the common doctrine of all devines.

Here if any will contend that these superfluous goods are not to be given unto the poore out of the rigour of the law, yet truly he cannot deny that they are to be given them out of charity, and it importeth little, God wot, whether a man go to hel for want of justice or for want of charity.[1]

Notwithstanding his stern views on the duties of Christians which, by the good leave of the Master of the Sacred Palace, are totally unoriginal and stem straight from the New Testament or the ascetic tradition of the Church, Robert Bellarmine was a peculiarly genial type of saint. His brethren in the purple had a great deal to say on this subject. The Cardinal of Santa Susanna testified that, despite his austerity of life and constant meditation on death, his speech was not stiff or solemn but ever "lovingly courteous and religiously urbane". The magnificent Cardinal Alessandro d'Este was yet more specific: "When I used to visit him, not to honour him as a cardinal but to venerate him as a saint, I would find myself irresistibly drawn to him, as though he were a magnet. In the consistories, I used to manoeuvre regularly to get the place next to his, and this, not because business required that I should be near him, but because I held him in such reverence and derived so much consolation from the sweet affability and open-heartedness of his converse." The Cardinal of Savoy spoke in the same vein: "I can say truthfully that I used to take the greatest delight in the holy charm of his conversation. His pleasant, playful manner attracted me immensely, so I used to

[1] When the Cardinal's little book was submitted for censorship, the Master of the Sacred Palace, a Dominican named Hyacinth Petronio, expressed strong disapproval of the views on almsgiving ventilated in it, and represented them to Pope Paul V as altogether new and strange. The Pope, whose speciality was canon law, did not agree and so a little classic of Christian spirituality went through to publication by Plantin's famous firm at Antwerp.

visit him very often and, no matter how long I stayed, it seemed to me only a few minutes, so great was the pleasure I took in his company. His conversation appeared to me to be like music, so much did his words accord with his perfect life." Cardinal Bandini spoke of his "singular gentleness, charming manners and pleasant geniality", and, not to draw out this litany of praises unduly, Cardinal de la Rochefoucault may be cited as a last witness: "The first of three things I noticed particularly in Robert Bellarmine was his humility which his vast learning left totally unaffected; the second was his unremitting self-denial in all things, joined with the most wonderful sweetness of manner, gaiety and affability in his dealings with other people; and the third thing that struck me was his perfect spirit of observance as a religious". Those testimonies, obtained by Bellarmine's first biographer, Giacomo Fuligatti, who knew him personally and published his *Vita* only two years after the Cardinal's death, seem fairly conclusive. Robert Bellarmine, on the natural as well as on the supernatural plane, was an exceptionally lovable man.

Bellarmine brings to mind another saint with whom he had much in common, his contemporary and friend, Francis de Sales. Francis depended almost entirely for his ammunition against the Calvinists of Savoy on the *Controversies* of Roberto. In the introduction to his great *Treatise on the Love of God*, published in 1616, he had referred in terms of enthusiastic praise to Roberto's *De Ascensione Mentis in Deum*, and followed this up with a letter from Annecy, dated September 12, 1617, in which he begged the Cardinal for some token treatment of the Epistles of St Paul, if only an exposition of those to Titus or Philemon. "Dear God," he writes, "how I wish and how great a number of wise and holy men wish, that we had, if not all, at least one or two, even of the shortest of St Paul's Epistles, explained in the three senses to which your Lordship alludes . . . to initiate us into this method". The allusion was in the dedication to Cardinal Farnese of the *De Aeterna Felicitate Sanctorum*, "whose sweet and admirable piety", wrote de Sales, "has refreshed the minds of the faithful and stirred them up to a better life". Pierre Camus, the excitable but delightful young Bishop of Belley, who worshipped St

Francis de Sales, though that dear man teased him mercilessly, enjoyed also the friendship of Cardinal Bellarmine and said two good things about him in his interminable *Esprit du Bienheureux François de Sales*, that "his name alone is his panegyric" and that he was "of a very gay disposition"—*d'humeur fort gaye*. In January, 1621, the year of Bellarmine's death, St Francis appealed to him on behalf of a Franciscan who was in distress and began his letter with the following words: "The odour of your meekness and kindness draws to your Illustrious Lordship all who are in debt or trouble, as to a place of strength and a house of refuge. If this is a burden to your Lordship you have only yourself to blame for choosing to be what you are."[1]

Bellarmine's letters of this last period of his life bear out the beautiful tribute of St Francis. It seems highly likely that he never in his life left a letter, no matter how unimportant, unanswered but, pressed as he nearly always was, he had to write at top speed, and the consequence was an illegibility that has made thousands of his extant letters unavailable to this present day. In 1618 he wrote to an old friend, Father John Gerard, whose dramatic escape from the Tower of London is celebrated among prison-breaking exploits, and remarked at the end, "Your Reverence will have hard work to read my bad writing".[2] To a young nephew in Florence he wrote in 1617: "I would gladly have sent you a copy of my little book *De Gemitu Columbae*, only that the postal charges on it would mount to much more than the book itself is worth. If you can think of any way of getting it to Florence, without putting the college to expense, do please let me know and you shall have it with the greatest pleasure." A

---

[1] *Oeuvres de St François de Sales* (Annecy ed.), vol. xx, p. 4.

[2] The letter, written in Latin, is in the Stonyhurst archives, and, indeed, an agony to decipher. Gerard had sent him as Christmas presents, an English pocket-knife, a little box in bone or ivory, and, most oddly, three small toothpicks, as if such things were unknown in Italy. He wanted a benefice for his friend Dr Singleton, who had been relieved of his post at Douay because of his friendship with the Jesuits of Louvain. Alas, though keen to help, the Cardinal found it out of his power. "I who was thought to have some influence with the Pope", he wrote ruefully, "have laboured for more than ten years for a Spanish priest, an excellent man and a great friend of mine, to obtain for him a benefice falling vacant in his own country."

Jesuit missionary returning to the Philippines sent him a bone ring acquired in that country, guaranteed as an antidote to poison. The Cardinal thanked him warmly for the ring as a token of friendship, "but as for wearing it, no, because I am not very much afraid of being poisoned. What I really covet is a share of your merits, for though we here in Europe also labour hard in the Lord's vineyard, I am very sure that your labours are more precious beyond compare in the eyes of God. Go on your way, Father, joyously and courageously, as now you do, and keep a little place for me in your holy prayers."

One short letter of St Robert may be given here *in extenso* as truly representative of his spirit. It was written in June, 1620, when his health, such as it was, had begun to break down completely, to a Jesuit in Mainz who had composed a little treatise on the Blessed Trinity and diffidently sent him a copy:

> Pardon my ingratitude, dear Father, in having delayed so long to thank you for your present to me, small in size but very great in quality. The reason for my delay was that at first I thought your work on the Trinity would be like many others, written in regular scholastic form, and consequently very dull and difficult to read. As I was then occupied from morning to night with matters of very great importance, I put off reading it seriously and attentively, for a considerable time. But as soon as I settled down to it properly, I found it sweeter than honey and more precious than gold or jewels. Now I am continually reading it, for I look upon it as a thoroughly spiritual book, most suited to inflame, elevate, and feed my mind. I have read it all through, and if God allows me a little more of life, I have planned to re-read and ponder it again and again. So I thank God who moved you to write such an admirable work, and I thank you, too, for having prepared such a feast for me.

The old Cardinal was reluctant to appeal to the Pope for help for the many who turned to him in their distress because he had learned from Paul V's various almoners that he was already disbursing as much as a hundred thousand crowns annually in direct charity and had besides to support entire colleges and seminaries, not only in Italy, but in Germany, Belgium, Greece, "and places as far away as Japan". But he did not hesitate to play the beggar when writing to people of wealth, such as the Prince Bishop of Würzburg. A German gentleman of good family who had fallen on evil days appealed to Bellarmine for assistance. "I shall not fail to speak to his Holiness again and again about the matter which you have entrusted to me," wrote the Cardinal to the Bishop. . . .

But meantime, I cannot refrain from recommending to you most warmly and earnestly Francis N., whom your Lordship knows well. I myself have begged the Pope to make such provision for his son out of some rich benefice as would be sufficient for the decent support of both father and children. But as these affairs cannot be arranged in a moment, I entreat you during the interval to add a little more to the liberality which you have often shown this unfortunate man in the past. I write this entirely of my own accord. Francis has told me in grateful terms about the assistance you are giving him out of your kindness, and he did not in any way suggest that I should ask you to increase the alms. It is because I feel so much pity for his poverty and have so much trust in the kind heart of your Lordship, that I am emboldened to commend his case to you again.

As for the Cardinal's own resources, he had none, because beyond the support of his modest household, he had given everything else away. "Do not be surprised," he wrote once to his brother Tommáso, "that I send you only sixty *scudi*, because we have not a farthing left in the house, and I had to borrow the sixty crowns from the bank."

The following letter, addressed to the Abbot General of the Spanish Benedictines, Antonio de Castro, on June 27, 1617, is typical of others in the files and speaks for itself:

Very Reverend and Most Religious Father,
    Juan Orozco has lately come to Rome in secular dress to seek a remedy for his soul from the Grand Penitentiary of our Lord the Pope, because out of fear of still more grievous imprisonment he had thrown aside his sacred habit and thus fallen into

a state of apostasy from his rule and vows. When the Penitentiary learned that he had come straight here and that he was most anxious to return to his order, he gave instructions that he was to be absolved *in foro conscientiae*, but for absolution *in foro externo* he referred him, according to custom, to your very Reverend Paternity, especially as it is impossible to know here in Rome whether what he says is true. For this reason in the letter written to you on parchment and stamped with the Penitentiary's seal, there is added the clause, "provided you see fit".

As this religious is very much afraid of the severity of his superiors and is consequently in great distress, I thought I might venture to intervene, trusting to the charity and kindness of your very Reverend Paternity. Owing to my great fear that the devil might grievously tempt this most afflicted servant of Christ, I have dared to intercede for him as a mediator, and with my whole heart to commend his peril to your charity lest, swallowed up by sadness, a soul should be lost for which Christ has died.

I appeal, then, to your goodness to consider whether, if what he says be true, his abbot did not proceed against him with too great severity. After putting him in prison, he wanted to thrust him into a still more dismal cell, and so gave the unfortunate man grounds for fearing even worse evils. At last, overcome by his forebodings, he took to flight. Still, he did not go back to the world but fled to the bosom of our universal Mother. Show, then, the tenderness of your compassion to this your son, and put a favourable construction on the words, *si sibi videbitur*. May your charity enable you to see your way to pardoning him, to lessening his punishment and to tempering the rigour of your rule. By such kindness he will be more and more strengthened in his good resolutions.

The last three years of Cardinal Bellarmine's life were the hardest he had ever known. An unusually severe Roman winter in 1619 caused his hands to bleed so much from tormenting chilblains that he was forced to wear gloves. Yet still he went on answering letters and attending faithfully the various congregations to which he was attached. His legs became so badly swollen that the gaiters he had acquired eighteen years earlier would no longer meet around his calves. He was told that a new pair could be had for a mere trifle of five or six *giulii* but answered that the sum would not be a trifle in some poor man's pocket, and had the old gaiters fitted with strings which would stretch them sufficiently. He wore his gaiters over the bare skin. His devoted gentleman, Pietro Guidotti, knew that they tormented him, and gave him a few pairs of woollen stockings, bought out of his own resources. The Cardinal thanked him warmly but, after his death, the stockings were found among his few belongings as new as on the day of their purchase, for he had never worn them.

At this time St Robert appears to have vacated his quarters in the Vatican and to have been residing in some rented house. A great longing came over him to lay aside his dignities and to end his days as a simple Jesuit. He drew up an elaborate petition to Paul V and began a systematic search for new posts for his domestic staff and gentlemen attendants. But the Pope, aging himself and near the end of his long reign, did not feel that he could dispense with the Cardinal's services just yet.

Pope Paul died in January, 1621, and St Robert, then in his seventy-ninth year, had to endure the rigours of his third conclave, which elected Pope Gregory XV. Fortunately the conclave was almost a record for brevity, less than a fortnight. The frail old Cardinal was distressed by some of the methods employed at papal elections, particularly that known by the technical name of "adoration", meaning simply a deep bow before the throne of a favoured candidate. If two-thirds of the cardinals performed this reverence, the candidate was understood to be elected. Bellarmine disliked the method because it frequently led to dissension among the cardinals and he submitted an earnest little paper to the new Pope, urging its abolition. Within the year Gregory XV published a bull of reform in which the custom was prohibited. St Robert died before its issue, but the Pope's nephew, Cardinal Ludovisi, bore witness that his advice had counted in bringing about the reform. "I particularly promised Cardinal Bellarmine, who is now at rest," he wrote, "and pledged him my word that I would employ all my authority and industry for the attainment of this result."

At his first audience with Pope Gregory, the Cardinal pleaded most earnestly to be allowed to return to the Society of Jesus, so that he might die as a simple Jesuit. Gregory, a kindly man who suffered much from ill-health himself, was deeply sympathetic but told the old man that the Church needed his services up to the last moment, and he must ask him, not to return to the Jesuits, but to take up his quarters once more in the Vatican. Bellarmine resignedly instructed Guidotti to make ready for the change and then fell gravely ill. He dictated a letter to Cardinal Bandini, whom he knew to be a close friend of the Pope, begging him to obtain for him from the Holy Father at least a dispensation from attendance at the consistories and congregations because his "deafness was getting worse every day". Bandini, who loved him, did his best, but the Pope still maintained that the old man was necessary and that his disappearance into retirement would cause general distress. So St Robert returned to the Vatican and did not require a pantechnicon to remove his scanty personal belongings. But the Pope could then see for himself how frail he was, and granted him his heart's desire a few months later.

CHAPTER XIV

THE DEATH OF A SAINT

ON August 25, 1621, Bellarmine retired very happily to the Jesuit novitiate of Sant' Andrea on the Quirinal, and three days later, the feast of St Augustine, to whom he was greatly devoted, "he fell sick and was taken with a very sharp and violent fever which deprived him of his senses for the tyme". Those words are from a little book called *A True Relation of the last Sickness and Death of Cardinall Bellarmine*, which was published at Saint-Omer in 1622. It was written by Father Edward Coffin, the Jesuit chaplain to the English students in Rome, who had translated the Cardinal's book, *The Eternal Happiness of the Saints*. Coffin knew Bellarmine intimately, loved him ardently, and was a privileged visitor to the sick-room where his old friend lay dying. Besides what he saw for himself, he drew in his *Relation* on a letter written by Father Giacomo Minutoli who, by direction of the Jesuit General, Muzio Vitelleschi, "remayned with Bellarmine from the beginning of his sickness till the last gasp". Minutoli wrote his detailed report at the request of Cardinal Farnese, one of St Robert's most devoted friends. The lay brother Giuseppe Finali, an educated man, who helped to nurse his illustrious patient, also wrote a report, so it may fairly be said that the passing of a saint has never been more adequately documented.

When the first attack of the fever had subsided, the patient "with great alacrity of mind began to discourse of the great gladness and comfort he had, for that he was so near his home, or as he did always in this sickness call it, *a casa mia*, to my house". In delirium, Finali noted that all his raving was of God. He preached snatches of a sermon on the love of God, and wept and prayed for unhappy people who would not love Him. To continue with Coffin's *Relation*:

When his vehemency was a little relented, he would make
the Signe of the Crosse and begin another prayer; never so
much as once in all these extreme fits speaking any idle word or
shewing the least signe of impatience. In so much as my selfe in
company of others often visiting him, and that at such tymes as
he was in this fever, I doe sincerely protest that I never saw
man in his best health repose more quietly or make lesse showe
of feeling the force of any disease, than alwayes I saw him in
this. For the most part his armes were decently layed acrosse
on his breast, he never moving (unlesse he were willed) any part
of his body, never sighing, never complayning. Nor though his
tongue was scorched with the raging heat of the ague, did he
ever so much as call for drinke, or once offered to refresh his
mouth, so as the beholders could make no other judgement of
him but that which the disciples made of Lazarus: *Si dormit
salvus erit*, if he sleep he will recover. For his magnanimity was
such he rather seemed to sleep than to be sicke, and thereby
gave greater signes of life than death. . .

When the Blessed Sacrament was brought he would needs
rise to receave it and prostrated himselfe on the ground with
singular devotion and humility. And this his piety upon every
occasion did manifest it selfe in all his sickness, in so much as he
desired the physicians leave to say the Office of his Breviary,
and that so earnestly as the doctors, though they denied it as
a worke too greate for his weakness, yet to satisfy his importunity they graunted that in lieu thereof he might say his
Beades, but with some pawse between every decade, lest his too
serious application might hurt his head. And seeing that no
more would be graunted to him, he sayd to those about him:
Me thinkes I am become a mere secular man, and am no more
Religious, for I neyther say Office nor Masse, I make no prayers,
I doe no good at all. And this seemed to afflict him more than
his sickness which yet was most violent and mortall.

Pope Gregory used to send his own medical adviser each
morning and evening to find out how the Cardinal was progres-
sing. On Tuesday, August 31, this man's report was very un-
favourable, and the Holy Father, who was deeply grieved by it,
sent to inform the dying man that he would visit him early the
following morning. When Bellarmine heard the news he was

much concerned and said anxiously to Finali: "I am sorry that his Holiness puts himself out for a poor thing like me—*per me poverino*. And our stairs, too, are very high and narrow." The number of steps the Pope would have to climb so worried the Cardinal that he asked one of his attendants to go and beg Gregory not to come. That appeal served but to strengthen the Holy Father's resolution, so on the morning of September 1 St Robert made whatever pathetic preparations he could to receive his august visitor. He struggled into a sitting posture in his bed and put on a coat:

When he saw the Pope enter his room, he sayd with the good Centurion, *non sum dignus ut intres sub tectum meum*, with other words of great dutifulness and humility. And when the Pope shewed the griefe of mynde he conceaved for his sickness and how much he esteemed his losse, the other answered as he had alwayes done that he had lived long enough and therefore desired no longer respit on earth. And I will pray God (quoth he) to graunt your Holiness as long life as he hath unto me. The Pope replied, but not in so lowd a voyce as the Cardinall could heare him, I have more need of Bellarmine's meritts than of his yeeres. Many wordes past betweene them, of great affection in the one and submissive humility in the other. The Pope, after that he had twice most lovingly imbraced him, being to depart, sayd that he would pray to God that he might recover. Not, quoth the Cardinal, that I may recover, but that God's will and pleasure may be done eyther for life or death.

After that the Pope was gone, he seemed to be much more cheerful than he was before, the cause whereof he disclosed unto Father Minutoli, saying: Now truly doe I well hope that I shall dye, for the Popes are never known to have visited Cardinalls but when they were in danger of death, or rather past all hope of life; to which effect he alleadged divers examples. Remayning therefore in his joyfull hope, when divers of the Society came to him and offered to say Masse and pray for him, he would very lovingly thank them all, but still accepted their curtesy with this *caveat*, that they should not pray for his longer life, but contrariwise that his passage might be safe and soone.

After meate, all his recreation was to heare the lives of Saintes read unto him, especially of bishops and above all of Saint

o

Francis. And in the hearing their rare and eminent vertues, he would alwayes weep and sigh after that perfection of life to which they had so happily arrived, and from which he thought himselfe to be much further than he was. . . . Besides this griefe conceaved for himselfe and his owne unworthiness, another thing also seemed to afflict him, to wit, the continual watch at the night with him. For he would ordinarily demaund of such as he saw about him in the morning whether they had watched with him all that night, and if they sayd yea, then would he reply: So much trouble, and of so many, for my sake, for me that am but a poore wretch and fit for nothing! And if he saw more together with him, he would say: One is sufficient to watch; let the rest sleepe, and yet another watch whiles he doth sleepe. The trouble of so many is a trouble unto me who deserve not so much attendance.

Likewise when he saw any extraordinary thing brought him to eate, as chickens or the like, he would say that such expense was ill bestowed upon him, and would be better on the poore, whom he so loved and was so bountifull unto them as he left himselfe so little as could hardly mainteyne him and satisfy his household. . . . He never respected his owne inconvenience, payne, or trouble, in so much as not only to Cardinals and Prelates, but to any other that came to see him (and there came many) he would take off his night-cap, lift himself up in his bed, and never endure that any should stand bare-headed in his presence. . . . Even to his owne servants he bare that respect as he would endure much, rather than put them to any trouble.

His resignation and indifferency of mind was very exact, without all contradiction or reply, whatsoever happened, whatsoever was determined. Nothing troubled his mind, one thing only excepted. Having from the beginning of his sickness prepared himselfe to dye, it fell out that the seventh day, held by the physicians for critical, he began to be somewhat better. Much joy was conceaved thereat, and the same signified unto the Cardinall, who, weighing the matter in another ballance, was somewhat troubled with this sudden resolution, and sayd myldly ynto the doctours: I had thought at this tyme to have gone into my house and home, and now I see that you will hinder me. I pray you let me goe. Their answere was that it belonged unto their office to preserve his life as long as they

could and was pleasing unto God, and he also was bound therein to concurre with them, to doe as they should ordayne, and
be contented to stay in this world until that God should otherwise dispose. Well then, quoth the Cardinall, his will be done.
. . . I shall follow your direction.

The cause why he desired the dissolution of his earthly
tabernacle was no other but that lest through the frailty of
body and mind he should hereafter offend God . . . whom now
he had rather dye than displease. This his fervent desire grounded
on the foresaid motive was so imprinted in his hart and fixt
therein so deeply as even when his violent ague bereaved him
of his senses, he was often heard to say: *Signore, vorrei andare
a casa mia*, O Lord I would gladly go home. . . . And the
eleventh day after his sickness he sayd unto all his physicians:
When shall I heare from you that happy news that I must
depart? When shall I be delivered from this body of death?
They answered as before, not so long as they could keep him
alive. Well (quoth he), God sees my desire, and how willing I
am to come unto him.

Non est fraudatus desiderio suo. God heard his prayer and that
very night he was seene to sob in such a manner as a learned
physician, watching with him held it for mortall, and forthwith
advertised the Generall (for so had the Cardinall before willed
them, when they should perceave him in evident danger),
who came early the next morning, and seeing how matters
went, thought it best plainly to acquaint him with the truth,
and sayd unto him: My Lord, I thinke that the ende of this
sickness will be the end of your life, and by all likelyhoode you
cannot escape long, for the physicians now give a very ill
censure of your disease, upon some signes they have seene, and
more and more discerne in you. So as it seemes, Almighty God
will call you unto him, and you shall doe well to make your-
selfe ready, and dispose of what you leave. The tyme is short
and delayes are dangerous.

At this unexpected but much desired message, the good
Cardinall replenished with inward joy, presently with cheerful
countenance and undaunted courage brake forth into these
wordes: *Buona nuova, buona nuova, O che buona nuova è questa!*
that is, Good news, good news, O what good news is this! . . .
After this joyfull exclamation, turning his speach unto Father

Generall, as answering unto that which he had suggested, he sayd: For disposing of my thinges, I have nothing left to dispose, and it grieveth me that I have nothing to bestow upon the Society, for I feare much that in making you mine heyres, as if I had something to leave you, I shall but charge you with new debts. The Generall replyed that therein he should not trouble himselfe. He had left the Society so much, and so much honoured it with his name and immortall labours as it esteemed that treasure more than all the riches of the world. . .

The Cardinal had in fact made three wills, all drawn up in full legal form. The first was at Capua when he was about to attain the age of sixty-three, the grand climacteric and supposedly a very dangerous year in a man's existence. The circumstances of his life having greatly changed, he made a second will, annulling the first, after his return to Rome. That too was annulled in 1611, and a final will drawn, "being of the age of three score and nine, and very near as I imagine to my last day". In this will he expressed an earnest desire to be buried, unembalmed, like any other Jesuit, without pomp of any description, in the presence only of his Jesuit brethren. "As for the place of my burial," he continued, "I would gladly have my body lain at the feet of Blessed Aloysius Gonzaga, once my ghostly child, but notwithstanding this, let the Superiors of the Society bury it where they list." Even then, ten years before he died, he had very little to bequeath, an image in a frame of Pope Clement VIII which he desired should go to his brother Tommáso. To his nephew Angelo, the future Bishop of Teano, he left "a little picture in a frame of Robert, Cardinal de Nobili", the young portent of learning and sanctity who had died at eighteen, "and one of the two in frames of St Charles Borromeo and one of the little crosses which I wear about my neck, with the relics that are in it". He wished restored to the Roman College six tomes of the *Annals* of Baronius, which it had lent him, together with another six given to him by the author, "and all my writings and my whole library, unless it shall please our most Reverend Father General to bestow the library on some other house of the Society that is more in need". Whatever else belonged to him or should belong, "whether immovables, movables, debts owing me, whether sacred things belonging to my chapel, or profane, belonging to my wardrobe, or to my cellars or other places, whether ready money or whatsoever else, I will that all entirely appertain to the House of the Professed Fathers in Rome".

The House of the Professed did not, in the event, benefit much, for the Cardinal at the time of his death had long since cancelled all the debts owing to him and had given his last *quattrino* to the poor. On the fabric of his titular church, Santa Maria in Via, of which the Servite Fathers had charge, he had spent considerable sums, and could only leave them at the end one of his three best vestments. There being no money as stipends for Masses for his soul, he threw himself upon the charity of the Society of Jesus. "I trust, or rather I know," he wrote, "the pious charity of my Mother, the Society, will not be wanting to help me, as myself have never been wanting all my life to offer Sacrifices and prayers for such as were departed of the same." He constituted Cardinal Aldobrandini executor of his will and hoped "there will need no labour in the execution thereof". There certainly was not when the time came. For any trouble the famous nephew of Clement VIII might be put to, he bequeathed to him, "than which I have nothing more dear, a wooden Cross filled with most precious relics, the names of which he shall find in a little desk covered with red silk".

The *True Relation*, from which comes also the text of Cardinal Bellarmine's will of 1611, summarized above, continues as follows:

He caused one to reade unto him the death of St Charles Borromeo, as desirous in his owne to imitate it. Which being ended, he desired to receive the Sacraments of Holy Church, and that as soone as might be, lest after he should be lesse able for indisposition both of body and minde to receave them, and to prevent also any suddayne accident that might in this weakness take him away ere he had armed himself with this so necessary and sovereigne defence.

Forthwith all thinges were made ready for receaving of the Blessed Sacrament of the Altar for his *Viaticum*, which was ministered unto him by the handes of the Generall, and receaved with exceeding devotion of the Cardinall. For notwithstanding his extreme weakness of body, he would needes agayne, as he had done before, rise out of his bed and kneele on the ground to receave It. And so earnest was he to receave It in this manner, as it was not possible, without his great griefe and distaste, to hinder him. The Generall perceaving his will so fervently bent on that devotion would not withstand him therein, lest the inward griefe might more afflict his mind than that exterior action endamage his body. Wherefore he receaved It kneeling on the ground with singular humility. And after some collection made according to his wont, which endured for some while, he began to talke with the Generall about his buriall and the manner of his funeralls, which he did with so great peace of minde, and so familiarly, as if in his health he had spoken of going to dinner, or some other light and ordinary matter.

The same day, some six or seven houres after his receaving, he demanded the other and last Sacrament of the sicke, Extreme Unction, I meane, which he requested the sooner to receave because he would be sure, he sayd, not to be deprived of it, or to take it when he should not know well what he did take. He was now in his perfect senses and therefore might receave it with devotion, as he did, and answered *Amen* with great compunction of hart at each several unction. And now with greater serenity of mynd than before, he expected his last call, and coming of our Lord to take him out of this vale of misery and bring him where he might see *bona Domini in terra viventium*, the joy of our Lord in the land of the living.

Being thus armed for his last encounter, and in great tranquillity and peace of mind, the Cardinall began agayne to cast backe his eyes on his life past to see what therein might trouble his conscience, or breede any feare in him at that straite account before God, which now hourely he did expect to be called unto. And after all his discussion and search, he said unto Father Minutoli that no one thing so much troubled him of all that he had done in his life past as that he had left his Church and Archbishopric of Capua, where by his continuall residence he might have done more good, to the honour and glory of God, than in any other place; and that heere in Rome it seemed that he had lost his time and had done nothing of any weight or

moment. Yet he was imployed in all matters of most importance which concerned the whole Church, the proper office of a
Cardinall, as the sayd Father told him. . . . Moreover sayd the
Father, you can have no scruple in this matter which you did
by command of the Pope, whome you were bound by your
rule to obey.

Indeed, sayd the Cardinall, so the matter passed. . . . But for
that he had learned of his deare Master, Blessed Father Ignatius,
not only to seek the glory of God, but the *greater* glory of God,
in all things, and because he thought that he might have done
more good in Capua than in Rome, therefore did he sorrow
and have this remorse. This scruple being removed, and his
mynd quieted, there remayned one difficulty touching his
temporall estate, to wit, for repayment of his Cardinalls ring;
for effecting of which he used the help of the Cardinall of S.
Susanna to his Holiness, alleadging this reason, that it could not
be paid, for he had not wherewithall to bury him, much lesse to
pay that debt.

When it was knowne in the City that the Pope had been with
the Cardinall, that he had taken his *Viaticum*, that he was
annealed, and that there was no hope left of longer life, wonder-
full it was, not only to heare the honorable reports which all
made of him, but to see the meanes and inventions used, and
that by men of quality, to come unto him. Some sued unto
the Cardinalls and great personages; some intreated the Fathers,
some used the help of his servants; and others made other
devices, and this not only to see him, but to kiss his handes,
his head, or some other thing about him. And when they had
satisfied their devotion, they would touch his body with their
bookes, their beads, handkerchiefs, crosses, medalles, and other
like thinges, and that very reverently on their knees. And in this
kynde none were more frequent than the Cardinalls themselves,
who by reason of their more frequent conversation did best
know him, and some of them mentioned his canonization.
When once they knew of his sickness they came very often
unto him, and ten of them sometymes in one day, who all
desired his blessing, but he constantly refused to give it. And
one of them taking him by the hand kissed the same, and then
touched his eyes and head therewith. At which Bellarmine
mervayling, when the other was gone asked those about him

what kind of curtesy this was, and how long it had beene in use amongst the Cardinalls.

Another tyme the Cardinalls that came would needs before they departed kisse his hands, at which he was much grieved, and would have withdrawne them backe, but was not able to resist their importunity, and therefore only sayd, *Non sum dignus*, I am not worthy of this honour especially from you my Lords. And he offered to have kissed theirs againe one by one, but they would not yield, and he was too weake to force them. And some Cardinalls agayne, togeather with other Prelates, would needs have his benediction, which he utterly refused to give. And they continuing to aske it, he craved theirs, so as the contention grew who should blesse the other; which a Cardinall perceiving decided the matter by taking Bellarmynes hand, and blessing himselfe therewith perforce. . .

Two Cardinalls, above the rest, seemed to be more solicitous of him, Aldobrandini and Farnesius. The first came very often to the Novitiate to enquire how he did, and out of courtesy forbare to visit him, as not willing to trouble him with his presence. Yet at length he resolved to see him, although his sight cost him teares.

And when he with others requested that when he came to Heaven he would remember them, although the Cardinall alwayes showed a great hope and confidence in Gods mercy, yet was this conjoined with no lesse distrust of himselfe, for he would earnestly crave every mans prayers, and to this petition of the Cardinalls, he answered more than once saying: To go to Heaven so soone is a great matter, and too great for me. Men use not to come thither in such haste, and for my selfe, I shall thinke it no small favour to be sure of Purgatory, and there to remayne a good while in those flames that must purge and cleanse the spotts of my offences, and satisfy the just wrath and justice of Almighty God. But when I am come Home, quoth he, I will not faile to pray for you all.

Cardinal Farnesius was at this tyme at his house of Caprarola, thirty miles from Rome, who hearing of the sickness of Bellarmine wrote many letters to Father Minutoli. . . . And as often as Farnesius his letters, still full of love, were read unto him, Bellarmine would in very effectuall wordes make remonstrance how far he was indeared unto him, and how little able to discharge that duty which he did owe him, of which in his health he was never unmyndfull. . .

And for the other Cardinalls, they did also so tenderly affect him as few or none of all those which came to visit him could forbeare weeping. And one of them, a very grave man, sayd unto Father Minutoli that he did greatly glory to have been made Cardinall by that Pope which had made Bellarmine Cardinall; and that *in toto genere* (I use his owne wordes) the world hath not had any of so singular learning accompanyed with so great humility and Religious maturity as he, for many ages, and perhaps may expect long ere it have another. And he did well to specify his humility, for though he were equal to any, yet he so still demeaned himselfe as though he had been servant to all, and this even until death. For to all that came unto him in his sickness, although he did speake with all respect and duty unto them, yet at their departure he would crave pardon of them, and say: My Lords, I pray you pardon me if I doe not as I would, or as I am bound, for I am not myne own man. I want strength of body; I can do no more. And indeed he did more than was convenient for one in his case, though much lesse than he desired to have done to them whom so hartily he did honour.

In fine, when the danger of his disease was once divulged over all the City, not only Cardinalls, but many Bishops, Prelates, and others of speciall note, repayred unto him, especially the three last dayes before his death. . . . In which tyme the foresaid Cardinalls, Bishops, Prelates, and others sent little cappes of silke, such as they use to weare under their square cappes, and others sent white nightcappes, which they desired might be put on his head, as they were, and with them they sent also little crosses of gold and silver, reliquaries, prayer-bookes, and other things, to touch him, and that in such multitudes as there were more than a hundred and fifty red, white, and other caps put on and taken from his head during this tyme, and since his death that number hath been much increased. . .

The devotion of others unto the Cardinall hath made me make the longer digression from his owne person. But now leaving them a little (to whom eftsoones I shall returne againe), let us a while contemplate and cast our eyes backe to the sicke man. . . . Drawing on apace to the last period of his life, he found more and more difficulty to take any meate, or keep what he had taken; and he had not only a great repugnance and aversion from eating but a great loathing and horrour to see anything brought him. Heere, what should his attendants do? To force him seemed too violent for one so weake, so meeke, and of that ranke and dignity; to persuade him was but lost labour, for such difficultyes are hardly overcome by persuasion. Nothing remayned but to urge him the physicians commaund, and that he was bound under obedience to eate.

Hereat, presently he would rise, take and eate whatsoever they brought him, and that very readily, though it were never so much agaynst his stomacke, and though he did presently cast it up againe; never looking or respecting what was given him, and which is more strange even when he was beside himselfe in the extremity of his bad fit, the very name of obedience would have made him take whatsoever they had brought him. So accustomed and affectioned he was to that vertue as nothing seemed hard unto him that came under that tytle, imitating therein his deere Maister, our Lord and Saviour Jesus Christ, *factus obediens usque ad mortem.*

The dying Cardinal suffered a great deal from the zeal of his doctors. Brother Finali tells how they applied blisters to his calves in the hopes of drawing out certain alleged humours from his body. The only humours which they did draw were the poor patient's tears, for the torture became so unbearable during the night that he cried like a child. He did not ask to have the blisters removed, however, but only clasped his crucifix more tightly. A crowd kept vigil outside the doors of the novitiate, and when they heard that he had become much worse, they pushed past the porter and swarmed up the stairs to his room. Brother Finali was at his wits' end, but there was no controlling the visitors. Some threw themselves on the floor, beating their breasts, while others knelt up against the bed, crying unrestrainedly, and saying "Why, O my God, do you not take me, and spare this great captain of the Church?"

After his visitors had departed the Cardinal got some quiet sleep which grew calmer and deeper as the dawn approached.

Finali was sitting at the foot of the bed when he at last awoke. "Lifting up the curtain I congratulated him on having obtained some sleep, and wished him good day. To this he answered in a clear voice: 'May God be praised, Brother, I shall live four days more and then go home'." That was Monday morning, September 13. When the night came, the fever returned with all its violence. In the midst of his agony the Cardinal was troubled by the sight of Finali's tired face. "Do go to bed, dear Brother", he said, and then turning to his crucifix, whispered: "See, Lord, how good a thing it will be for me to go home when thou doest call me, for the only purpose I serve now is to be a burden and trouble to my dear brothers".

Among the many visitors the following day were the Oratorian Fathers, the brethren of Baronius. When the dying man noticed them, he begged their forgiveness for not being able to bring the cause of their Founder, Blessed Philip, to a conclusion, as he had ardently desired. "I have to go where I am called," he said, smiling up at them, "even leaving unfinished the letter that I had begun, as our rule commands." The rooms of the sick man on the Wednesday morning reminded Brother Finali of the apartments of a Cardinal in power, crowded with high-born aspirants for his favour. The doctors had decided the previous evening to apply leeches to their patient's head, and the visitors had now come with richly embroidered handkerchiefs and napkins to catch any blood that flowed from the wounds. Worn-out by all these well-meant attentions, Finali reported, the Cardinal turned to the doctors and said mildly: "So much trouble, Sirs, is not worth while over one who cares so little either for escape or for delay. God's determination is something quite beyond the power of your physic. I am on my way home, and you could not do me a better turn than to let me go whither my Lord calls me." Then, fixing his eyes on the crucifix, he added: "Still, do just what you think best, I am content". All the time his bed remained covered with rosaries, pictures, books, and various objects of devotion, so that it looked to Finali like one of the stalls that are to be found at the doors of churches. The dying man thought that they had been placed there to protect him from the assaults of the devil.

The last night of his life which was the 23. of his sickness, the former signes still increasing brought him into a certaine dulness or insensibility, especially some five or six houres before his death, which made all who were about him to thinke that now every houre might be his last. . . . Having an little Crosse of silver in his hand, he kissed it very often, and blessed himselfe divers times therewith, saying some prayers by himselfe, some togeather with them that were with him and kneeled at his bed side.

Afterwards taking into his hand a greater Crosse that stood by, which had the picture of our Saviours body fixed thereon, he did oftentimes very devoutly kisse the same. A little after he layed it on his eyes, and taking it from thence he layed it on his left shoulder, imbracing it very hard between both his armes, being put across one over the other. And so he continued a good while, till removing it a little towards his brest, he lifted his hand up to take off his night-cap, but could not doe it. And such as kneeled by him knew not what he meant, till at last by conjecture Father Minutoli gathered that he meant to doe some act of devotion, and therefore took off his cap for him. Then the Cardinall tooke the Crosse with both his handes, and so much forced himselfe as he placed it on his bare head. . . . Finally, he layed it on his brest, under the coverlet, where it remayned till he was dead, so as he seemed unwilling to see, thinke, or desire anything but Christ and him crucified.

Now was he come to the last houre of his life, and though his paines were greater, yet his courage, his patience, his quiet and peaceable repose the same. The holy man began his prayers, sayd the *Pater Noster*, and *Ave Maria* and began againe the *Pater Noster*, which being ended he sayd distinctly the Psalme *Miserere*. And being warned to say also the Creed, in protestation of his beliefe, and that he dyed a member of the Catholik, Apostolik and Roman Church, presently he began the same, and sayd it all through, and with the end of the Creed he ended his speach, these being the last wordes that ever he spake clearly and distinctly in this life: *Et vitam aeternam, Amen*. After which his voice so fayled that they could scant, with all diligence used, heare him, yet he sayd very softly to himselfe, in such manner as he was able, Jesus, Jesus, Jesus, and continued still in the same until the last gaspe, which of such as beheld him was in a manner insensible, in so still, quiet, and peaceable fashion as it seemed a sleep rather than death.

He left this world the seventeenth day of September, betweene six and seaven of the clocke, in the morning, wanting not three weeks of three score and nyneteene yeares, for he was borne on the fourth of October, being St Francis day, and dyed on the feast of the same Saint, dedicated to his sacred woundes, which miraculously he had receaved; the solemnity of which feast the Cardinall much laboured with Paul the Fifth to have graunted to the Religious of that Order.

The dead Cardinal's desire for a simple and private funeral, attended only by his Jesuit brethren, had to be overruled by the Pope, owing to the extraordinary scenes of veneration which followed. Bellarmine's emaciated body had been clothed in one of the very much faded purple robes which Pope Clement VIII had given him twenty-two years before, but this had been quickly reduced to tatters and divested of its ermine, lining and buttons by the scissors and knives of prelates who crowded around the sacred remains. The Cardinal's other articles of dress had disappeared completely and Brother Finali was obliged to borrow what was necessary from the novices' stock. At last, the faithful Guidotti, aided by three of the fathers, succeeded in smuggling the mortal remains of his beloved master through the novitiate garden to a gate at the back where a vehicle was waiting to take them to the infirmary of the Gesù. To avoid a tumult at Sant' Andrea, Finali was then obliged to unlock the doors and admit the waiting crowd to the room where he whom they already called their "Santo" had died. Others followed them all day long and then hastened to the Gesù and forced their way into the room where the "Santo" lay, bringing with them masses of flowers and taking away snippets of his grave-clothes, which had to be replaced completely that night. The Pope sent his own physician and a surgeon to carry out the embalming, but at this ceremony, too, which took place after dark, many eminent men and venerable prelates crowded around. "We had no need of any vessels or basins," wrote Brother Finali, "to receive the blood and water from his holy breast. The important thing was to get all the linen in the house under lock and key, for the distinguished visitors were scouring the house for pieces of cloth, and appropriated whatever they found without hesitation. Indeed it was astonishing to see consciences ordinarily so delicate allowing themselves so much latitude about other people's property."

The rest of the story may be given in the words of the *True Relation:*

> The next morning, September 18, the Nobility and Gentry of the Congregation of our Blessed Lady got his body into their Oratory or Chapell, where being all assembled they sayd the Office of the Dead for him, two gentlemen alwayes standing at his head to keep the multitude from kissing his bare face, permitting them only the hands and feet. He lay on a fayre hearse, vested like an Archbishop, with his myter and pall. The Office being ended, the narrowness of this place was not capable of so great concourse, and to avoid the inconvenience of such presse of people, the more haste was made to carry him into the Church, where being layd on a bed prepared for the same, there came to behold it, or rather to reverence and worship it, as though not the dead body of Cardinall Bellar-myne newly departed, but eyther the body of S. Augustine, or S. Ambrose, or S. Athanasius, or some auncient Doctour, Bishop or Patriarke had been exposed and layed open to be honoured. And I know not what more devotion the people could have used unto their sacred reliques, than now they did unto the body of this Cardinall.

> For they came not as ordinarily on such occasions they use to doe, to gaze and see the pompe of the funeralls (which heere was very little), not to pray for the party deceased, not to enquire of his heires, his testament, his wealth, his buriall, or the like more curious than necessary matters; but to see as they called him, the Saint, to pray unto him, to reverence his body, and that in such sort as if already he had been canonized.

> And for that it was now placed higher than they were able to reach, and compassed by some of the Popes Guard and Macebearers of the Cardinalls that came to be present at the *Dirige*, they wearyed them all with giving their beades unto them, which the one on the top of their truncheons, the other, of their Maces, lifted up to touch his bare face. And so many

beades being given to touch, and that so continually without any intermission, all looked or rather feared that his face would have been disfigured therewith, for it was touched, as most conjecture, by more than twenty thousand payre of beades. And there had been no end of touching it, had not the Fathers, with helpe of the Popes Guarde, after more than three houres within night caryed it away perforce, as presently shall be said.

And not withstanding that the body lay aloft, and was well guarded with truncheons and halbardes, yet were there of these pious thieves so cunning that some of them cut away pieces of his myter that he wore, others the tassells and knots of his Cardinall's hat, others, the skirts of his vestments, others, other things; and what each would get, with great devotion he kissed the same, lapping it up in cleane linnen, silke, etc. And two Prelates brought each a short staff under his garment, and when they came over against one the other at the lower end of the hearse, where the hat lay at the Cardinall's feet, they cast it off from thence very dexterously with their staves into the bosome of one of their servaunts ready at hand to receave it, who had conveyed it cleane away, had not one of the Fathers by chance espyed him, who by help of the Popes Guard recovered it out of his hands and carryed it into the Vestry. In fine, had not his body been well guarded, I thinke that neyther hat, or myter, or vestment, or anything else had been left, and perhaps the very body itselfe had been taken away and devided for pious spoile.

And although his body were thus exposed in more plaine and positive manner, with lesse splendour and majesty, than is accustomed for Cardinalls, yet were his exequies in other respectes very honourable. For contrary to that which both in his will had designed, and desired of the General on his death-bed to have no Cardinals present thereat, there came so many that more have not beene seene at any buriall; for excepting two or three for exceeding great age, sickness, or some other business absent, all the rest were there, and stayed untill the very end of the office, which was performed by the General in his cope, and the Fathers of the Society. And further there was such resort as none living ever saw more, or perhaps so many at once, in that Church. When the Office was done, to satisfy the importunate request of so many as desired it, the body was taken downe, layed on a Beare covered with black velvet, and caryed to the Chappell of Our Blessed Lady in the same Church, not without a strong guard, where such as entered at one dore passing out at another gave way for more to satisfy their desires.

But it was not possible to satisfy all; for though it remayned there untill after three houres in the night (as I sayd), yet were the Fathers forced to send away many that were still flocking thither; much agaynst their will and not without mayne force of the Guard and others, that commaunded and compelled them out of the Church and shut the dores, to their no small regret.

The multitude being excluded, the body was put into a plaine coffin of wood and layed in the ordinary vault where others of the Society are wont to be buryed; therein condescending to the Cardinalls desire, who would needes lye with them in the grave, with whome he had lived, whome he had loved, and to whome for many years before his death he would have returned, and led agayne a Religious life under the common Rule if it might have been permitted him.

After the translation of the relics of St Ignatius in February, 1622, to his new shrine in the Gesù, Cardinal Farnese erected a monument to Bellarmine over the spot where the Founder of the Jesuits had lain. On this monument the Cardinal's bust by the sculptor Bernini was placed, and at each side of it, statues representing Religion and Wisdom. The inscription bore the following words: "Edward Cardinal Farnese erected this monument of undying love towards one whom he ever revered as though he was his father". A year later the Cardinal's body was placed in a new coffin and laid in the vault which had contained the remains of St Ignatius. In the middle of the nineteenth century some architectural changes were made in the interior of the Gesù. A new tomb of white marble was then constructed for the Jesuit Cardinal's relics, over the false door which formed part of the original monument erected by Cardinal Farnese. There they remained until their solemn translation to the feet of his "ghostly child", St Aloysius, in the Church of St Ignatius, on June 21, 1923.

Cardinal Bellarmine's beloved patron, St Francis of Assisi, was solemnly canonized in July, 1228, less than two years after his death. Bellarmine himself was not beatified until more than three centuries had passed over his grave. Few "causes" in the annals of sanctity have suffered such and so many vicissitudes as his, but as they were due to political and religious opposition, Gallicanism and Jansenism, which had nothing to do with his reputation for sanctity, asserted by nobody more strongly than the great authority on canonizations, Pope Benedict XIV, they need not be recorded here. Suffice it to say that Cardinal Bellarmine was declared *Beatus* by Pope Pius XI on May 13, 1923, canonized by the same Holy Father in 1930, and given the crowning honour of Doctor of the Church in 1931.

THE END

INDEX